SMART!
A Reading Tutor's Guide

SMART!
A Reading Tutor's Guide

Helping Teens Read, Think, and Act Smarter

Sylvia Keepers

KEYSTONE COURT PRESS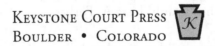
BOULDER • COLORADO

Printed in the United States of America
First Printing, 2014

Keystone Court Press
1204 Keystone Court
Boulder, CO 80304
http://keystonecourtpress.com

Publisher's Cataloging-in-Publication
(Provided by Quality Books, Inc.)

Keepers, Sylvia.
    Smart! : a reading tutor's guide : helping teens
        read, think and act smarter / Sylvia Keepers.
    pages cm
    Includes bibliographical references and index.
    LCCN 2012955962
    ISBN 978-0-9885320-1-4
    1. Tutors and tutoring. 2. Teenagers--Education. I. Title.
    LC41.K44 2014 371.39'4 QBI14-600067

Cover design and art, Jen McCleary
Author photograph, Lissa A. Forbes

Credits for quoted material and illustrations are found on p. viii.

For my Grandmother (Granny) Crawford,
who ran a school out of her West Texas home
and gave me the idea that teaching was something to aspire to.

And for Clarissa Pinkola Estés,
whose lessons in individuation set me on the way.

When you teach students to read skillfully, you offer them the keys to academic success and more satisfying career choices. These are wonderful gifts in themselves, but for some individuals tutoring goes beyond these outward benefits and opens a door inward, offering them a degree of introspection and imagination that otherwise would have remained out of reach. You are giving these students the key to a rich inner life, sparked by the tutoring relationship and nurtured by the world of books.

—SK

Credits

Numbers in bold refer to pages in this book.

69, 177, 186. Excerpts from T. Walter Wallbank, et al., *History and Life*, 4th ed., 11, 22. By permission of the T. Walter Wallbank Family. **144-45**. Excerpts from Velma Wallis, *Two Old Women: An Alaska Legend of Betrayal, Courage and Survival*, 1-2. By permission of Epicenter Press. **151-52**. Based on story plot in Lois Lowry, *Number the Stars*, 1-10. **153, 403**. Based on story plot in S. E. Hinton, *That Was Then, This Is Now*. **190**. Excerpt from Edward Fry, *Reading Drills for Speed and Comprehension, Advanced Level*, "Glass," 23. By permission of the author. **194-96**. Excerpts from Irwin L. Joffe, *Opportunity for Skillful Reading*, 3d ed., 73-74, 75, © 1980 by Wadsworth, a part of Cengage Learning, Inc. Reproduced by permission. www.cengage.com/permissions. **196**. Excerpt from John W. Kimball, **Biology**, 64. **199**. Excerpt from Thomas Bulfinch, *Bulfinch's Mythology: The Age of Fable; The Age of Chivalry; Legends of Charlemagne*, v. **199**. Excerpt from Daniel J. Boorstin, *The Discoverers: A History of Man's Search to Know His World and Himself*, 338. By permission of Random House, Inc. **200**. Excerpt from Amy Cruse, *The Englishman and His Books in the Early Nineteenth Century*, 108. **200**. Excerpt from Bertha Morris Parker, *The Golden Book Encyclopedia*, Volume VII, 612. By permission of Random House, Inc. **274-75**. After a concept in William Kottmeyer, *Conquests in Reading*, 2d ed., 104-112. **292**. Figure 14.3, adapted from Dorothy Ellen Babcock and Terry D. Keepers, *Raising Kids O.K.: Transactional Analysis in Human Growth and Development*, 40. By permission of the author. **293**. Excerpt from Thomas H. Huxley, *Collected Essays*, Volume III, 404. **325, 337, 339**. Excerpts from David Keirsey and Marilyn Bates, *Please Understand Me, Character and Temperament Types*, 5th ed., 1, 21, 24. By permission of Prometheus Nemesis Book Company. **328-29**. Excerpt from Linda Kreger Silverman, Ph.D., "Understanding Introverted Kids." By permission of the author. **350-51; 391; 394**. Excerpts from Joanne Carlisle, *Beginning Reasoning Skills, Beginning Reasoning and Reading*, 20-25, 44. By permission of Educators Publishing Service, www.eps-books.com. **360**. Excerpt from Sally Shaywitz, M.D., *Overcoming Dyslexia: A new and complete science-based program for reading problems at any level*, 132. By permission of Random House, Inc. **386-87**. Hugh B. Cave, "Two Were Left" in *Aiming High: Stirring Tales and Poems*, Annette Sloan and Albert Capaccio, eds. Used by permission of the Hugh B. Cave Irrevocable Trust. **395-99**. Excerpts from Edward Fry, *Reading Drills for Speed and Comprehension, Advanced Level*, "Magic," 18-19, 20, 179. By permission of the author. **401-02**. PBS LearningMedia "Developing Active Reading with Effective Questions." **409-12**. Maxine Rock, "Human moms teach chimps it's all in the family." *Smithsonian* magazine, March 1995 issue. By permission of the author. **417-20**. Adapted from flash cards concept in Romalda Bishop Spalding, Mary E. North, Ph.D., editor, *The Writing Road to Reading: The Spalding Method for Teaching Speech, Spelling, Writing, and Reading*, 5th ed., 213-21.

Contents

Part III: Reading Nonfiction   165

Part IV: Reading Speed   223

Appendices:

Supporting Materials for Student and Tutor   377

Illustrations

Tables

Foreword

READING WAS ALWAYS EASY FOR ME. I still remember how much I wanted to start school so I could learn to read, and I can also remember the thrill of bringing home the Tip and Mitten books we used. I was always a "bluebird" and by fourth grade, I was reading a book a night. In junior high, with access to my first real library, I continued my habits of extensive reading. I decided in eighth grade that I wanted to be an English teacher so I could, 1) keep on reading and 2) teach kids to love reading as much as I did.

Flash forward eight years to my first classroom in a rural district where I taught 7th, 8th, 9th, and 11th grade English. I was ever so confident about my knowledge of my content and my abilities to create great lessons and reach my students . . . until I realized some of my students could not understand the text. Some could read aloud but had no comprehension; some couldn't even do that. And—because reading had always been so easy for me—I didn't know what to do to help them.

Flash forward again, to a day in 2013 when I was considering books for a book study with our district reading interventionists. Secondary English teachers do have better pre-service training than I did, but they are still stymied when it comes to students in their classroom who struggle with reading. There are many great books to help these teachers find ways to address individual student reading issues along with covering the curriculum/standards, but many of them run heavy into theory and light on practicality. During my search, I stumbled upon Sylvia Keeper's website and read about *SMART! A Reading Tutor's Guide*, which sounded very promising. My heart sank when I found it was not yet available, but Sylvia graciously let me see a draft.

I knew shortly after I began, this was the book I wanted. I couldn't wait to put it into the hands of our teachers. At every meeting, I told them about this fabulous book we were going to read as soon as it was published. This book would be the bridge between all the wonderful things we want to teach our students and their reading limitations. It would answer those questions that began "I have this student who . . ." This book would do what our pre-service courses hadn't: it would tell us exactly what to do to help all of our students.

An abundance of detail provides readers with a deeper understanding of assessment (especially initial assessment), how nonfiction reading differs from fiction reading, when to employ phonics instruction (and when not to), and students with special needs. Resources are also abundant in the appendices, and Sylvia's stories of her work with students give a human face to these ideas.

This book is rich in specific activities and strategies for specific reading problems. It would be worth the price if that were all it offered, but there's more. Although my use of the book is aimed at classroom teachers, the book's audience is the reading tutor. Information on how to set up a tutoring business, how to deal with parents, how to advertise and more is practical and welcome. Many teachers supplement their incomes with extra jobs, and working as a private tutor is a way to make some extra money and gain experience working with struggling readers.

On my desk, I have a collection of the books that have most impacted my practice. The first copy of *SMART! A Reading Tutor's Guide* that comes in will join them (after I've annotated it, of course). Then I am going to take the other thirty-something copies and do what I have been wanting to do for almost a year: place each one in the hands of a reading teacher.

Thank you, Sylvia, for your life's work and for this amazing book. Your influence will spread farther than we can know.

—Ramona Lowe, Ph.D.
Lewisville (TX) ISD
Innovation & Integration/Embedded Literacy SDC

Preface

SMART! A Reading Tutor's Guide is a comprehensive guide to individual reading instruction for adolescents. The aim is to help teachers and tutors become skilled reading instructors and insightful mentors. The book is about transformations, both academic and personal.

As a tutor, I know that my work makes a difference in students' lives. Students often succeed in school (and in life) as a result of my efforts, even when all previous attempts to help them have failed. No one has a monopoly on the ability to help kids do their best, however. My success with these students was founded on principles and techniques I believe any caring teacher can learn.

Over the years, whenever a technique worked well, I made a note of it so I could pass it along. This book grew out of those notes. It is a collection of practices and approaches that I hope will allow tutors and teachers to experience a new level of success with their own students.

Recently I began tutoring a bright 17-year-old girl, Carli, in ACT (American College Testing) preparation. Carli wanted to attend the Coast Guard Academy. Her reading scores on her initial practice test were quite poor, however, and she was due to take the ACT test in two weeks. Unless her scores improved, she would be turned down by the school she wished to attend.

During my years of tutoring, I have seen many kids come from behind and catch up, but this situation seemed truly hopeless. Still, I worked with Carli to do the readings in her test preparation book with the close attention they required, weighing the meaning of each sentence and seeing relationships within and between readings.

At the end of our second session, I asked her what she had learned that day. Her unexpected answer: "That I have been reading mindlessly." This realization in itself helped Carli enter a new stage in her studies and in her awareness. From then on, she made surprising progress. She dramatically improved her analytical reading skills, doubled her reading speed in a week, and went on to ace the test. Her ACT average score for reading and English had gone from an 18 to a 21 to a 30 with no further instruction. There was no reason she couldn't attend the Coast Guard Academy as she wished.

Carli's experience demonstrates how we can sometimes help young people make near-miraculous changes in their lives through reading instruction. This incident is an example of what propelled me into tutoring reading in the first place and what prompted me to write this book.

Sometimes the transformations that take place in tutoring can seem like miracles, as with Carli. The purpose of *SMART! A Reading Tutor's Guide* is to help you learn to perform these "miracles" yourself. You will find techniques, methods, and attitudes in this book that hold the possibility of creating dramatic academic breakthroughs for students. And although these breakthroughs might seem miraculous, they are what can be expected when young people are provided with the correct learning experiences in an order that makes sense and in the context of a supportive and savvy emotional environment. For these changes to take place, however, the stage needs to be set with patience and perseverance.

Almost all tutors and students have within themselves the makings of great teachers and learners, and whether you are setting the stage or seizing an inspired moment, the goal of this book is to help you unlock the best in yourself and in your student.

Acknowledgments

By necessity, a book this size is the product of a group effort, and I couldn't have asked for a better team to back me up in its writing and production. Bonnie Simrell, my editor and production manager, played an indispensable role in the creation of this book from its beginnings as a slim pamphlet to the volume it is now. She saw the value of my project before I was convinced of it, and she encouraged me at every step. Specifically, I owe much to Bonnie's top-notch writing instruction and editorial advice. Add to those jobs, perhaps the most important of all—that of friend. Without her expert help in all those areas, *SMART!* simply would not exist.

This book also owes its existence to the moral and logistical support of my husband, Terry Keepers. Terry showed me by example how to be a writer and backed it up with good advice and an interest in my work. He was always ready to make suggestions about a passage or offer a phrase when needed. I thank him for believing in this book even when I didn't.

My thanks to Joseph Hutchison of Full Scale, Inc., for his detailed and thoughtful copyediting; to Jen McCleary for her beautiful cover design and art; to John Ransom for his line drawings; and to Joan Hewitt for her careful proofreading. Sara Schwartz Kendall proofread an early draft of the manuscript and offered suggestions for its improvement.

Kathy Sherman, founder and head of Hillside School, an independent school in Boulder County, Colorado, shared helpful information and references, particularly about dyslexia.

Several teachers who studied with me to become reading tutors helped fine-tune the ideas in the book by trying them out and commenting on them. Thanks also to my sister, Peggy Dart, for her persistent questions: "OK, tell me again, how do you teach that? You must have left something out." My work with Peggy kept me focused on the correct sequence for the teaching activities in the book.

Special appreciation goes to Ramona Lowe, Ph.D., for her professional encouragement and generous Foreword.

Finally, I would be remiss if I did not acknowledge those many students from whom I learned so much over the years—not only about which tutoring methods were most effective in different circumstances, but about the kids themselves. Each presented new challenges and often inspiration that advanced my work in important ways. Some made material contributions to this book, if anonymously, as their stories illustrate.

—Sylvia Keepers
Boulder, Colorado

SMART!
A Reading Tutor's Guide

Introduction

To TUTOR IS TO TEACH, GUIDE, OR INSTRUCT on an individual basis in a special subject for a particular purpose (based on *Webster's Third New International Dictionary* 1993). The goal of tutoring is to help students help themselves: to guide them to become independent learners who no longer need the services of a tutor.

Tutoring is a time-honored practice. The ancient Chinese nobility relied on tutors to educate their sons for civil service. And the Romans even kidnapped educated Greeks to tutor their own, presumably ignorant, children. The British university system uses tutors, as anyone who's watched an episode of Inspector Lewis will be aware. Today tutoring has become much more democratic—and democratizing.

An internet search will turn up scores of websites for tutoring businesses, and there is even a "tutoring sector" whose worth is given in billions of dollars as a share of the US economy.

Thus there is both a respected tradition and a burgeoning industry connected with tutoring. Let's take a look now at the demand side of the equation—that of the learner.

Literacy in the United States

Reading problems are more widespread than casual observation or anecdotal evidence might indicate. According to literacy experts there is an epidemic of poor reading comprehension in the United States, a trend that makes a compelling argument for better literacy instruction for young adults (ACT, Inc. 2006; Haynes 2005).

The following statistics emphasize the need for an increase in all types of reading instruction, including tutoring. Except for the last two points, this information was reported in *Reading between the Lines* (ACT, Inc. 2006), which concludes that too many American high school students are graduating without the reading skills they'll need to succeed in college and in workforce training programs.

- 2.4 million students are labeled "Special Education" simply because they cannot read (Administrator Magazine 2009).
- Sixty-six percent of eighth graders read below the proficient level (National Assessment of Educational Progress 2007, 27).
- Three thousand students will drop out of high school today; the majority are poor readers (Alliance for Excellent Education 2003).
- According to the National Assessment of Educational Progress (NAEP), a third of boys and a fifth of girls cannot read or write at the basic level by the end of high school, and even teens who can read well often need help with complex texts they must master in high school.
- Only about half of our nation's ACT-tested high school students are ready for college-level reading.
- About forty percent of high school graduates lack the literacy skills employers seek (Achieve, Inc. 2005, 8).
- Not enough high school teachers are teaching reading skills or strategies and many students are victims of teachers' low expectations (Ericson 2001; Meltzer 2002).
- "To Read or Not to Read," a report from the National Endowment for the Arts (2007), says Americans are reading less and reading less well, and that the "declines have civic, social and economic implications." Though reading scores of elementary school students have been improving, scores are flat among middle school students and slightly declining among high school seniors.

Clearly, we have a "reading problem" at the national level. Reversing this trend will require a concerted effort by government, schools, and teachers. Solutions rest with public policy and broad social trends, forces that are notoriously hard to direct. Rather than dwell on these difficulties, however, this book focuses on an area in which we can truly have some influence—that of individual students.

The Need for Tutoring

Granted, there is a reading problem in the United States, but does it necessarily follow that teens need tutoring? Can't they just learn on their own? If they have the basics, can't we just give them more reading assignments or ask them to pay better attention at school? And why do older students need to work on their reading at all? Beyond a certain level, isn't reading just reading?

Let's take the last question first. Reading isn't just reading, of course. Levels of reading proficiency vary greatly. For instance, an eighth-grade reading level is not adequate for an Advanced Placement (AP) history class, and a student who reads only for facts will not understand a newspaper editorial. This book is about building reading skills, starting wherever we find students and helping them achieve the level of expertise needed to meet the challenges in their lives and to reach their own goals. Even more than that, however, it's about helping students develop their potential to be all they can be, and for some, it's about being more than they thought they could be.

As to the first point, about just having students read more, it's true that it sometimes does help for students simply to read more. However, for an unskilled reader, practice without guidance often simply reinforces errors, and forcing students to read may backfire, making them more balky and uncooperative.

I often work with pre-med students, quite a few of them college graduates, to improve their scores on the verbal section of the medical school entrance exam. Some have spent a year or more practicing intensively on their own, attempting to improve their reading comprehension and speed, often with disappointing results. A few weeks of effective reading tutoring can make all the difference in the world for these students. When they have the tools to improve their own reading, their practice finally achieves results. It's not an exaggeration to say that the techniques presented here have saved a number of students, now in medical school, from nervous breakdowns.

Furthermore, in my experience teaching speed reading to adults, I've found that slow reading is common even among people who read frequently, including doctors and lawyers, and comprehension problems are surprisingly common even among people who enjoy reading. Clearly, focused instruction is often what's needed for people to improve their reading.

Just as reading more might not solve a reading problem, neither will simply paying closer attention in school. Schools might not assign enough reading to students, might not know how to intervene when teens are having difficulty, or might not have adequate continuity or follow-through in reading development programs. Even worse, the school might not even know that a teen is experiencing a reading problem. (This is not entirely the school's fault, however, because kids are good at hiding deficiencies under the guise of coping.)

Who This Book Is For

This book is for anyone who wants to help teens improve their reading. It is geared toward individual instruction, but many of the ideas could also be used with groups. In addition, while it is meant to be used with teens, with some minor variations, most of the exercises and activities could be used with other age groups. I've mainly taught in middle- to upper-class white suburbs, but the ideas and techniques presented here can work anywhere, and I hope they will help tutors and students from many different backgrounds.

If you are interested in becoming a reading tutor, the tips and information provided in this book can help you get started on a profitable and rewarding career. If you are already a tutor and would like to help your students read faster, increase their understanding of what they read, and enjoy their reading more, *SMART! A Reading Tutor's Guide* can be your consultant in book form.

If you are a classroom teacher whose students are held back by negative behaviors and attitudes, you can use the concepts explained here to help your students develop confidence and a willingness to learn. Whether you are a homeschool parent with the goal of helping your teen achieve reading excellence or a classroom teacher wishing to initiate a speed-reading program for your students, this book takes you through the tutoring process one step at a time.

SMART! A Reading Tutor's Guide was written for use by an educated individual who has never taught before, but it is also for classroom teachers who want to tutor individual students. The tutoring relationship is unique, and so is the type of teaching it allows. Teachers can use methods and activities in tutoring that are unworkable in the classroom. One goal of this book is to help classroom teachers recognize and make the most of the opportunities offered by one-on-one instruction.

Some tutors are merely homework helpers. They can help a student understand and complete a school assignment, but most college-educated adults would be capable of doing the same. A tutor who simply wants to help students with their homework does not need this book. However, what if a student is impulsive or careless with his work? What if he reads slowly or misinterprets his reading? Helping such a student learn to focus, understand, and read skillfully requires more than homework help: it requires teaching students to think, and that calls for a distinct kind of tutoring. *SMART! A Reading Tutor's Guide* is a resource for teachers who want to help their students develop fully. In other words, it is not just a guide for reading tutors; it is for reading mentors.

Good Tutors Are in Demand

According to the U.S. Census Bureau, the number of tutors in the U.S. more than doubled from the years 2002 to 2011 (American Fact Finder, U.S. Census Bureau, Economic Census). Large commercial franchises like Sylvan account for most of this growth, but opportunities for private tutoring are increasing as well. Many parents want help with SAT (Scholastic Aptitude Test) and ACT test preparation for their college-bound (or college-hopeful) students; they want tutoring for high school students who are in AP (advanced placement) classes; and they want their teens to actually be able to get through their school reading rather than relying on online study guides such as CliffsNotes.

At the other end of the academic spectrum, parents are eager for tutoring to help a child reverse a pattern of failure. Tutors who are skillful at helping underachieving students learn to read better and care about their schoolwork are likely to be as busy as they want to be.

Not only do parents want tutoring for their teens, they are willing to pay for it. Nationwide in 2007, parents spent $5 billion to $7 billion on tutoring sessions, an increase of 18 percent from 2005, according to the Education Industry Association (EIA), an organization that supports private providers of education services. (These findings are from proprietary research conducted by Eduventures for their subscribers, which include the EIA.)

Most parents whose children need outside help consider tutoring a necessity rather than a luxury. If they believe their child will benefit from tutoring, they will find a way to afford it. If you have any doubts about this, see how busy the Sylvan, Kaplan, or Princeton Review classes are in your area. These are nationally known commercial tutoring and test preparation franchises that serve a large customer base, and their success indicates how much demand exists for tutoring services nationally. The market is there—you just need to learn how to tap into it. The information provided in this book can help you do that.

Qualities of a Good Tutor

Tutors come in all varieties. Classroom teachers, peer tutors, parents, and even neighbors can be effective reading tutors. Math tutors are often in a position to see a child's reading difficulties while working on story problems, and they can teach both subjects as the need arises. And contrary to what many people believe, it is not necessary to be a reading specialist to teach reading improvement.

A tutor's personal characteristics and outlook are far more important than previous training. Here's a list of characteristics of successful tutors. Don't worry if you don't embody them all to start with, however. The process of tutoring can help you develop them. Effective tutors:

- remember their own childhood and how it feels to be a kid
- are good at getting others to cooperate
- are perceptive observers of student behavior
- love to read and write and are generally well-educated and literate
- enjoy young people, including those who are uninformed and apathetic at first
- are able to see the potentially competent person underneath a troubled exterior
- can explain clearly
- are patient and can tolerate both repetition and change
- are imaginative at coming up with different ways to teach a particular skill or idea
- know when to put their foot down and won't allow others to take advantage of them
- feel sympathetic toward parents and are willing to work cooperatively with them

The Gifts of Tutoring

The value of tutoring goes beyond teaching reading: you can also use the tutoring process to help your students develop as individuals. When you teach students to read skillfully, you offer them the keys to academic success and more satisfying career choices. These are wonderful gifts in themselves, but for some individuals tutoring goes beyond these outward benefits and opens a door inward, offering them a degree of introspection and imagination that otherwise would have remained out of reach. You are giving these students the key to a rich inner life, sparked by the tutoring relationship and nurtured by the world of books.

If you have decided to tutor, you have chosen a job that will reward you over and over as you see your students grow and mature. Your satisfaction at seeing your students' progress can be all the more pleasurable when you realize you have not sacrificed yourself to accomplish it but have only gained in the process.

Tutoring is one of the best jobs in the world, and I would like the privilege of sharing it with you. As a tutor, you can set your own hours, accept only the students you choose, and arrange the details of the setting to your liking. You have the rewards of teaching without the busywork and distractions of a classroom.

Tutoring also has its share of stress, however. You see kids and families in crisis, you are asked to help young people with a history of failure, and you occasionally need to deliver bad news to parents. Tutoring can be difficult, but that doesn't keep it from being one of the most exciting and satisfying careers available to anyone who enjoys teaching.

About This Book: Principles and Organization

SMART! A Reading Tutor's Guide offers a balanced, comprehensive approach to individual reading instruction for adolescents: balanced because it doesn't avoid or overemphasize subjects such as phonics, and comprehensive because it provides complete rather than cursory explanations of important topics. In deciding how much detail to include on a given topic, I asked myself: "If I didn't know how to teach a subject at all, would I be able to actually teach it based on this explanation alone?"

This book is *holistic*, focusing on students' inner workings—the thoughts and feelings that detract from learning or move it along. Knowing the "secrets" of the adolescent mind can put you in a position of power—not power over your student, but the power to work cooperatively with an adolescent who may never have had a close, trusting relationship with an adult.

By teaching skills and strategies, *SMART! A Reading Tutor's Guide* provides a practical approach to intervene in the vicious cycle of student failure and avoidance of reading (Figure 1). It contains a series of stepwise, interconnected exercises you can use to teach your students the skills they need to become proficient, thoughtful readers. The book is arranged so that you can use all the exercises or choose a few to fill a particular need. You will also find vignettes, case descriptions, and scripts that explain how to teach a particular skill or get an idea across.

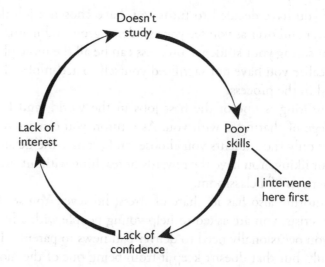

Figure 1. Breaking the vicious cycle of failure and avoidance.

The exercises are arranged in order from easy to hard, simple to complex; they are also incremental in that each learning activity is based on the one before and leads smoothly into the next. Thus the entire book can be used as a flow chart. This "stair-step" organization reinforces continuity of learning and makes it easy for the tutor to individualize a curriculum for a particular student. A tutor who is able to pinpoint the simplest skill with which a student is experiencing difficulty can locate that skill in the book and begin teaching from that point forward, including subsequent skills for instruction or skipping over them as needed.

The book is also organized so that it can be used from start to finish. As a result, the same skill or technique might be presented in several different places in the book. For instance, a skill could be introduced in one chapter, elaborated in the next, and concluded later on. That is because the exercises are arranged in increasing order of difficulty and depth, with room to introduce, practice, combine, and repeat each skill. This arrangement makes for a less linear organization but hopefully will result in a more useful guide.

SMART! A Reading Tutor's Guide comprises 18 chapters organized into six parts and focuses on three main subject areas: the business of tutoring (Part I); academic content (Parts II through V); and student psychology and the interpersonal dynamics of the tutor-student relationship (Part VI). Each chapter closes with a summary of key points. Supporting materials for tutor and students are presented in Appendices A through I, followed by References for works cited in the text, a bibliography, and detailed subject index.

The theoretical basis for emotional learning in Part VI uses the ideas of such writers as Eric Berne (1996) and David Keirsey and Marilyn Bates (Keirsey and Bates 1984). Drawing on this foundation, the book shows teachers how to deal with problems that arise in the tutoring relationship. Discussions of the concepts of "strokes" and "temperament types," for example, reveal the inner workings of student behavior. Using the principles in this book, tutors will be able to deal more effectively with such common problems as distractibility, apathy, and oppositional behavior.

Chapters about motivation show how to bring out the best in every student, no matter how deeply buried that child's positive qualities may seem. Numerous explanations and teaching scripts help tutors combine emotional guidance with academic instruction. In many cases tutors will observe transformational results for their students as unproductive work habits and attitudes fall away, to be replaced by focus, competence, and success.

A note about language referring to gender

To avoid sexism and tortured sentences, masculine and feminine pronouns alternate from chapter to chapter throughout the book.

Summary of Key Points

- *SMART! A Reading Tutor's Guide* is a comprehensive guide to one-on-one reading instruction for adolescents. Its aim is to help tutors become skilled reading instructors and insightful mentors.
- This book is written both for educated individuals who have never taught before and for classroom teachers who want to tutor individual students. Homeschool parents will also find something of value here.
- The book was designed to be used with individual teens, but it can be adapted for students of other ages and for groups.
- Tutoring holds the potential to transform students' lives. This book is not meant for homework helpers, but for educators who want to give their students the means to develop fully as human beings.
- Tutoring is not only a rewarding career, it is also a booming business with a strong demand for qualified tutors.
- Tutors come in all varieties. Academic background is less important than awareness and outlook.

- Effective tutors are skilled, empathetic people who have clear personal boundaries.
- *SMART! A Reading Tutor's Guide* uses stepwise, interconnected exercises to teach whatever skills students need to learn to become proficient readers.
- Competence leads to confidence, and as tutors we can intervene in the cycle of failure and avoidance by helping students build skills that lead to success.

Part I: Getting Started

PART I BEGINS WITH A PRACTICAL COMPENDIUM of educational psychology in Chapter 1, "The Art of Tutoring." In this chapter, tutors learn to recognize reading problems and understand the principles of effective teaching. Chapter 2, "Setting up Business," discusses the ins and outs of establishing a tutoring business and poses questions that prospective tutors should ask themselves (but might overlook) before opening a business. Sample forms and policy information are provided, together with guidance for the initial exchanges with prospective students and their parents. Chapter 3, "Initial Consultation and Informal Evaluation," provides a plan for an informal reading evaluation of a prospective student, and Chapter 4, "Introduction to Reading Comprehension," lays the groundwork for helping students understand and remember what they read.

1 | The Art of Tutoring

THIS EVENT HAPPENED 30 years ago but is still fresh in my mind. I had been working with a 14-year-old girl for about six months, tutoring her in reading. When we started, not only was her reading very poor, but she didn't seem to care about anything. She was dismissive and angry and seemed unwilling even to try. Over the months, however, both her attitude and her ability to read greatly improved. She moved from a second-grade to a fifth-grade reading level, and more importantly, she now considered tutoring an opportunity, not a punishment. She still had a lot to learn, but she was on a steady course of improvement, and I felt confident her reading skills would continue to improve, even without tutoring.

I had heard occasionally from the girl's mother, mostly by phone; she seldom had anything too remarkable to say. Now she requested a visit in person. I imagined the mother would be happy about the girl's progress, but other than that I didn't know what to expect.

The woman who appeared in my office was quite different than the person I had met six months earlier. Now her eyes were sunken and her hair wispy. She wasted no time explaining the purpose of the visit. "I am dying of cancer," she said. "The doctors tell me I have only a few months to live." She wanted to thank me for "giving my daughter back and for giving her a future."

She had a lot of grief, but at least she was free of fear about what would happen to her child, something that had been a constant worry for her before. "Now that she can read," she said, "she'll be able to take care of herself, and knowing she's happy about herself makes it a little easier for me to let go and say goodbye."

I wanted to tell her that I was just a bystander and couldn't really take credit for much. Instead, I reached for her hand, thanked her, and promised to continue to do my best for her daughter. In hindsight, it's clear to me that although in one way I was just a bystander, I had also been allowed a greater role. I was able to do what that mother needed simply by my willingness to teach her child to read and help her do her best.

Though the stakes are rarely as high as in this situation, new tutors will certainly meet families and students for whom they can make a major difference. And although you may think you are simply tutoring, you are also supporting families in ways you aren't even able to foresee.

Who Needs a Tutor?

Evidence points to an epidemic of poor reading in the United States, and reading problems are widespread at both the middle school and high school levels. Tutoring can provide relief for these common problems: trouble decoding (sounding out) unfamiliar words, trouble concentrating, not understanding, not remembering, reading slowly, not doing reading assignments, and not enjoying reading. Tutoring also can help students who are adequate or even good readers improve their note-taking abilities, understand more advanced literature and science texts, and master close reading of the kind required by the ACT and SAT.

Poor readers often do not recognize their own problems, and even teachers and parents might not be able to pinpoint what is wrong. Although some students are able to master these skills on their own, self-improvement is not a dependable solution. Kids are far more likely to hide their problems than find true solutions on their own. If you talk with several adults about their school experiences you will find that reading problems do not ordinarily just "go away"; instead, they go underground and may persist into adulthood. With some questioning, adults in a student's life may observe the following indicators of reading problems:

- doesn't like to read and puts off assignments
- may be the last in the class to finish reading assignments
- gets poor verbal scores on standardized tests, including the SAT and ACT
- thinks she has read and understood a selection but, when questioned, demonstrates only a sketchy understanding or unwittingly makes up ideas, seriously misinterpreting what she's read
- understands and enjoys fiction reading but finds textbook reading difficult, or vice versa
- appears apathetic and unmotivated, but a closer look shows a reading problem at the heart of the difficulty

- had talked with enthusiasm about going to college but hasn't mentioned college recently. An unidentified reading problem could be to blame.

As a tutor, you might notice other problems as well. The student:

- scores poorly on reading tests. To find out, ask to see test scores, including state assessments (the TCAP, or Transitional Colorado Assessment Program, for example), the Preliminary Scholastic Aptitude Test (PSAT), and the ACT Assessment (ACT). Unfinished reading sections indicate slow reading speed, while poor vocabulary scores often show lack of reading experience.
- depends entirely on class discussion because she doesn't do—or doesn't understand—the readings
- slogs through everything slowly and deliberately, or conversely, only skims for generalities
- does not read recreationally

Symptoms of reading problems can be fairly straightforward, such as the ones listed above, but others can be more difficult to spot. I work with many students at the upper end of the academic scale, but being in an AP (advanced placement) class or an IB (International Baccalaureate) program doesn't preclude having reading difficulties. Here are a couple of high-end reading problems I've dealt with. Knowing these problems exist will help you identify them and offer help when needed.

In the first case, students are so overloaded with reading assignments from their advanced classes that there is no way they can actually do all the reading. Instead, they use CliffsNotes and hope for the best. They are so overworked that they never read for fun, and needless to say, their reading does not improve. Tutoring can help these students by giving them the tools to actually do their reading, although the problem of unreasonable assignments may remain.

A slightly different problem occurs when a bright student becomes obsessed with doing everything perfectly. It might take that student hours to read a textbook chapter her classmates complete in an hour or less. Although these academically talented students don't fit our preconceived ideas of who needs help, they can still benefit from tutoring.

Because tutors are in a position to see reading problems before others might be aware of them, they are ideally situated to remedy them. The problems described above should not be considered permanent or enduring: They are symptoms that can be resolved quickly once the underlying reading problems are addressed.

Inspiring Transformation

Tutoring can be for enrichment as well as remediation, and qualified tutors can do more than simply correct problems. Parents may realize that just because their teens are making good grades does not necessarily mean they are receiving a quality education, and they may want enrichment to fill in what's missing. One advantage of an enrichment program is that it can be based largely on students' interests.

As a tutor it is possible for you to have a strong and lasting positive effect on your students' lives. The close personal relationship that often develops in tutoring can be transformative for students. In a supportive and responsive environment, students not only become good readers and thinkers, they also grow as individuals. In tutoring, insecure children gain confidence, impatient or impulsive youngsters learn to persevere, and those with simplistic views become willing to consider new ideas and broaden their outlooks. These transformations do not occur in every case, of course, but in my experience, they happen more often than not.

Keys to Effective Tutoring

Almost all young people want to do well in school, but they may fail because of barriers they themselves or others put in the way. Even students who seem lazy or turned off by school usually want to succeed at some level. To understand the mixed motives teens might have about their studies, first think of the student as the individual he or she actually is, then add the idea that the person comprises an internal cast of characters, each with a different agenda. One figure in this internal cast might want to work hard, but another might be alienated by school. These aspects of the personality may take turns on stage, and they might even struggle for control. The tutor must find and strengthen the aspects that want to succeed. (To learn more about this internal "cast of characters," read about ego states in Chapter 14.) The following keys to effective tutoring offer ways to ally yourself with the desire for success within each student and help it grow.

Find out what your student knows—don't assume

The directors of a peer-tutoring program at our local high school say that when students are not learning satisfactorily from their tutors, one of the most common reasons is that the students fake a level of understanding they don't have, and it doesn't occur to the tutors to challenge them. The question, "Do you understand this?" will almost always be met with an automatic "Yes."

It is important to check your student's understanding of a subject before, during and after you teach it. Question her to find out what she knows, and if there's any doubt, have her teach the material back to you. She will listen more carefully if she expects to be questioned whenever she hears an explanation.

By the same token, when a student begins working with a tutor, both the student and parent may maintain that the student is a "good reader," but it's best to take that opinion with a grain of salt. Reading problems are not always obvious to those who have them, and teens often cover up a problem to save face, so check a student's reading before accepting anyone else's word on the matter. To these students, being a "good reader" might mean reading aloud correctly or loving to read novels—real strengths, but not the whole picture. (For more about how to check a student's reading comprehension, see Chapter 3.)

Direct students' attention to their own learning process

At the same time you are checking the student's factual understanding, it is also important to find out about her internal process and emotional reactions. To do this, you might ask:

- How did this speed-reading technique work for you?
- How was your concentration?
- Were you able to visualize?
- How do you feel about doing this?
- Do you notice any change in your comprehension?

Answers to questions like these have the important function of allowing the tutor to adjust instruction to the individual student. In addition, these questions can start students thinking about their own learning process.

Many students, especially less experienced ones, have rarely given any thought to their own learning. They think about grades or whether or not they are "smart," but not about the internal process of learning. In fact, they usually do not even realize that learning is a process and that they must develop strategies and hone skills if they want to succeed academically. The tutor's questions can help them begin to see that reading is a series of internal steps, that choices are involved, and that skills evolve with strategic practice. This knowledge instills hope.

Control your message with conscious use of body language and tone of voice

We all send subtle, and sometimes not so subtle, messages through posture, movement, and vocal expression whether we are aware of them or not. We transmit at this nonverbal level all the time, and usually our communications are readable but not particularly important. When we teach, however, it is a different matter. Kids are highly attuned to nonverbal communications and respond to them whether or not they themselves are aware of them.

Becoming more aware of the cues you send can help you gain conscious control of your communications, and will in turn contribute to your students' learning. Through body language and tone of voice you can assert your authority, make your point, or communicate a particular attitude. For instance, if you want to show you are listening, you sit one way, but if you want your student to listen, you sit another.

Though it's beyond our scope to teach details of nonverbal communication, here are a few keys.

- Kids want to be seen. Nobody likes to be stared at, of course, but kids do want to be noticed, so some eye contact is good. In addition, spend time simply observing.
- Avoid the tone of voice that says, "Now we are speaking to children." It's the way some kindergarten teachers talk to little kids, but teachers of secondary students sometimes use the same tone! Kids rightly interpret it as condescending.
- Choose vocabulary that is encouraging even when you are making demands. "I think you can do this. Show me your best."
- Offer to show the student how to do something rather than teaching it to her. It's just a matter of word choice, but being shown is sometimes easier to accept than being taught.
- Encourage students to lean forward so they can see clearly what you are pointing out in the paper or book on the desk. Most kids have a tendency to lean back, letting the teacher do all the work. Leaning forward leads to more active engagement.
- Choose seating for yourself and your student carefully. For instance, a student who constantly challenges your authority might be moved to a lower chair. It's hard to be controlling when you are looking up at someone. By the same token, sit on the same side of the table to show you're "on the same team."

- Ask a colleague to observe and critique your nonverbal communications. It is often difficult to see ourselves as others see us, so this can be an eye-opener. Tape recordings and videos are useful as well. This type of criticism can be hard on the ego in the short term but is worth it in the long run.

The idea behind the conscious use of voice and body language is not to be picture perfect but to ensure we are sending the messages we want to send.

Keep it simple

Try to keep explanations as short as possible and still cover the subject. One reason given by teens about why they prefer not to work with their parents on academic subjects is that their parents overwhelm them with explanations. Students will be more open about asking questions if they aren't deluged when they do.

"What you stroke is what you get"

According to psychologist Eric Berne, strokes are units of attention (Berne 1996, 15). Everybody needs and wants attention. It's a biologically determined, inborn need, and people will go to great lengths to get it. So, if you pay attention to positive behavior in your students, you'll see more positive behavior. If you comment often and ineffectually about their negative behavior, you'll reinforce (reward) it, and that will generate more unwanted behavior. That doesn't mean we should simply ignore bad behavior. It only means we should observe which behaviors we pay attention to, comment on, question kids about and smile at. Those are the behaviors we will get more of in the future.

Here is one way to use strokes to achieve a positive outcome. David, 13, comes in to tutoring. He's fidgeting, can't sit still. He's bored, and he isn't looking at you or listening. At some point in the future, you might need to tell him to be still and listen, but now isn't the time for that. Don't comment on his inattentiveness at all for now. Simply get him to do something he's likely to focus on. Ask him to answer questions, talk about himself, read something interesting and tell about it, listen to directions and follow them—anything that's likely to cut down on his fidgeting. Then, when he's calmer and more focused, comment on his response: "What you just did (said) was interesting (clear or correct)."

After that, continue with activities that require focus to accomplish, and keep commenting on the good results. In other words, comment on his actions, not on his personality, and avoid making comments such as,

"Wow, you are really paying attention," because few self-respecting teenagers would want to please a teacher that much! Here is an example.

"What you stroke is what you get"

A psychologist's teenage patient was often late. Without mentioning the lateness, the doctor offered the boy a Coke whenever the boy was on time, but did not give him a Coke when he was late. The boy started coming on time more and more frequently, until he was almost always there when he was supposed to be. So the boy was getting a "secret reward" for being on time, and it worked. This story shows that rewards don't have to be big, they don't have to be talked about, and they work even when the recipient is not aware that they are rewards. This anecdote encourages us to be aware of the small, unspoken ways in which we reward—and punish—our students' behavior.

It is possible to over-reward, so make room in the process for comments such as "I think you could do better. Try again."

Reward students' best efforts

In psychological lingo, rewarding a student's best efforts in a consistent, organized way is known as "rewarding successive approximations." This means that you begin by rewarding any move in the right direction, but then gradually raise your expectations until nothing but success will do. Rewarding your students' best efforts is a simple idea with some big payoffs.

To put the principle into practice, first come up with an objective, something that requires the student to attain a certain level of skill in a particular area. This might be a goal that you and your student set together or one that you assign. For example, you might ask the student to aim for a particular reading speed or to correctly identify the main ideas in a certain number of paragraphs in a row.

When you have a goal in mind, begin by rewarding (commenting on, paying attention to) any step in the right direction, no matter how small. After that, keep "raising the bar," rewarding each effort that moves closer to the goal than the previous attempt. The "reward" can be a stroke: a comment about a job well done, simply saying "right!" at the end of a task (this really works!), or giving the student the chance to quit one activity and start another.

This method works because it doesn't expect too much too soon, cuts down on frustration, and provides a way for teachers to break tasks down to size without compromising their standards. The way expectations are expressed can make a difference—for instance, "That's great! Now, the next step is for you to _____." Most teens respond positively to this approach, which acknowledges the gains a student has made while requesting more.

"Grandma's Rule"

Grandma's Rule states, "First you do what I want you to do, then you can do what you want to do" (Becker 1971, 24). Grandma's Rule has obvious applications for a parent, who might require younger kids to wipe their muddy boots before they come inside for a snack, or to go to bed in time for a story. But it also works well for teachers, even at the secondary level.

For instance, making up stories together is fun, and students like to be asked their opinions about things, but phonics instruction and analysis of paragraph structure are less motivating. According to Grandma's Rule, if the student works hard on the tedious but worthwhile things first, she gets to do some of the fun stuff later. So you might leave five minutes at the end of the lesson for some relaxed conversation as a reward for a child who has successfully curbed her urge to interrupt. A teenage student who needs to work on basic skills (word identification, for instance) but doesn't really enjoy it will probably agree to do it if she knows that afterward she'll get some help on her homework assignment that's due tomorrow.

The trick with older students is not to be too obvious with the sticks and carrots. The tutor might simply say, near the end of a successful lesson, "We've worked hard and I think you've learned a lot. How about some down time? Would you like to . . . (play the Mad Libs parts-of-speech game, look at art books that fit in with your history reading, make up a character for your science fiction story)?"

Immature teens with attention or behavior problems may need a more direct approach. For instance, you could put a clock or timer in front of a student and say "this part of the lesson will be over when you've concentrated for 'x' number of minutes." Far from being resistant, most kids respond well to this approach because it actually gives them some control over the course of the lesson. It follows Grandma's Rule because the student gets to do what she wants (get on with the lesson) after she does what you want (pay attention).

Find out what is interesting and rewarding to students

Determine what a student finds interesting and rewarding, and if it fits with your program, give it to her. Five minutes of talking time might make Barbara happy, but Brad wants to illustrate a story he's read, and Ed simply wants to learn how to read faster and better. To find out what kids like, ask them, and also ask their parents.

In working with teens it's not usually a good idea to use actual physical rewards such as tokens, teddy bears, or T-shirts, as some commercial tutoring centers do. Instead, try to be aware of the ways in which the lesson itself rewards students. For instance, fun books should be strategically interspersed with more difficult ones. A chance to laugh over an activity gives a welcome break, and a reading game can follow a grammar lesson. Remember that negative strokes—a teacher griping or complaining about a student's behavior—can have unintended results. I'm not saying that punishments, or negative consequences, should be avoided altogether, but only that they should be used strategically.

In a slightly different vein, if you inquire—not necessarily every time, but occasionally—about students' ideas and opinions before offering your own, it will help them feel listened to and might provide you with some interesting insights into their thinking.

Manage repetition and quit while you're ahead

Repetition and drill are necessary, and even desirable—it's *un*necessary drill that creates student foot-dragging and grumpiness. One of the greatest rewards at your disposal in tutoring is to allow a student to move on to a new activity as soon as she has met a specific goal. If you quit *before* the student gets bored or frustrated, she'll be happier about doing the activity next time. Also, it is important to quit right after the student has been successful at a task, not when she has failed. Always try to end on a note of success.

One way to avoid unnecessary repetition and keep students engaged is to know your goals for each student and have a clear idea of the steps the student will need to take as she progresses. In other words, you need a road map. Setting up this map—or list of sequential learning tasks—can be difficult at first but gets easier with experience. In addition, if you share the map with your student, you're that much farther ahead. If she knows where you're going, she'll be more willing to go along.

"Why are we doing this?"

We know that if something is relevant for us we are more likely to do it. You might be teaching some crucial skill to your student, but the fact that you know it's important won't convince the typical ninth grader that it is. She will want to know what it's good for and why she should bother with it, so it's helpful to have some answers ready beforehand.

Skepticism can often be headed off in the way a topic is introduced. Stating the benefits of learning a subject can help. In a matter of fact way, tell the student that if she learns such-and-such a subject or skill, then she'll be able to _____. And if she doesn't, then _____ is likely to happen. Here's an example. To introduce speed reading, I offer to teach the student to read 50 percent faster than her current speed. I point out that reading faster can help her get through her work more easily and quickly and even help her concentrate better. "Easily and quickly" is a good selling point for teens. Then I have the student look over a chart showing how many books a month a person can read at various reading rates, and I preview one or two of the techniques she will be learning in the speed-reading course. I close by reminding her of some of the skills she has already mastered in tutoring. If she has her past successes in mind, she is more likely to believe that the new skill is achievable. This preview helps assure the student will be "on board" from the beginning.

If the student seems doubtful or resistant, I might also explain the likely natural consequences of her actions if she continues on a certain course. For example, in the case of speed reading, I might say, "You'll be assigned more and more reading as you go through school. If you continue reading at your current rate, it will take you several hours a day to do your assignments. You might feel extremely burdened with the heavy workload, but it's more likely that you'll just decide not to do your reading, with all that means—poor grades, unhappy parents, and a slim chance of getting into the college of your choice." An explanation like this will have most students nodding.

Here is a simple step that goes a long way toward answering the question "Why are we doing this?" It is an almost foolproof measure you can take to make sure your students enter tutoring willing to learn. When I teach students to read for detail using a textbook, I point out that the actual details of the reading selection are of less importance than the skill itself, and that the passage is merely something to practice on. In other words, it's not important in the grand scheme of things for the student to remember the main exports of Brazil, but it is important for her to know how to remember such things if she chooses. It's the ability that counts, not the specific facts.

As we know from our own teen years, most adolescents have very active B.S. alarms, and acknowledging trivia for what it is keeps things in perspective for the student. In addition, most teens agree that expanding a mental ability gives them more control. (For more on teaching recall of factual information, see Chapter 7.)

When starting a new activity, it is informative to ask the student what she thinks the activity is good for. Not surprisingly, kids who always want to know "what good is it?" often haven't thought through the real-life implications of their learning. For example:

"Why do you need to know how to spell in adult life? Why not just depend on a spell checker?"

Answers: To write notes to your employees, write a love letter, write a note to your child's teacher that will be taken seriously.

"How could reading faster help you?" Answers: To get through assigned reading, to do better on the SAT.

"When would you need to be able to read factual material with 100 percent understanding?"

Answers: To follow a recipe, put a bike together, prepare for a test, do taxes.

In addition, you can provide plenty of reading opportunities in real life. Work with maps, TV guides, phone books, want ads, menus, job applications and the driver's education booklet. Using practical materials helps students see the relevance of their reading to everyday life and provides practice in useful skills.

Avoid shaming

It is easier for students to make changes in their behavior if they are not humiliated or shamed. Sarcasm, a favorite form of humor for teachers, might be funny, but it can also be used to humiliate. You don't have to avoid using ironic humor altogether, but try to be aware of the consequences of your remarks.

CONSEQUENCES OF SHAMING

Carl is a high school junior. Although he is capable, he is notorious for not turning in work or for handing in slap-dash papers. Carl presents a jolly façade, so when one of his teachers teased him about not getting his work in, he laughed right along with the rest of the class.

Last semester Carl decided to try to do better in class, and he began completing his work and getting it in on time. The teacher said nothing for a couple of days, but about the third day commented, in a sarcastic tone of voice, "Well, Carl, this is earth-shattering! What's going on? What's got into you?" This comment was not said in an encouraging way, but with a needling undertone. Carl laughed, but he clearly felt angry and embarrassed. Soon afterward the boy fell back into his old ways and quit doing his work.

It would have been better for the teacher simply to have remarked to Carl in private that he noticed the boy had recently been getting his work in. That comment, delivered with a smile, would have allowed Carl to save face and provided the emotional space to continue doing well. As it was, the teacher embarrassed or shamed Carl in public and the boy fought back, mistakenly thinking, as most teens do, that the work is done for the teacher's sake, not the student's, and that not doing his work would be his revenge.

One of my friends says the main motivator of humankind is not power, sex, money, or any of the other common prods and enticements that make people do both good and evil. Rather, it is simply face-saving: the desire to look good and avoid embarrassment. "If you look at the reasons behind the actions of most individuals," she says, "after the public façade is stripped away, you find a large measure of face-saving. This applies to public and private figures, and even nations." She has a point. In tutoring we find that many of the unpleasant, uncooperative, disrespectful, or challenging behaviors of the people we work with are fundamentally attempts to save face. Apathy, bragging, and avoidance are common face-saving ploys.

Minimize reminders

Reminding students about when, where, and how to do their work is a time-honored way of controlling student behavior; the trouble is, it doesn't work. Even simple reminders, if repeated many times, are like shaming: they might appear to work in the short run, but in the long term they almost always backfire, producing passivity, dependence, and resentment.

If we call reminding what it really is—nagging—it brings some clarity to the issue. Any time you ask a student more than once or twice to do something, it is probably nagging. Some teachers and parents nag almost continually. Parents ask if kids have homework to do, they tell them to start their work, and they ask if the work is done. They remind kids to slow down or speed up, to work carefully, and to check their work.

Teachers issue repeated reminders for students to complete assignments or arrive on time. Students are also reminded to be quiet, be still, and stay on task. Beyond their first or second appearance, however, none of these reminders or requests has a place in teaching if your goal is to produce self-disciplined, independent individuals. In fact, for students who are passive and resentful, the cure might be to quit nagging.

On the other hand, when teachers and parents quit reminding students to do their work, kids may quit performing entirely, so it's not enough simply to quit nagging. Instead, tutors need to use a stick and carrot, or consequences, approach to shape student behavior, and they should encourage parents to do the same.

DISCIPLINE AND INDEPENDENCE

Sam, age 12, suffered seriously from ADHD (attention deficit hyperactivity disorder) and was very disorganized and undisciplined. As a result, his parents had developed the habit of telling him when and how to do almost everything in his life. Not surprisingly, Sam took very little initiative at home, in school, or in tutoring. The boy and his parents were caught in a vicious cycle from which it was difficult for either side to disengage.

Once I knew Sam was on board emotionally, the first step was to assign tutoring homework. At the same time, I requested that his mother not ask him what the assignment was or whether he had done it. I wanted to make sure the tutoring assignments were entirely between Sam and myself.

"You're so used to your mom telling you what to do that it might be a little hard for you to do your assignments for me at first," I said. "You'll have to take on the job your mom has been doing and start telling yourself what to do for a change. It'll be different for you, but I think you can do it. If you don't have your work finished, I'll keep you after the tutoring session. If you have finished your work, I'll tell you a story for the last five or 10 minutes of the lesson." (Sam loved stories, so this was a good carrot.)

Sam slipped up several times in a row, then one day came in with the pronouncement that he had to get his act together, which he proceeded to do. After that, except for once or twice, Sam was prepared for his lessons. Sam's mother had a little more trouble backing off than her son, and Sam tattled on her frequently, but she definitely allowed him more independence. The first step toward independence for Sam was for the grown-ups in his life to quit reminding him to do his work. This plan only works, however, if the tutor is consistent in keeping track of the student's tutoring assignments and in applying rewards and consequences.

Instead of nagging, tell the student what's expected once, then ask her to explain it back to you so you know she's got it, ask her how she can remember it (or tell her how), then expect her to do it, on time and correctly. If and when she doesn't, you rely on consequences, not reminders, to steer her in the right direction. If you do this consistently, in conjunction with an interesting and challenging program, you will end up with a student who is self-directed and can take initiative for her own learning. To work, consequences do not have to be odious punishments. In fact, it's best if they're not. (For more on consequences, see "Student Motivation and Behavior" in Chapter 4.)

Like a comedy routine, a lot depends on timing

The best lesson plans and learning methods in the world can flop if they are taught at the wrong time. It's crucial to develop a sense of what needs to be done when. It's hard for one person to tell another how to develop a good sense of timing in tutoring, just as it would be in stand-up comedy, but the key is to develop and pay attention to your own intuition. Knowing when to teach one subject or another, when to let things slide and when to demand results, when to confront a behavior or ignore it, when to ask parents to intervene or to back off, and when to scold a child or to sympathize—all depend ultimately on timing.

A good sense of timing comes from good intuition, which, in turn, is based on a combination of sound instincts and thoroughly examined experience. Although it might not be possible to teach intuition directly, you can still work on developing your own intuitive nature. One of the best ways to do that is to participate in a peer supervision group to review and critique videotapes or recordings of your tutoring sessions. I can attest to the value of such a group. For a year and a half I brought in the worst examples of my tutoring each week to have a group of peers pick apart what I had done and offer suggestions for improvement. The result was both a harrowing and an exhilarating experience, and it changed my life as a teacher.

Self-Esteem through Accomplishment

Many parents want tutoring for their children specifically to help them develop self-confidence. They are correct in assuming that children who see themselves as learners and believe in their own abilities can learn better and will feel better about themselves. Confidence isn't taught in a vacuum, however, and experience shows that confidence comes from competence. How can educators help students develop self-esteem and confidence? And how do academic accomplishment and a feeling of self-worth fit together? Here is a guide to helping students develop a can-do attitude:

- Instead of addressing self-esteem problems directly, start with clear-cut, realistic expectations that demand responsibility and active learning. Add interesting educational activities in which the student continually feels both challenged and successful. Then comment on the student's successes, even if they are small at first.
- Teach essential skills rapidly so she can see immediate progress.
- Let the student know what she's learning and why she's learning it so that she doesn't feel she's having something done to her.
- Increase the number of responses required of the student.
- Remember that *what you stroke is what you get*, so give plenty of praise, provided it's sincere.

- To encourage independence, ask the student to critique her own work and help choose assignments.
- Provide a wide variety of language activities involving reading, writing, speaking, and listening to build all-round language skills.
- For the same reason, include inspiring, funny, or thought-provoking materials to read and discuss.
- Finally, remember that the goal of tutoring, as with all education, should be to help our students become as independent and self-reliant as possible—in other words, to work ourselves out of a job. When a student comes to a tutoring session ready to conduct the lesson herself, that's a real mark of success for both tutor and student.

Exercises

Here are some activities to strengthen your ability to direct student behavior in positive ways:

1. Teach somebody how to make or do something (bake a cake, tie a fly, do a dance, bat a ball) using only positive feedback. Telling people what not to do is often necessary, but this lesson is about teaching positively, so confine your actions to giving instructions or having the student imitate you and commenting on what she did right.

2. Interview three teenagers and find out their interests, likes, skills, and strengths, as well as their dislikes and weaknesses, both in and out of school. Kids don't like to have "weaknesses," however, so instead of using that word, ask them what's hard for them. Take notes during the interviews and write a paragraph about each student. This exercise is similar to what you will be doing in your initial interviews with the student and parents (Chapter 3), so it is good practice.

3. Ask a student who has trouble reading aloud to read a few paragraphs to you. Pick a subject she likes. Give immediate feedback when she has read correctly by saying, "Right" or "Mm-hmm" at the end of each sentence. If she makes mistakes, read the word or the sentence back to her correctly. You don't have to get her to sound out words or even try to teach her anything at this point. All you're doing is seeing the effect that immediate positive feedback can have on a person's performance. How do you think it worked?

Summary of Key Points

- Reading problems are widespread and difficult to overcome without skillful help.
- Reading difficulties include inability to decode (sound out) unfamiliar words, trouble concentrating, slow reading, and lack of understanding, particularly at more abstract levels.
- Reading problems frequently go unrecognized.
- Tutors are in an ideal position to notice reading problems and remedy them.
- Reading tutors can provide enrichment and college preparation in addition to helping struggling readers.
- The close personal relationship that often develops in tutoring can transform students' lives.
- Effective tutors ascertain what their students know, help students understand their own learning process, attend to behaviors they wish to encourage, reward students' best efforts, and negotiate skillfully.
- Effective tutors also appeal to students' interests, make a point of quitting while they're ahead, take time to explain the purpose of the tutoring activities, discipline without shaming, and understand the importance of good timing.
- Confidence comes from competence.

Perhaps the pointers and tips we've worked on so far have you wishing you could begin tutoring right away, but if you don't have students yet, the next step is to turn your attention to setting up a practice. Chapter 2 starts with suggestions for promoting your tutoring services then turns to setting up the business itself. Next come the first actual tutoring activities: the initial consultation and evaluation.

2 | Setting up Your Business

IF YOU AREN'T TEACHING YET and don't have many contacts with teens, how do you find customers? And if you already have a tutoring practice, how do you maintain your business so that people continue to refer to you? These are important questions, but because the answers are highly individual, it's not possible to include many ready-made answers here. Instead, I've tried to set out choices and alternatives, explain the various pros and cons, and suggest additional questions to consider. I hope this approach will help you find solutions and form a plan that fits for your own circumstances and personality.

Developing a Referral Base and Finding Students

To start your business, you need ways to get the word out about your services and build professional contacts. However, who you talk to and how you talk to them are only part of the equation. How you see the situation and your own emotional response are also important. For instance, if you start with the idea that you are imposing on the people you meet and wasting their time, your results will probably reflect that attitude.

Keep in mind that you are providing a valuable service to students and parents in the community through your tutoring. Furthermore, you are offering administrators and teachers a way to help their own students, which is probably one of their primary goals. Concentrating on these ideas will allow you to move beyond the feeling that you are begging, selling, or convincing. Your job then becomes one of informing others of opportunities they are happy to learn about.

This chapter includes a list of tips for building contacts, some of which require prior experience. For instance, how do you give a talk about your tutoring services to school counselors if you have no tutoring experience? Here are some ideas.

Consider volunteering

The way around the obstacle of inexperience may be to start by volunteering, perhaps at your local high school or at a family learning center run by social services in your city. Libraries often need volunteers for their free literacy and homework help programs. The advantage of volunteer work is that students are easy to find and the environment is forgiving. In addition, the students really need the help, and some may be glad to receive it. The disadvantage is that people often will not value what you do because they aren't paying for it. Furthermore, it's hard to be firm about expectations with drop-ins, who might just decide not to show up for the next lesson. Obviously, you must weigh the pros and cons in deciding whether to volunteer.

Contact other educators

If you already have school contacts, by all means use them. Teachers, aides, and librarians who have worked in schools have an "in," and they may simply need to let their associates know they are tutoring to receive referrals. For most people, however, it's not that easy.

When I first moved to Boulder, I didn't know anyone and was at a loss about how to get started tutoring in a new town. Looking back on it many years later, one of the best ways I used to get acquainted was to call all the other tutors and private educational services listed in the yellow pages of the phone book. I introduced myself and asked about the other tutors' services. (Today, internet listings are worth checking as well.) The results weren't spectacular. Hardly anyone called me back when I left a message, but of the three who did, I still keep in contact with two and receive referrals from them, so it was worth the effort.

Most tutors are friendly and eager to meet one another and will refer back and forth when they know each other's work. Unfortunately, in my experience, this cooperative spirit does not always extend to classroom teachers. While many of them are receptive and will turn out to be good referral sources, some teachers may see the tutor as a competitor and act accordingly.

The ratio of effort to success

This leads to a question about the ratio of effort to results. My estimate is that you will have to phone or visit or send letters to 10 potential referral sources to get one referral. This seeming lack of response could be discouraging to someone who is not aware of the ratio. Visualizing the ratio as an image, you have to sow about 10 seeds for one to take hold and grow; you just don't know which one that will be. Far from being discouraging, this image kept me going when I was starting out.

School visits: putting your best foot forward

Let's talk about how to put yourself in the best light when you make public relations visits to potential referral sources such as school counselors and administrators. A school visit might follow this sequence: Ask about the other person's services; give an overview of your own services, including anecdotes and pertinent examples; and finally, find out who else your contact thinks you should talk to. Practice what you plan to say beforehand. You might even write it down. You should be able to give an elevator talk—one lasting about three minutes—describing what you do and what your strengths are.

It is important to find out something about the other person. Then, when you talk about your services, you can emphasize how you might help that person's clientele. You can also point out that referring to you would be a two-way street. For instance, a school counselor would probably be interested to know that you do SAT preparation and therefore could help students who will be taking the test. If you are visiting a private school, you could say you want to learn more about community resources and that you would like information about the school to pass along to the parents of your students, assuming that is the case. Doing this shows that you are not just looking out for your own business but are also a team player—a positive quality in a tutor.

People's eyes may begin to glaze over after hearing more than three or four factual statements about your tutoring, but they will perk up with an anecdote or story. It also helps to have some special interest or project to talk about in addition to day-to-day tutoring. For instance, counselors are polite and mildly interested when I tell them about my tutoring, but they get excited when they hear I am working on a homeschool program or have been training tutors to teach speed reading. You will add to your own store of anecdotes as you gain experience.

Building a Practice

After you have had some experience tutoring, the following suggestions will be helpful for building a practice. Have photos of yourself with your students and samples of student writing. Before and after examples showing students' progress in tutoring can be highly persuasive. Leave a folder of materials with your potential referral source, but keep it simple and try not to deluge the person.

Hand out business cards, flyers, and maybe an article you have written on an educational topic. Giving your business a name other than your own adds a professional look to your cards and flyers. I came up with my business name by looking at what other people were calling their tutoring services—in another state—and adapted a name I liked to reflect the unique character of my own work.

In approaching a school for the first time, you could offer a reduced rate for one student on the condition that the school administrator agrees to refer more students to you if he or she is happy with the results of your tutoring. I did this once and a counselor sent me a boy with a serious case of Tourette's Syndrome. I suppose she wanted to see what I could do. She must have liked the outcome because she continued to refer to me until she retired 15 years later.

Even when your tutoring business is well established, you need to continue promoting it. An annual visit to your referral sources will keep your name and services fresh in their minds. People might stop referring not because they are dissatisfied, but because they've forgotten about you or think you're no longer in business. "Oh, are you still tutoring?" a counselor or teacher sometimes asks. "I thought maybe you were retired." In the words of our family business advisor, "Let them know you're still alive."

Promotional Activities

Now for the promotional activities, starting with the ones that have worked best for me. The rest might work for some people in some circumstances, so they're worth considering but are not sure bets. You might want to begin with contacts that are less important to you just for the practice. You could feel more comfortable if you know not much is riding on the outcome of a visit, and the practice will help you gear up for more important calls. Here are activities that I found useful.

- Give an informative talk to the counselors at your local high school. (See possible presentation topics below.) A few minutes at the end of a faculty meeting is an excellent chance to get the word out. Direct advertising is frowned on in this situation, but include your credentials when you introduce yourself and set out cards, flyers, and articles for people to take.
- Meet individually with each counselor in the next few weeks.

- Talk to private (independent) school principals and admissions counselors.
- Ask private schools if they can refer teens to you who applied to their school but were not accepted. These are likely candidates for tutoring because they probably need help and have parents who can pay.
- When your tutoring business is up and running ask parents to tell their friends about you. Give them cards and flyers to hand out. Satisfied parents are your best promoters.
- See if you can meet with child psychologists and psychiatrists in your area. Doctors can be great referral sources. Find out about their services and special interests and spend a few minutes explaining how you handle a particular problem that might be of interest to them.

Other promotion approaches

- Does your community have a directory of youth services? If so, you might want to get on that list. You might not receive students directly from the list, but being able to point out the listing to school administrators enhances credibility and is good PR.
- Give a talk for parents at your local library.
- Put cards and flyers on bulletin boards, particularly at schools.
- Write and publish an article in a newsletter or local magazine for parents.
- Buy a commercial mailing list. Some lists are age and sex specific. These are expensive, so you might team up to buy a list with others who do not compete directly with you. One tutor I know started her math tutoring business just by using a mailing list.
- Some companies have metal display racks in public places and rent out space for displaying your flyer and keeping it stocked. This is an expensive service, but some tutors claim it's worth it. Again, maybe you could team up with another tutor, make a joint brochure and share the cost.
- High school plays and concerts sometimes have printed programs that include paid advertising, and parent newsletters sometimes accept classified ads.
- I have never had any luck with newspaper ads, but some tutors use them. To be successful, your ad must run continuously.

Informative talks

Besides the short description of your services mentioned earlier, you might want to prepare an informative talk to present to groups. Here are some possibilities. These suggestions are not intended for beginning tutors since they require a certain amount of experience, but keep them in mind and work up to them.

Topics for parents

Parents who are concerned about their children just want to know what they can do to help them. Give them suggestions for what they can do at home, include some anecdotes, and offer guidelines on when to get professional help. This might mean a tutor (you), a private school, or a therapist. Have your promotional material at hand, but slant the talk toward solutions that don't require tutoring.

For example:

- How parents can help their teens get organized. This might include a weekly notebook and planner check. (See Chapter 4 for study skills.)
- How parents can help teens improve their reading. For example, parents might ask kids to do tellbacks (oral summaries, Chapters 5 and 7) or the family could read aloud at the dinner table. Books on tape can boost reading skills without much parental supervision if the student reads along as he listens.
- Suggest books teens would like. Learn about teen reading trends by talking with a librarian and asking bookstore sales people.

Topics for counselors

When talking to school counselors you can discuss:

- How you teach study skills or SAT preparation. Include some tips or handouts that counselors can pass along to kids and parents.
- How you encourage students to be self-directed.
- How you can help students increase their reading speed. Counselors might be interested in learning about some speed-reading techniques themselves.

Topics for psychiatrists

Most psychiatrists will be interested in your approach to teaching students with ADHD, dyslexia, or learning disabilities (Chapter 18). The doctor may be the expert on medications, but mental health practitioners do not have much experience teaching their patients—that's not their job. Therefore, your perspective as a teacher may be quite welcome.

Tell doctors how you help students learn to be more focused and responsible. Psychiatrists work with many teens who have ADD (attention deficit disorder), and many of those students, by definition, have problems following through and staying focused. If doctors are going to refer to a tutor, they want to know how the tutor is likely to deal with problems common to their practice. (Tips on teaching responsibility are covered in Chapter 4, "Troubleshooting Motivational Problems." See Part VI for more on responsibility and focus.)

Where to Tutor, What to Charge, and How to Keep Track

Will you tutor in your home, your student's home, or at the library? How do you set your fees? What's the easiest way of keeping track of your billing? These are all necessary decisions as you set up your tutoring business. They are also personal choices, based on your own needs and preferences. Some options to consider are outlined here.

Where to tutor

Some tutors have a room in their home set up especially for tutoring. Others meet their students in a public place such as the library or a café. Still others travel to their students' homes or meet at the students' school. Let's look at the pros and cons of these arrangements.

At the tutor's home

First, tutoring in your home is probably the easiest. You have all your materials at hand, and the commute is short. Because it is your home, the student feels that he is a guest there and is likely to be better behaved than he would in his own home or at school, which is his turf and where he likely feels he is cock of the walk.

One possible disadvantage of tutoring in your home is the need to provide a quiet, orderly place—fine if your home is quiet and orderly, but a challenge if it's not. Students gossip about their previous tutors, and I have heard stories about housewives who tutor at the kitchen table with their own children underfoot, the phone ringing, and the dog wandering through. Imagine a kid with ADHD in that situation! If you do tutor at home it's important to have a space that is set aside primarily for your work. One math tutor I know tutored in a one-room apartment but used screens to separate his teaching and living areas.

A major concern for a male tutor is the risk of accusations of sexual misconduct if he is alone with a female student at his home. Because of these concerns, many male tutors meet at the student's home when family members are present or opt for a public setting.

Café or other public place

Meeting in a café also has its pros and cons. It can mean a pleasant outing, but some students are so distractible that they don't learn much in a public place. At one time I ran a homeschool program in the school library, and a considerable part of my students' attention was taken up with people-watching.

The student's home

Meeting in the student's home works for many tutors but requires some boundary-setting that isn't necessary in other environments. First, will the student be there and be prepared when you arrive? I once tutored a third-grader who was home alone after school when I came for his lesson. He would conveniently ignore my knocking at the door and then later tell his dad I hadn't come! It's not usually this bad, but kids who have lessons at home often do take advantage of the situation. Some firm rules will help set things straight, though, and you will surely have more business if you can tutor at the student's home.

The student's school

Tutoring at the student's school is also an option. A teen might meet with you during his study hall or lunch period. Of course the particular arrangements depend on the school. An advantage is that it is easy to meet with teachers and they are likely to consider you part of their team if they see you with the student at school. One major problem is that the students you tutor at school will undoubtedly lump you into the category of school teachers, an assessment that can be to your disadvantage, even with a student who likes his teachers.

Avoiding isolation

Whether you choose to teach at a student's home, in a public place, or in your own home, one thing is certain: you will be isolated. It's the nature of tutoring. You will be in a world of kids, and the adults you do spend time with are customers, not confidantes. How much of a problem this will be for you depends partly on your own personal needs—how introverted or extraverted you are—but even introverts will eventually want contacts with others, so it's best to make arrangements ahead of time to satisfy your social needs. If you wait, you might end up quitting tutoring, not out of dissatisfaction with the work itself, but because you feel lonely.

Starting a professional group is a good way to spend quality time with like-minded people. A few months ago I asked two other tutors if they would like to get together, and after these first two asked their friends, things snowballed and we ended up with a wonderful educators' seminar and support group. Our group includes tutors, administrators, psychotherapists, and school placement consultants. Besides sharing ideas, we refer students to each other, use the group as a sounding board, and do some joint advertising. The group also helps us feel connected—an antidote to isolation.

How location can affect results

I once tutored several students at a nearby private college prep high school where they had recently transferred from a public school. Because of poor reading skills, these students were failing Social Studies at the prep school although they had received A's and B's in their public school Social Studies classes. At about the same time, I also took on a couple of students from the same school who came to my home. All the students were at roughly the same level to start with and were learning similar material. The students who were tutored at the school did learn, but their progress was much slower than the ones I taught at home. And this wasn't just a one-time thing. I noticed it again and again. The students who had their lessons at school learned more slowly. Why was this? I think I know part of the answer.

When I taught at home, the students were on my turf. I owned the place and I controlled it, and so I was seen as being more in charge of the learning situation. I felt that the kids trusted the process more (believed that I would be able to help them) and were more willing to accept my frame of reference (learning is good). When I told them that they needed to improve their reading comprehension, they believed it.

At school, on the other hand, the kids and I both fit into a larger framework that, in a way, had already defined us. I was the teacher, and of course I would tell them learning is good. And they would push against it. That's what teachers do; that's what students do.

How much to charge

How much will you charge? If you don't charge enough, people might not take you seriously. Charge too much, or overcharge for your level of experience, and you will have trouble finding customers. The best way to set fees is to ask around and see what others are charging. The commercial tutoring centers usually charge top dollar. An arbitrary formula, but one that strikes me as being workable, is to start by charging about 60 percent what Sylvan is asking, and then to raise your fees as you gain experience. You will find that many tutors undercharge for what they do, while still others may charge very little but not offer much. The latter actually might only be doing homework help rather than offering a complete educational experience.

Whatever your rates, eventually you will run into potential customers who want your services but who cannot pay what you charge. Will you offer a sliding scale or keep your rates the same for everyone? These are business considerations, but the outcome reflects your values.

Once I tutored a boy whose parents asked me to cut my rates for them. I did, but a few weeks later, the boy said casually, "I get to choose where we will go on our family vacation this summer. I am choosing Nepal. Last year my sister chose a game park in Kenya." Naturally, I felt I'd been had. Now, my husband and I have a half-joking policy that I should not cut my rates until he checks to see what kind of car the child arrives in. I do still occasionally cut my rates, but it takes more than a casual request for me to agree to it.

Then there's the matter of barter or trade. Would you accept work from a parent or student in exchange for your services? Barter can be a nuisance—people sometimes don't show up to work, for instance—but it can also help the student's family out and provide you with some services you might not get otherwise. I once had the mother of a student build wooden storage cabinets for my garage. Yard work or housework from a teen in return for a discount on their bill may be helpful to both the tutor and student. Then there's my all-time favorite bartering experience.

A BARTERING WIN-WIN

Greta was 13 and couldn't be bothered with schoolwork or reading. She was pretty, and in her eyes that should have been enough. I could practically see her looking cross-eyed at the books I asked her to read—until her mother began working for me in trade for the girl's lessons. The window of the tutoring room overlooked the backyard where Greta's mother gardened. We traded an hour of yard work for an hour of tutoring. Greta's mother worked hard, weeding, mowing, planting, fertilizing. As my garden improved, so did Greta's attitude. She could not miss seeing how hard her mother was working to provide lessons for her, and she would have been hardhearted not to respond with some serious work of her own.

How to keep track

Setting up a business, even a small one, requires having an organized way of keeping track of your money. This sounds simple, and it can be, but it's amazing to me how many years it took for me to come up with a simple, workable system. You need to track the time you spend, the amount you charge, and what your customers pay, along with a running total of their balance. This can be done easily using three-column ledger paper, with "charges," "payments," and "balance" heading the columns. One ledger, or billing sheet, for each student, conveniently tucked in the front of his or her tutoring folder and updated with each lesson will keep things straight. To bill the family, simply send a copy of the billing sheet with a note to pay the last balance.

Here are a couple of random tidbits I hope are useful. If I address my bill to a student's mother rather than the father, I often receive payment sooner and more reliably. Another observation: I've discovered that I need to overbook students by about 25 percent to get the right number of teaching hours after cancellations.

Books and Materials

Books you will need

You will need the following books to do the exercises in *SMART!*, depending on your student's reading level. You'll probably want two copies of each. Full publication data are provided in the References section.

My Side of the Mountain by Jean Craighead George
Number the Stars by Lois Lowery
That was Then, This is Now by S. E. Hinton
Tiger Eyes by Judy Blume
Two Old Women by Velma Wallis

Books you likely will want to have

ACT and SAT test preparation booklets and books, but obtain them only from the actual test companies (not Barron's or Kaplan).
History and Life by T. Walter Wallbank. Used copies of the 1990 hardcover 4th edition are available online.

The House on Mango Street by Sandra Cisneros

Reasoning and Reading by Joanne Carlisle

Reading Drills for Speed and Comprehension, Advanced Level, by Edward Fry. This title is out of print but available online.

Sadlier Oxford Vocabulary Workshop by William Sadlier

Books you might need, depending on the student

Learning to Learn: Strengthening Study Skills and Brain Power by Gloria Frender

Matthew and the Sea Singer by Jill Paton Walsh. This title is out of print but available online.

The Mythic Tarot by Juliet Sharman-Burke and Liz Greene. This title is out of print, but copies of the 1986 edition are available online. There is a new version that was illustrated by a different artist, but it is more realistic, so not as "mythic."

Night Journey by Kathryn Lasky.

Rand McNally Illustrated History Encyclopedia. This title is out of print but available online.

Summary of Key Points

- Volunteering is one way to get started tutoring.
- When contacting a potential referral source, learn about the other person's business and emphasize how your services might help his or her clientele.
- Prepare a short presentation, take visual aids, and have a project to talk about.
- Focus on the idea that you are offering your contacts a means of helping their students by referring to you. This will help you maintain an attitude of confidence as you make promotional calls.
- Give informative talks to counselors, doctors and parents to expand your business.
- Keep up your advertising and PR contacts even after your business is established.
- Deciding where to tutor, how much to charge, and how to keep track of your billing requires thoughtful planning.

Setting up a practice may seem daunting at first, and it could take years to get a tutoring business running at full speed, but once you begin making contacts to promote your business, you might find you like the experience of meeting new people and discussing topics of mutual interest. In that case, selling your services will go from stressful to fun.

With the preliminaries of setting up a business out of the way, the next step is to meet with prospective students and parents. This important meeting will set the tone for future sessions.

3 | Initial Consultation and Informal Evaluation

WHEN YOU FIRST MEET with students and parents, devote some time to getting acquainted and exchanging information before you actually begin tutoring. The initial consultation is an opportunity for you to provide information about your services to the family and also gain a first impression of your student and her educational needs. During the consultation, you may wish to conduct a short interview with the student and possibly give a "sample" lesson. These will allow you to refine your first impressions and will provide information to facilitate planning.

In some cases, you will realize you need further information about a student's abilities and needs. If so, you can do an informal evaluation to fill out your picture of her general behavior and reading proficiency. After the initial meeting and the student interview and evaluation, you will be able to come up with a preliminary teaching plan. Here are the steps in detail.

The Initial Consultation

When people enter a business arrangement, they want a chance to look the situation over before they commit themselves, and tutoring is no different. The initial one-hour consultation, which you might describe to parents as a get-acquainted session, allows you to find out how the parents view the problem and what services they want for their child. If you give a sample lesson it helps you get a feel for the student's strengths and weaknesses and gives the student an idea of what the lessons will be like.

The session might be divided this way. You meet with the parents and student together for about 10 minutes, then with the teen alone for another half-hour or so. Toward the end of the session, you talk to the parents again, usually alone, though you can give the student the option to stay and listen. At that time you tell the parents about what you've observed during the sample lesson and how you propose to help the student.

Information and policy forms

At the beginning of the consultation, you can ask the parents how they heard about you, and give them your card, flyer, and an information form to fill out at their leisure. Ask the family for their ideas regarding their child's needs. Ask the student for her opinion, but keep in mind that teens might be reluctant to answer in front of their parents, so you can talk in more depth later.

If the parents know there is a problem but don't know what help to ask for, you can use a skills checklist to give them some ideas. My list is included in Appendix A, but make up your own to fit what you do. It's also good to hand out an information form and a tutoring policy sheet (Appendix A). As soon as you can, write an article describing some aspect of your tutoring approach and provide that to parents. If parents are on the fence, reading a well-thought-out article can often swing them in your direction.

Now let's look at problems that might come up in the consultation and possible ways to handle them.

Parents or students who start worst foot forward

Offer parents time to speak with you privately about a student's difficulties. This anecdote illustrates why.

Seeds of a quarrel

Zak was 13, with a big personality and definite opinions on almost everything. It didn't help that his parents wanted to explain, in front of him, exactly what they thought was wrong with his schoolwork. Naturally, this brought out the boy's fighting instinct.

"Zak watches TV while he's trying to study."

"No, I don't."

"Well, then, what's the TV doing on while you've got your books out?"

"Oh, so you'd rather I'd put my books away!?"

To keep from having this kind of quarrel on your hands, explain to the parents beforehand that the main purpose of the consultation is just to get acquainted and that you will learn more about the student's problems as you work together. It's not essential for you to know everything at the beginning. Even if you put it this way, some parents will want to tell you their child's entire educational and psychological history at the outset, sometimes before you even meet the student. When that happens, I just assume the parents really need to tell someone their story, so I usually listen.

Most of the parents and children you meet in your business will be cooperative from the outset. However, a few parents will be extremely stressed about their teen's schoolwork, with the result that you are seeing them at their worst. People with failing children can feel like failures themselves. Even if parents seem negative at first, however, after they've calmed down they will often turn out to be delightful, helpful people and will often become your allies as your work progresses.

THE INSECURE PARENT

Cho's mother seemed both insecure and critical in the first session. She spent considerable time explaining irately how the school had failed her child. I felt that the only reason I did not come in for a similar scolding was that I hadn't yet had a chance to open my mouth. Within a few months, though, Cho's mother and I were hitting it off. Of course, it helped that the girl was reading better and that her writing had improved. Mom herself had gone from negative complainer to a warm, accepting person. A big part of the turnaround was a reduced level of stress for the mother.

In tutoring we need parents to be involved partners. This is in contrast to the way schools sometimes view parents. Parents can be our best informants about what is going on with a student and they can help by working with students at home. The more we keep communications with parents clear and cordial, the better it is for everyone.

The need for education is not limited to teens. Parents, too, may benefit from instruction. The tutoring situation is a natural avenue for educating parents about their teen's school and homework issues, and in some cases can even serve as a classroom for parenting skills. Such opportunities arise naturally when we cultivate a relationship of mutual trust.

Mini-interview

The best way to obtain useful information about a student is to ask the student! The first time you work with a student you might say you'd like to do a mini-interview, and if she has no objection, proceed to ask questions and take notes. Most teens actually like the process of being interviewed and warm up when they see you nodding encouragingly and writing down their words. This is your first chance, and an important one, to cut through a student's defensiveness, bring out a shy child, or listen to a teenager who feels no one understands.

It's important to be nonjudgmental during the interview, even though that can sometimes be difficult. You will hear things that make you cringe: "I hate to read." "I don't want to be here." "My mother didn't even tell me where we were going until we got in the car to come here." Try to respond as an interested bystander, friendly but somewhat detached. To the student who says she doesn't want to be here, you might respond, not unsympathetically, "I'm sorry to hear that," but decline to ask for more detail until you know her better.

Here are some sample questions for the student interview. Naturally you wouldn't ask all or even most of these questions. The questions you ask and how you ask them depend on your student's age and personality. Some teens love being interviewed while others just want to get on with the instruction, so your student's reaction is your best guide.

- How do you think I can help you best?
- What do you like and dislike about school?
- What are your strengths in school?
- What do you need to work on?
- What are your interests outside of school?
- How do you spend your time other than on sports and TV?
- How much homework do you do?
- How do you feel when you are doing your homework?
- How are you at knowing what your assignments are? Getting your work done on time?
- What do you think about your reading? (This question is purposely a little vague. It's a sort of projective technique.)
- Do you read for fun?
- What books have you enjoyed?
- If you don't read, what kinds of books might you be interested in if you *did* read?
- Are you interested in college?
- Do you have any particular career interests? (What do you want to be when you grow up?)
- For an older student: Have you taken the PSAT, SAT, or ACT? May I have a copy of your scores? Do you have the test booklet you used?
- How do you and your folks get along about your schoolwork?
- How is your reading speed? When you read in class do you finish first, in the middle, or near the end compared to others?

The teacher's turn

In the initial evaluation, take time to share information about how you tutor and allow the student to ask questions about tutoring. First, rehearse what you might tell a student about yourself and about how you hope to help her. A few sentences are sufficient. I might tell a student, for instance, that I use exercises and activities that are like stair-steps to get her from where she is now to a place she can do even better and feel more confident. If she is average at reading now, for example, our goal could be to help her attain above-average reading skills. Then mention two or three skills you might work on. To avoid making the tutoring sessions sound like a remedial program, emphasize subjects that sound fairly advanced like reading speed and in-depth understanding.

Provide a sample lesson

After you interview the student, if you have time before you meet with the parents again, you can provide a short sample lesson. The purpose of this lesson is to give the student a taste of what tutoring is like as well as to provide you with preliminary information about her skills and attitudes. During this session, ask the student to do a task that will give you some insight into her difficulties, but arrange the lesson so it ends on a positive note. A sample lesson with a student who is a slow reader might start with a brief comprehension check and timing (see "The Informal Evaluation" below). A student with poor test-taking skills could do the "How to Take a Test" activity from the informal evaluation (see also Appendix B).

To avoid putting students on the spot, delay any heavy-duty testing. Most teens respond well to activities that give them insight into their own learning, and the information from a brief testing activity may encourage an undecided teen to continue tutoring.

If you can end the sample lesson by teaching a learning strategy or technique that works for the student, you have made a convert. You could show the student a speed-reading technique, for example, or demonstrate how to group items in a reading passage to remember them. A breakthrough in the first session isn't always possible, but you can at least end on a positive emotional note: "Yes, your reading is slow, but the good news is it's fairly easy to learn to read faster."

Younger children and even some teens think that if they are in tutoring it must mean there's something wrong with them. In the same situation, a grown-up, or an individual with a more mature outlook, might decide to work hard and learn what was needed to get out of tutoring. Kids don't usually think this way, though. Instead, they might say to themselves, "I'm in tutoring because I'm dumb, and if I'm so dumb I'll just act dumb." Be aware that a student who needs tutoring might resist it, not because she's actually against doing it, but for what she imagines tutoring might mean about her.

Expectations

Before the student makes the decision to sign on for tutoring, I explain my general rules and expectations. The student will be asked to do some work, and under most circumstances I do expect it to be done. Tutoring assignments will always take second place to schoolwork, and I'll work with the student to make sure she's not overloaded. In many cases the student can kill two birds with one stone and do my work and her homework from school at the same time. For instance, she might practice some comprehension techniques she learned in tutoring while she reads her history assignment from school. Knowing that tutoring and class assignments can often be combined will go far to relieve the student's worries about being overloaded. (See also "Preparing the student for tutoring assignments" in Chapter 4).

At the end of the session, I provide the parents a brief, fairly general run-down. What parents want to know at this point is whether I can help their child. I try to be encouraging but honest. I might say that I've had good luck with other teens who had similar problems and offer names and numbers of references. Later I can explain more of the process involved and what the parents can expect of tutoring.

Parents often want to know how long the tutoring will take. The most truthful answer is that there is no way to tell at the beginning, but I tell them I might be able to make a prediction after a few tutoring sessions. Parents are rarely satisfied with this answer, so I often relent and try to give them a ballpark figure. I explain that though there is no way to know for sure, it usually takes between four and nine months to bring a student up to an adequate reading level—if the main goal of tutoring is general reading improvement, if the student is motivated, and if no serious learning problems exist.

Some students stay in tutoring much longer, occasionally for two or three years, not out of necessity, but because they enjoy the lessons and value the support and encouragement they receive. Not all learning is measured on such a long scale, however. It might take several months for a student to become a skillful and independent reader, but parents and students will probably begin to see results much sooner, possibly after only two or three sessions.

Time limits

Toward the end of the consultation, if we're running out of time and still haven't scheduled more lessons, I ask the parents to call during the week so we can finish up our business over the phone. It's important to try to wind up the session on time. You want to be responsive but don't want people to think they can impose on your time.

The same applies to phone conversations. In fact, if you spend more than 10 or 15 minutes on the initial phone call, you are actually less likely to get the student than if you had kept the conversation brief and asked the parent to set a time to come in!

The Informal Evaluation

The best time to conduct an evaluation is during the first two or three sessions following the initial consultation. You may even want to include an activity from the evaluation during the first meeting.

It is not necessary to do an evaluation with every student. Sometimes, the initial consultation will give you a clear idea about what needs to be done, and at other times you know that during the course of tutoring you will find your way soon enough. There are times, however, when the situation is puzzling and you need more information before you can proceed. In that case, an evaluation can reveal possible solutions and suggest a course of action.

In any case, it always pays to do a quick check of all students' reading comprehension to rule out hidden problems. Students, parents, and even teachers may be unaware of teens' reading difficulties. Parents and student alike may even maintain that a student is a good reader, but "good reading" may only mean "good bluffing," so find out for yourself. A student might be referred for some other problem—organizational difficulties, for instance—but if you routinely check all your students' reading levels, you will discover, and be able to help, those with hidden reading problems.

Informal evaluation vs. standardized test: pros and cons

Why use an informal evaluation rather than a standardized test? The answer is that sometimes you shouldn't. Standardized testing is preferable in some situations, especially if the parents suspect undiagnosed ADD or dyslexia, or if a student has experienced several years of failure and the parents are confused and frustrated. It is often to the tutor's advantage to have the testing conducted by an outside party because the test results can put parents' expectations in perspective and can also provide valuable information for tutoring.

Unless you are qualified to do the testing yourself, it is best to have one or two qualified people you can refer parents to for evaluations. Professionals trained in educational testing administer standardized reading, language, and psychological assessments, then include their findings and interpretations in a written report. Not all assessments are equal, so see whether the testing report is clear to both you and the parents and especially whether it provides useful recommendations for remediation.

In the absence of a serious problem, an informal evaluation offers several advantages over standardized testing. It is less expensive for the parents, it may keep the student from identifying herself as a special case, and it could even provide valuable information not available from more formal tests. For instance, few formal evaluations test a student's response to instruction, but it is easy to observe learning behavior in an informal evaluation. How well a student responds to instruction may not be quantifiable (one reason it's not included in standardized tests), but it is observable.

Preparing for the evaluation

Before we discuss the evaluation in depth, we'll go over some preliminaries, including a brief discussion of intelligence, reading level, and how to introduce the evaluation. While it takes years to become a pro at pinpointing reading problems based on an evaluation such as this, most people can learn to do a useful job in a few weeks' time.

Adjusting for intelligence quotient (IQ)

When you evaluate a student's reading, you are not looking at reading in a vacuum. You also receive impressions of an individual's personality and intelligence. IQ doesn't figure prominently in this book because students of various ability levels can learn from similar exercises if the activities are suited to their interests. Still, the topic of IQ does merit a look. In the process of conducting the evaluation, you will gather an impression, either consciously or intuitively, of your student's relative level of intelligence. This impression should be regarded as just that—an impression. Wait to decide on how smart (or not) a student is until you've worked with her several months. Here's why.

IQ is more fluid than many people believe. You've probably read about the studies of teachers who were told that their average students actually had superior IQs. The teachers, as a result, did a much better job of teaching those students and did indeed help them perform at higher than average levels. That's because kids usually rise to the challenge.

We don't really know what students are capable of achieving until we've worked with them, with an open mind, for a sufficient period of time. Many times I've had high school students who were considered "too ADD" or too slow to succeed in regular academic classes subsequently test out of their special programs and move to mainstream classes after a year or two of tutoring.

Students can surprise us with what they are able to accomplish. On the other hand, IQ is not infinitely malleable, and it is possible for parents and teachers to have unrealistically high expectations of students. Expecting too much can create frustration and disappointment for both the student and the teacher and is as destructive as expecting too little. In my husband's work as a clinical child psychologist, he often observed how demands for overachievement led to anxiety, depression, and social withdrawal created by shame at being unable to satisfy parents and teachers.

Unrealistically high expectations can come from the best of intentions. Once, a young woman who wanted to learn the ins and outs of tutoring was observing me tutor a 14-year-old boy. The boy was trying unsuccessfully to do some exercises from a book on reasoning skills. The task was to find one word in a list that didn't belong with the others and then say what the remaining words had in common: for instance, "laugh, cry, sit, talk, yell." No matter how I presented the activity, the boy just couldn't do the exercise.

After the boy's lesson I mentioned that I thought the task was beyond him and perhaps I should change tactics and just work on oral reading. "But," the woman objected, "the boy can do anything he wants. His potential is unlimited. By saying it's impossible, you're making it impossible." On a philosophical level this idea might have some merit, but I knew I was watching a child butt his head against a brick wall, and I knew it wasn't doing anybody any good. I needed to discover what the boy *could* do, then work with his family to help them make realistic plans for his education, not focus on some pie-in-the-sky "potential."

On the other end of the scale, you might be asked to work with highly intelligent teens, either because they are failing school subjects or because they are anxious about their performance. In working with gifted teens, it's important to let the students themselves guide you in putting together a program for them. One characteristic of gifted children is that they have strong interests and compelling ideas about what they want to learn and how they need to learn it.

In a nutshell, expect much from all your students and do push them up to a limit—even a little beyond that limit—but seek to do it in a way that's both realistic and compassionate. Skillful teachers constantly adjust their words and actions to fit students' interests, temperament, and IQ. Mostly this is accomplished on a subconscious level. If you are working successfully with a student, you are probably estimating his IQ accurately.

Reading levels

The idea behind the reading evaluation is to start with material you predict will be challenging but not frustrating for the student and switch to harder or easier material as needed until you find a comfortable reading level for that student. This will allow you to come up with reading material that is just right for that person, Goldilocks style. To turn this activity into an evaluation, you see where the student's abilities fall compared with others—and, even more useful, where he is compared with where he needs to be to succeed in school.

The student's reading level. To perform an informal evaluation, it is necessary to understand what constitutes average, above, and below average reading levels for students of various ages. There are plenty of books on the subject, but I prefer the seat-of-the-pants approach. To use this method, find some cooperative teenage volunteers who already are pegged as poor, average, or good readers according to themselves, their parents, and/or their teachers, and spend some time with them reading and discussing what they've read. Ask them to read silently and tell you about what they've read, then orally to hear how they sound. To ensure a valid comparison, have all the students do at least one reading of the same passage. This should give you a feel for the reading level of a particular student. In addition, if you can get standardized test scores for these students, you'll be that much further along in understanding how reading levels correspond to actual reading material.

Sitting down with a book and a child and reading and discussing might come naturally to you, but in case you need something to get you started, here are some sample questions you can ask to further the exchange:

- Can you summarize what you've read for me?
- What did you think of the part where _____?
- What do you think the point of this paragraph is?
- What's your reaction to _____?
- Put this passage in simple terms. To do that, pretend that you're explaining this to a younger child, say a sixth grader.
- Find the part that indicates the author thinks such-and-such.

- What does this phrase or word mean?
- How would you describe the style or tone of the piece? This question, if it applies, may take some explanation. Using the words *attitude*, *mood*, and *viewpoint* may help.
- Tell me about this character. How did he feel about such-and-such? Why did he act as he did?
- Have you ever known a person like this or been in a situation like this?
- What do you guess might happen next, based on what you read?

Don't forget to add your own reactions as a reader. If you treat the situation as if you were talking to a friend about a book (within limits), it takes the discussion out of the realm of interrogation and turns it into a friendly exchange.

The book's reading level. Besides having an idea about students' reading levels, it's also necessary to know something about the difficulty of the books you'll be asking your students to read. This will allow you to interpret the information you get in the evaluation and will help you choose appropriate books for your students later on. To build your awareness of reading grade levels, it would be helpful to meet with the local librarian who knows the most about books for young adults, as teens are called in the publishing business. Ask around to find out who that person is. Ask her or him to show you examples of books that would be considered appropriate for students of various age groups. Ask what books are currently the most popular, and also get a list of all-time favorites. A visit with middle and high school English teachers may also be helpful, and they might have their own list of favorites. However, schools are not always discriminating about level of difficulty, so use school lists cautiously.

Another way to learn about reading level as well as finding out about exciting books, is to read reviews of children's books in trade publications, newspapers and magazines. Local or state chapters of the International Reading Association (IRA) publish newsletters with good book reviews. State IRA branches have exciting and informative annual conferences on literacy, with dozens of worthwhile speakers and an amazing array of books for sale. You can take a look at the IRA on the internet at www.reading.org.

In addition, spend time browsing the young adult section of your local bookstore to find out what's selling. Finally, read lots of young adult books yourself, and find out from your teenage friends what they like to read. Teens, maybe even more than grown-ups, like to read what their friends are reading. It's a wonderful way to have fun while learning more about young adult reading tastes and abilities.

Levels of understanding

We've been talking about reading level, but there's another sort of level that needs to be taken into account in the evaluation, and that is the student's level of understanding. More specifically, we need to determine the level at which a student's misunderstandings occur in a given reading. It is important to pinpoint just where the problem lies, and these questions can help you do that. The skills referred to in the questions could be considered as points on a continuum of difficulty and abstractness. The informal evaluation is based on these same questions and follows them in roughly the order they appear here. After the evaluation, remediation begins with the lowest level of skill or understanding at which the student first encountered difficulty on the test and proceeds from there.

If a student reads a selection:

- Was he able to read the words and understand their meanings?
- Did he remember the details?
- Did he get the main idea of the paragraph?
- Was he able to read several paragraphs at a time and summarize them?

Introducing the evaluation

At the beginning of the evaluation I tell students that I would like to learn more about their reading level to see how to help them best. It helps students to hear that you need the information to help them, and not because of some failing on their part. I explain I am not giving a standardized test, so they won't get a percentile score, but I will ask them to do several different reading activities. During the evaluation, I take notes on my observations and share them with the student.

I reassure students that I will not talk to their parents about anything I haven't shared with them first. Sometimes people in authority talk about students in a way that does not respect their privacy. Not talking behind a person's back is an important part of gaining anyone's trust and is particularly important with teens. When I talk to the parents, I might cover a subject in more detail or put a different slant on things than I have with the student, but I try to avoid tattling. And, of course, I avoid talking about students in their presence as if they weren't there.

Main Elements of the Informal Evaluation

What should you teach and how should you teach it? Those are the big questions all tutors face in planning instruction for a student. The tasks in this evaluation are designed to help you answer those questions. The evaluation is only a collection of tasks with no ready-made meaning, and its usefulness depends largely on the experience and powers of observation you bring to it. Still, the tasks described here mark a starting place for building the experience and sharpening the perceptions that will turn the evaluation into a truly useful tool for you.

With practice, the information you gain from the evaluation will provide both an overview and a detailed picture of a student's strengths and weaknesses in reading and will also shed light on a student's typical approach to tasks requiring problem-solving.

In the informal evaluation process the student reads silently first and then out loud, from fiction and nonfiction, on various levels, then does a pencil and paper test. You discuss and ask questions about the readings, observe carefully and analyze the student's responses. Then you use the information from the evaluation to develop a learning plan, which you share with the parents and student. Here is a list of tasks used in the evaluation, which is followed by a more detailed discussion of the informal evaluation itself.

Fiction reading

Task: the student reads a passage from a short story and summarizes from memory.

1. Before asking the student to read, check her understanding of individual words from the passage. This will give you a rough idea of her vocabulary.
2. Ask the student to read silently and tell you as much as possible from memory. Then ask questions. How much concrete detail is she able to remember? (Can she tell you "who, where, and what" about the passage?)
3. Can she understand and explain clearly what she has read?
   a. Does she provide adequate detail and show a grasp of main ideas?
   b. Does she use clear referents? (That is, do you know what she is referring to with words such as *it, he,* or *they*?) This task gives a suggestion of the student's ear for the language.

4. In this evaluation, it's fine to teach while you are testing.
   a. After your student reads the passage, go through it with her and point out what she remembered correctly and what she missed.
   b. If she had difficulty, teach:
      (1) the puzzle pieces analogy to aid recall of detail (see the next section, The Informal Evaluation in Detail, below)
      (2) visualization (forming mental images)
5. Oral reading. Have the student read aloud and observe
   a. word recognition, application of phonics skills
   b. fluency and accuracy
   c. student's attention to punctuation, meaningful and natural expression. Poor oral expression often indicates a lack of understanding in a student's silent reading. To promote fluency, you can teach a brief oral reading lesson during the evaluation.
6. Ask questions to discover more about your student's higher-level (abstract) thinking skills. Abstract thinking is reflected in
   a. the ability to follow a story
   b. the ability to predict what might happen in a story
   c. understanding character and motivation
7. Note how well your student learns during the testing. Improvement predicts success in tutoring.

Nonfiction reading

1. *Textbook reading.* The student reads a passage from a textbook and relates from memory what she has read.
   a. Can she identify the main idea of the passage?
   b. Does she include important details? Is she able to remember important names and dates?
   c. Can she answer questions about the text such as, "What does that mean?" and "Why was this important?" Answers offer insight into her level of understanding.
2. *Timed reading.* The student does a timed reading of a nonfiction article and answers a set of questions that follow it. This exercise provides a check of each of the following skills:
3. *Comprehension.* Questions test the student's ability to remember information read, identify main ideas, and draw conclusions. If all test results have been satisfactory so far, a low comprehension score

at this point calls for exercises to improve comprehension of non-fiction reading. Another possible explanation of a low score on the timed reading is that the student understands the reading but lacks test-taking skills. More observation may be needed to pinpoint the cause of the problem, but test-taking skills can be taught if needed.

4. *Vocabulary.* Before the timed reading, check the student's ability to determine the meaning of words in context. Low performance here requires a further look at reading vocabulary. The student may need a vocabulary development program.

5. *Reading Speed.* Time your student's reading and figure her reading rate in words per minute. A low reading speed without other reading problems is relatively simple to improve, requiring four to six weeks of daily practice with weekly lessons.

Test-taking and reasoning skills

The student does a mock test, answering questions about unfamiliar material (Appendix B, "How to Take Tests" worksheet).

1. To introduce the task, explain, "This is to see what you do when you don't know the answers. On unfamiliar material, how do you figure things out using logic?"

2. Try to answer these questions about the student's performance on the mock test:

   a. Is she able to synthesize, or combine, background information with which she is already familiar to solve problems?

   b. Will the student try a question again if she doesn't get the answer the first time?

   c. Does she use a process of elimination in answering multiple choice questions?

Writing, listening, and organizing

It is important to know whether a student is able to write well, listen competently, and organize materials and time efficiently. The informal evaluation does not cover these subjects in detail, but sources of additional information are provided in the Bibliography.

1. Obtain a sample of your student's writing (composition, not handwriting). Though writing is not covered in this book, it is an important subject and should be taught along with reading. See "Suggestions for remediation" later in this chapter for references on teaching writing.

2. Observe your student's listening habits. For example, does she understand and remember directions you give during the testing?
3. Ask the student and her parents about her organizational skills. If pertinent, ask to look over her notebook and planner.

The Informal Evaluation in Detail

Remember, an evaluation is only useful if it suggests ways to remedy the problems it uncovers. Accordingly, many of the skills covered in the evaluation refer to sections in the book in which they are discussed in detail.

Fiction reading

Studies show that students who read recreationally are better readers than those who do not, so helping students improve their fiction reading (a recreational favorite) will help them become better readers all around. Students also need to be able to read fiction skillfully for language arts and literature classes at school.

For this part of the test, locate a short story on about a sixth- or seventh-grade reading level. Once you find materials you like for the evaluation, stick with them. The more you use these materials with your students, the more you'll be able to make comparisons and understand how a particular student is faring.

The story you choose should have some twists and turns to see if students can follow the plot. Also some important aspects of the story should only be implied, not spelled out. You want to see how the student does with "reading between the lines" as well as picking up the obvious. Choose a story that will lend itself to telling why things happened as they did, how the characters in the story feel, and what is likely to happen next. It's preferable to use a short story so the student can finish it in one sitting and get a sense of closure.

The story I use to test fiction reading is called "Two Were Left" (Cave 1983). This story, included in Appendix A, can be used with most middle school students. It can also be used with high school students who might have a low reading level based on your predictions from the interview. "Two Were Left" is used to demonstrate some of the test items in this chapter. If you are already sure a student would do well on a story of this level, you could use a more difficult short story to check fiction reading such as "Paul's Case" by Willa Cather (Cather 1999). Regardless of the difficulty of the material, you are still observing the same habits and abilities, just on a different level.

Reading silently for detail

Some students gain only a general impression of what they read because they skip details or can't remember them. Reading for detail is basic to understanding. Therefore it is one of the first skills to test for and, if needed, to teach. Have the student read the first paragraph of the short story silently and tell you everything she remembers without looking at the text. You really want her to go into detail—this isn't just a brief summary. Jot down what she remembered and what she did not. Don't ask questions yet, but do note any misinterpretations.

Soon you will ask questions about how the characters felt and why they acted as they did, but for now you are only checking for the concrete details: the answers to the questions, "who?," "where?," and "what?" For instance, can the student tell you where and when the story takes place? In "Two Were Left," the answer is: The far North, maybe Alaska or Canada. More questions and their answers might be:

Q: What is the problem in the story (the conflict)?
A: A boy is stranded on a piece of ice with no food or supplies.
Q: Who is in the story (characters)?
A: A boy (or a man) and his dog. (It's not essential to remember names.)

You would be surprised at how many kids aren't sure about the answers to these simple questions.

After your student has run out of things to say about the passage, start asking more in-depth questions. That way, you'll find out how much material the student has in both active and passive memory. Material in active memory can be accessed deliberately and independent of reminders. Passive memory refers to material a person can remember if prompted or reminded, but by definition, material in passive memory cannot be accessed spontaneously.

Both kinds of memory count, but it's good to distinguish them so you can teach active memory if needed. Contrary to what one might assume from observing the typical public school classroom, reading memory can (and should) be taught directly. (Fiction reading in general is covered in Chapter 4 and all of Part II, reading memory in Chapter 5.)

Clarity of verbal expression

As you listen to your student's verbal expression, ask yourself: "Can she understand and explain clearly what she read? Does she provide adequate detail and show a grasp of main ideas? When she refers to someone in the story, can she clearly explain who she is talking about?"

When students communicate clearly, it's an indication they are thinking clearly. The opposite is also true. Though verbal expression is not specifically taught in this book, as a tutor you can help a student sharpen her verbal skills (and her thinking) by questioning her when she is not clear, and by modeling and calling attention to your own communications. For instance, you might say "Here are two ways to say the same thing. Which one is better? Why?" Having students do "oral essays" and oral book reports also makes a noticeable difference in communication skills. At the beginning, you choose a topic and show the student how to organize her thoughts about it into an essay. Later, the student chooses a topic and reports on it aloud in essay form, complete with introduction and conclusion, topic sentences, explanations, and examples.

A student's verbal expression also gives you a suggestion of her "ear" for the language. I think of this as being similar to an ear for music or an eye for color. Students who lack this talent still can learn good verbal skills, in my experience, but it may take them more time, effort, and guidance.

Do a reading critique with your student

Finally, if the student omitted or misunderstood material in telling about the short story, have her follow along while you read the passage aloud. This step is important. Call attention to what was actually stated in the passage, remark on what the student remembered correctly and point out or ask questions about anything she missed.

Developing readers don't do this kind of reflection on their own: It is the missing piece, and one that only you can supply. By explaining "This is what the writer said, this is what you got, and this is what you missed," you are providing an essential new perspective for your student.

Teaching while testing

When working one-on-one, you can teach while testing. After all, your goal is to gain insight into the student's reading, not to come up with a score, so there's no need to worry about contaminating the results. And since the ultimate aim is to select the best educational strategies to use with a student rather than simply compiling a list of deficiencies, it is not necessary to have a static, unchanging picture. If a student does poorly on the first part of a test but does better with some instruction and the tools to improve her work, you note that in your educational planning.

From this standpoint, it is desirable to start teaching while you are still testing. The evaluation is a dynamic process, and you and your student are both learning from it. If your student had trouble remembering what she read, try using the "puzzle pieces" activity and the visualization exercise referred to below. If her oral reading was halting, teach the oral reading exercise. These activities work well in the evaluation because they are relatively simple and offer help quickly. If you teach these exercises as part of the evaluation, keep instruction brief, spending only a few minutes on each one, and take notes on the student's progress before, during, and after each exercise.

One caution: When a student does poorly on a task during the testing but improves with instruction, she is likely to forget the material quickly. This isn't unusual; it simply means that you need to check occasionally and re-teach if needed. Your notes from the testing will help you remember what to teach and re-teach, so you'll want to consult them frequently over the next few weeks.

"Puzzle pieces" to introduce recall

This teaching activity will help students see the importance of paying attention to details as they read. Young people have a tendency to discard information unless they see it as immediately relevant; however, they will remember what they read better if they can be convinced to keep track of information even though they may not see how it fits together at the moment. The "puzzle pieces" activity, an explanation in the form of an analogy, should help your students do that. (To teach it, see "Puzzle pieces" in Chapter 6.)

Visualization

Skillful readers see in their mind's eye what they read, but poor readers often do not, which prevents them from understanding, much less enjoying, their reading. Fortunately, visualization is a teachable skill, and reading improves quickly when people learn to visualize and make it a habit to see with their mind's eye. Introducing visualization in the evaluation gives your student a strong start in learning to read for meaning. To get started now, see "Visualization" in Chapter 5.

Oral reading

Having your student read aloud can alert you to problems that might not otherwise be apparent. Waiting until this point in the evaluation to have her read orally gives your student time to get into the story before you put her on the spot. Select a paragraph for her to read aloud and note what you hear. See if she uses good phrasing and sounds as if she understands what she is reading about. Does she stop at the periods? Pronounce words correctly? Any errors you notice can provide information about what you will need to work on later.

In some cases, people can read well enough silently, but stumble when they read orally. If you think this may be the case with your student, ask her about it. If your student seems to be able to read individual words correctly but is still having difficulty with oral reading, you can teach a short oral reading lesson now. (See "Oral reading and phrasing" in Chapter 5.)

If she misses words, do you see her trying to sound them out but unable to do so? Is she not even trying? Is there a pattern of missing certain parts of words, perhaps the middles or endings? Noticing and categorizing errors will help you tailor remediation to the student's needs. Problems with reading words aloud may indicate your student needs help with phonics, covered in Part V.

Questions for abstract thinking

Until now you have been checking mostly for concrete understanding. Now it is time to find out more about the student's higher-level thinking skills. You want to see if she can "read between the lines," predict outcomes, and tell something about characters and their motivation. Though abstract thinking reflects intelligence, habits of abstract thinking can also be taught. Teaching reading without helping students learn to think more effectively would be like a doctor treating only the symptoms of an illness but ignoring its causes.

In "Two Were Left," the boy and his dog, marooned on the ice, are eyeing each other "warily." To gain an idea of your student's abstract thinking, ask these questions and note the responses you get:

"Why would they be wary?"
"What are they afraid of?"

Further along, the story explains that in the face of starvation, the boy and dog might try to kill each other. However, the student has not reached this passage yet, and before she does, see if she picks up on the implication that this may happen. This task involves the ability to predict and requires thinking about character and motivation. Both require abstract thought.

Finally, using the same paragraph, ask how the boy and dog feel about each other. As with all discussions of this type, follow up by asking, "How do you know?" Abstract thinking is discussed in detail in Chapter 6.

Learning from the test

Most students do much better after they read and discuss the first few paragraphs of the short story. Based on the teacher's questions, they see what is expected of them and will read accordingly. This can be a breakthrough for a student who is a sloppy reader simply because she has never been expected to read carefully or, more precisely, to read carefully *by someone sitting right beside her*. How a student responds to this instruction is a predictor of success in tutoring.

Vocabulary check

Vocabulary refers to knowing the meanings of words, not simply being able to pronounce them. It is important to have an idea of your student's vocabulary because what looks like a reading problem may be a vocabulary problem in disguise. If students don't know the meanings of even a few words in a passage, they may miss the meaning of much of their reading.

So before your student reads the passage, check her understanding of the vocabulary used in the story by asking her the meanings of any words you think might be difficult. For the story "Two Were Left" I ask students to tell the meanings of "iceberg," "warily," "wedged," and "intently."

Having one or two students tell you the meanings of words on a list won't reveal much, but after several students define the same words, you will begin to form a mental "bell curve" to help you judge where one student's vocabulary falls relative to others. With a list this short, the results of the vocabulary check can't be conclusive, but they will at least alert you to the need for more testing. To follow up, you can use the Sadlier vocabulary series for both testing and remediation (Sadlier 2001). Each book comes with a pretest for the proficiency level it addresses. I have several books and try students out in two or three to find the right level on which to start.

Besides looking at word meanings, see if your student understands idiomatic language. Some teens miss the meanings of fairly common expressions and sayings because they are overly concrete in their thinking or else unfamiliar with the wording. Idiomatic language is not covered in the evaluation, but it is something to be aware of as you work with your student.

Quite often, a student understands the meaning of a word but is unable to explain it. If this is the case (or you suspect it is) working on defining words will add to a student's verbal skills. Joanne Carlisle's *Reasoning and Reading* contains a useful exercise on defining words (Carlisle 2000, 32-34).

Though vocabulary development is an important component of any reading program, it is usually less pressing than reading comprehension, so you may wish to wait to start vocabulary instruction until your student has made progress in developing other, possibly more urgently needed skills. (Suggestions for helping students build vocabulary can be found in Chapters 6, 7, and 11.)

Nonfiction: Textbook reading

In this part of the evaluation we look at textbook reading. It might seem that fiction and nonfiction reading are so similar that it would be unnecessary to test them separately. They require very different skills, however, and students who are good at one may do poorly on the other.

Being able to read a textbook well is an essential academic skill even for students who do not have assigned textbook reading at school. A student who is adept at textbook reading will be able to apply her skills to many other types of nonfiction reading. Test-taking, reading magazine or newspaper articles for class, or following instructions for science labs all depend on similar reading skills, and those skills can be taught first and best with a textbook.

One purpose of the evaluation is to find the most difficult level at which a student can read successfully. Start by trying your student on a ninth-grade history textbook. If she does not succeed at this level of textbook reading, go down a level and test nonfiction reading using a children's science book such as *Six-Way Paragraphs: Introductory* by Walter Pauk (1999).

At the other end of the continuum, if the ninth grade textbook is too easy, you could choose a reading selection from a sample PSAT, SAT, or ACT test. (You can get free tests online or from your local high school counselor's office.) It is also possible to use the student's own textbook for this part of the test, but this only works if you can use the same selection for a number of students.

Materials

Choose a passage from a textbook to use for the evaluation. The material should be both well-organized and heavy on facts. You will be checking to see how much information your student can understand and remember and also whether she can identify the main idea of a paragraph (an essential skill and a good indication of reasoning level). The passage I use is from a ninth-grade World History textbook. It's easy enough for most eighth graders and not too far below the level of many older students. I like to start with this passage on the origins of ancient Sumeria:

The oldest civilization began in Mesopotamia

Mesopotamia, which means "land between the rivers," was the eastern portion of the Fertile Crescent, the well-watered region that extends in an arc from the Mediterranean Sea to the Persian Gulf.

The Sumerians built city-states in southern Mesopotamia

About 3500 B.C. a people known as the Sumerians moved into the southern portion of the fertile plain of Shinar between the Tigris and Euphrates rivers. This area is in present-day Iraq where the Tigris and Euphrates rivers flow into the Persian Gulf. The Sumerians probably migrated from the southeast, for their language is unrelated to those of the Semitic people of Mesopotamia who lived to the northwest. (Wallbank 1990, 11)

Process

The process for testing textbook reading is much the same as for fiction reading in that you check for recall of concrete details as well as for abstract thinking. Start by asking your student to read the textbook passage silently and then tell you as much as she can without looking back at the book. Proceed one paragraph at a time. Can she relate the main idea of the passage? Recall important details? Remember the most important names and dates? Did she look at the map that appears in the book to locate the places she read about? As you watch and listen, take notes.

When the student has told you everything she can remember, start asking questions to see if she picked up more from the passage than she was able to relate. How much information should your student be able to recall? Counting the titles, the two paragraphs on Sumer contain about 14 separate facts. Add to that a couple of main ideas, and there are about 16 pieces of information in the passage a student might have remembered. If a student remembers fewer than seven after questioning for the whole passage, she would probably benefit from working on textbook reading. With instruction, the majority of students will be able to remember most (10 or more) details in a passage such as the one on Sumer.

Just recalling facts isn't enough, however. It's also necessary to prioritize information: What ideas and facts are more (or less) important to pay attention to? Some students remember many random details but leave out the most important ones. And of course, we want students to understand the ideas and concepts presented in the text, not just the details.

Reading speed

In this part of the evaluation you will be testing your student's reading speed to discover whether she could benefit from speed-reading instruction. Slow reading can lead to school problems, but since "slowness" itself may not register as a problem with parents, teachers, or students themselves, inadequate reading speed often goes unnoticed. However, slow reading speed can hold a student back just as surely as poor comprehension. Students who read slowly may become bogged down in their work and lose sight of the overview. In other words, they might see a few trees but miss the whole forest. In addition, they may neglect their work or quit doing it altogether. Poor reading speed will cause a student to do poorly on standardized tests, hold her back in literature classes, and may prevent her from enjoying reading generally. Learning to read faster will help teens overcome these problems. Reading speed is easy to teach, but first the problem must be recognized.

The goal of teaching speed reading (Part IV) is to increase speed while improving or maintaining comprehension. Thus, from the beginning we test for comprehension along with speed. Low reading speed without other reading problems is relatively simple to remedy, requiring four to six weeks of daily practice with weekly lessons. Most students enjoy learning to read faster, so instruction is usually readily accepted.

Materials

Test your student's speed and comprehension by timing her reading using a short nonfiction passage then having her answer questions about the reading. For this part of the test it is useful to obtain a book of interesting short articles for timed readings followed by questions. Several speed-reading texts or workbooks have readings that are well-suited to the task. See, for example, *Triple Your Reading Speed* by Wade Cutler (2003).

You will also need a good stopwatch or timer. (Watching the second hand of a clock can be confusing and is not recommended.) This task tests comprehension, speed, recall and test-taking skills. Check to see that the questions accompanying the article cover facts, deductions, and the main idea. If they also ask about author's purpose and figurative language, so much the better.

Choose an article that's on an easy to mid-high-school reading level and is long enough to present a memory challenge. A desirable length is about a thousand words. In my experience, anything shorter tests only immediate recall, not functional reading memory. You want your student to remember what she's read for a few minutes, not just a few seconds. If you prefer to find your own book, look at a community college bookstore for texts used by students enrolled in basic reading courses, since these books are often written on a high school level.

The book I use, *Reading Drills for Speed and Comprehension*, has articles of about 1000 words in length, ideal since students can finish in a few minutes but still have a memory challenge (Fry 1975). The article titled "Magic" and the accompanying questions for comprehension are from this book (see Appendix C). Some students will do well on all parts of the testing until this point but will have trouble with reading speed. In that case, you can jump right into speed reading.

Process

Have your student read the article, and note the time it took her to read the passage in minutes and seconds. Then have her answer the questions (un-timed) and go over the answers together. Finally, compute her speed.

Before you do the timing, here are some points to bring up with your student. Ask her to read the passage at a speed close to her regular rate, but reassure her that it's all right for her to push herself to go a little faster than normal as long as her comprehension doesn't suffer. Ask her to read with the same care as if she were doing a school assignment on which she would be quizzed the next day but not to reread or try to memorize the material. She should pay attention both to details and ideas since the questions cover both. After the reading, have the student answer the questions without looking back at the article.

After she reads and answers the questions, go through them together. Mark them right or wrong, of course, but also show your student why she missed the questions she did. It's not too soon to start teaching test-taking skills. For instance, teach the student to weigh the meaning of questions carefully and to use a process of elimination in answering multiple choice questions. Surprisingly, some students don't do either of these.

When you are finished discussing the reading and the questions, calculate your student's reading speed by following the instructions in the speed-reading text you have used. (If the nonfiction article you use is not part of a speed-reading text and you wish to know how to determine reading speed, see "Calculating baseline reading speed" in Chapter 10.)

Show your student her reading speed along with the percentage of answers she got right and tell her how these scores compare with those of others her age. An appropriate goal for eighth- and ninth-graders would be 80 percent comprehension with a speed of 225 words per minute. For comparisons, Chapter 10 contains a list of speed goals for other grades. If your student scored below those speed goals but achieved a decent comprehension score (over 70 percent), speed-reading instruction is called for. If comprehension fell below 70 percent, start with comprehension and wait to introduce speed reading until the student has mastered the basics of understanding and memory.

Students with passable speed scores may still wish to learn to read faster. For example, students who are anxious about the time it takes them to study or who are extremely painstaking and conscientious about their work would be helped by speed reading.

Test-taking and reasoning skills

To learn more about your student's test-taking and reasoning ability, have her complete the worksheet titled "How To Take Tests" (Appendix B). Each question in this mock test is based on a slightly different test-taking skill. Going over the test with the student can suggest ideas for remediation and can also provide a useful lesson in test-taking strategies.

The explanations that follow the test are for both the tutor and student. Don't simply tell your student the answer to a question she got wrong, but see if you can help her work it out by giving clues and pointers. Whether she was right or wrong, ask the student why she picked the answer she did. Doing so will help you understand the student's thinking better and give her practice reflecting on her own learning process.

Writing, listening, and organizing

It is important to know whether a student is able to write well, listen competently, and organize materials and time efficiently. Even if you choose not to teach these skills, you still need to be aware of your student's level of competence in these areas, if only to refer her to another tutor or advise parents that a problem exists.

Although writing (composition, not handwriting) is covered only briefly in this book, lack of space does not signify lack of importance. Students benefit when reading and writing are taught together. Start by asking your student to give you a page or so of her best writing. I ask students to write about an accomplishment. (For other writing ideas, see "Book Reports and

Higher-level Thinking" and "Putting Character and Theme Together" in Chapter 6.)

Though listening skills and organization are covered in this book, they are not included in the evaluation. In my experience, it is easier to discover what you need to know about your student's competence in these subjects as you work together rather than testing them in advance. You can start early on, however, by observing your student's listening habits during the interview and evaluation. For example, does she understand and remember directions given during the testing? If you suspect a problem, see "Lessons in Listening," Chapter 18.

To learn about a student's organizational and study skills, ask her and her parents. You might wish to look over the student's notebook and planner. You could even arrange to talk to the student's teachers. For more on organization, see "Homework policies and guidelines" in Chapter 4.

Suggestions for Remediation

As noted, the sequence of tasks in the evaluation suggests a stepwise approach to planning remedial strategies. Within limits, the tasks in the evaluation move from basic to more advanced skills, and the recommended remedial activities do the same, so remediation could start with the first task in the evaluation with which the student has difficulty and proceed from there, teaching each skill in order. The book itself is arranged similarly, making it easy to teach the necessary skills in an orderly way.

Here is an overview of teaching activities that might be suggested by the evaluation.

Oral reading exercise

The student reads aloud each day for a specified time. Students gain more natural expression by dividing sentences into phrases. The listener (a parent or aide) follows a certain procedure for corrections, modeling and rewarding accurate, expressive reading. (See "Oral Reading and Phrasing" in Chapter 5.)

Silent reading

Students read books chosen for their individual skill level and interests. They write summaries and discuss what they've read. For students who have trouble concentrating, a hand technique can help, for example, the *long smooth underline* introduced in Chapter 5. Parts II and III offer many activities to improve silent reading.

Vocabulary

Chapters 6, 7, and 11 contain sections on vocabulary. Also, Sadlier company publishes workbooks that emphasize building concepts rather than merely memorizing word meanings (Sadlier 2001). Activities for vocabulary building include keeping a log of unfamiliar words, making up sentences using new words, and using words in a story.

Phonics

Phonics instruction can help students of any age read unfamiliar words more fluently and can also help with spelling. Phonics, or sounding out words, is taught through exercises and flash cards (Part V).

Reasoning

The book *Reasoning and Reading* (Carlisle 2000), used over a period of several months, can teach students to think better in a number of areas, including categorizing, defining and comparing. On a higher level, the verbal sections of the PSAT or SSAT may be useful. (See "Main Idea" in Chapter 8.)

Test-taking

Students can practice test-taking and reading at the same time by using *Reading Drills, Reasoning and Reading,* and *Barron's* SSAT (2013), as well as readings from PSAT tests. Learning better note-taking skills will help students arrive at tests prepared. If you'd like to learn more about teaching test-taking skills, you may wish to consult *Learning to Learn: Strengthening Study Skills and Brain Power* (Frender 2013). See particularly the section on "intelligent guessing strategies" under test-taking skills.

Nonfiction reading

It is important to have the right level of reading material for the student to use for practice, then to proceed stepwise. There are several techniques or exercises that can be used to help students improve their ability to understand and remember what they read. These include learning to visualize, counting facts on fingers, and telling themselves what they have just read. Students should learn the SQ3R method to preview, read and review their textbooks (Part III).

Reading speed

Almost all students can increase their reading speed by 50 percent or more while maintaining or improving their comprehension. It takes about

18 hours of practice for a student to achieve and maintain these higher reading rates (Part IV).

Writing, listening, and organizing

Combine writing and reading by having students write summaries, notes, and reports about their reading. Creative writing inspired by novels and stories is fun and motivating. Students can improve their listening habits and abilities by following oral directions or listening to a story and repeating what they hear (Chapter 18).

When people use the term "organization" they may mean study skills, the organization of time and materials, or motivation and self-control. Students can learn to take good reading notes by summarizing aloud what they have read without looking back at the book and then writing the main idea and two or three important details from memory (Chapter 8). See "Starting with study skills" in Chapter 4 for references to other study skills books.

To help with motivation and attitude, interview parents and students, then help parents set up appropriate routines at home. See "Homework policies and guidelines" in Chapter 4.

Handling Feedback from the Evaluation

Talking with the student

Students are much less likely to be resistant when they have their problems acknowledged but not overemphasized, and the solution to those problems accentuated. People, especially kids, resist having "things done to them." By explaining what you are going to teach, as well as how and why, and leaving the way open for a response, you bring the student into a more equal and cooperative role.

Suppose a student reads haltingly or has trouble remembering what she has read. How do you talk to her about her difficulties? You don't want to embarrass her, but if she doesn't know she has a problem, she might not realize she needs tutoring. In this case, you would explain that a problem exists, but you do it in a way that's easy on her pride. Be gentle but straightforward and stay information-oriented. Explain how the student's problem might hold her back. You might say, for instance, "Your reading is slow enough that it's probably making your schoolwork more difficult than it needs to be." After you have explained the problem, tell the student how you plan to help her.

EVALUATION FEEDBACK: TALKING WITH THE STUDENT

Susan's reading comprehension is poor. She's in tenth grade and finds it nearly impossible to read and take notes from her textbook. She tries to survive by paying careful attention to class discussions and lectures. That worked in earlier grades, but is growing increasingly difficult as her schoolwork becomes harder.

In the evaluation Susan did poorly on the first part of the short story ("Two Were Left"). In contrast, she did all right on the oral reading part of the test. She also did better at reporting what she read for the rest of the story after some instruction on visualization and after she saw what kinds of questions I might ask.

On the textbook reading task, she was able to recall only about half the facts in the paragraph and even invented information that was not in the passage. In other words, she had some significant problems, but her strengths (good oral reading and her ability to learn the visualization technique) made me think she simply needed instruction to help her make use of her abilities.

Susan was discouraged about her schoolwork and worried about her grades. Clearly, she needed an explanation and some encouragement. "I can see that textbook reading must be hard for you," I said. "You probably are putting a lot of time into reading and trying to take notes but not getting much in return for your effort." Then I explained that I could show her some techniques that would help her understand and remember what she read better. We would do this by continuing to work on visualizing. I reassured her that with only a few weeks of practice, most students are able to remember 10 out of 10 pieces of information in a paragraph, and I pointed out that her good oral reading was a sign she could probably succeed at this.

"There is also a technique—almost a formula—for learning to find the main idea of a paragraph. Being able to find the main idea will help you in taking notes, writing reports, and understanding what you've read. After you are able to find the main idea and remember the details of one paragraph, we increase the amount you can read to two, then three paragraphs, and finally to a whole chapter."

I explained we would work on note-taking and even how to study for a test. I assured her that these were all skills she could learn. "You have to make an effort—you have to practice—but the skills we've talked about are not ones that only the smartest kids in the class have the ability to use. You can use those skills, too. The first thing you have to do is decide you want to get better at your reading."

As adults, we would assume that the benefits of reading faster would be obvious, but that's not always so with kids. To explain the value of learning to read faster, for instance, one might say, "There are some techniques you can learn that will help you get through your reading faster, and that could give you more free time and make your studies easier." Teens need reasons, but they respond to certain ones and not others. One way to find out which reasons will appeal to a particular student is to ask the parents. They are the ones who know whether their child dreams of getting better grades, impressing her friends, or having more play time.

If your student did well on a particular section of the evaluation, be sure to let her know that as well. Even though encouraging comparative thinking should usually be avoided, maybe it's all right to offer comparisons in this case, since kids are thrilled to hear that they are "better than average" at something. So I might tell a student (if true) that she did better than most of my other students at a certain task, or that her skill took me by surprise. When people compete only with themselves they are more likely to become self-directed than if they aim to do better—or worse—than others; but comparative thinking is sort of like refined sugar: even if you're against it, a little bit won't hurt.

Talking with parents

Parents mainly want to know whether you can help their teen. They are interested in finding out what's wrong and how you hope to remedy the situation, of course, but their immediate concern is whether you can help their student. So unless they show by their questions they want more, offer a short summary of the testing, what you did and what you observed, and how you propose to help the student. It helps to ask a few questions. Doing so indicates you're open and interested in their views. It will also fill out your picture of the situation. Then tell the parents whether you think you can help their teen. There's an inherent problem here, though. How will you know you can help a student until you try? Here are some ways to stay honest but still sell your program. If true:

- Tell the parents about teens you've helped with similar problems.
- Emphasize that you have had good results with other teens who've worked on the same problem (if you have).
- Provide references—names and phone numbers of parents of students with similar problems with whom you've been successful. (Clear this with the parents beforehand, of course.)
- Reassure the parents that most students enjoy the program and will work hard at it.
- Show the parents a few of the books and worksheets you plan to use with the student.

- Show writing done by previous students. "Before and after" examples with dates are really helpful.

If you are just starting out, you obviously can't rely on your experience, but you can describe in positive terms a program or book you intend to use.

Occasionally you will find that the consultation and evaluation can be bypassed altogether. For instance, I've had parents send a teen to the first session alone and ask that I start tutoring a particular subject immediately. They are quite clear about what they want. This is rare, however, and most of the time the consultation and evaluation are needed to make sure everyone is on the same page.

Now that you have taken these first steps, you have an idea of what the parents want and need for their teen, what the student's interests and abilities are, and what subjects you need to work on with the student.

Summary of Key Points

- An initial consultation provides valuable information for the tutor, parents and student. It is an opportunity to let your program and your approach sell themselves.
- A sample lesson will allow the student to experience tutoring before committing to it.
- Don't be afraid to tell students what you expect of them. Wording expectations in a way that says "I'm on your side" will put you in the role of helper and team-mate rather than taskmaster.
- An informal evaluation done by an intuitive and observant tutor can provide valuable information about a child's emotional state, as well as her willingness and ability to learn. It is no substitute for a formal evaluation when that's needed, but can be an important addition.
- Having a plan to follow and a set of testing materials of different types and levels will allow you to "standardize" your own evaluation over time.
- The informal evaluation may uncover hidden reading problems.
- It will also provide information to help you decide whether to work on fiction, textbook reading, speed reading, or a combination of these with your student.
- In the evaluation, you will check on the student's ability to read for detail, summarize, and read aloud. You may also wish to determine her reading speed and get a rough idea of her vocabulary.

- It is possible to begin teaching during the evaluation. Exercises begun now can be followed up and re-taught later. Visualizing, oral reading and recalling aloud (tellbacks) are good introductory learning activities.
- Students respond well to a learning plan that is honest but upbeat.

With the interview and evaluation completed, we turn to the most essential topic in the book, teaching reading comprehension.

4 | Introduction to Reading Comprehension

READING IS THE PROCESS of deriving meaning from the printed word. Reading without comprehension isn't really reading at all. When I first started to teach reading, back in the late 1950s, I thought that if I could just teach children to read words accurately, the sense would take care of itself, and if the students didn't understand what they were reading, maybe it just meant they weren't up to the task mentally. At the time, many thought that intelligence can't be taught.

After a while it became clear that I was turning out students who could read words. Period. I tried some new methods to teach comprehension, and to my surprise, students who had once seemed dull appeared to become a lot more intelligent.

There were still difficulties, however. When I tried simply asking "comprehension questions"—"Who did what, and why did they do it?"—the students' answers were as simplistic as the questions. It would take a more thorough and thoughtful approach to help students become the critical, emotionally involved readers I wanted them to be.

Eventually, after much trial and error, I was able to help students meet those goals consistently, often in the space of only a few months. When I began getting the "failures" from other tutoring programs and was able to teach them successfully, I knew I finally had a system that worked.

THE BOY ON THE ROOF—READING!

Bart, or Bortje, as he was called by his Dutch family, was my young neighbor at the time I was trying to master the intricacies of reading instruction. His mother, Elizabeta Van der Pool, a good friend of mine, asked if I would tutor Bart. I agreed, but declined to take any payment since my results until then had been mixed.

The Van der Pool's house was across the street, so I had a fairly good view of the goings on over there, and there were many. Eleven-year-old Bart and his brothers and sisters thrived on pranks and high jinks.

81

One day, after several months of free tutoring, I got a phone call from Elizabeta, who sounded . . . well, I wasn't sure if she was proud or upset. "Bortje's up on the roof reading, and he won't come down!" she sputtered. I looked across the street, and sure enough, there was Bart, atop the garage roof with his nose in a book. This was probably the only place he could get away from chores and the constant rough and tumble of his brothers and sisters.

That's when I decided to start charging for my tutoring. Bart's reading on the roof was a mark of success for both of us. He must have started comprehending what he was reading, because there would have been no point in stolen moments for something he didn't understand—and he must have learned it as a result of the work he did with me. Succeeding with Bart helped me define my approach to teaching reading comprehension.

The methods I developed for teaching reading comprehension are summarized here. Though the techniques are simple, it may take months of practice before you are ready to call this approach your own. The good news is that by capitalizing on my experience (and mistakes) you could save yourself years of experimentation. This chapter:

- discusses the importance of incremental, or stepwise learning
- takes a more detailed look at reading level
- offers planning guidelines for comprehension instruction such as which skills to introduce first
- provides notes on lesson planning
- outlines possible interventions for study and behavior problems

Chapters 5 through 9 present the actual teaching activities and exercises, and Chapters 14 through 18 more fully address attitude and behavior. At this point, however, we're simply gaining an overview of issues concerning educational planning and student behavior. These matters may seem less essential than actual reading instruction, but giving them extra thought now will improve your chances of success in the long run.

Incremental Learning

Effective learning is incremental

The steps toward successful learning must be relatively small and orderly. This principle applies to selecting books as much as it does to choosing educational activities. Thus, an important part of reading instruction is to choose books that are interesting and at a comfortable reading level for the student, and to proceed stepwise, neither skipping needed skills nor repeating any unnecessarily.

Some educators seem to feel that since the goal of education is to get students to read challenging material and to think conceptually, then higher-level thinking must be where they should start. These are the teachers who assign *Romeo and Juliet* to eighth graders who may never have read a novel in their lives. Obviously, the students can't read a book like this on their own, so the assignment becomes an in-class reading project. It's OK as a classroom activity, but does little or nothing to further students' reading skills. In this situation students do not progress, since both their reading level and reading histories are ignored. At the opposite extreme, some middle school and high school students are not required to read novels at all.

Incremental learning, on the other hand, keeps the learner's changing needs and capabilities in mind and moves stepwise from skill to skill, each new learning experience growing out of and building on the last. Moreover, review ensures mastery and students are willing to take risks because they have a history of success.

Skipping ahead only leaves gaps in a student's understanding that may never be properly filled in. Proper preparation, not avoiding difficult material, is the key. For instance, a student may need to read 10 or 20 novels before tackling *Romeo and Juliet* or *The Odyssey*.

The "process of success"

Young people often misunderstand what is involved in learning. They need to understand that gaining better reading comprehension, recall, and speed are not like "clothes they put on" but competencies they develop in the same way they would master a sport or a musical instrument. They also need to know it's not just "the smart kids" who succeed, and that succeeding is a *process*.

Explain to the student that you'll get him to the advanced level of understanding (interpretation: "good grades") that he wants, but that first you have to build a foundation. Here's a way to get the point across. Sketch a few stair steps and label each of them, from bottom to top, with these phrases in order: "reading individual words, reading for detail, main idea, note-taking, reading a whole chapter, studying for tests, and writing reports and essay questions." Using information from the evaluation, point out where you think the student is currently located on the "stairs," what he's already mastered, and where you're heading. A gap in a student's knowledge or skills could be drawn as a missing stair step. Knowing that you're "filling in a gap" can help a student accept work on fairly elementary material without "chomping at the bit" too much.

Point out that each of these skills is quite learnable, and that in class you will be relying on a series of exercises that focuses on the individual student's needs. You will work only on what the student actually needs, and as soon as he has mastered a skill, you will move on to new material rather than repeating old work *ad nauseum*, as sometimes happens at school. Though these ideas sound simple, hearing this explanation can be a turning point for students who may never have thought of learning in this way before. For many teens, success is a mystery, or a matter of luck, or else it is for "those other people," whoever they might be. Help your students understand what "causes" success.

The value of repetition

For learning to progress stepwise, it is not enough merely to have the exercises arranged correctly. The learning process itself—what goes on in kids' minds—must also be sequenced so that each intellectual step is grasped and entered into memory before it is put on the back burner and the teacher introduces a new skill.

Successful teaching requires the effective use of repetition. It is possible to have a wonderful tutoring program—one that is emotionally in tune with kids and uses interesting books and well-chosen teaching activities—and still have it fail because it lacked a provision for repetition and review. This was the downfall of a local tutor, now out of business, who introduced phonics, spelling, and even paragraph analysis to students in a promising way, but then moved on before the students had a chance to master each component skill.

Of course, repetition must be done correctly. Most people have horror stories about the senseless repetition they had to endure in school. Here are some pointers for using repetition successfully:

- *Check to see what your student knows.* You don't want to waste time on material your student has already mastered, but neither should you assume that he or she knows *anything* about a subject. To find out for sure, pretest for the desired knowledge and skills, teach and practice if needed, check again, give the student time to forget, and then re-check.
- *Overlearn.* To make sure your student remembers what he learns, have him overlearn. Overlearning prevents forgetting by moving material from short-term into long-term memory through repetition. To overlearn, the student should practice something until he gets it right three lessons in a row. Encourage students to practice

independently this way as well. Overlearning does not come naturally to teens, and you may need to lean on your student a bit.

- *Write it down*. Keep a written log of what you teach, the methods you use to teach, and how your student is doing on each task. At the end of each lesson, while the subject is still fresh in your mind, make a quick note on what to do in the next lesson. That way you'll only repeat purposely.

- *Wait if necessary*. It's OK to set a task aside for a while and return to it later. A clear written log will allow you to do this without dropping the ball.

- *Use variety*. Fortunately there are usually many different ways to teach the same material. Vary your methods and materials to keep the lesson from getting stale. For example, tellbacks can be used on the sports page as well as in a history lesson.

- *Alternate periods of drill with other activities*. One way to incorporate repetition is to alternate short periods of drill between more interesting topics in the lesson. Begin a lesson with something cut and dried such as a spelling test or a phonics drill and end with an imaginative exercise such as discussing a story the student is writing.

- *Explain*. Explain the need for repetition to students and, if called for, even apologize. For instance, "This isn't the most interesting activity, but it's really going to help you."

- *Give feedback*. Continually let your student know how he is doing. He may not like doing more tellbacks, for example, but he'll tolerate them if he sees he is improving.

Level of the Reading Material

To start where the student is and teach incrementally, we need to determine the level of any reading material we're thinking of using. An important element in putting together a successful reading course is finding the right book for a particular student at a particular time. Let's frame the question this way: How difficult is the book I am thinking of using? We can evaluate books for difficulty according to the following four factors, each of which can be imagined as a continuum:

- the length of the reading passage and the amount of information it contains
- how concrete or abstract the material is

- the difficulty of vocabulary and sentence structure
- the background knowledge required to understand the book

It is important to consider all four factors, not just one, when determining a book's level of difficulty for a student.

Length and amount of information

Aside from the level of the material itself, there are also various ways to manage the difficulty of the reading task for the student. For example, on the continuum called "length of the reading passage," reading an entire chapter in a history textbook might be nearly impossible for a student, but if we start with one paragraph at a time, he might be successful and then could move on to progressively longer sections.

Concrete vs. abstract content

Similarly, a book with easy words but rather abstract ideas might be difficult for a student, much to a parent's or teacher's puzzlement: "It looks easy; how come the kid's not getting it?" *Tiger Eyes* (Blume 2010) is a case in point. When using this book and others like it (easy words, complicated feelings), an in-depth discussion on why the characters feel and act as they do would be necessary to move a student along the continuum from concrete thinking (what happened) to a more abstract level (why it happened).

Vocabulary level and sentence structure

In addition to the length of a passage and how abstract it is, we need to consider vocabulary, sentence structure, and background information or general knowledge required to read the books we assign. Take *The Hobbit* (Tolkien 2007), for instance. Since it's a book whose subject appeals to children and teens, and because it was a book we ourselves may have loved, many parents, teachers, and kids themselves think it would be a good choice for a young person with reading difficulties. But the book is harder than it looks. The vocabulary is not that easy and the wording is sometimes archaic. That is not to say *The Hobbit* should be kept out of kids' hands. For some students it will be just right. However, if a student is having a problem with a book, we need to consider its readability and not assume it is at an appropriate level just because it's appealing or looks easy at first glance.

The S. E. Hinton novel *That Was Then, This Is Now* (2008) is a good example of a book that kids like but that needs some explaining to be understandable to teens today. What was "in" during the seventies, when the book was set, can be incomprehensible now.

Oddly enough, teens can get bogged down in books and not even be aware they're stuck. They honestly don't know why it's taken them two weeks to read the first chapter, and they will often claim to be "reading" a book that has languished at the bottom of their backpack for days. Furthermore, studies have shown that poor readers consistently pick books that are either too hard or too easy for them. Thus, choosing books of an inappropriate level may of itself indicate a reading problem. It falls to us as teachers to help students choose interesting books that are at an appropriate reading level for them until they learn to do it for themselves.

Exceptions to the rule

On the other hand, it's not always necessary for students to start by reading easy material in small sections. Individual interest goes a long way toward allowing students to read more challenging books without frustration. We still need to keep reading level in mind and generally progress in our instruction from shorter to longer, easier to more difficult, and concrete to more abstract tasks. But there are exceptions.

FROM MISDIAGNOSIS TO MIRACLE

After I'd worked with Verne a couple of months, his mother called and asked me if I thought he was learning disabled. Verne was one of my first students, and the concept of learning disabilities was new to me. I thought about it for a minute, and since I really knew nothing about the subject and didn't know what to look for, I hedged. "I'm not seeing it," I said. "That doesn't mean he doesn't have learning disabilities, but there's nothing obvious that would indicate he does."

"But the doctors in Texas where we had him tested said he was learning disabled."

Well, great, what did I know? On the other hand, how much did the doctors know?

So I said, "I will let you know if I become aware of anything significant that is blocking his ability to learn. In the meantime, I will continue working with Verne on his reading comprehension. It's important for him to be reading material that is interesting to him. Maybe you can help him find something he likes and have him bring it in. In any event, I'll keep you posted." I had no idea what I was looking for, but there's nothing like beginner's mind (or dumb luck) to carry the day.

So, Verne comes in for his next lesson with a rather advanced-looking book on auto mechanics and car racing.

"Verne, are you sure you want to read this? Isn't it a little hard?"

"No, I like it. I'm going to be a race car driver."

So Verne, who is 16 and reading on a second grade level, plowed into *Be a Racing Pro*.

Then the miracle happened. He started the book in early spring. By the time the June flowers were out, he had moved from painstakingly picking out one word at a time to a semblance of reading.

Every week was better than the last, and my frequent question "Are you sure you want to read this?" was met with the same scoffing "Are you crazy?" look. He might as well have said "What, you want me to give up?" So Verne persevered, and both of us learned a great deal about professional racing.

By fall Verne could read—really read. What do those bumper stickers say? "Expect miracles?" I hadn't expected a miracle but I got one anyway.

By the book

To balance Verne's story with one where its opposite—"doing it right"—worked, let's look at Will's situation. He was not a teen, but a third-grader, and was a nonreader when he first appeared for tutoring. This was in the late eighties, and children who were still not reading by third grade were more common then, perhaps because it was wrongly assumed that a child who had a slow start in the primary grades would catch up later.

THE READING LEVEL MISMATCH

Not only had Will not learned to read in first and second grade, he now had the misfortune of being in a third grade classroom that used a one-size-fits-all kind of Whole Language instruction. (Whole Language emphasizes using good literature to teach reading and downplays teaching skills in isolation. Good theory, bad application in Will's case.)

Maybe "instruction" is the wrong word. From what I could tell, Will's teacher used the sink-or-swim method, with no instruction at all. I visited his classroom once and found the children being assigned some wonderful classics—such as *Heidi*, *Black Beauty*, *Swiss Family Robinson*—but without regard for whether they were actually able to read them. Needless to say, Will's reading was not improving, and his hangdog look was witness to his frustration.

Fortunately, the cure for Will was easy. All I had to do was to start him at the beginning and provide stepwise instruction, making sure that each new book was not too big a step up from the last. I also made a point of finding stories that appealed to Will and teaching him new words before he had a chance to be confused by them in his reading. There was nothing mysterious or difficult about it, nor was there anything wrong with Will's abilities. He simply needed smaller steps and more instruction than his teacher had provided.

So far we've talked about incremental learning and attention to reading level as ways to make instruction accessible to students. Now we'll turn to lesson planning.

Planning for Comprehension Instruction

Create a written plan

Earlier we noted the need to have a plan or "road map" to share with the student and the need to have a written log of the evaluation and the tutoring sessions. The written plan goes one step further. It is important to have a learning plan for each student—not just for a lesson or two, but a long-term plan specifying which abilities and skills the student needs to improve, and the techniques or exercises you will use to help him meet those goals.

If you are just beginning to tutor a student, or if you are new at teaching, you may not have enough information to form a plan yet, but try to work one out as soon as you are able. A written plan can help you keep on target, and it also gives you a quick answer when you get those surprise phone calls from parents asking what you are teaching their son or daughter. It is handy to keep the plan at the front of the student's folder so you can look it over often and change it as needed. Check off each skill as you work on it, making notes on what the student has already mastered, what you're currently working on, and what you want to start on next. Your comments are helpful, too: Did your student do well? Did he enjoy an activity? Do you need to review later? In short, making a plan and keeping track of how you implement it can mean the difference between a quality program and a haphazard one.

Now let's take a look at some general principles for implementing a plan to teach reading comprehension.

Keep comprehension instruction short at first

It's best to keep the time spent on reading comprehension fairly short in the beginning sessions. Half an hour out of an hour lesson is a good amount of time to begin with. Later, when the student has become used to concentrating on detailed work, spending an hour on comprehension is fine.

Work only on what the student needs

This harks back to the "rules of repetition." Explain to the parents and student that some people can read stories and novels well but have trouble with textbook reading, and vice versa. And, of course, some students could use help on both. In any event, you'll just be working on whatever the student actually needs. That's different from what happens in school, and should be a good selling point for tutoring.

Try all the exercises in coming chapters unless you are certain your student doesn't need them. If the student is able to do an exercise right away, simply move on to the next one. If he is having trouble, stay with the activity until he shows an acceptable level of competence. By moving as soon as possible from one exercise to the next you won't skip anything important, but you won't bore the student with exercises he doesn't need, either.

Prioritize academic needs

If all academic problems were equally pressing, it would be impossible to prioritize solutions. But since some are more urgent than others, it is possible to put them in order of importance. To gain focus, ask yourself frequently, "What is my student's weakest skill at this point in time?" And, "What is his most pressing academic need at the moment?" The answers will help you lay out a plan and revise it in response to changing circumstances. For instance, a tutor might ask, "Does the student need to learn to read faster because he's swamped by major school assignments now, or does he need to understand better before he works on speed?" Weighing the answers to such questions will help you develop a responsive, timely plan.

Deciding on a Sequence: What to Teach First

In general, begin a course of tutoring by teaching only one skill, and when the student is making some headway on that one, introduce another. Continue introducing subjects until you have a balanced assortment of activities to draw on for each lesson. When a student masters one skill, discontinue that subject (except for review) and put a new one in its place.

This book is arranged in such a way that it is theoretically possible to start at the beginning and continue in first-to-last order through all the exercises and activities, teaching one after the other. In practice, however, it may be desirable to omit exercises and vary the sequence in which you introduce skills.

Here are some guidelines to help you decide what subject to teach first.

Fiction

Begin the course of instruction with fiction reading (Chapters 5 and 6) if the student fits at least *one* of these categories:

- He is 12-14 years old and not yet required to do textbook reading in school.
- He is an older student who enjoys fiction but dislikes academic reading.

- He is uninterested in schoolwork.
- He has a low vocabulary and level of comprehension that would prevent him from reading factual material successfully until he has improved those skills.

Nonfiction reading

Begin the course of instruction with nonfiction reading (Chapter 7) if *one* of these characteristics is true of your student:

- He needs to read textbooks and articles for school.
- He is 16 or older.
- He does not need immediate help in a literature class.
- He wants to start SAT or ACT instruction.
- He prefers information to stories.

Speed reading

Start tutoring with speed reading if the student:

- has good comprehension in either fiction or nonfiction reading
- needs to read faster to get through school assignments
- will be taking the ACT soon
- is motivated and would enjoy reading faster
- or (paradoxically) is unmotivated and needs something to spark his interest.

Starting with study skills

Sometimes it will be necessary for you to tackle study skills before you can do much to help a student improve his reading skills. This may be true even for students who are very poor readers. For instance, if a teen is reading two years below grade level, is "studying" in front of the TV, and has no idea what his assignments are, you start with the problems that are easiest to fix and will pay off the fastest, namely study habits. Teaching a study skills course is a way to initiate the necessary change. There are many excellent books written on the subject of study skills, so I will include some main points here and encourage you to fill in the gaps with your own reading. A good place to start is *How To Study in College* (Pauk and Owens 2013); see also *Learning to Learn: Strengthening Study Skills and Brain Power* (Frender 2013).

Before setting up a study plan, gather information about your student's study habits. Does he hand in assignments? What's the state of his locker, his backpack and his desk at home? How long can he concentrate at a time?

How does he feel emotionally when he is studying? In what way are his parents involved in his studies?

Young people often know exactly what to do to solve their own study problems, but it helps when an adult directs their attention toward the knowledge they already possess. It's as if the information about how to study is "in there" but they're not paying attention to it. For any given task, your student's answers to the following questions will help you plan instruction and will also start your student thinking about the process of improving his own study habits.

- What have you tried?
- What have you noticed about doing it that way?
- How did it work?
- What do you think you should do?

For a reality check, ask the parents for their take on a student's study habits, as well. ("He says he's studying, but he's really just watching TV" is a common answer.)

Some tutors see themselves as study coaches. If you have a student who needs help with organization, and if the study coach role is one you wish to take on, you can do quite a bit to help a student become better organized. For instance, you could check his planner and notebook and discuss ways for him to set up a workable study area at home. Set aside a lesson or two to help the student set up a system, then continue with weekly notebook and planner checks. (For more on study skills, see the final section of this chapter, "Student Motivation and Behavior.")

A note about phonics

If a student is able to read words adequately but is deficient in comprehension or higher-level thinking skills, it is fairly easy to see where to begin: The teacher simply determines the highest level at which the student has a good grasp of the ideas he is reading and starts from there with comprehension instruction. In contrast, if a student is having difficulty with word recognition, deciding where to begin can be problematic.

At first glance it might seem logical simply to teach word recognition, including phonics, early in the course of tutoring. If the student is having trouble reading individual words, it might seem like a good idea to start at that level, and it makes theoretical sense, too, since we usually start with smaller pieces (sounds and single words in this case) and move to larger ones (passages). Despite appearances, though, starting with phonics does not usually work well because of the human component. It's just not motivating enough, so I believe it is best to wait to introduce phonics instruction and begin tutoring with other subjects instead.

In this book, the chapter on phonics is placed after comprehension and speed, since those topics are usually introduced first. A good time to start phonics instruction is when the student has had enough work on comprehension and recall to have gained some degree of confidence as a reader and when it is apparent that lack of phonics skills has become the weakest link in that student's chain of abilities. Also, it's best to wait until you feel you've built enough credibility with a student that he will believe your assertion that phonics will help him.

Combining subjects

Even though the exercises in this book are arranged in a logical order for presenting them, don't be reluctant to overlap, switch or omit activities if you feel that is what's needed. It is possible and often preferable to teach three or four different skills in the same lesson. And combining reading with writing and study skills instruction enhances all three subjects.

Planning Balanced Lessons

The goal of lesson planning is to create an interesting and rewarding experience for the student but also to balance that with the goal of meeting the student's greatest academic need at any given time. To understand the idea of constructing a balanced lesson, imagine a continuum: At one end are lessons that are fragmented, fast-moving, and lacking follow-through—a kind of educational MTV; on the other is the ponderous, stodgy lesson based on one particular subject taught the same way week after week. Obviously, neither extreme is desirable. Instead, you want to find the middle ground between chaos and boredom. To find that balance, put yourself in your student's place and see what would both engage you and also help you learn in an orderly fashion.

Putting together a lesson

For a student who is beyond the beginning stages of tutoring and seems to be progressing smoothly, an hour lesson might be divided as follows. Devote the first 15 minutes to spelling, handwriting or grammar. The next 15 minutes might be spent on reasoning skills, then 20 minutes on reading comprehension, and the last 10 on reading speed. Take care not to spread things too thin by doing too many activities. Two to four activities in one lesson usually works well. The goal is to give enough instruction in each area to develop the forward momentum necessary for the student to learn a subject successfully but also to cover enough different subjects so that he doesn't become bored or feel that he's missing out on something important. ("Why aren't we working on my homework? When are we going to get to SAT preparation?")

The hard/soft principle

In the *Whole Earth Catalog* of the 1970s there was a review of a book about a private school that had a "hard/soft" philosophy of education. The term "hard/soft" referred both to the way classes were conducted and to the way the school was laid out physically. Some school subjects would be taught in a "hard," or strictly academic, way (grammar, presumably), and others would be "soft," or less structured, and more experiential (maybe writing poetry or painting a mural). The school grounds had their more and less structured areas, too, with traditional classrooms in the front, and a vegetable garden and chicken pen in back.

It was a delightful notion. There would be a healthy balance of the emotional and intellectual, the creative and structured. After reading that review, I set out to apply the "hard/soft" principle in my own teaching. The following guidelines on lesson planning owe much to this concept. As you try your own lesson planning, you will find that attention to the sequence of activities within a lesson does make a difference, leading to a smoother flow and less resistance from the student.

Sequence and timing of teaching activities

- It works well to start with a "cut and dried" activity such as spelling or punctuation practice.
- Allow time near the beginning to review points from the last lesson.
- Ask if the student has anything from school he needs to work on (but be choosy about what you work on in the session).
- For a teen with study problems, ask him at each lesson how he is doing in his classes. Ask him to be specific. "What are you doing in that class?" "Did you get all your work in this week?" "Why not?" "How did that happen?" "What can you do so it doesn't happen again?" "What's your current grade in that class?"
- Find out if what you worked on in tutoring last week helped your student in school.
- Alternate easy and hard activities to give kids a breather.

- Alternate more interesting and less interesting parts of the lesson, and apologize for the boring stuff.
- Tasks requiring more concentration often work best in the middle 20 minutes of the lesson.
- Creative and more "personal" activities fit well in the last 20 minutes: poetry, creative writing, or a literature discussion that has a bearing on the student's life.
- At the end of the lesson, you might ask the student what he learned. Ask for specifics as well as broader ideas.
- Give an assignment at the end of the lesson. It can be simple, "Observe such-and-such during the week and report back," or more demanding, "Bring in five pages of reading notes, plus your lecture notes for the week's classes."
- Sometimes you will give the assignment you think the student needs, sometimes you will ask the student what *he* thinks he should do, and sometimes you will decide together.

Student Motivation and Behavior

In this chapter we've looked at incremental learning and lesson planning, two important topics in preparing to teach reading comprehension. Ultimately, however, the success of the program rests with the student. Does he want to learn and will he cooperate? The choice is his alone. Still, I believe we have much more power to influence the situation than we might assume at first.

Although helping students become engaged, responsible learners can take weeks or even months, a few steps at the beginning can set the tone and head off future problems. The first measure is to make sure the student knows what to expect—and what is expected of him.

Preparing the student for tutoring assignments

During the consultation or first few lessons, I explain that I teach skills—reading, comprehension, and memory—mostly through exercises and activities. As part of this conversation, sometimes it is helpful to sketch and explain the "vicious cycle" (Introduction, Figure 1) and the "good cycle" of *reading skill, practice, and enjoyment*. I explain that no one can "make" the student like reading but that people usually like to do what they're good at, so just gaining a few skills can go a long way toward making reading enjoyable. Kids often get this analogy: "If I was seriously out of shape and went out and tried to ride my bike, I probably wouldn't enjoy it because it would wear me out. If I took an exercise class and built up some strength, though, I would be a lot more likely to enjoy riding my bike. Tutoring is like an exercise class to help you build strength." This explanation in itself sometimes will turn an unwilling teen around.

I point out that it may be possible for the student to master many of the skills we work on in a short period, perhaps only two or three weeks, provided he practices the way I ask him to. First, he'll need to put in about half an hour a day on his tutoring assignments. This might be separate from his schoolwork, or if he has reading from school that he could practice on, he could do both my assignment and his schoolwork at the same time. Since I have already warned him he might have some work to do in tutoring, this shouldn't come as a shock, but I do want to give kids a chance to object, or at least negotiate, if homework from tutoring class is not feasible.

Some students are willing to do assignments but honestly do not have the time. Many teenagers are seriously over-scheduled. They barely have time to eat or sleep, much less do extra assignments. In this case, I may need to set aside time for reading practice in the tutoring session rather than having the student do it at home. Then I explain to the parents and student that it will take longer to complete the course of tutoring that way.

If it is unclear whether a student is unmotivated or simply does not have time, an easy solution is to ask the parents how much time their teen spends studying. In addition, asking parents to send a note explaining that the student did not have enough time to do a tutoring assignment can allow the tutor to ease up when it's appropriate without seeming lax.

Make a no-homework contingency plan

It is important to decide what to do when (not "if") your student comes to his lesson without his assignments. This will happen sooner or later, and it needs to be dealt with consistently and firmly, or your entire program, which might otherwise be very promising, could fail before you even get off to a good start. Here are some guidelines to consider:

- Give the student "one free miss" (one assignment not completed). Use this first miss as an opportunity to review your expectations and policies.
- It is counterproductive to get mad, threaten, or shame.
  o Aim for voice tone and body language that is interested, involved, friendly, and absolutely determined.
  o Embarrassing students, even in a playful way, never works.

- Tell your student you can help him only if he does his part. You want his tutoring assignments to be between the two of you and you'd like not to get his parents involved, but that may be necessary in the future if he's not doing his work. (For most kids parental involvement is something to be avoided.)
- Make sure the student has an organized way of keeping track of assignments, both for you and for school.
  o Ask the student if he has a system for remembering to do things. Some kids, especially those with ADHD, mean well but are disorganized.
  o If necessary, show the student how to keep a planner or an assignment sheet and check jobs off as he does them.
  o You can also have him put sticky notes detailing your assignments on the cover of a book he will be carrying with him.
  o Check at each session to see if he is actually using his system.

Constructive consequences

As noted, simply reminding students to do their work is usually ineffective. Consequences may be needed. Here are a few that usually work well.

Additional lesson

If the student comes to a lesson without an assignment, have him do the missed work during the tutoring session, then come back later in the week for an extra lesson, since he didn't get a real lesson the first time. Discuss with the parents beforehand to see if they're agreeable. You might charge less than your regular rate for the extra lesson, and if a student seems not to be taking it seriously, you could suggest he pay part of it.

Stay after

Instead of having him come in for an extra lesson, you could just have him stay an extra 15 minutes or half an hour at the end of his regular session. This doesn't seem like much of a punishment, but it usually works as well as more time-consuming consequences.

"World's most boring lesson"

One consequence that I've used with good results is intentionally giving a boring lesson to a student who has come to a tutoring session unprepared. Boring means that I keep any chatting or socializing to a minimum, and rather than teach as usual, I have the student read and take notes, or even copy from an uninteresting textbook. To be successful, this consequence must be treated with a little humor and the student should be warned beforehand that "world's most boring lesson" is coming if he neglects his assignment again, but other than that, he should not be informed about any of the details.

Tell the student that if he doesn't like an assignment, doesn't have time for it, or doesn't know how to do it, he needs to call you and discuss it. Then you'll know his heart's in the right place. Kids will hardly ever call, but simply making this suggestion seems to help them get the work done.

Additional ideas

Explain matter-of-factly but gently what the consequence will be and why you are imposing it. Ordinarily you want to keep things as brief as possible and still get the idea across. Here are some ideas to choose from.

"It's been three weeks now that you've forgotten to bring your assignment in. This isn't working. We need to do something different. If you forget your work next time, I'm going to ask you to stay after class." Explain that staying after class is not supposed to be a big punishment and its purpose is not to make the student feel bad or guilty. Instead, "It's necessary because if we don't do something different you will probably keep coming in with no assignment, and that's going to add months and months to the time you're in tutoring. And that could definitely discourage you." Explain that having a consequence is simply a reminder. "Not doing your work isn't about right and wrong; it's just a habit, and like all habits it can be changed. Sometimes you simply need something to interrupt the habit, and that's what this is."

When a student neglects to complete tutoring assignments, the tutor is being offered an opportunity to help build the character traits he needs. For many students, this marks the first time in their lives they have been held accountable for consistently meeting deadlines and producing quality work; thus, meeting the tutor's expectations can mark a major positive turning point in a young person's view of himself and his responsibilities. (See Chapter 18 for a more thorough discussion of this topic.)

Troubleshooting motivational problems

The best way to deal with most motivation and behavior problems is by giving students a taste of success. That success, along with an adult's undivided attention for an hour or two a week, is a powerful motivator for most teens. Sometimes, though, a young person is so caught up in negative attitudes about himself, school, tutoring, or life in general, that he needs more than the ordinary interventions.

Some problems are so serious they are beyond the scope of tutoring. Children with severe mental illness may not be good candidates for tutoring, and the tutor may need to bow out of those cases. On the other hand, for some troubled young people, the structure and positive emotional environment of tutoring can be life-changing, sometimes even accomplishing more than could be achieved in psychotherapy. To quote my husband Terry, a clinical child psychologist for 30 years, "Tutoring is the treatment of choice for some teens."

If you do take on students with serious problems, the beginning sessions are important ones for establishing expectations. The same is true of any behavior challenge, serious or not. The tutor must intervene in a timely way to correct behavior and motivational problems. Allowing problems to continue will reinforce students' existing patterns of avoidance and failure.

Here are a few pointers for troubleshooting the more difficult motivational and attitude problems you will face in your tutoring. Part VI addresses some of the relevant psychological and physiological aspects of learning in greater detail.

Problem

The student does not see himself as a learner. "I'm not really into school. I'm just a . . . (punk, redneck, artist, athlete, other)."

Interventions

Arrange an activity in which the student is likely to succeed and then comment on the results. Be circumspect, though. The student may feel that if he "gives in" and does his schoolwork correctly he has lost face.

Adolescents may select identities almost like they choose clothes, so help them see they can be inclusive. For instance, a student can be artistic *and* smart. One of my high school students recently discovered she could be a disreputable looking snowboarder on the weekends and a straight A student the rest of the week. This choice hit a good balance for an ambitious kid with a rebellious streak. As always, use the student's own interests to involve him. For example:

- Help a future artist write a business plan.
- Ask an athlete to write an essay on steroid use or nutritional supplements.

- A student who is motivated by the typical TV fare of sex and violence may be able to shift gears enough to read a novel about war and scandal instead.

Problem

The student is hyperactive or overly distractible. He interrupts, changes the subject, and can't stick with his reading.

Interventions

Set limits. "Don't interrupt me. I listen to you carefully when you speak and I want you to do the same with me."

Use a carrot *and* a stick. "I see that it's hard for you to stay on the subject. Let's stick with this for the next 10 minutes and then we'll have some time for whatever you want to talk about." Or, "I notice that you don't like listening to explanations. I'll keep it short, but I must have your complete attention. If you're not focused, I'll feel I need to keep explaining, and you won't like that."

Discuss the problem head-on. "I can see that you're distractible. What might help you pay attention better?" If the parents seem receptive, you might recommend a meditation class for the teen.

Possible additional aids include:

- background music
- short breaks
- physical prompts
  - o Touch the child's arm, look directly at him and say, "We're talking about *X* right now. Let's stick with it."
  - o Or, tapping the page, "Keep your eyes here, please. Move up closer so you can see better."

Medication can be helpful, but the topic is controversial. Avoid bringing it up directly, but if nothing else works and the child is so hyperactive it affects his quality of life, you might refer the family to an M.D. who is experienced with kids and is known to have a balanced approach with medication.

Problem

The student is irritable and dismissive.

Interventions

Discuss the problem directly.

Tutor: "You seem annoyed. What's wrong?"

Student: "My mom is making me come here."

Tutor: "What would make you happier about being here?"

Student: "Nothing." Or, "Just help me get this paper done." Or, "Maybe if I didn't have to repeat this grade."

Tutor: Acknowledges what the student has said and adds, "I'll try to keep the lesson as interesting as I can and still have you learning what you need to, but I'd like you to keep an open mind."

Get the student started on creative writing or some other form of expression so he can get his feelings out in an acceptable way. For a passive-aggressive or openly angry student, psychotherapy may be helpful. Whether to refer to a psychotherapist or not depends on the openness of the parents and the availability of a good therapist. In any case, wait to refer until you have built a trusting relationship with the family.

Problem

The student is dreamy or "spacey," perhaps gazing around the room, not focused on work. This student's eyes may even seem unfocused.

Interventions

Have the student read for a purpose. Ask him to read so that he can do something afterward, such as draw a picture from written directions, make a map, illustrate what he's read, or act out a part in a skit or dialog.

Teach a subject that requires focus to understand, such as parts of speech or rules for syllable division, and expect the student to get it. "I'm going to explain something rather complicated, and you will need to focus your brain completely to understand it. When I'm done I will ask you to explain it back to me." (This may take several tries.)

Comment nonjudgmentally on the student's lack of focus, but explain that he will need to focus in tutoring. "I see you drifting pleasantly through life. Sometimes that's OK, but I'd like you to try focusing more in tutoring. Focusing your brain is similar in some ways to focusing your eyes."

Explain that expectations are different in tutoring than in school. "At school if you don't pay attention you might get a bad grade and your Mom might be unhappy, but nothing very bad is going to happen. In tutoring it's different. There's no bad grade but we'll go over things until you get them. If you don't want to listen to me repeating lesson material, the solution is to focus your brain and pick up on things the first time around.

Find out what the student's responsibilities are at home. More demanding and complex tasks can teach concentration and initiative. Parents often want to come in each week to discuss progress at home. (There's more in Chapter 18 on using household chores to promote learning.)

If the child is missing work at school, teach study skills, including keeping a planner to track assignments. Allow class time to organize.

Some students read so slowly they nearly fall asleep over their books. These students are more likely to understand the material better if they read faster. Teach the *long smooth underline* (LSU), a hand technique for increasing concentration and speed. The LSU is introduced in Chapter 5 and discussed further in Chapter 10, "Reading Speed with Comprehension." Explain why you want the students to read faster, and with their agreement, put time limits or at least set goals on passages they read in the tutoring session.

Ask students who are slow to respond, "Are you stuck or do you just need time to think?" The question will probably cut down on daydreaming without interrupting the students unnecessarily.

Guided reading will help. "Read this paragraph and tell me three things you thought were interesting or important. At the end of this section, I will ask you who was in the scene, what each person said, and how he or she felt."

Problem

The student is dismissive and has a sense of entitlement. The unspoken attitude is, "I'm too good for this class."

Interventions

- *Set personal goals.* Find out what the student thinks is important and help him set personal goals. It's hard to feel "too good" for your own goals. Talk about how tutoring can help him reach his goals.
- *Teach ego states and drama triangle.* It is helpful for the student to learn about the internal Parent, Adult, and Child aspects of the personality and their roles in learning. Knowing about Persecutor, Rescuer, and Victim roles can also raise awareness. Curiosity about these new subjects will pull the student in at the beginning, then when he has advanced enough to listen dispassionately, point out how his current attitudes may not serve him well and discuss more adaptive approaches. (See Chapter 14 for more on ego states and Chapter 16 for a discussion of the drama triangle.)

- *Volunteer work.* Working as a volunteer on community projects will often deflate a superiority complex. I've known parents to take their teens to Mexico to volunteer in an orphanage. This is a sure cure, but extreme. Closer to home, some teens benefit from working with animals at the Humane Society or at a horse rescue mission. Working on a trail-building crew can help both kids and the environment.

The interventions suggested above are not limited to use with only one problem, and in many cases the solutions are interchangeable. Your intuition will guide you in choosing and combining the right strategies for your student.

Improving study habits

Problem

The student is disorganized, does little studying, and fails to hand in work at school.

Interventions

Since most studying happens (or doesn't happen) at home, talk to parents about appropriate "sticks and carrots" they can use to establish good study behavior. Avoid giving direct advice on parenting, which can backfire. Simply tell parents what has worked for other families in similar circumstances, present some choices, then let them choose a course of action themselves.

Learning about the rules, expectations, interventions, rewards, and punishments that work best for a variety of families will require experience on your part, but you can start now to build that experience. Begin by asking the questions, "How do you handle (homework time, TV time, computer games) in your family?" and, "How does it work to do it that way?" Your mental file of useful parenting tips will grow along with your tutoring experience.

Homework policies and guidelines

These homework policies, rules, and guidelines have grown out of my conversations with teens and their families regarding study problems.

- Most students already know what needs to be done to solve their own study problems, so discuss possible solutions with them first. Most kids can come up with surprisingly good plans for themselves when asked and, given some encouragement, may even stick with them.

- Students who frequently miss turning in school assignments, either because they are resistant or disorganized, can be asked to keep an assignment notebook that includes the signatures of their school-teachers as well as a parent. (One mother I know pays the student a set amount for each signature, including one from the tutor!)
- If kids are recalcitrant or just easily tempted, do not allow them to study in their own rooms. Instead, have them study in a shared family area such as the dining room, and ask parents to be sure to control the traffic and noise in that area.
- Some families lead lives that are just too chaotic to allow teens to study well at home, so help parents make other arrangements. Some parents drop their teen at the library or even the book store to study.
- Occasionally I have a teen study at my office while I tutor another student. I charge a small fee and check on the student's progress before, during, and after the study session.
- Some families arrange to have a college-age study helper take the teen to the library or a café to study.
- If students study in their rooms, work with them to minimize distractions. Ask them to give up the cell phone, the computer, and the TV if those are in the bedroom.

If a student seems receptive, the following guidelines may also be helpful. Go over these together.

- It's best to study in the same time and place every day. Your mind will be in the habit of thinking at that time just as your stomach expects to eat at a certain time. (The teen should help decide where and when to study but then should be held to his decision.)
- Treat studying as you would exercise. Here are some pointers from an article on how to stay physically fit, but the same principles would apply to mental "workouts" (Rocky Mountain Health Plans 2005).
    o Don't overdo it. Gradually increase the length of your workout (study time) and its intensity.
    o Divide and conquer. Do three 20 minute workouts (study periods) a day instead of one 60 minute session.
    o Create structure. Exercise with a buddy or head for the gym. For

a student, set up a standing study date or schedule study time in the library.

o Set measurable goals. For individuals trying to become fit, this might mean losing a pound a week. For a student, it could be completing all the reading assignments for history class for the week.

The log-in study plan

It's best to allow students to study on their own, or at least give them the chance to see how they get along by themselves. If the teen continues to skip home study, parents may need to step in and supervise. Even if it's needed, however, a parent supervising a teen's study sessions is a set-up for rebellion. The "log-in study plan" is an antidote—a method parents can use to keep tabs on their teen's study habits without micromanaging. It will help put some space between an over-involved parent and a teen who needs to be out from under the parental thumb. The plan is based on the honor system, however, so it only works if both parties are honest. And though it lets parents off the hook and allows parents and teens a time out from their struggles, it may put the tutor in the "hot seat" instead, so use it with some caution.

Under the log-in plan, the teen sets a time and place to study daily, and the parent agrees not to ask if he has homework or whether he has done it. Instead, a log book is kept in the kitchen or some other public family area. Each day, the teen enters the time he began studying, the time he finished, and the subjects he studied along with page numbers. He leaves the log book, his planner containing the assignments, his textbooks, and any papers or assignments out for his parents to see.

The parent promises to simply observe, not to question or drill, and the teen gives his word to be honest in recording his hours and work accomplished. Teens feel less rebellious when they can leave notes for their parents instead of answering questions, and doing it this way allows parents to avoid nagging while staying informed. Even though the parent isn't to ask questions, consequences are still allowed—it's just that consequences must be based on external information, such as a poor weekly report from school, for instance, or seeing that the student is not being honest with the log.

Here's the catch: The tutor is the designated arbiter, so if there are worries or disagreements, either party is to phone you. When you receive a call from a parent or teen, you listen to both sides then propose a solution.

Solutions might range from a reminder to a parent not to question the teen, to consequences I might suggest for work not done. This intervention really works to cut down on the emotionally charged cycle of nagging and passive-aggressive behaviors that goes on in many families between teens and parents about schoolwork, so it has its advantages. If you are comfortable being a referee, and if both parties are well-intentioned, this plan should work. If not, something else may be needed.

If the log-in study plan is too low-key for a particular student, see what can be done at school to persuade the student to complete his work. Some schools have what is called supervised study hall. One study hall teacher I know gets a weekly report from a student's teachers, and if the teen is behind in his work, he remains in study hall until his work is reasonably caught up.

Behavior problems can get out of hand quickly, and if they do, it is hard to bring the situation back under control. Hopefully, these guides to student motivation and behavior will help you head off trouble before that happens. (See Part VI to learn more about student behavior.)

Summary of Key Points

- To be effective, learning must be incremental. Steps must be small, each step should build on the ones before, and meaningful repetition and review must be provided.
- Teens who have trouble with initiative and follow-through often don't understand that success comes as the result of steps they may take themselves, so presenting the concept of stepwise learning to students may be helpful.
- Being aware of reading level allows a teacher to plan a stepwise curriculum (and ignore the rules when they get in the way).
- To keep instruction palatable, begin by devoting only a part of each lesson to comprehension.
- Work only on what the student needs.
- A written plan can lend an overview and sense of purpose.
- Generally it works well to include several different activities in a one-hour lesson. Over a course of several months, introduce new subjects as your student masters old ones.
- Attention to the sequence of activities within a lesson may lead to a smoother flow and less resistance.
- Constructive consequences can redirect students' learning for the better.

- Many troublesome attitudes and behavioral problems can be "headed off at the pass" with strategic interventions.

Now we'll take the ideas about teaching comprehension covered in this chapter—incremental learning, reading level, and lesson planning—and apply them in actual tutoring situations, beginning with fiction reading.

Part II: Reading Fiction

PART II PRESENTS STEPWISE, or incremental, exercises and activities that will help teens understand, remember, and enjoy the stories and novels they read. The strategies presented here will work for a wide range of students, from those who have never read a book in their lives to readers who need to be challenged at the college level. Chapter 5, "Fiction: Reading Comprehension and Recall," outlines strategies to boost basic reading skills. Chapter 6, "Teaching Higher-Level Thinking Skills," discusses ways to take students beyond the surface reading typical of beginners to a new level of insight and reflection.

5 | Fiction: Reading Comprehension and Recall

IN CHAPTER 4 WE REVIEWED possible reasons to begin tutoring with either fiction or nonfiction. Even if you decide to start tutoring with textbook (nonfiction) reading, however, it is recommended that you read this chapter on fiction first, since many of the exercises used later are introduced here in their most complete form.

Studying fiction helps students develop an appreciation for stories (the basis of literature study), and students who spend time with good stories will be prompted to think about their own lives as they read about the lives of others. In addition, by practicing on fiction in tutoring they will learn the important strategies to improve their understanding and recall, build a springboard for more analytical reading, and put in place the skills needed to work on reading speed.

Choosing a Book

To begin, you'll need to choose a book to practice the exercises in this chapter. Do the exercises with the student in the tutoring session and then, when you think she is ready to work on her own, lend her the book to practice with at home. Oddly enough, students with reading problems would rather "practice" something than "read" it at this stage. Maybe it sounds less intimidating.

For the first few weeks of tutoring, it's important to have the student read books that are fairly easy so that you can work only on the skills you choose to teach at the moment—visualizing, tellbacks, phrasing, and long smooth underline—without interference from other challenges. Advanced vocabulary or the symbolism of the *Scarlet Letter* will have to wait. Make sure you explain the reason for the easy book to both student and parents. One time when I neglected to do this I got an irate call from a mother who wanted to know why I had her high school daughter reading "baby books."

Offer the student two or three books you think she might like and let her choose one. The discussion in Chapter 3 concerning reading level and choosing books for the evaluation may help you narrow the field. It's a good idea to read the books before you recommend them to your student so you can describe them accurately.

The number of great books to choose from is almost limitless, but these are usually well-liked and will keep your student going for a while. For kids who like the outdoors, you could use *My Side of the Mountain* by Jean Craighead George (2004). If that is too easy, try *Two Old Women* by Velma Wallis (2004). For a teen who is a little more citified, maybe with a touch of "tough guy," try S. E. Hinton's (2008) *That Was Then, This Is Now*. A girl who likes some emotional drama would probably respond to *Tiger Eyes* by Judy Blume (2010). An older student might gravitate toward *Speak* by Laurie Anderson (2006).

The exercises that follow are the backbone of the reading improvement program presented in this book. *Visualizing* can help students remember and enjoy what they read; *oral phrasing* promotes fluency; *tellbacks*, both for detail and main idea, can build a thorough grasp of the material; and the *long smooth underline* (LSU) helps concentration and speed. Other exercises will help students read aloud with confidence, understand more about how a novel is structured, and begin to think more abstractly.

Visualization

Why do some students remember what they read in great detail, while others, seemingly as intelligent, are unable to recall even a few simple facts? Often the answer lies in their ability to visualize, or to form a mental image, of what they read. Fortunately, visualizing is a skill that can be taught, and learning to visualize and practicing it until it is automatic can work wonders for students' reading comprehension.

First find out if your student is visualizing what she reads. If she isn't, explain that you can help her read novels and stories more easily, get more out of them and enjoy them more by learning to visualize. Here's how I present it:

> When you read, do you see what's happening in your mind's eye? If you
> don't, that could explain why you either aren't understanding or aren't enjoy-
> ing your reading as much as you could. The writer is painting a picture for the
> reader with words. The kids you know who really enjoy reading are probably
> seeing what's happening as if they are watching a movie. Students often are

glad to hear this. They know there is some reason they aren't enjoying their reading, but they're not sure what it is.

As you read, make a conscious effort to form a mental image of everything that's mentioned in the passage. Keep up the effort to see what you're reading for a while until pictures start coming to you more automatically. Make these images as real as you can, as if you were watching a movie. Imagine what the people look like, where they are standing, even how things sound and smell. This will make reading more fun for you, and it will also help you remember more. This technique is called *visualization*.

For the student to practice this kind of "seeing," select a story that contains strong visual images. I use the story from the evaluation, "Two Were Left," which is reproduced in Appendix A. In "Two Were Left," an Eskimo boy has lost all his belongings in the breakup of an ice floe: his food, his knife, and his furs. These are items that would be important for the boy's survival. I want the student to picture each object as she reads about it. Then I tell her to imagine all these things grouped together—in this case, piled on a sled. Seeing them together will help the reader remember them. I close by noting that *it's a lot easier to remember mental images than it is words*, and if the student will practice this visualizing technique, it will come in handy in a number of situations, including textbook reading.

You can teach more about visualization and provide practice for your student using *My Side of the Mountain*, a story about a boy who runs away from home and survives alone in the wilderness. The book opens with a description of the boy's hollowed-out tree house, an image that lends itself well to visualization (George 2004, 3). Have your student read the first couple of paragraphs and tell you what she remembers in as much detail as possible. If she did well, give her an enthusiastic "good work!" and move on to the next exercise. But if she wasn't able to remember many details, or if she seemed foggy about where the story took place, continue as follows.

Out loud, go through the description, one item at a time, *sketching* each object as you talk. Your sketch could include a hollowed out log used as a dwelling, a bed of slats (what's a "slat?"), a handmade stove, and a notched stick used as a calendar. Don't worry if you aren't a good artist. Any drawing you do is sure to interest your student.

Put things into perspective by explaining that it's not the detail per se that's important, it's the *ability to grasp the detail*. Teens will appreciate the distinction, and just hearing this from an adult is sometimes all it takes for a previously disaffected reader to make a commitment to understanding.

The power of visualization

Visualization is a powerful tool with many applications. An adult student, Marietta, had suffered a serious brain injury in a horseback riding accident and, tragically, had lost her ability to read on all but the most rudimentary level. Before the accident she was a Ph.D. divinity student. Afterward she was reading on a second or third grade level.

One reason she could not read better, I discovered, was that she had lost the ability to visualize what she was reading. I realized that she must learn again to translate what she was reading into images, but this would be hard because she was unable to see *anything* in her mind's eye. After some discussion, I discovered that her disability was pervasive, even preventing her from maneuvering around a puddle in the street or placing new furniture in a room, since visually she could not imagine a route to follow or a "look" to aim for.

I asked Marietta to do some drawing exercises, first looking at an object, or an arrangement of objects, then looking away and sketching what she had seen from memory. This was an impossible task at first, but with practice she became better at it. Finally, she reported that puddles were no longer puzzling. She could see her way around them! We resumed our reading visualization exercises, which had been discontinued earlier as being too frustrating, and she was able to progress through several grade levels quickly, thanks to her recaptured ability to "see her way around."

I'm not necessarily recommending drawing lessons, but this example demonstrates the important connection between seeing—both in the external world and through the imagination—and reading comprehension.

Now the disclaimer. From discussions with skilled adult readers, I've learned that a few good readers do not visualize much of what they read. So it's possible that not everyone needs to visualize, but if a student who is having trouble with comprehension is *not* visualizing, then teaching visualizing will be extremely helpful.

Continue practicing by having the student read from a novel or nonfiction book, describing what she sees in her mind's eye. Include some visualization as a part of each lesson until she has mastered it. If she is having trouble, demonstrate by taking a passage one line at a time and telling her exactly what *you* see in a particular section. For example, from Jean George's *Julie of the Wolves*, "Now I am reading about the wolves returning to their den, greeting their pups. I imagine them playing, tumbling, chewing on each other, just like dogs do." You might suppose a teenager would be turned off by hearing an adult detail her internal process in this way, but your student will likely be captivated as you draw her into the story. You are engaging her imagination, and she will respond positively.

Tellbacks

The tellback exercise consists of having a student read and then "tell back" from memory what she just read. You are already acquainted with tellbacks. You used them in the evaluation when your student recalled what she read and more recently when she described what she was visualizing. This next step builds on your previous work.

Tellbacks are an ideal exercise for tutoring. In the classroom, students are often asked to answer written questions about what they've read. The practice of asking study questions of this sort may be a convenient way of tracking understanding with many students in a classroom, but it has its drawbacks. Children can easily guess or parrot answers without understanding what they've read, and they will read more passively if they do not have to come up with a summary in their own words. Also, answering questions may distance a reader emotionally from a passage. Using tellbacks helps avoid these drawbacks.

Tellbacks provide an easy way to keep tabs on a student's comprehension. They are definitely more useful than random questions about what a student has read. Used in a consistent and organized way, tellbacks are a powerful tool for developing understanding and memory.

Just because tellbacks have great potential to help doesn't mean they always work right away, however. Some students read and report on paragraph after paragraph with little understanding. This section outlines some steps for helping students get more out of their tellbacks. (For using tellbacks in longer readings, see Chapter 6.)

As soon as the student is doing well with tellbacks, the tutor may begin asking more thought questions, particularly about why things happened as they did in the readings. Interpreting and analyzing are covered later, but it's never too early to start discussing character, motivation, and how we respond personally to what we've read.

Tellbacks to teach recall of detail

First we'll consider using tellbacks for developing memory for detail in fiction reading. Tellbacks for identifying main idea and in textbook reading come later. Emphasizing memory for detail might seem opposed to the idea of thoughtful reading since it focuses on recall rather than interpretation, but it is actually an essential first step in building comprehension, memory, and ultimately higher-level thinking skills. Trying to bypass this concrete level of reading to make faster progress is like trying to skip walking and go straight to bike riding: it is frustrating and often ends in failure.

To do a tellback, simply have the student read a paragraph and tell everything she remembers on her own, then ask her questions. The long-term goal is for the student to be able to recall 90 to 100 percent of the details or facts she has read in a paragraph without looking back at the book. If she has to mix up the order in which she relates the information, that is all right.

After the student tells what she remembers, have her follow along in the book while you reread the paragraph aloud. Just as you did with visualization, acknowledge what the student got right and call her attention to anything she missed or didn't understand. Using the reading material, you might explain how you yourself got the facts and ideas you did from the passage.

Learning by imitation is one of the best educational methods available. Some teachers feel they always have to get the student to come up with the answer themselves, but try to strike a balance and don't be afraid to model or demonstrate how to do things, especially when it comes to getting the meaning from reading.

There's no telling how much practice a student will need to meet the goal of 90 to 100 percent recall in tellbacks. Success may come after only a few tries or it may take several weeks. A student who needs to work on this skill should practice at home, either independently or with a parent. If she does need to work with a parent, the tutor should help set up the home practice sessions.

As simple as the tellback exercise is, it holds enormous potential for helping students improve both their memory and concentration. Many students report that it even helps them think better generally. Tellbacks provide a way for the student and teacher to know exactly how much the student understands and remembers from a passage, and this may be the first time a student has really felt responsible for knowing what she's read.

Tellbacks and vocabulary

When doing tellbacks, make sure your student knows the meanings of words in the passage. This may seem too obvious to mention, but there are a couple of reasons to bring it up. First, students may appear to be having trouble with the concepts and incidents of a story, but with closer attention you may find that they simply didn't understand the meanings of some of the words. If you explain the word meanings, the student understands the ideas. If you weren't aware of the vocabulary component, you might waste a lot of time unnecessarily practicing on tellbacks or trying to fill the student in on plot and character. You would also incorrectly estimate the student's capabilities.

Second, don't assume a student knows the vocabulary, even if she claims to! Just as students who need tutoring often do not have the self-monitoring skills to pick an appropriate level book for themselves, they also lack the awareness to determine what they know and don't know, especially when it comes to reading vocabulary. The way around this is to question the student about the words in the reading that might possibly be unfamiliar. "What does this word mean? Can you use it in a sentence?"

The goal, of course, is to get the student to ask about unfamiliar words on her own, to ask for help when she needs it, and eventually to use the dictionary. The process can be a difficult one to get rolling, but it may work to say, "If you don't ask me any questions, I'm going to assume that you know all the words in this paragraph and hold you responsible for them, so don't just skip words you don't know." After that, question the student about the meanings of any words that might be unfamiliar and keep a running list of any words she misses to review occasionally.

Provide each of your students with a folder for important papers. They will bring their folders to class each week and take them home to use for reference. Make notes, or have the student make notes as you teach, and store them in the folder.

Keeping score

This simple activity works to increase reading memory rapidly. It is motivating for people to see in black and white how they're doing, and students often like having the tutor keep score of how they are progressing with their tellbacks.

To keep score of students' reading recall, tally everything they remember and anything important that they miss. Draw a line down the middle of a sheet of paper and jot down a mark in the left column for each piece of information the student is able to recall correctly from a paragraph, even if you had to question her to get it. Then put marks in the opposite column for anything important that she missed from the same paragraph. At the end of each paragraph these tick marks can be turned into fractions, then percentages, showing the student how much she got right for each paragraph. For example, if there were eight possible facts in a paragraph, and the student remembered six, note it as 6/8, or about 75 percent.

I have known quite a few students who were not motivated to remember what they read until they saw their reading memory scored and expressed as a percentage. Keep it up so your student can see her progress over a period of several weeks. If the student doesn't enjoy the scorekeeping exercise, there's no need to push it. It's just a game, nothing crucial. Still, it can be quite motivating for some teens.

Talking with the student about tellbacks

After the student has done a few tellbacks, remind her that the separate facts or pieces of information are not really important in and of themselves: *the important part is the skill.* Being able to remember exactly what you have read *when you choose to* is crucial, not just for school but for the rest of your life. Discuss situations in real life when the student might need to read and remember details, such as recipes, a driving booklet, or instructions on putting a bike together.

Kids really understand the distinction between learning in order to accumulate facts, especially facts they consider insignificant, and *learning to practice a useful mental skill.* "Turned off" adolescents can become more positive when they see that the teacher knows the difference between pedantic trivia and a useful skill, and they're usually quite willing to do "brain exercises" if they know that's what they are.

When you teach tellbacks or any other reading exercise, stop occasionally and ask the student, "How is reading this way working for you?" Kids who might not ordinarily say anything about their reading experience may have important questions or concerns that will be revealed with this prompting.

IS READING THIS WAY WORKING FOR YOU?

Rachael was a young teen with good word recognition skills but very low reading comprehension. She was doing tellbacks at my request, but this was a tedious and discouraging exercise for both of us since she seemed to understand so little of what she was reading. I asked her to read a few sentences to herself, visualizing as she went, and then stop, look away, and tell herself what she had read. Her reading comprehension improved a little with this exercise, but she still looked glum. My question, "How is reading this way working for you?" brought a response I didn't expect. "This is so slow. Will I have to read this way all the time now—looking away and saying what I read? I'll never get through my work!"

I had forgotten to explain the purpose of the visualizing and tellbacks, or had explained in a way Rachael didn't connect with the work she was doing at the moment. "No, this is just temporary. It's a brain exercise. As soon as you can do it well, you get to quit." Rachael gave me a nod that said she understood. Without my question, though, she probably would not have voiced what was on her mind. Asking kids "How is this working for you?" is sometimes more important than we realize.

Stick with it

Although it is easy to become impatient with teaching tellbacks, it is important not to cut this phase of instruction short. Be prepared to stick with the concrete level of tellbacks for several weeks (interspersed with other learning activities, of course) if that's what's needed: "What did you read? How did the scene look? Who said what? What did they do?" Patience now will pay off later. If you omit this step the student may never move beyond the concrete level of reading. However, if you run up against a brick wall when it comes to helping your student recall detail, you may wish to skip ahead temporarily to learn some of the memory techniques described in the chapters on factual reading in Part III, and then return later to tellbacks aided by this new information to help your student build memory skills.

Assigning tellbacks for home practice

If your student has made a successful start on visualization and one-paragraph tellbacks but needs more work than can be done in class, you may wish to assign home practice. A reasonable assignment might be six one-paragraph tellbacks a day, followed by a short period of regular reading not using tellbacks.

Naturally, the total amount of reading time you assign depends on the student, how much homework she has from school, and what her home situation is. Workable goals could be a half-hour a day for sixth through eighth graders and forty minutes for ninth graders and above. Teens who are not yet "broken in," unused to concentrating for longer periods, should be assigned less reading time, regardless of age. But do warn students that the light assignments are just to ease them gradually into the work, and that you will expect more later. Many students already have reading assignments from school, so combining assignments may be possible.

Encourage your student to continue visualizing along with the tellbacks. She can practice tellbacks either with a parent or alone, but if she does work alone, it is important to do the tellbacks out loud. When she's done with one tellback she can go back and reread the material to see how much she got right. If she left anything important out, she should simply make note of it mentally as she reviews.

For a middle school student, you may want to show a parent how to keep score on the tellbacks the way you did in class and have the student bring in a "score sheet" from home that includes the date of each practice session and a score for each paragraph. The dated sheet will help you keep track of the student's progress, but keep tabs by having her go through a paragraph or two each time you meet. Also find out how the student and her parents are getting along doing the tellbacks together. If there are conflicts, try decreasing work with parents in favor of having the student do more alone or in tutoring sessions.

TELLBACKS CAN TURN THE TIDE

Belva was an adult college student with a couple of school-age children. She wanted to work on her reading comprehension, and after some discussion I discovered she wasn't reading at all. She had been getting through her community college courses with good grades only because she tape-recorded every lecture and spent hours listening to the tapes. She also memorized verbatim the answers in the Q and A study guide that came with the texts. Her ability to memorize was as remarkable as her lack of understanding.

We started on tellbacks right away, using a sixth-grade social studies book, an account of village life in India that interested her. At first she was at sea, focusing on trivia and neglecting key ideas. Slowly, as she read along and listened to my own tellbacks, she began to zero in on the more important details for herself, recalling first a sentence and then whole paragraphs.

"So that's how you do it!" she said. "I always wondered what I should be paying attention to when I read." So far, I was simply demonstrating, and she was following intuitively. I had not begun any specific teaching of main idea, and I was not yet attempting to work on higher-level thinking skills. At this point, it was important for Belva simply to remember content.

I discovered she had never read a book in her life! One of her assignments from my class was to read to her sons. Gradually, as her understanding improved, we moved on to main idea (quite a challenge), interpretation, and tackled more and more difficult books. Eventually she was reading college material and taking notes with assurance. The tellbacks had worked to turn the tide, at least on an academic level.

On an emotional level, there was more to the story. Belva had a history of mental illness, and though she was intelligent, her low self-esteem made it difficult for her to pay attention in her tutoring sessions. While she sobbed her way through her first few lessons, I tried to provide a safe, caring place for her to "fall apart." I knew she needed psychotherapy, but was aware that because of her financial situation and cultural background, she was not likely to get it soon. So, for want of anything better, I was "it" in the emotional help department, at least for the time being.

Two and a half years later, Belva had made remarkable strides, earning several promotions at work and getting herself into therapy, on top of being able to do college work. For Belva it all began with tellbacks—and a shoulder to cry on.

Oral Reading and Phrasing

After the hard work of visualization and tellbacks, the next exercise allows for a breather. If you noticed in the evaluation that your student read aloud awkwardly, working on oral phrasing will help. Teaching phrasing will allow students to read more fluently and expressively and will improve their reading generally. In phrasing, students group words rather than reading one word at a time as is typical of poor readers. Oral phrasing is motivating and easy to teach, and it doesn't have a lot riding on it so is low pressure.

Although oral reading is not of great importance in itself, it is still worth paying attention to because *it can be used to identify and correct problems that occur in silent reading.* Besides its diagnostic value for the teacher, being able to read aloud is a big morale booster for a student. Since it is not an essential skill, however, and can be considered optional, the decision to work on oral reading is best left up to the student.

Phrasing can be used for two quite different purposes. It's both a speed-reading technique and an oral reading aid. After learning this technique, the reader can use it either for oral or silent reading and can vary the speed to suit her purpose. Phrasing for speed reading is covered in Chapter 11; at this point we are only using it in oral reading.

Teaching oral phrasing

To demonstrate the need for attention to oral phrasing, the teacher reads a passage aloud the wrong way, haltingly and word for word, then the right way, more smoothly and in phrases. Ham it up a little. Point out that it's easier to understand words in groups than it is single words.

Here's a script that explains the process in detail for the student:

> Each phrase should be about two to four words in length and should consist of words that make sense together. You are the one who decides if they make sense together, so you need to be thinking about the meaning as you read. Use your hand, with the fingers together and slightly curved, to underline, or point out, each phrase as you come to it. Read the phrase aloud as you point to it. Don't rush yourself. (It is necessary to be this specific in teaching this skill. Without this advice, teens have a tendency to become sloppy and flail around.)
>
> Decide which hand you want to use for phrasing and then stick with it. Switching hands can be confusing. Keep your hand far enough below the line so it doesn't distract you or interfere with your view of what you are reading.

The object here is to extend the reader's visual range, so don't allow the student to point with only one finger, since that would encourage her to continue reading one word at a time. This phrasing technique is similar to the *long smooth underline* introduced in the next section.

As the student continues reading aloud using the hand technique, you will probably need to encourage her to slow down and leave pauses between phrases. When she comes to a comma or period, have her use the pause to catch her breath (many kids don't do this) and to look ahead at what's coming next. Explain that reading aloud is easier if *your eyes are slightly ahead of your voice.* Make sure the student continues pointing out the phrases, and remember to say "right" or "yes" at the end of the sentence she phrases correctly. Immediate feedback is essential in improving oral reading, and you may be surprised by how much your responses will shape your student's reading. Sometimes little else is required to change a student's reading behavior.

Continue to show the student how to separate the phrases and, after a few sessions, how to run them together smoothly, using good inflection. Though oral reading instruction starts with phrase reading, it is important to move beyond phrases into "regular," or smooth, reading.

If the student is reading passably in the tutoring sessions, have her take the book home to practice by reading several paragraphs aloud each day. Then check out her progress each time you meet. Lend her a book rather than letting her use one she already owns. I don't understand why, but kids hardly ever do the assignments if you let them use their own books.

Some students understand the idea of phrasing but still read in a monotone. It will help if you read aloud yourself and have your student pay attention to how you use your voice to get across the meaning of a passage. Explain that you're aiming for oral expression that is easy for the listener to understand and interesting to listen to. You wouldn't think it would be necessary to mention that we read aloud to get an idea or a feeling across. To many kids, though, the entire purpose of schoolwork up until now has been to please a teacher or a parent by meeting some hazily understood rules, and the goal of actually communicating with another person may not have occurred to them.

Talking about the listener's experience can further your student's insights concerning the connection between the tasks she is learning and the purpose of communicating. You can add to this understanding by commenting on your experience as you listen to her read aloud. "I was really able to follow that," "The way you read it made me want to find out more," or, "I'm having trouble following. Could you say that again more clearly?"

Some students find it difficult to understand what they read orally. They can do it if they read silently, but for them, oral reading takes so much mental energy they don't have any to spare for comprehension and recall. If that is the case, don't push for comprehension when the student reads aloud. Save the comprehension for later and just work on inflection and phrasing for now.

PRACTICING ORAL READING

Tory was a bright 12-year-old, and from what I could tell, a fairly good silent reader, but his oral reading was an embarrassment to him. He made many errors when he read aloud, almost as if he had a speech impediment. A "take-charge" kind of kid, Tory insisted that we work on his oral reading each time. We had spent several months practicing word recognition, so Tory was definitely ready for oral reading. We read aloud from *Call It Courage* by Armstrong Sperry (1990), a book chosen for its dramatic language and challenging vocabulary. Tory practiced looking ahead while he was reading, reading in phrases, and taking plenty of time for dramatic pauses.

I encouraged him to be persistent in sounding out unfamiliar words. Tory reads aloud quite well now but still wants to continue his practice. Maybe that's because it's fun and because the story is getting exciting!

Some students need several minutes to warm up when reading aloud, and in such cases you and your student both have to keep this in mind. After about five minutes of oral reading, the error rate should fall noticeably. Experiment and see how much your student benefits from warming up, then allow for warm-up time when reading orally. Also, it is important to teach teens to allow for their own warm-up time.

Students also need warm-up time when reading silently. For most people, less than 20 minutes of silent reading is useless. It takes that long to get warmed up in the first place, and not much learning happens during the warm up time. For that reason, require practice sessions of at least half an hour when assigning homework.

Reading aloud at home

You can use this next exercise to promote oral reading at home, whether or not you are aiming specifically at improving phrasing, so put it in your bag of tricks to use now and draw on in the future.

Both my adult children are passionate readers, and when I asked them what they thought contributed to their love of reading, they both mentioned this next activity, "Dishwasher's Choice," which we did many times while they were growing up.

DISHWASHER'S CHOICE

I used to hate washing the dishes. This was in the days before we had a dishwasher. To distribute the burden more evenly I insisted that my two children, ages 10 and 14, pitch in. We'd take turns. To keep the bellyaching down, we came up with the rule that whoever complained would have to take an extra turn. So we started washing the dishes, but it felt dismal. The kids hated it, and my daughter always cried when it was her turn.

To cheer everyone up, I came up with a new twist. Whoever was washing the dishes got to ask one of the other two to read aloud for entertainment, but the choice of books always belonged to the dishwasher. The reader would stand or sit near enough to be heard over the clank of dishes—an important part of the exercise since it demanded a clear voice—and read away at whatever the dishwasher wanted to hear.

It was great! The kids were decent readers, but they said later that reading out of the books I chose for them (when I washed and they read) improved their vocabularies and made them curious to learn what exactly these challenging but mysterious books were about. They were not books the kids would have selected on their own, and it is true they did not understand whole chunks of what they read, but it didn't matter. They were hooked. And I often noticed the other child hanging around to listen.

They read passages to me from *The Lord of the Rings* by J.R.R. Tolkien (2005) and *Watership Down* by Richard Adams (reprint edition 2005). And I read whatever they asked for. They both liked Tolkien's *The Hobbit* (2007), and the younger one wanted factual articles from *Big Book of Tell Me Why* (Leokum 1989). Soon the older one was asking for *The Lord of the Rings*, too. We worked out a rotation so that everyone got to read, just as everyone had to wash dishes.

"Dishwasher's Choice" was a big hit in my household. (It works just as well for homes with dishwashers, too.) Here's why it helped. First, the reader felt privileged. Reading meant you didn't have to do the dreaded dishes. So reading was a "plum." Second, the dishwasher paid attention and would complain if the reader was unclear or uninteresting. Finally, the kids were exposed to more advanced vocabulary and concepts than they might have been on their own.

You can help your students and their parents set up a similar exercise. Other chores might work as well as dishwashing. Another activity that helps some teens become enthusiastic about reading at home is what I call "the after dinner family read together."

THE AFTER DINNER FAMILY READ TOGETHER

Helena was a bright girl with mild dyslexia who resisted the reading practice she so badly needed. She had many tearful battles with her parents, who were doing everything they could think of to get her to read at home.

While working with Helena, I remembered hearing at an IRA (International Reading Association) conference that children may resist reading not because they dislike it, but that they feel lonely when engaged in such a solitary activity. So I suggested to Helena's parents that they all sit down together and read every day after dinner. Everyone was to participate. The only requirement was that they all be in the same room with their books. They could read aloud or tell about their books if they wished, but that was their choice. This family activity worked wonders! Helena never resisted reading again, and her busy parents liked having a chance to get caught up on their reading, too.

Reading aloud can also help students improve their listening skills. (See "Read and repeat" in Chapter 18.)

Long Smooth Underline (LSU)

Previously masked reading difficulties may become apparent now that your student can visualize and recall what she's read. For example, perhaps she reports being so bored with her school reading or so distracted that she doesn't remember anything she's read. Or perhaps she keeps losing her place and missing material or rereading unnecessarily. Fortunately, there is help available for these problems in a technique called the *long smooth underline* (LSU).

Importance of the LSU

The LSU is so simple that people are sometimes fooled into minimizing its importance. However, using this simple technique for yourself and teaching it to your students can be a godsend, and in some instances can make the difference between failure and success with a student. Like phrasing, the LSU is a speed-reading exercise that also can be used at slower speeds to aid concentration and comprehension. (Chapter 10 describes the use of the LSU as a tool for increasing reading speed.) The LSU is helpful for anyone with visual tracking problems or for individuals who report "spacing out" while reading. It may even tame resistant readers by making reading more accessible to them.

Preparing for the LSU

With a student who has trouble concentrating, begin by speaking directly about that problem, then offer the idea that there is a way to concentrate better. In discussions with a teen, it works best to treat lack of concentration not as a defect or attitude issue but as a legitimate reading problem, an "honest problem," and one worth serious attention. This gives the teacher a chance to talk to the student about concentration in a way that says, "We can solve this together."

Of course, in reality, it's more complicated than this, since lack of concentration almost always involves both skills *and* attitude, but it is easier to teach concentration if the student doesn't start out on the defensive. For a teen who needs a pep talk, either because she is discouraged or because she insists "that's just the way I am, and there is nothing I can do about it," explain that everybody has concentration problems at one time or another—even reading experts tune out—but concentration is a skill *and a habit* that can be learned and practiced just like other skills and habits. It is important to point out that the LSU will help the student improve her concentration, but only if she wants it to and if she tries.

Teaching the LSU

The LSU is a hand technique much like phrasing, except that the reader keeps his hand moving *smoothly* under the line rather than pausing or pointing, and it's used for silent, not oral, reading. The following instructions are for both tutor and student.

When you use the LSU, keep your hand low enough under the line so that it doesn't interfere visually with what you're reading. Move your hand, and your eye will be automatically drawn along by the motion of your hand. When you get to the end of the line, do not pick your hand up, but pull it down *diagonally* to the left, to the beginning of the next line. You're now in position to start the next line.

Although we are not aiming for speed at the moment, the reader can vary her speed by changing how fast she moves her hand. The purpose of the LSU at this stage is to help the student keep her place on the page, coordinate eye movements, and keep moving ahead at a steady pace, all of which can improve visual tracking and counteract daydreaming. In addition, like phrasing, LSU encourages the reader to see words in groups and so improves comprehension, speed, and focus.

The LSU automatically improves visual tracking. Inefficient readers often have problems because of difficulties with visual coordination. If these problems are serious, they could require professional help, but for most people simply practicing the LSU is sufficient. Not only does it help readers keep their place on the page, but it gets the left and right eyes to work together more efficiently.

The hand can be held with the fingers straight out and flat on the page or curled a little as with oral phrasing. Discourage the student from pointing at individual words with one finger because that will slow her reading down. Tell your student that when she uses the LSU, she will still *see* all the words, but only the more important ones will register in her mind.

Advise your student not to read faster than she is able to understand the material. Watch to make sure the student has not speeded up dramatically. Some kids just jump in and take off racing before they are ready for it. They don't even necessarily do it on purpose. Maybe their hands "run away with them." (It wouldn't be the first time that has happened to an adolescent.)

One last caution. The student should avoid moving her mouth or throat when she reads unless she must do so to understand. Chapter 10 provides more information about decreasing unintentional vocal movements.

The LSU is tedious to use for long periods, but fortunately it's not necessary to do it for long stretches, since the benefits the student derives from it (such as better visual habits) will generalize to her other reading even when she's not using the technique. For home practice, have your student use the LSU for the first 10 or 15 minutes of each reading practice session, and then for another 10 minutes at the end of the session. If students continue to practice the LSU, their reading speed and comprehension will continue to improve for up to a year even with no further instruction.

The two underlining techniques you have learned, phrasing and LSU, work seamlessly with the tellbacks your student has been doing. If a student's reading improves dramatically as a result of using the LSU technique it probably means that the original problem was one of poor visual tracking. In such a case, consider referring the student to an optometrist who specializes in reading difficulties to see if she could benefit even further from being fitted with special reading glasses. A combination of the LSU and special glasses has actually worked some "miracle cures" in which remedial students required less than a month of tutoring to get up to grade level after years of lagging behind.

Brain benefits

From what I've observed, the benefit readers derive from using the LSU technique goes far beyond an improvement in visual tracking. My theory is that when readers use the LSU regularly over a period of several weeks or months, their improvement in visual tracking brings about a parallel advance in brain organization and development. In other words, the coordinated, repetitive hand and eye movements of LSU not only improve visual habits, but also engage and bring to life new brain connections, resulting in better cognitive skills. I can't prove this, but I can attest to the hundreds of children, teens, and adults who demonstrate the ability to "think better" after using the LSU for a period of time.

Now for the disclaimer. Although the LSU helps most people, it is not for everyone, and even when it does turn out to be a good technique for a student, it may take days of tedious and sometimes frustrating practice before knowing for sure it will work. For this reason, it helps to explain to the student beforehand that it takes about a week of practice to find out if LSU is actually going to work for her. Encourage her not to give up if she doesn't see good results right away, but to keep practicing. After a week or two, if the student still does not feel it is helping and she genuinely dislikes doing it, and if you are sure she actually gave it a good try, let her drop it. About one out of 10 students is not successful with the LSU, though some may come back to it months later and succeed.

Tell Yourself What You've Read

If your program is progressing well, your student can now read a section in a story or novel with good concentration, is able to visualize, can tell you what she's read, and can keep moving ahead through a book at a steady pace. But what about the students who are still not comprehending? And what about the ones who are doing all right but just need something extra? This next exercise is for them.

Instruct the student to "tell herself" what she has just read, stopping right after she reads something important and going over it silently in her mind. She could pause at the end of a sentence, a paragraph, or even a section. It can even be done while the student actually is reading. This is kind of like an internal tellback, but since it's silent, it only takes a few seconds. The student should avoid rereading. Explain that the internal tellback is better than rereading because it is a memory (brain-building) exercise.

Some people are reluctant to take the time to tell themselves what they've read, believing, oddly enough, that "thinking takes more time than reading," and that they should keep on pushing ahead with the reading, sometimes rather blindly, or else reread, rather than taking a few extra seconds to think about what they've read. You can show the student that the internal tellback works well and doesn't take long by demonstrating how to do it yourself and then having the student read while you time her, first with and then without using the silent tellback.

Working with Greg was educational for both of us. Greg was about 17 and was coming to me to learn to read. His word recognition was all right, but his reading comprehension was "zero." He had no idea at all of the meaning of anything he read. I guessed that he probably had an IQ on the low end of normal but was not developmentally disabled. Though his IQ was comparatively low, I didn't think that in itself should be enough to prevent him from reading better. I tried one activity after another, one interesting and hopefully motivating book after another, to no avail. Greg still had not one glimmer of understanding. Finally, I asked him what he was (or was not) doing inside his head as he read.

"Well," admitted Greg, "I can read it, but I just don't listen to myself."

"Oh," I said, "I see. And could you change what you're doing? Could you tell yourself what you are reading, and listen to yourself?" Greg said that he would try and proceeded to read—first a sentence, then a paragraph—with passable comprehension. He was not only telling himself, but he was listening, and that made all the difference.

This next activity is a tellback with a difference. For some teens it works wonders to have them pretend to explain what they've read to a younger child. I ask them to interpret for about a 12-year-old child. Trying to explain material to a teacher, who, after all, already understands it, can be unrewarding, even daunting. Doing it for an imaginary buddy can help. And sometimes, to lighten things up, the teacher can even play the part of the earnest but ignorant 12-year-old.

Results

What changes have you noticed in your students as a result of using the exercises in this chapter? Perhaps an unfocused student is able to concentrate better because of using the LSU, or maybe a child who used to read haltingly has gained confidence and fluency through the phrasing technique.

Summary of Key Points

- After you have an overview of your student's reading level and have chosen an appropriate book for practice, select exercises to help her understand and remember what she's read.
- To improve comprehension and recall, students should make a conscious effort to visualize, or see in their mind's eye, as they read.
- Having students read and tell back what they remember consistently over a period of weeks is a powerful tool for building concentration and comprehension. Keeping score adds to the benefits.

- Be aware of your student's understanding of vocabulary.
- Working on oral reading can be fun and help students gain self-confidence. Phrasing is an important component of reading aloud and is easily taught.
- Underlining reading material with the hand, a technique called the LSU, improves eye coordination, aids concentration, and can pave the way for speed reading. It may even have long-term cognitive benefits.
- Students who "tune out" can be encouraged to tell themselves what they are reading, and more important, to listen. Asking students to listen to themselves as they read may work better than the directive to pay attention.
- The reading exercises in this chapter can be used alone or together to help a student break free of inefficiency, boredom and failure.

A student who has succeeded with the exercises described in this chapter should now be reading stories and novels with increased concentration and understanding, and, if all goes well, with renewed interest. Up to this point, we've concentrated on helping students understand what they read at a fairly basic, concrete, level. Achieving concrete understanding—knowing who, what, where, and when—is a necessary first step in becoming a skillful reader.

Still, it is only a first step. With the next chapter, we move into higher-level thinking skills and discuss ways to help our students read with more depth and maturity—that is, to move beyond the concrete and begin to think abstractly about what they read.

6 | Teaching Higher-level Thinking Skills

UNTIL NOW WE HAVE BEEN CONCERNED primarily with concrete understanding. "Who was in the story? What did they do? What happened next?" Though concrete understanding forms a necessary foundation for higher-level thinking skills, it is clearly only a small part of what is involved in reading. Now we turn to abstract thinking.

Abstract Thinking

Abstract thinking is also referred to as conceptual thinking, generalization, reasoning, and higher-level thinking skill. *Webster's Third International Dictionary* defines *abstract thinking* as both the ability to summarize and "the ability to consider a characteristic of a thing without referring to the thing itself, such as 'whiteness, triangularity, and honesty.'"

Higher-level thinking is teachable

Contrary to widely held opinion, abstract thinking is not just a static reflection of intelligence; it can be taught. Some of the reading skills you will be teaching soon—summarizing and main idea—require a higher degree of abstract thinking from your students than our previous work. Many students will be able to summarize and identify main idea right away, but those who are not yet ready for these activities can *become* ready through the use of "brain exercises" and other activities to foster abstract thinking skills.

Of course, abstract thinking encompasses much more than just summarizing a passage or identifying its main idea. If things go well, children will grow into young adults who understand symbolism and figurative language in literature and can think metaphorically about poetry and myth. They may even be able to do the "hard things" like identifying the author's purpose and answering the SAT questions that ask "which of the following are true EXCEPT . . ."

131

Abstract thinking requires maturation

Jean Piaget, a scientist exploring cognitive development in the 1930s and '40s, noticed that children below a certain age did not understand certain concepts pertaining to the physical world that older children and adults grasped readily. Based on his studies, Piaget concluded that before the age of about 14, children have not yet acquired the brain development necessary to master certain abstract concepts.

That's all well and good. It is knowledge that can help us form realistic expectations of children. But we're still left with this question: what should teachers do when they are faced with students who have not yet developed a sufficient level of abstract thinking to tackle the work that is expected of them in school?

What goes wrong in school

Unfortunately, when faced with students operating at a concrete level beyond the age when they are expected to be able to handle abstract concepts, teachers often deal with the situation in unhelpful ways. An experienced teacher who manages a peer tutoring program at a local high school explained the situation this way.

"In my job I supervise peer tutors, and I also spend enough time with the students that I get to know what problems they are having with particular teachers. If a number of kids are having similar problems in the same class, I like to go talk to the teacher and see if I can pin down what's happening. Sometimes I can give the teacher suggestions that will help that person teach in a way that's more understandable for the kids.

"I've noticed over and over that kids are coming into ninth grade without much ability to think abstractly, and the teachers in math, science, and literature are having a tough time figuring out how to present the required material for that grade level to kids who aren't ready for it.

"For instance, algebra in ninth grade is pretty abstract, but most kids just aren't at the level they need to be to understand it. So we've got a lot of kids failing ninth grade algebra. The teachers either try to water the course down, in which case the kids don't learn the material needed for the higher-level courses, or the teachers keep the coursework difficult and blame the kids for not trying or for acting dumb. And then the kids are frustrated and *do* feel dumb.

"As a result, the students simply fail a course in math, science, or history, or else they come into our tutoring center looking for 'first aid' tutoring, which isn't really enough. A third possibility is that the parents end up hiring tutors to teach kids what they ought to be learning at school. Obviously, none of this is what should be happening.

"When I talk to the teachers about it, however, they are at a loss. They realize the kids are not thinking abstractly enough to understand the material, but the teachers don't believe there's anything they can do about it. I tell them that they should work with the kids to help them learn to think more abstractly first, and *then* teach the more difficult material, but the teachers don't know how to do that and wouldn't have the time if they did. Usually they just argue that you can't teach abstract thinking.

"But I know better," she concluded.

After seeing hundreds of students move from concrete thinking typical of younger children to the more abstract level characteristic of adults through the focused instruction of tutoring, I agree that abstract thinking not only *can* be taught, it *must* be taught if we are going to help students reach their potential.

What tutors can do

Public school teachers face a challenging dilemma. They can't change themselves overnight, and school systems are notoriously unwieldy, so there is not much hope for positive change there. As tutors, however, we have the ability to make a real difference. What happens at school may be beyond our reach, but as private reading teachers we are free of the time, money, and political constraints that limit the public schools, and we can use this freedom to put into place outstanding programs to help adolescents develop the thinking skills they need to excel.

To teach higher-level thinking well, we must provide students with adequate exposure to abstract thought; give them the language to express concepts; incorporate good books; understand that there will be transfer of ideas from one subject to another when it comes to teaching abstract thinking but that it will not be complete; and, most of all, to keep at it.

Exposure to conceptual thinking

Children who have been exposed to higher-level thinking at home or school are more likely to develop this cognitive approach themselves at an earlier age than if they were not exposed. In other words, experience as well as maturation is at play. Unfortunately, a subgroup of Waldorf educators (perhaps because of an over-literal interpretation of Piaget) wants to withhold abstract concepts from children who, based solely on age, are deemed "not ready for them yet."

While these misguided individuals purposely want to restrict children's access to ideas to "protect them" from frustration, another more pervasive, insidious force restricts the access of many children to ideas, not purposely, but by default. The effects of the second force are incalculable since they permeate our entire culture.

Consider an ordinary American household: The main source of news is the TV or the internet; the main reading material is the bestseller, either violent or romantic; and both entertainment and religion are delivered cut, dried, and prepackaged to bypass thinking or feeling of any depth. The household I've just described does not provide many opportunities to learn what the poet Robert Bly calls "metaphoric thinking." In *The Sibling Society* (1996), Bly warns that metaphoric, or symbolic, thinking is dying out in our national discourse as people become increasingly literal-minded.

Even though our focus in tutoring is at a more immediate and personal level, it is necessary to realize that we are dealing with a wider problem—not just with this or that child who cannot think well about literature or politics or science, but with a whole group of children.

Bly goes even further. He says people's over-literalness is not just random and accidental, but has actually been engineered. Read *The Sibling Society* to understand how television, consumerism, and the peddling of "the illusion of equality" have overtaken our national values. You may not agree with Bly, but he is an interesting writer and builds a good argument. His explanation of how a child's brain develops with (and without) the influence of television is a revelation.

It is not easy to oppose broad cultural forces. It's important to know what we're up against, but as tutors we're in a good position to counter what I call the "dark forces of literalness." The fact that we are doing it one child at a time doesn't diminish the importance of the task.

How do we go about it, though? The first step in any struggle is to have a plan, and that's what the following sections are about.

Vocabulary: language to express concepts

Having the language to express complex ideas allows us to form and use those ideas. That is, learning the words allows us to think the thoughts. For instance, students can learn terms to talk about classification, comparison, character, and emotion. As you teach, try using challenging vocabulary, translating aloud into simpler terms as you go. (Additional suggestions for helping students build vocabulary are found in Chapters 7 and 11.)

Many teens who are unable to answer a teacher's questions about theme, motivation, and main idea correctly in a class discussion may simply need to be shown how to discuss these subjects. It's not the concepts that are so difficult: students just don't know what teachers want and don't understand the language we use.

Try putting your questions into different words that teens can understand. For example, the theme of a novel can be described as what the author is trying to teach us, or "what he wants us to know about human nature." Simply reading well-written book reports or summaries can be a turning point for many. A variety of book summaries written by teens can be found at http://teenink.com. The state associations of the IRA also publish concise, interesting book reviews suitable for students.

Any work on vocabulary helps build concepts. A common way of teaching vocabulary is to use the student's own reading as a source of vocabulary words. He keeps a log of new words, looks them up in the dictionary, memorizes the definitions and uses them in sentences. This is no doubt the proper way to learn vocabulary. But given a choice, most students will opt to use a vocabulary book instead. I let the student choose. If he picks the vocabulary book, I find out what vocabulary he is learning at school and if appropriate, supplement it with the Sadlier vocabulary series (Sadlier 2001). These are by far the best vocabulary workbooks around, and most kids actually enjoy using them.

A positive aspect of vocabulary study is that students can do it largely on their own once they've started, freeing lesson time for activities that require more teacher input. If needed, parents make good partners in helping teens practice new vocabulary at home. I know one family that practices the new words through discussion over the dinner table. When students work at home, class work can be pared down to asking the student to pick a few words to review each time and having him use these words in original sentences. Working on vocabulary together can definitely be fun. I use vocabulary practice as a way to get to know my students better and to let them see me in a little different light.

Make sure students are able to use new words in sentences and stories of their own and are not simply parroting definitions. For example, instead of asking "What does 'obdurate' mean?," you might ask "Do you know anyone who is obdurate? What does this person do that makes you think so?" Also, when students make up their own sentences to illustrate word meanings, the sentences should clarify the meanings, not simply contain the vocabulary words. An example of a poor sentence: "The flood was *devastating*." Better: "The flood was *devastating* because it destroyed homes and killed people."

It works well to have students make flash cards for the new words they learn. Flash cards should be kept in one place and brought to each lesson. (Three-by-five note cards cut in half save paper and are handy to carry. Some copy centers have a machine that cuts them in one slice.)

If a student is still unsure how to use words after making an effort to learn them, try this. First have him spread out the vocabulary cards so he sees the words but not the definitions. Use sentences of your own to illustrate the word meanings. Then, to quiz the student, make up sentences aloud, leaving blanks for him to fill in with the appropriate words. He will have to choose between several words to see which one fits, without looking at the definitions. This activity can be entertaining, especially if you try putting the sentences into a story. Then give the student a turn to create a story.

Make sure the student knows how to pronounce the words and is able to decipher the diacritical (pronunciation) marks used in the vocabulary workbook. Finally, keep tabs on your student's progress and make sure he schedules time for reviewing previous lessons. In school, students rarely remember the words they study after they are tested on them. You want to be sure that doesn't happen in tutoring.

Use written programs to teach abstract thinking

It might be tempting to skip the following skill-building work on abstract thinking and instead go straight to abstract thinking: taking outlined notes or discussing newspaper editorials, for instance. For some students that's fine, but for others—the ones who still can't tell you the main idea of a paragraph after you've worked on it a month—that is a recipe for failure. Kids who are concrete thinkers will never attain higher levels if we don't start where they are and draw them along gradually.

Several workbooks and courses exist for teaching higher-level thinking skills. They really work! Working on classification, similarities and differences, and analogies, for example, are all great ways to teach "entry level" abstract thinking. *Reasoning and Reading* teaches these skills effectively on the word, sentence, and paragraph levels. Other books to help students sharpen their higher-level thinking skills include *Building Power in Reading* by Henry I. Christ and *Revisit, Reflect, Retell: Strategies for Improving Reading Comprehension* by Linda Hoyt.

Here are a few tips on using these books. Explaining the purpose of the reasoning course to the parents and student at the outset will enlist their cooperation for an activity they might otherwise see as a "frill." Most kids are quite happy to do it if the teacher introduces the book as a series of "brain exercises."

Imagine you have a 13- or 14-year-old student who needs to start on the "bottom rung" of the ladder. This is where *Reasoning and Reading* comes in. The best candidate for this book is a middle school student who has trouble with book reports and other forms of summarizing and who often misses the point of his reading. Some high school students can also benefit, especially those who have a limited vocabulary and whose low reading and conceptual skills prevent them from succeeding at more difficult exercises.

Reasoning and Reading is set up as a workbook, so it is well suited for the teacher and student to use together in the tutoring session. Ordinarily, sending the book home does not help much unless the student is simply practicing something he already knows how to do. For best results, kids need immediate feedback when they are learning conceptual skills.

In teaching abstract thinking from these books or others, you will need to supplement the exercises with your own explanations. For instance, you can illustrate what the terms "category," "group," and "member" mean by using a simple drawing. Ask the student to name three breeds of dogs. Write the word "dogs" on a line, then below that draw a large circle with three X's in it. Each X stands for one of the breeds named by the student, and can be labeled. Explain that "dogs" is the group, or category, and "cocker spaniel" or "bulldog" is a "member of the group." Then have the student come up with "categories" and "members" of her own. "Trees," "flowers," and "mammals" are interesting to ask about since they also tell you something about the student's grasp of general information.

Try spending about 20 minutes of each lesson on the reasoning skills book. At that rate, your student should have progressed far enough in two or three months for you to discontinue the workbook and put your efforts directly into schoolwork that requires abstract thought, such as summarizing and note-taking.

Expect transfer

How much can we expect learning in one area of abstract thought to transfer to another? Obviously, transfer is not perfect. If it were, teaching equations would ready a child for literary discussion, and doing word analogies would render him proficient in outlining.

On the other hand, skills learned in one situation definitely do rub off on other situations. For example, *Reasoning and Reading* does not address schoolwork directly, but students who have gone through the exercises in the book are able to write better summaries and book reports and can take notes and outline better than they did before. Parents sometimes report that students who are being tutored become less impulsive and less given to acting out socially. This could be due to the overall therapeutic effect of the tutoring relationship, but perhaps learning to think clearly about academic work also transfers to better thinking about behavior. In short, the student's new thinking skills are not confined to the type of work done in the tutoring session—analogies, classification, etc.—but do actually transfer to other types of learning, both in and out of school.

When in doubt, don't bail out

Abstract thinking is related to intelligence, at least to some degree. This means that if you have a student who is getting the facts but missing the ideas and no amount of teaching seems to help, it could be because the child lacks the mental wherewithal to do what you want him to do. In this case, badgering the student is simply cruel.

On the other hand, what if your student has missed the experiences or vocabulary necessary to become proficient at abstract thinking? Or what if he is merely immature and not ready to do what you are asking *at this time*? You won't know whether your student is capable of learning to think abstractly unless you try, and that means making a concerted effort to teach him to think conceptually over a period of several months.

If a student is not capable of moving beyond the literal level, all that can be done is to teach him to use the concrete skills he does have. This is such a rare circumstance, however, that it usually works to assume the best and continue doing all you can to teach higher-level thinking skills.

So far, we've talked about the need for young people to have exposure to higher-level thinking, to give them the language they need to express concepts, to use written programs to teach reasoning, and to persevere. Now let's move on to the next step, asking questions that lead to more in-depth thinking.

Asking "How" and "Why" Questions

How is your student doing on tellbacks? When he is consistently getting 80 to 90 percent recall, start asking more in-depth or abstract questions about what he's read: "How did so-and-so feel? Why did he do what he did? What kind of a person is he? What do you think might happen next? Do you see a pattern in that person's behavior?" Explain to your student that since he can "do facts" now, it is time to start thinking more about reasons for things, and of course people's feelings figure into why things happen as they do.

If your student has trouble with this new dimension in the discussion, take a passage and show him the key words and phrases that point to the answers. Even more important, ask questions and make comments yourself on the behavior of the novel's characters. For instance, in *Tiger Eyes*, the main character, Davey, is attending her father's funeral but seems to be quite unfeeling about his death, focusing instead on how her shoes hurt (Blume 2010, 3). Most teenagers understand that Davey is in shock because of her father's death, and may comment that "she's still in denial." Often teens will pick up on these ideas right away on their own, but asking a few questions will help the ones who need a leg up.

For students who need it, here are some questions to guide the discussion. "How is Davey acting at the funeral? What is she *not* doing that you might expect her to do? Why do you think she is acting that way? How is she feeling?" Then, and this is important, have your student find words and sentences that back up his answers. "What makes you think so?" is one of the most useful questions you can ask. If the student is unable to respond, simply answer the questions yourself and see if he can answer next time.

Here are some "why" questions based on the first two pages of *The House on Mango Street* by Sandra Cisneros (1997). The main character in the story says she and her family have moved many times, often in a hurry, and that she wishes they had a house with a lawn. So the conversation with the student could go like this:

Question: Why do you guess the family moves so much? What does that tell you about them?

Answer: Maybe they are poor.

Q: Why would poor people have to move suddenly?

A: Maybe because the dad loses his job or there are fights in the neighborhood or the landlord does something bad.

Q: What do you know about the house so far?

A: It's small and there's no lawn.

Q: What does this tell you?

A: It's not the house they wanted.

Q: The girl says her mom's hair looks like candy rosettes and smells like sweet bread. What does this tell you about how the girl feels about her mom?

A: They're close. She loves her.

Here's another example. In *Jason's Women*, by Jean Okimoto (2000), Jason, the main character, is a neglected and isolated teen. When I ask a student to describe Jason's relationship with his father, I sometimes get the answer that Jason's divorced dad is busy going out on dates with a lot of women. That's true, but not exactly an answer to the question. After some discussion, guidance, and questioning, a student might come up with the more thoughtful answer that Jason's dad ignores him and that Jason probably feels lonely. For some students, this type of discussion is new territory. Mastery is not crucial. You need only make a start. (*Jason's Women* has some sexual innuendo, so you might want to read it first to see if you think it is suitable.)

The education website of PBS (Public Broadcasting Service) published a list of excellent general reading questions not geared to any one specific piece of literature. The PBS list (2006) is provided in Appendix D, Developing Active Reading with Effective Questions. Here is a sample:

"Who or what do you predict this story will be about?"
"Where and when do you think the story will take place?"
"What questions do you have about this story?"
"What can we learn about the characters from what they say and do?"
"What is the most important event in each chapter or section of the story?"
"Does the author make you want to keep reading? If so, how?"
"Can you relate any part of this story to an event in your life?"
"What could be an alternate ending for the story?"
"How did the author use imagery to tell the story?"

For more on literature discussion questions, the internet is full of helpful websites. Some of these are included in the "Online Resources" section of the Bibliography.

Understanding the Beginning of a Novel

Even though the student has been reading fiction for a while, it is time to direct his attention to the beginning pages of a novel. Inexperienced readers often get stuck in the first few pages of a book. A student will start a book only to put it down a short while later. He may not even know why he is not able to continue: "It's boring," or "I couldn't figure out what was happening," he might say, or simply, "I didn't like it."

Of course, all these comments might be true. But if the student can learn what to look for at the beginning of a book, it may shortcut his frustration and keep him reading long enough to judge more accurately whether or not he likes the book.

With that in mind, here are some tips to help students get started on a novel. Introduce the topic by telling the student that getting through the first chapter or two of a novel is hard for everyone, even experienced tutors, but there are some tricks and methods for getting through the first few pages easily.

Puzzle pieces

Unskilled readers often ignore material at the beginning of a book if they don't understand what it means or how it fits together. By contrast, skillful readers collect and mentally file such introductory information for future reference. You can help your student read the first pages of a book more actively through an explanation, or analogy, using "puzzle pieces."

For this exercise, I choose a paragraph from the beginning of a story or novel, one that contains quite a bit of information. Reading the paragraph aloud, I point out how the author has included some details that may seem to be puzzling or unimportant at first, but that end up being crucial to understanding the story. I explain that the author is giving the reader "puzzle pieces" that don't make any sense by themselves, but when put together with other pieces of the puzzle (information from the book), they will actually mean something.

To demonstrate, I sketch some *unconnected* jigsaw puzzle pieces, each with part of a person's face drawn on it—eyes, mouth, or nose. These features, though unconnected, are in the correct positions, relative to each other, for forming a face as we proceed. Even inattentive students will pay attention if the teacher draws to illustrate a point, so regardless of your artistic skills, give it a try. The purpose of drawing in this exercise is simply to get the student to pay attention to your explanation.

As I read aloud, each time I come to a new fact in the book that's worth noting, I draw in another puzzle piece, with another part of the face, eventually connecting all the pieces—and by extension, all the information. The paragraph I'm reading will likely not have anything to do with puzzles, or even people. Each piece simply represents a fact to be remembered. At the end of the portion of the book I've chosen to read, the face is completed.

At that moment, the student sees how all the details fit together, and he has a drawing of a person's face made of "joined" puzzle pieces to reinforce his understanding. This moment can be a revelation for the haphazard reader.

I explain the process this way:

> When you read, be careful not to discard the things you learn even if you don't understand yet where they fit in. You hang on to each small piece of information and then fit them together as you read. That will help you understand the characters, the setting, and even the beginnings of conflict in the book. This picture of the finished face is to remind you of how you can get an overview based on the separate pieces of information.
>
> The author spreads the information around to make it more interesting to discover. Books for little kids often tell all the information in the first couple of pages, but they aren't as interesting as books for teens or adults.

To demonstrate, you might read aloud from the beginning pages of a children's book.

Know what to look for

Next ask the student what ideas or information an author needs to get across to the reader in the first few pages of a novel. This may sound like a simple question, but is a difficult one for most teens, and it may take some discussion to guide the student to the answers. In the end, you may give more answers on this subject than the student does, but that's all right. The purpose is just to get him thinking about things from the author's perspective—something most young readers have never done.

Explain that in the first few pages the author must get across who is in the story (the characters), names, ages, looks, and a bit about their personalities; where the story takes place (setting), when (if it's a historical novel), and what the conflict or problem is. Jot these points down as you discuss. Of course, not every book contains all this information in the first few pages, but compared to books for adults, books for teens are more likely to have all this material up front.

Conflict is the main problem of the story. Explain that all stories must have a conflict; otherwise you end up with "a very nice girl lived in a pretty town and was very happy. End of story." Give examples of various conflicts from your own reading or from movies you and the student have both seen. Add that the immediate conflict usually isn't the main conflict for the entire book. For example, at the beginning of *My Side of the Mountain*, the boy is snowed in, but you know there's going to be a broader conflict later.

After the student is familiar with the ideas of setting, character, and conflict, along with some pointers to help find them, have him try out his new knowledge. Ask him to read the first few pages of S. E. Hinton's *That Was Then, This Is Now* and look for answers to the following questions: "Who is in the story? What are their names? What do you know about them? Where and when does the story take place? What problems do the characters have?" It helps to have the questions written down.

As the student reads, have him find the answers to the questions you've posed and jot down the answers as he discovers them. For a slow starter, have him dictate his answers for you to write down. Your enthusiasm can turn the search into a lively exchange: "Wow, I didn't know if you'd find that one. It was kind of hidden." The finished product will be a list of all the characters introduced in the first few pages of the book with several descriptive words or phrases about each one. It will also have a brief description of the setting and conflict.

Even if they aren't actually enjoying reading yet, students usually like the list of characters they've just made and feel that making the list was an accomplishment. After a student has gone through this exercise with two or three different books, he will probably find it easier to get started reading a new book. That's because the information at the beginning of a book will now seem like an opportunity for a treasure hunt instead of extraneous material. Explain that even experienced readers sometimes find it necessary to keep a list of characters and their identifying characteristics. I may pull out my own list from the most recent mystery or spy novel I've read—the more characters, the better.

Introduction to Identifying the Main Idea

Being able to identify the main idea is the foundation for many other important academic skills. For a student who is unable to identify the main idea of a passage, it will be difficult to summarize, outline, take organized notes, write paragraphs with good topic sentences, or understand the point of an article, lecture, or a piece of literature.

Many of the exercises your student has done so far lead up to identifying main idea, or "what all the sentences in a paragraph have in common." Students who have worked on categorization in *Reasoning and Reading*, for example, will know that categories are groups containing members that all have something in common but also show differences. It is a short step from that idea to locating the topic sentence and the supporting sentences in a paragraph. That is because the topic sentence or main idea gives us the name or subject of the group and the supporting sentences are like its members. The work you have done so far will put your student in a good position to take the next important step, that of finding a theme common to all the sentences in a paragraph even when the theme is not stated directly in the topic sentence. Though many teens will intuitively be able to identify the main ideas in their reading, others may need some specific instruction. The following explanations and exercises should help.

Many students will understand the idea of "finding the common theme" of the sentences in a paragraph, but for those who don't, explain that telling the main idea simply means to "tell what it's about in just a few words." Here's an example most teens can identify with: "You go baby-sitting and the kid you're sitting won't go to bed, tears up magazines, throws food, and screams. What's the main idea? Answer: The kid's a brat." Here, these details add up to a theme, or main idea.

Some teenagers enjoy examples from fairy tales. For instance, ask for a summary of Goldilocks in three or four sentences. Have students do summaries of entire stories as well as paragraphs, since they will need to do both in their actual reading. To start things off I might provide this summary of the Goldilocks tale. "Goldilocks went in the bears' house and messed with stuff. She ate their cereal, then tried out their chairs and beds. She fell asleep and the bears discovered her when they came home." What's the main idea? It was in the first sentence: "Goldilocks went to the bears' house and messed with their stuff." Do a few more story summaries and then try some paragraphs from a novel.

In the book *Two Old Women*, for instance, discussion of the first three paragraphs might proceed as follows:

First paragraph:

The air stretched tight, quiet and cold over the vast land. Tall spruce branches hung heavily laden with snow, awaiting distant spring winds. The frosted willows seemed to tremble in the freezing temperatures. (Wallis 2004, 1)

Before asking about main idea, have the student tell you in detail what he read. Since the details in this paragraph are mostly for atmosphere and not really important in and of themselves, it's OK to gloss over them a little and say something like, "The air is cold, it's snowy, and the trees also seem cold." The details lead right into the main idea, which is super simple: "It was cold."

Second paragraph:

Far off in this seemingly dismal land were bands of people dressed in furs and animal skins, huddled close to small campfires. Their weather-burnt faces were stricken with looks of hopelessness as they faced starvation, and the future held little promise of better days. (Wallis 2004, 1-2)

Again, ask for details and then main idea. A student might report the main idea in one phrase as, "A tribe of people is starving."

Third paragraph:

These nomads were The People of the arctic region of Alaska, always on the move in search of food. Where the caribou and other migrating animals roamed, The People followed. But the deep cold of winter presented special problems. The moose, their favorite source of food, took refuge from the penetrating cold by staying in one place and were difficult to find. Smaller, more accessible animals such as rabbits and tree squirrels could not sustain a large band such as this one. And during the cold spells, even the smaller animals either disappeared in hiding or were thinned by predators, man and animal alike. . . . (Wallis 2004, 2)

This paragraph has a lot more detail, so just ask for three or four most important points, which might be, "The people were nomads who followed big animals for food, but the animals they depended on, including smaller ones had disappeared." And main idea: "The people were starving because their food animals were gone."

When your student does tellbacks for detail and main idea, try to get him to do as much as he can himself, but don't be afraid to tell him the answers if he can't get them. If he has the general idea but is missing parts or has worded things unclearly, fill in for him. "Yes, and another way to say that would be. . . ."

Kids' minds often shift into neutral as soon as the teacher starts talking, so, obvious as it may sound, you may need to make sure the student understands he's expected to learn by listening to you rephrase his tellbacks. Also, point out that making some educated guesses, or putting two and two together, is a good thing, then demonstrate. Without this permission teens often will stick strictly to the facts and avoid attempting any sort of interpretation.

Keep practicing both the detail and main idea tellbacks until the student is doing fairly well with them. Then you can discontinue the detail tellbacks. When the student is able to identify main ideas, have him practice at home by writing the main idea of each paragraph for a section of a novel. When he brings in his list of main ideas, show him that it would be possible to use the list as the basis for a book summary.

If your student still isn't picking up on main idea tellbacks, don't be too concerned. Main idea appears again in the factual reading section, along with more exercises. If the student is doing well on one-paragraph tellbacks, however, you can take the next step and help him extend his range.

Longer Tellbacks

In this exercise the student starts with short sections and moves into reading and remembering increasingly longer ones. Go from asking for tellbacks after each paragraph to a tellback after two and then three paragraphs. Expand this to a page, a section, then a chapter. Some students may soon be ready to read an entire book and summarize. Doing these longer tellbacks is similar to shorter ones, with one important step added, as follows.

Recalling material from longer sections can be difficult. Try it yourself to see. It is easy to remember the first and last paragraphs, but readers often find "the middle has disappeared" from their minds. Here's a simple, effective way of remembering an entire section. At the end of each paragraph, have the student do a tellback *silently* instead of aloud. He should stop at the end of the paragraph, look away from the book, and tell himself what he just read before he moves on. His silent tellback should include the main idea in a short phrase and two to four important details. Doing a silent tellback after each paragraph can go a long way toward helping him remember what he has read by the time he has reached the end of the section. He should do the silent tellbacks for the entire section and then review all of them mentally before summarizing the section aloud for you.

As soon as he hands you the book to do the summary (oral tellback) for the entire section, he is required to do it from memory. This point is important. Inexperienced students often believe they understand or remember something when really they have only given it a cursory glance. The tellback is a great reality check, quickly revealing what a student knows and does not know. In this situation, the teacher can afford to be kind and supportive, allowing the tellback to reflect the sometimes unpleasant truth.

For this reason, doing a silent tellback after each paragraph is an (almost) certain cure for lack of concentration, as it will immediately make the student aware of an unfocused mind. Ordinarily, when a person becomes aware that he is not understanding, he will gather his resources and concentrate.

Make sure your student is actually doing the mental tellbacks, however. Some readers try to skip this step. Encourage the student to model his silent tellbacks on the oral ones he's already been doing. "Imagine you're telling me what you read, but do it in your own mind."

For oral tellbacks that cover longer sections (more than a page or two), it is not necessary to ask for a huge amount of information. One or two ideas from most of the paragraphs is fine. Assure the student that these longer readings will be a big help with social studies and science reading at school.

Some students ask to take notes to help them remember what they have read, but since the object of this exercise is to develop memory, it is counterproductive to use notes at this time. There will be plenty of opportunity for note-taking later.

That said, if a student is reading an entire book outside of the tutoring session, it works best to have him write a one- or two-paragraph summary after each chapter rather than waiting to summarize until the end.

In the next chapter we will cover several additional memory techniques, so if your student is currently having trouble on the longer tellbacks, you can try again later with the help of these new methods.

On a different note, it's now time to start requiring your student to use the LSU technique consistently if he's not already doing so. Even when teens know the LSU helps them, they may still need to be reminded to keep using it.

When to Introduce Reading Speed

In Chapter 4 we discussed which reading skills to introduce first. Now, before we continue with comprehension strategies, let's revisit the question of when to introduce speed reading. Learning to read faster can be an important boost for students both intellectually and emotionally, so there are plenty of reasons to introduce reading speed as soon as it is practical.

Still, a balance needs to be struck. Start speed reading too soon—before a student really knows what he's reading—and he will still be reading "gibberish," only faster. On the other hand, if you wait too long to introduce speed reading, you will unnecessarily postpone an opportunity to do your student some good.

With these considerations in mind, *if* you feel your student's comprehension is adequate, now is the time to introduce reading speed. "Adequate" might mean a student is able to remember 70 to 80 percent of the important ideas and facts from his reading, provided the material is on a suitable reading level for him.

Regarding a "suitable level," if a student is reading more than two years below grade level, it's best to help him raise his reading skills before beginning speed reading. If a student is that far behind, he has a serious reading problem, and you will want to focus all your efforts on helping him improve his comprehension. If the student is reading less than two years below grade level, and if his comprehension is adequate at his current level, it's fine to start on speed reading. In this case, it's simply a matter of providing the right material and allowing plenty of time to work on comprehension as well as speed. Fortunately, comprehension and speed reading can be taught simultaneously, so you can continue on with the following comprehension exercises after you introduce speed reading. (Speed reading is detailed in Chapter 10.)

Summarizing

Summarizing means relating the main idea and a few well-chosen details for a reading passage (or any other subject). An example of a summary would be an informative but concise answer to any of these questions:

"What was the movie (or book) about?"
"What was growing up in the Depression like?"
"How did hostile relations develop between the Israelis and Palestinians?"

Since summarizing is such an essential skill, have you ever wondered why so few people can do it well? The problem isn't confined to young people or the uneducated, either. Have you ever been in a meeting with school personnel who are planning an individual educational plan (IEP) for a student? Ninety percent of the meeting may be taken up with details explaining the testing procedure or exactly what the teachers have tried (unsuccessfully) to teach the student. Any planning usually takes place in the last 10 minutes of the meeting, seemingly as an afterthought.

Problems with summarizing may be widespread, but fortunately summarizing itself is a teachable skill. When you help your students learn to summarize, you are doing more than simply teaching a reading skill—you are also giving them valuable tools for effective communication and analytical thinking.

Like most subjects in this book, summarizing is approached incrementally. When students first start reading novels, and before they are ready to summarize, they will still be able to do one thing that makes everybody happy: They can you tell the plot. This fits in with the longer tellbacks they've been doing. Kids love to tell you what happened, blow by blow, start to finish. Let them do it for a few chapters, then start asking them to summarize instead of giving you the whole plot line.

Let's look at why people may have trouble summarizing and what we can do about it.

Overdetailing and overgeneralization

STUCK IN THE DETAILS

Nicky was a 15-year-old girl enrolled in my first homeschooling program. From Nicky I learned the problems some students face in gaining an overview. Nicky was now living with her father and stepmother, but she had been raised by her birth mother, who by all accounts was psychotic. In spite of a difficult and painful upbringing, Nicky seemed relatively "together." I noticed one thing that was really off, however: it was impossible for Nicky to get an overview, not just in academics, but in any situation. She headed straight for the details.

I got the full effect when I tutored her at the library. I had accompanied her to the stacks to help her pick out some reference books on the history of the violin for a paper she was writing. Instead of looking at the shelves to see where the books on violins or musical instruments started and stopped, however, she went straight to the first book she saw, pulled it off the shelf and started reading. She didn't look around first to see what her choices were or how many books there might be on her subject. And this wasn't even a particularly appealing book. Her stepmother told me this was how Nicky went through life. Everything was a detail for her. There were no overviews.

Not surprisingly, when Nicky started her work with me, she didn't get much out of her reading except for some random details. She made good progress, though, and her comprehension improved. Summarizing, SQ3R, and outlining (Chapter 9) all proved useful. I don't know whether our work helped Nicky in other areas, but however things turned out for her, Nicky provided an important lesson for me. Since then I've kept my eyes open for students who were stuck in detail mode, and I have tried to come up with ways to help them see both the trees *and the forest*. (See "Helping Students Get the Point" in Chapter 18.)

Difficulty summarizing can show up as overdetailing or its opposite, overgeneralization. And it's not uncommon for one person to do both. Students can be made aware of these pitfalls through role-playing. First, the teacher demonstrates overdetailing by launching into a story with no introduction at all. For example, the tutor might say, out of the blue, "The cookies are baked and now she's starting on the punch. After a while she'll change into her new clothes. The house looks pretty good." After a while the teacher stops and says, "Did you understand what I was talking about? Why not? What was wrong? What could I have done differently?" Then provide the overview: "My friend is getting ready for a party. Here's what she's done so far."

Something similar could be done with overgeneralization. For example, "I have an idea for a new business. I'll sell stuff and get a lot of money. Does that sound like a good business plan?" When the student looks doubtful, you add, "Maybe I need more specifics. Like what kind of stuff I'm going to sell and who's going to buy it." This provides an entry into talking about what should be included in a summary.

It will help that the student has had experience identifying both main idea and detail. To move into summarizing he simply needs to list the main ideas for several paragraphs and add a few details for each, then come up with a one- or two-sentence introduction that explains the main idea of the entire section. All this should be done from memory, or at least as much from memory as possible.

With these elements, the student is on his way to being able to do a good summary. "On his way," but not quite there, perhaps. Many students' book summaries are confined to the plot, but there's more to a book than just the plot. This next step is about helping students come up with more in-depth, balanced summaries of their reading.

Balanced summaries

As with previous comprehension exercises, if your student needs to be eased into this activity, start with summarizing movies and fairy tales. In doing summaries, teens have a tendency to cover only facts and incidents (plot), so they need to be encouraged to include how the characters feel about things and any actions or comments that reveal relationships among people. Character description, reviewed in the next section, should be included as well.

In addition to conveying the characters' feelings and motivation, some books like *The Night Journey* by Kathryn Lasky or *Number the Stars* by Lois Lowry, require a degree of political or historical understanding. These are children's books, but young teens may enjoy them, and they provide an ideal arena for teaching about character, political thought—and of course summarizing.

For the exercises that follow, have two copies of *Number the Stars* on hand, one for you and one for the student. To start, provide background on concepts such as the German occupation of Denmark and other European countries in the Second World War and also the Resistance. Then ask your student to watch for and include comments or incidents that explain the political or historical elements in the story. This may sound difficult, but even fifth and sixth graders can be taught to include political ideas in their summaries. Just ask them to "put in anything you read about the government," then show them how.

This summary of the first chapter of *Number the Stars* should give an idea of how to incorporate these elements. I might provide a summary like this *after* the student has had an opportunity to read and summarize the material himself.

> Two girls, Annemarie and Ellen, are racing each other down a city street in Copenhagen, Denmark. Of the two, Annemarie is bolder, Ellen more reserved. (I would add the information, not yet apparent in the story, that Annemarie is Christian, Ellen Jewish.) The city is occupied by Nazi soldiers. The girls nearly run into some soldiers, who question them, along with Annemarie's little sister, Kirsti, then send them on their way. When the girls' mothers hear about this run-in with the soldiers from Kirsti, who's a bit of a "blabbermouth," the mothers are afraid for the girls and caution them to go to school another way.

> The mothers talk quietly about how the Germans are on edge because of recent bombings by the Resistance. Annemarie goes over in her mind what she knows about the Resistance, and we learn that a family friend, Peter, delivers an illegal newspaper to Annemarie's parents, leaving us to wonder whether Peter himself is a member of the Resistance.

> The chapter closes with Kirsti asking her mother when they will have cupcakes to eat again. We might wonder what else Annemarie's family—and the Danish people—are being deprived of besides cupcakes.

The summary includes the necessary elements: plot, character description, a little about how the characters relate to each other, and a mention of the political situation.

The "accordion" summary

An excellent activity for developing flexibility in summarizing is the "accordion" summary. It's called an "accordion" because it can be expanded and contracted depending on your purposes. In this example, we'll start large and gradually contract.

Begin with a tellback: Have your student read a section that includes from three pages to an entire chapter, and without looking back at the book, tell everything he can remember of what he read. Then have him pare that tellback down to a summary of about eight to ten sentences. You can facilitate by writing down what he says. (A laptop computer is useful here.) Next ask him to boil that summary down even further to three or four sentences containing the kernel of the story. Finally, you should give an even shorter summary. This will be just a statement of the main idea of the passage, maybe only one or two sentences long.

After you have gone through a few of these "accordion" exercises orally, expanding or contracting the length of the summary for practice, it is helpful to have the student write them himself. This is a good homework assignment, and one he can use with his school reading.

Here are some examples of accordion summaries based on the eight- to ten-sentence summary given above from *Number the Stars*. First, the three- to four-sentence version:

> It is WWII, and Copenhagen, Denmark, is occupied by Nazi soldiers. Three girls, Annemarie, her friend Ellen, and her sister, Kirsti, are racing when they have a run-in with some German soldiers. The girls' mothers caution them to avoid the soldiers. We learn a little about the Resistance and the deprivations of the war.

Second is the tutor's "main idea" of the chapter in one sentence:

> We meet three girls living in Nazi-occupied Denmark and learn something of the problems and tensions afflicting their families.

Kids' wording will be different, but they could include the same ideas.

The entire process of learning to summarize can take several months if you are devoting 20 minutes or so to it out of a weekly lesson. Helping your student learn to summarize is a commitment, but since the outcome is so important—and so gratifying—it is definitely worth the effort.

Character Description

If your student is doing a decent job of answering "how and why" questions about his reading, it is time to return to character description. This time, though, you want the student to go into more depth than before, and you are going to show him how to do it.

Describing character is difficult for many students because it involves an unfamiliar way of thinking and talking. They need a template. The following exercise works well because it reduces the task into do-able parts and gives the student a series of steps to follow.

First have the student pick one character from a book he is reading and ask him to give three suitable adjectives or nouns to describe that character. An adjective could be "angry" or "smart" and a noun could be "a criminal" or "an artist." Don't accept more than one word describing physical appearance. Instead, ask for words that tell about personality or character. Examples: "brave, independent, observant" (the boy in *My Side of the Mountain*); "wimpy, anxious, shy" (Jason in *Jason's Women*).

To teach parts of speech, you also can use a *Mad Libs* game. *Mad Libs* are collections of stories with key words missing. Players fill in the blanks with parts of speech requested by a leader to complete the stories. The results can be quite funny. The *Mad Libs* series has many titles, various publishers, and was written over about a 50-year period by Roger Price and Leonard Stern.

Using Hinton's *That Was Then, This Is Now*, ask the student for three descriptive words about the character Mark. Make a note of the three words. Then ask him to tell something the character felt or did in the story to show why he picked each of the words. Jot it all down. To describe the character Mark in *That Was Then, This Is Now*, your student might say:

> He's a "con artist" because he scams people into playing pool with him and always wins; a "crook" because when he needs a ride he steals a car, though he usually returns it. He's "loyal" toward his friend Bryon, backing him in the street fights they get into.

Then take what you have—the three descriptive terms and the pieces of evidence that back them up—and roll them together into a paragraph that you write yourself. Point out that the resulting paragraph would fit nicely into a book report, something that will seem useful to most students. The sentences, put into paragraph form by the teacher, might read like the following, where words in italics are the ones supplied by the student.

> Mark is a *con artist* and a petty *criminal*. He tricks people into playing pool with him so he can fleece them. He steals cars when he needs a ride and is on probation for hotwiring a car. Mark's sheer gall is amusing, while his sense of *loyalty* makes him human and even likeable. For instance, it is the principal's car he hotwires to drive to a meeting with his probation officer. When Mark and his best friend Bryon are threatened by two thugs in a street fight, he puts himself at risk to protect Bryon.

Teens usually are delighted to see the results of their efforts in making the list of descriptive words and turning them into sentences, and then seeing their ideas turned into a good paragraph can seem almost magical. Even though they know the teacher guided them, the process gives them a glimpse of their own potential, so this small activity can be an inspiration.

Character description of the kind we've been doing is a good activity for several reasons. Since teenagers are so interested in people—themselves and each other—it appeals strongly to teens to talk about people in books—how they feel, what they're like, and why they do things—even when teens don't have a sophisticated vocabulary to get their ideas across. Discussing people in books is a great first step in the study of literature, and a good way to build rapport with a child who is reserved or disengaged. Moreover, character descriptions require (and teach) abstract thinking. Discussing literature generally and characterization in particular gives a good opportunity to talk about values in a way that is thought-provoking but not heavy handed.

Some students need more help to get them started than was described here. For those students, pick a movie you've both seen or use a fairy tale to practice describing the characters. For instance, if you choose to describe "Goldilocks" (she figures quite a bit in our literary discussions), you might say she was "impulsive," "self-centered," and maybe even "not very bright." By now, kids are usually laughing and they get the point. Next it's the student's turn. He might try "Little Red Riding Hood." Does the student know the word *naïve*? If not he can learn it now. Don't accept the words "nice" or "mean" in this exercise.

From now on, every time you have the student read a book, ask for a description of the main characters. For this purpose, *Tiger Eyes* is a good book to use with girls, while boys age 15 to 19 may enjoy *Jason's Women*. This work on character description builds the foundation for more sophisticated discussions about theme and issues in literature. Some teachers put together lists of words to describe people to use for such occasions. Table 6.1 presents some of my own.

Require Plenty of Reading

At this point, the amount and frequency of a student's reading takes on greater importance than it has previously. Students will not become highly adept readers if they are not immersed in reading, and now that they have an array of skills and know-how to build on, this is an ideal time for them to plunge in. Some students will read without being asked, but many teens need an adult (or another student) to help them stay on track. Beyond the preliminary stages of tutoring, I want my students to be reading a book at all times. If the student is reading a book for school, he doesn't need to be reading anything extra for me, but he isn't to be "between books" for more

Table 6.1. Words to describe people.		
Positive	**Negative**	**Other**
pleasant	over-demanding	shy
good-natured	cruel	bashful
kindly, kind-hearted	critical	timid
thoughtful	controlling	wishy-washy
sympathetic	rigid	wimp
understanding	manipulative	repressed
supportive	bossy	conformist
friendly	scheming	ordinary
spunky	cold-hearted	secretive
lively	unresponsive	immature
open	unsympathetic	worry-wart
outgoing	evil	pessimistic
polite	a villain	fatalistic
brave	self-centered	withdrawn
resilient	self-absorbed	uninvolved
heroic	narcissistic	wild
spirited	arrogant	weird
intelligent	neglectful	eccentric
observant	angry	
resourceful	shrill	
honest	tough	
tough	insensitive	
optimistic	unruly	
ambitious	hypocritical	
hardworking	stupid	
creative	ignorant	
dignified	spiteful	
generous	bad-tempered	
cheerful	greedy	
affectionate	temperamental	
loving	dishonest	
caring	undignified	

than two or three days. After a few weeks of speed-reading instruction as described in Chapter 10, a student could be expected to complete a book every two weeks.

It's easy to determine how many chapters or pages to assign based on students' current reading speed and the amount of time you wish them to spend daily on their reading. Most students below ninth grade can handle about 30 minutes of reading each day, while high school students can be expected to put in around 45 minutes if you ease them into it. Even so, you will probably find that asking for a specific number of pages works better than assigning an amount of time to be spent reading. Time suggestions are included here primarily to help you determine how many pages to assign.

You can assign books by telling students they need to have something to practice their speed reading on. *Practicing* a skill seems more palatable to many teens than "becoming a reader," at least for now. They understand practice, especially if it's compared to music or sports practice, and oddly enough, the idea of *practicing*, rather than simply reading, is more appealing. Most students comment that they've read more in their first few months of tutoring than they've ever read before in their lives—and they're not complaining.

Choose Books That Help Students Grow

In discussing books with adolescents, we touch on the great universal themes: love, hate, loyalty, betrayal, courage, sacrifice, survival and transcendence. And these subjects are not confined to words on a page or talk in a classroom. It doesn't happen with every book or with every child, but often enough we get the opportunity to influence character and even, occasionally, to touch souls in our work. Some of this learning is unplanned and happens naturally in the course of tutoring, but as teachers we are also in a position to help the process along by choosing books that will encourage our students to develop as individuals.

When students become skillful readers, they naturally become more engaged with books on a personal level, and they will choose books for themselves with no prompting. They will read recreationally and to inform themselves. They may sample a variety of books and will respond with emotion and intelligence to what they read. Above all, they have the capacity to choose the books they need to continue to grow emotionally themselves. In short, they become independent readers. But it can take between several months and a couple of years of tutoring for students to reach this level. When they have reached it, they are self-starters who do not need others to help them choose books. Before that, however, our help as reading mentors can play a central role in their lives.

As you worked through Chapter 2, you may have interviewed teachers, librarians, and students to learn what books they recommended for teen readers. At that time you were primarily interested in learning about reading level, but many of the books you learned about then will have a renewed interest for you now as a way to help teens learn about themselves and other people. Taking a college class in literature for adolescents is an interesting way to learn about books for teens.

If you start with the suggestions in this book, combine them with recommendations from other educators and librarians, and add or subtract as you see fit, you should end up with a list—and ultimately a tutoring library—on which you can depend as both a practical resource and a source of inspiration.

In Bibliotherapy, a form of therapy similar to art or dance therapy, trained therapists use books to help students deal with particular issues in their lives. We may not be bibliotherapists, but as tutors we can still help students address personal problems and learn emotionally through their reading. The way to achieve this is not by simply giving your student a book in which the protagonist has a problem similar to his own. Instead, try to find a book that has an emotional message to which the student will relate. For instance, you wouldn't necessarily choose a book about a teen whose parents are getting a divorce for a young person in the same situation. Instead, you might choose a fantasy with themes of betrayal and heroism.

Chapter 17 contains suggestions for choosing books that will appeal to the various temperament and character types. The bibliography includes "Books for Students," a list of the books teens have said were transformative for them. Some students prefer books for adults rather than ones written for teens. One girl told me she thought grownups had more interesting problems!

Book Reports and Higher-level Thinking Skills

What good are book reports? Kids usually dislike doing them and often go through the motions without learning anything. The opposite can be true, however, and if book reports are used as a springboard for teaching about broader issues, real learning often takes place.

Not surprisingly, few of the students who come your way will have experienced success at writing book reports. To avoid reinforcing their negative experiences, proceed gradually. You could start with discussion, do oral reports together, have students write in class, and then assign book reports as homework. A simplified form to use for younger teens is provided in Appendix E. If the student can write a successful report using this format in tutoring, he will probably be able to do what is expected at school.

Older teens don't usually have to do book reports at school but are often asked to write literary analysis papers. Many of the higher-level thinking skills you and your student have worked on so far will be needed both for book reports and literature papers. A book report and a paper for a literature class may seem miles apart, but discussing the larger issues, or the unifying themes of books, can help students prepare for either type of writing.

Putting Character and Theme Together

Whether the task is writing a book report or discussing literature, one very difficult job for almost every student is identifying and discussing the "theme" of a book—and, therefore, it is difficult to teach. Generally, the more abstract the task is, the less predictable the results will be. Try the following and see what happens.

Begin by asking if the student has had any experience in identifying the theme of a book. He may say that, yes, the teacher has talked about it in class and has explained all about the theme of say, *Animal Farm* by George Orwell or *Lord of the Flies* by William Golding. In discussing theme, some teachers just hand students the ideas rather than drawing out insights through discussion and helping students arrive at ideas on their own.

Ask the student if he'd like to learn something that could help him figure out the theme on his own so that he could do a better job on book reports or literature papers. I've never met a student who didn't want to do better at recognizing and writing about theme, so this is a safe question.

Using a book you and your student have both read, ask what the lesson or the moral of the story is, what the author is teaching us through the story, or what the theme of the book is. Though the moral and the theme are not exactly the same, it helps to start with this idea and refine as you go. For *Izzy Willy Nilly* by Cynthia Voigt, the answer might be, "You never know who your real friends are until a crisis hits." Or, for *Two Old Women*, "Never say die."

Another approach is to have the student give you a couple of adjectives to describe the main character and turn those words into qualities that identify the theme. So, if the main character was brave, as in *Number the Stars*, the theme could be "courage." Finally, you can list for the student words and phrases that are often used to describe theme. Of course, it's important to practice identifying theme—sometimes for several weeks.

Students have learned at school that books can show "man against man," "man against nature," etc., and they want to offer those phrases when asked for theme, but those words describe the conflict, not the theme. Following is a more detailed lesson plan, including a script, to encourage students to think about the theme of a part of a book or story. This opening ploy has been used for other lessons, but kids don't seem to mind running into this character again.

> First, tell me the basic plot of "Little Red Riding Hood." What do you think the lesson, or the moral, of the story is? What could it be warning people to do or not do? Not be too trusting? Look at who is under the bonnet or behind the disguise? Or who you are getting into bed with?
> Now we'll talk about the moral or "lesson" of a movie.

It's good to have the student watch a movie in preparation for this. For younger teens good movies are *The Secret Garden* and *The Indian in the Cupboard*. *Breaking Away* and *Shawshank Redemption* are great for older teens. *Shawshank Redemption* contains rough language and violence, so you should watch it yourself first and maybe even ask parents to take a look before assigning it. *Smoke Signals* is another good movie for older students.

Here are some of the words that can be used to describe the themes of these movies. In working with your student, be sure to draw out the ideas through questioning and discussion, not give them away at the beginning.

> *The Indian in the Cupboard*—It's not good to mess with other people's lives. You can't play God. Rephrased, people deserve dignity and self-determination regardless of who they are.
> *Breaking Away*—Have goals and go for your dreams, but be who you really are, not just pretend. Also: growing up, "breaking away," class struggle, disillusionment and ultimately triumph.
> *Shawshank Redemption*—Perseverance, never lose hope, don't let the bastards grind you down. Freedom of spirit, "you can chain my body but you can't destroy my soul."

One neat assignment for a student who isn't quite ready to be turned loose to find theme on his own: Give him one word to write about or discuss in connection with his movie. For instance, you might ask a student to watch *Shawshank Redemption* and have him pick out at least three incidents or quotes that have to do with "freedom," a main theme of the movie. Since you've given him the word *freedom* beforehand, he simply needs to look for quotes and incidents about freedom. My favorite is the scene in which an opera aria is played over the public address system from the locked and forbidden library. That, I explain, is freedom of spirit.

THEMES: THE TWO TOWERS AND THE SECRET GARDEN

In a lesson about theme with a 13-year-old boy, Aaron, I began by saying, "In the movie *The Two Towers*, the theme might be good versus evil. That's the theme of a lot of movies, especially action films."

Aaron then volunteered that he thought the theme was the same as the plot. "No, the plot is what happened. In *The Two Towers*, Frodo gets the ring, the Gollum follows him, the trees go on the march, and so forth. The plot is just incidents. The theme, though, is the emotional or moral aspect of what's happening. To find that, ask yourself what values the author wants to get across. These are like the lessons in 'Little Red Riding Hood', something the author is teaching us through the movie."

"First, let's describe some of the characters and come back to theme in a minute. That will help make it clear. Take Frodo. Pick a couple of words to describe him."

"He was brave," Aaron said, "and he kept trying even when he felt like what he was trying to do was impossible."

"Right. What do you call that, when someone keeps going instead of giving up?"

"I'm not sure."

"I'll write it: *persistence*."

"Oh, yeah, I've heard of that."

"Right. So, Frodo was persistent. That's how we describe him. But we can also say that the theme of the book is 'persistence,' or 'the value of persistence.'"

"The theme is the message, then," said Aaron. He'd obviously had some of this in school, and it was coming back to him.

"Yes, exactly. Now let's look at the movie *The Secret Garden*." (We go through the plot and character description briefly, to make sure we're on the same page.) "How did the bratty girl and the crippled boy change in the course of the movie?"

"The girl got nicer and the boy started walking."

"That's right. And what were the things that helped them overcome their problems?" After some discussion, Aaron thinks they might have to do with making friends and being outside. I rephrase this as, "friendship" and "nature," and add, "These are themes of the book, then: 'the healing power of friendship and of nature.'

"But the theme is not always something good," I say. "Where is the boy's dad during the story? He's not around, is he? How does he treat his son? *Neglect* is the word that fits here. So some of the emotions we are talking about in the movie are 'neglect' and 'grief.' Let's try including the word *neglect* in our statement of the theme: 'Two children overcome past neglect through the healing power of friendship and nature.'"

"Yeah," says Aaron. "I get it, but if you're watching TV, you're not going to be able to pick out many themes like what we've been talking about."

"That's probably true. That's one difference between literature and TV shows—TV might not have much of a theme."

Here's a list of "starter" theme topics: overcoming weakness, striking out on your own, surviving, learning to trust, and learning when not to trust. For teens who still need an extra boost when it comes to finding theme, you could just jot down the following list and see if they can come up with other words and phrases that are similar.

- All the emotions: love, hate, jealousy, fear . . .
- Personal characteristics: Courage, perseverance, prejudice, friendship
- Facing up to reality, being real, finding out the truth, being your own person, finding your place
- Standing up against government, family or religious repression and abuse

Teens who haven't understood theme until now usually get the picture when they see this list. They even joke about taking it to school and using it for their book reports.

Introducing Symbolism

Literary symbolism is one topic that is often well taught at school, and though students might need some practice interpreting symbolism, they usually don't need major work to understand the concept. Literary symbolism means using one thing (an object or action) to refer to another in a work of literature. The symbol is visible, but what it refers to is not. Examples: A dove stands for peace. The ring in *Lord of the Rings* stands for the seductive, destructive temptations of absolute power.

After some talk about the meaning of symbolism, ask your student to explain some symbols from his own reading. Example:

Q. What does it mean that the aunt in *Tiger Eyes* bakes cookies with Davey's little brother?

A. She's treating him like a girl and a baby instead of helping him be a boy and grow up.

Here's my all-time favorite exercise to help students become familiar with interpreting symbolism. It is also excellent for teaching about detail and overview. Obtain a pack of Tarot cards, the kind used for fortune telling. My choice for this purpose is a deck called the "Mythic Tarot" (Sharman-Burke and Liz Greene 1986), but any will do. (Check first to make sure the student's parents don't object to their child using what some people consider a "pagan" device.) Start by showing your student a card from the deck and analyzing it yourself. After you have done one card, have your student do the same for others. Students usually love this exercise and kids will often beg to do it.

Here's a procedure that works well. Tell the student to give an overview of what he sees on the card. For the 10 of pentacles, for instance, "Here is a family enjoying themselves outside. A father, mother, baby, and little boy are together on a lush lawn. They seem happy and prosperous."

Give the details you see that led to this generalization. For the same card, "The father is holding the baby, who is playing. The mother looks on proudly. The boy is playing with a golden toy. They are richly dressed. In front of the family are two columns entwined with grapes. Large coins also hang on the columns. Behind them there is a lake."

Analyze the symbolism in the picture. "This card stands for happiness and prosperity. In fortune-telling, if you drew this card it would mean you will have those qualities in your life. The lush grass and the golden toy stand for richness, the golden coins for money, or again, the richness of life, the grapes for abundance and pleasure. The family grouped together shows harmony. The lake is full of life-giving water."

When your student analyzes a card, ask him *not* to show it to you beforehand and see if you can visualize it clearly from what he describes. Insist on clear referents (who's doing what). After that, it's a small step from working with symbolism in pictures to analyzing literary passages.

Taking Stock

If you've gotten this far, your students have learned a great deal, and I imagine you have, too. Remember, it is good practice to point out to students each step of the way how their abilities are improving, and it is even better if you can be specific about it. "Notice how you can tell back most of what you are reading now. That compares really well with how you started out, when you were able to remember only one or two facts out of a paragraph." Also, when you teach new material, as you will in the next few chapters on factual reading, try to compare it as much as possible with an exercise or material your student has already mastered.

While you are taking stock of your student's accomplishments, turn the light on your own. In what ways has your teaching changed since the beginning of this course? How do your communications with your students differ? And, finally, how would you rate your job satisfaction? I hope the answer is that you are feeling richly rewarded.

Summary of Key Points

- For students who are still at the concrete level, teaching abstract thinking is an essential part of teaching reading.
- Tasks requiring abstract thinking include summarizing a passage, identifying the main idea, understanding symbolism and figurative language in literature, and thinking metaphorically about poetry and myth.
- Children must reach a certain level of intellectual maturity before they are able to think abstractly, but teachers can help them gain that maturity.
- Teachers can provide exposure to abstract thinking, give students the language to express concepts, and use written programs to teach abstract thought.
- Learning to think abstractly in one area may transfer to others.
- It may take months of instruction for a student to begin thinking more abstractly. Persevere.
- To encourage conceptualizing, teach students to look for clues to character, setting, and conflict at the beginning of a novel.
- Have students begin identifying main ideas as they read.
- It is important to ask students how and why things happened in a story, not simply what happened.
- Move to longer tellbacks and summaries.
- Assign plenty of reading.
- Choose books that help young people grow.
- Make use of book reports.
- Introduce the idea of theme and teach it step by step.

Reading fiction can inspire and entertain; it can help grow the imagination, encourage students to reflect on the values and relationships in their own lives, and develop an introspective eye. Yet a student who reads only fiction will possess just a portion of the skills needed for adult reading tasks. In fact, if a family has the time and money for a student to work on only one type of reading, I believe it should be nonfiction because reading textbooks and articles translates most directly into academic success.

Reading fiction and nonfiction are different enough that nonfiction merits its own section. In Part III, Reading Nonfiction, we revisit comprehension, reading memory, and identifying main idea, then branch out into the higher level analytical reading that is required for high school advanced placement classes, college entrance examinations, and college-level reading.

Part III: Reading Nonfiction

PART III BUILDS ON EXERCISES introduced in the previous section to teach students to read textbooks and factual articles with skill and understanding. The section starts with simple information-gathering and then moves on to abstract thinking. Chapter 7, "Nonfiction: Reading Comprehension and Recall," contains concepts and exercises for helping your student understand and remember factual material. Chapter 8, "Paraphrasing, Predicting, and Identifying Main Idea," presents strategies for active reading, identifying main idea, and summarizing. In Chapter 9, "Branching Out: Higher-level Nonfiction Reading," tutors learn to help students look at an entire chapter in depth and then come away with an overview.

7 | Nonfiction: Reading Comprehension and Recall

FOR MOST STUDENTS the ability to understand and remember textbook readings and other nonfiction (factual) material does not come automatically. Rather, it must be developed through instruction and practice. Even though it requires work, teaching students to read nonfiction skillfully is simpler in some respects than teaching fiction reading. This is because the materials used in nonfiction reading are more straightforward and less open to interpretation. In addition, the process of teaching nonfiction depends less on developing awareness and emotional understanding and more on simply using exercises and activities to build necessary skills.

Because of the simplicity of the process, students can go from having almost no comprehension or memory of the nonfiction material they read to almost total recall and understanding in a matter of weeks. Nevertheless, they can easily become bored with textbook and other nonfiction reading unless the tutor makes an effort to keep the process lively and relevant. This chapter is devoted to not only helping students learn to read factual material better, but also engaging them in the process.

Surveying Your Student's Skills in Factual Reading

Before beginning the exercises in this chapter, it will be helpful to spend some time getting an idea of your student's factual reading skills, behaviors, and habits. A few minutes of reflection and discussion now can help you determine a starting point for instruction as well as suggest areas that need work. Here are some questions to consider:

- What strengths or weaknesses did you notice in your student's performance on the factual reading section in the evaluation?
- How is her fiction reading now? If it's fairly good, you can expect some of her skills in that area to transfer to nonfiction reading.
- Does she have textbook reading assignments for school, and does

she do them? Students who have no textbook assignments at school may need to be convinced of the value of this skill.

- In which classes does she receive reading assignments? For example, social studies is preferable to math when it comes to practicing textbook reading.

- How often does she have assignments? How long and what type are they? For instance, is she expected to read and discuss in class? Read and take notes? Outline? Answer study questions? Take quizzes or write essays based on the reading? If her assignments are light, you can add to them, but if she's already reading a fair amount for class, ask for copies of that material to use in tutoring.

- Does her classroom teacher hand out study or reading guides? If so, the teacher could be spoon-feeding the students by telling them exactly what will be on the test, thus reducing the amount of reading skill required.

- Do her teachers hand out magazine or newspaper articles to read, and if so, is she allowed to underline in them? If not, make copies so you can teach underlining.

- Finally, ask the student to bring any recent reading notes to tutoring, along with the book from which they were taken. Make sure they are her reading notes and not just items copied from the board in class.

- If your student does bring in clear, well-organized notes, question her to see if she understands and remembers what is in them, since good-looking notes can sometimes be deceptive.

It is not necessary to determine the exact truth about a student's study habits at this point. In discussions based on questions like the ones above, some youngsters will "fudge" and tell you what they think you want to hear, while others, well-meaning but unobservant, will overestimate their reading skills. However, the fact that kids are not always accurate does not decrease the value of learning about their opinions and their general "take" on their studies. You will find out how things really stand as you continue.

If your student seems fairly adept at handling abstract concepts, it may work to skip over the next few exercises and go directly to the section on main idea, later in this chapter. You will probably want to read the intervening material, but you may not need to teach it. To find out for certain, try teaching main idea first, and if your student catches on, you'll know you can skip the preliminaries.

Introducing Factual Reading

The benefits of developing factual reading skills are obvious to us as adults, but they are less so to kids. That's because teens may make blanket statements about their abilities without thinking about what particular skills they might be lacking, so the idea of spending time on developing a particular reading skill doesn't occur to them. Don't assume your student will automatically understand why she should read, much less remember, an explanation of photosynthesis or the causes of the Great Depression. As you talk with your student, list some of the situations in which good comprehension and recall are necessary, both in and out of school. The list could include:

- *for school*: reading to prepare for class discussion, taking notes, and taking tests
- *out of school*: following written directions for building something (making a model, following a recipe, or assembling a bike)
- *for adult life*: understanding tax instructions, learning about health matters, reading the newspaper

If the student is receptive, I add my own story.

READING SAVES A LIFE

A few years ago I saved my own life, and though it may sound strange, if it weren't for my skill in reading, I wouldn't be here now to tell the story.

I was quite ill. In fact, looking back on it, I know now that I was dying. I had lost nearly a quarter of my body weight, and was continuing to lose pounds for no reason I could put my finger on. My body was wasting away and no one knew why. I had been to so many doctors I had to make a list to keep track of them all, but no one was able to help me. No one even had any helpful suggestions. Besides looking hollow-eyed, I was nearly incapacitated. My eyes burned so badly I had to tutor with them shut! I had to ask my students, "Read that again. It doesn't sound right."

One day I awoke with the realization that I would surely die if I didn't find help right away, but from my experiences with my doctors I knew that the only one I could depend on was myself. Oddly, it was a calming thought.

"All right," I told myself, "I'll just have to think if there's even a tiny clue that could help me." And then I remembered that when I took high school biology, the teacher had told the class about two children he knew who were victims of a disease which allowed them to eat only bananas. Well, that was a clue. I was already eating a lot of bananas because they agreed with me when nothing else did. But what was the name of the disease I had heard about? I didn't remember, but I felt sure that finding out was going to save my life. How should I start, though? This is where reading comes in.

I went to the University Hospital medical library and proceeded to read everything I could find in the medical books, first about my symptoms, and then about the diseases that could possibly cause them. This was difficult to do with my sore eyes, but my curiosity pulled me along and I was able to narrow the possible culprits down to one ailment in particular, celiac disease. For someone with celiac, gluten, mostly found in wheat, acts as a poison. Having discovered that much, I continued to read everything I could find on celiac disease.

Finally, after three days of reading and taking notes, I called my doctor and insisted he test me for celiac disease. "Oh, you don't have that," he protested. "Test me anyway," I insisted. The test was done, and it showed that I did indeed have celiac. The doctor said, "Well, I'll be darned! Who would have thought?" To that I had nothing to say—out loud, at least.

After I went on a wheat-free diet, it took only a couple of days to start feeling some improvement, though it was months before I was back to normal. I will never be able to eat wheat again (that means anything made with flour, not just whole wheat), but I have my health back, and that's what counts.

I don't believe it is an exaggeration to say that my good reading skills saved my life. Though nothing this dramatic happens to most people, reading could be a "lifesaver" for almost anybody. Maybe you have a story of your own in which good factual reading helped you or others through a tight spot.

Choosing a Nonfiction Book

To teach textbook reading you will need a clear, well-written social studies or science book that is somewhat challenging but not frustrating for your student. If the student's own textbook meets these requirements, by all means use it. Quite often, however, students are in tutoring precisely because they are unable to read their assigned textbooks. In that case, you will need to choose an easier book to use for a few lessons until the student has gained the skill needed to read her own textbooks.

If you found a nonfiction book you liked for the evaluation (Chapter 3), great. If not, you will need to find one now. You might try calling the administrative offices of your school district to find out if they have a curriculum library, a professional library for teachers, or a textbook adoption center. You may be able to borrow books from one of those places even if you're not a public school teacher.

Look for a textbook that is interesting and intelligently written but not too difficult, one that is strong on concepts as well as facts, and one that is well-organized without being visually distracting. "Visually distracting" means lots of little boxes, many different type fonts, and short passages scattered all over the page. Also avoid books that contain subheadings for every paragraph, since you will want your student to come up with these on her own.

If you choose a clearly written ninth-grade history text, it is likely that most students, including sixth and seventh graders, will do well with it. On the other hand, if you your student is a younger teen who lacks background knowledge and has difficulty with word recognition, you will probably need to start on an easier level. Work up to a more advanced level as quickly as you can, however, since textbooks for grades six and seven are usually watered down and are not interesting enough to keep kids engaged for long.

If a student has a textbook from school and the level is suitable, of course it's preferable to use that. Geography and history books are best for beginners. Science is more difficult since content can be challenging. (It's best not to be struggling with main idea *and* photosynthesis.)

These two textbooks work well for younger readers: *Our World Yesterday and Today* by Dorothy Drummond and Bruce Kraig is an easy sixth- or seventh-grade history/geography book. *America, Pathways to the Present*, by Andrew Cayton, Ph.D., emphasizes social history and why things happened as they did. It is excellent for teaching higher-level thinking to students of any age. The 1999 edition is preferable to later ones, which omit significant material about indigenous people.

Factual Reading: An Overview

Many students who can read fiction adequately have trouble reading factual material. Reading a textbook, taking notes, and studying for a test from the book can be daunting for them. The problem is due partly to the very different kinds of reading skills required for reading a novel and for textbook reading. Also, though the need is clear, most students do not receive instruction in school on *how* to read a textbook, and many of them believe they are reading and remembering textbook material well even when they aren't. The result is an essential skill that is sadly neglected. Fortunately though, most students can learn to read, understand, and remember factual material with a few weeks of instruction and practice. The process can even be fun—or at least painless and mildly interesting.

The following section outlines the key steps I use to help students improve their skills in nonfiction reading. After this introductory overview, the steps are explained in detail in the remainder of this chapter and in Chapters 8 and 9.

Introducing factual detail

If a student is able to read words adequately, the next step is to read factual material for detail, answering the questions *who, what, where, when?* (The question *why* comes later.) Using a variety of materials, from a children's encyclopedia to a novel, the student does one-paragraph tellbacks. That is, she reads a paragraph, then tells what she read without looking back at the book. A good goal is 80-100 percent recall.

Most students are able to read a paragraph and tell what they have read after a few tries, *if* the material is interesting and at a suitable level. Tips and pointers from you on "how to remember" are helpful. These include forming a visual image, stopping often to review mentally, "counting" facts on fingers, and saying unfamiliar words (especially names) out loud. Students may like to keep score of the facts they were able to recall. Keeping track of "points" this way can be a good motivator.

When students read, they can gain much essential information from visual cues in the textbook such as maps, timelines, graphs, and diagrams. Teen readers may skip these aids if they have not been taught to attend to them, however, so it is important for them to learn to interpret the visual aids found in their texts.

The following skills, detailed in Chapters 8 and 9, are taught mostly by question, discussion, and example. Now it's time for the student to start asking "Why?" about her reading. Students should be encouraged to "tell themselves" what they are reading and to constantly ask themselves "why?" as they read. A useful question is "What is this sentence doing here?" Students need to spend a lot of time explaining out loud what they've read—not just the facts, but the concepts as well. It helps if they pretend to explain their reading to a younger child rather than to the tutor, who, after all, already knows it. When a student can do a fairly good job orally, writing a sentence to sum up each paragraph is helpful. Use a variety of reading material, including textbooks, novels, and (depending on the student's age) newspaper editorials.

Main idea

Begin by having students identify main idea and detail, first in illustrations, then in short oral passages. Next look for main idea in written material, working with progressively longer and more abstract selections. There is also a trick, or formula, students can learn to help with identifying main idea. If a student is having trouble with main idea, working on classification from the book *Reasoning and Reading* can help.

Note-taking

Many students have trouble prioritizing; they either copy everything into their notes or write nothing. So I do a lot of modeling (teaching by example), explaining why I included or left out material in the notes. I go through a whole series of steps to teach note-taking, including how to organize the notes in the notebook and how to review for a test using notes. Students can compile a list of note-taking tips for later reference.

Test questions

Many students believe they have studied well for a test but still perform poorly. Students can be helped to anticipate test questions by studying past tests and then making up their own questions.

Putting it all together

Next, the student combines all the above strategies and skills—recall of detail, rephrasing concepts, and identifying main idea—in a thorough and thoughtful reading. Note-taking is incorporated into the process.

Branching out

To become thoughtful, mature readers, students must move from reading relatively easy, concrete material to texts that are more varied and abstract. Students will enjoy choosing nonfiction articles and books to match their own interests. Learning to read college or adult level books can be challenging, but several weeks of intensive, guided practice will likely bring students to new levels of understanding. The following methods are detailed in Chapter 9.

SQ3R

The letters stand for "Survey, Question, Read, Recite, and Review." This is a method for studying a whole chapter in a social studies or science textbook. Many students learn this technique in school but never use it. They will use SQ3R, however, if you can show them how it will help them. In SQ3R we preview, work with titles and subtitles, and help kids ask good questions and make use of what they already know to understand new material.

Outlining

Knowing how to outline can help students organize their notes—and their own thinking. This task will be easy after all the work we've done on main idea and detail. Students like to learn outlining using note cards that can be moved around.

Paragraph structure

Understanding how paragraphs are organized can save effort and increase comprehension. This more formal study of the structure of written material includes prediction, cause and effect, comparison and contrast, etc. The student identifies structures and tries to predict content based on signal words and transitions. We also take a look at author's point of view or bias.

Final exam

The student demonstrates mastery of the above skills by reading and passing an exam on an entire textbook chapter. No guidance is given during the reading, but the student is encouraged to use all the skills learned so far.

This marks the end of the overview of factual reading. Now we'll reexamine each topic in detail.

Reading for Factual Detail, Step by Step

Following is a detailed, step-by-step guide on how to teach students to read a textbook for maximum understanding and efficiency. We begin with two old standbys from Chapters 5 and 6, tellbacks and visualization. After reviewing these exercises in the context of textbook reading, we will look at several new learning activities. These exercises and techniques are helpful with any kind of expository material, not just textbooks.

Tellbacks and visualization in textbook reading

Since textbook reading is associated in most students' minds with boring material that no one would want to understand even if they were able to, we need to pique the student's interest before we ask her to read. Here are a couple of simple ways to do this.

Use pictures to set the stage

Put together some interesting photographs and illustrations on the subject your student will be reading about and take a few minutes to look them over together. A student who has seen pictures of Phoenician sailing ships and art works, for instance, will be much more interested in reading a paragraph about Phoenician trade routes than one who has no visual images to associate with the subject. Spend some time collecting pictures to go with the textbooks you use. You can almost always find what you are looking for on the internet. In particular, try searching Google Images and the photography sharing website Flickr (http://flickr.com). Your students' interest will repay you for your effort.

Keep a store of stories

Prepare students for textbook reading by providing pertinent background information in the form of interesting stories or anecdotes. Students who need help with textbook reading almost always lack general information about a variety of subjects, and storytelling helps fill in the gaps. Since reading involves making connections between what we already know and the new material we encounter, students will be more likely to understand what they read if they are not starting cold. Providing background information helps set the scene for success.

A background story can draw the student in and awaken her imagination. For some teens, this may be the first time in their lives they have been exposed to information about history or about the natural world in a way that engages their curiosity. Exploring the subjects your student will be reading about will give you the tools you need to amaze and entertain—or, at the very least, make your student a more willing participant in textbook reading. Here are some examples of background stories, or lead-ins to stories, chosen to pique the curiosity of inexperienced readers:

- Walking down into the Grand Canyon is like walking through time.
- The scablands of Washington State are the result of unimaginably huge floods released when glaciers melted.
- Plants and animals both exhale what the other needs to breathe.
- Butterflies use smell to find their mates and can sense another butterfly several blocks away.
- Traders in ancient Africa set out trade goods then walked away, returning a few hours later to see what their Arab trade partners left in exchange.

The importance of vocabulary

As your student reads for nonfiction tellbacks, remember, as in fiction reading, to quiz her on any words that might be unfamiliar. It's even more important now, since textbook material is more "dense"—packed with more information than fiction—and the meaning of a whole section can hinge on only one or two words. In this way, nonfiction is less forgiving than fiction reading.

Make a list with your student of important vocabulary words from the textbook—not terms referring to particular places and people but words needed to understand the concepts in the book, such as *alliance, democracy, protest, conservative, trade,* and *economic.* Keep the list handy so you can review and add to it often. Isolated words on a list are of limited value, however, so work for depth of understanding through stories and explanations, as before.

As you work on vocabulary, gradually expect your student to take on more responsibility for flagging, recording, and learning unfamiliar words. (See "SAT Vocabulary and Reading" in Chapter 11.)

Adapting visualization to factual reading

In school, students are routinely expected to understand and remember what they read in their textbooks, but they are hardly ever shown *how* to do these things. Students who lack skills in reading expository material may gain only a vague general impression from a passage or else completely misunderstand what they've read. Worse yet, they may simply avoid textbook reading altogether.

To counter these problems, tutors can teach students to do close reading by showing them how to "take a paragraph apart" and analyze it. This type of focused attention to detail gives students an alternative to the vague reading for general impression that is common with many inexperienced readers.

A good place to begin is with two relatively simple and easy-to-teach techniques, visualizing and grouping. These are two of the most important methods that can be used to understand and remember nonfiction material, yet it only takes a few minutes for you to start your student using them, and since visualizing was already introduced under fiction reading, it will require only a short review.

Teaching visualization and grouping using a "moving diorama"

The following lesson provides an "aha!" experience for many teen readers, including students who are doing fairly well. This is one of the more important lessons of the book in terms of producing results quickly for modest effort, so quite a bit of detail follows.

Begin by saying that if the student uses the techniques you are going to demonstrate, it is likely she will be able to remember almost all of what she reads in a paragraph. That might mean remembering 10 out of 10 possible pieces of information from a paragraph in a history or social studies book, for example.

Before reading the sample paragraph, make sure your student has adequate background information to put it in context. Include these points in a preliminary discussion.

- The Ice Age ended about 12,000 years ago.
- At that time, the snow started melting and the ice pack receded north.
- Areas that had been under ice were now exposed.
- Because the weather was growing milder and the soil was moist, the newly opened areas were covered with lush grass and attracted herds of animals.
- Europe was like the Serengeti in Africa, with endless herds of animals.
- People moved into these areas, and life for them must have been very easy. Maybe it was like a paradise.
- Since life was easy in the Mesolithic age, people had time to invent and discover new things.

Then have the student read carefully the following passage from *History and Life*. It is about some of the inventions, or innovations, of Mesolithic people. Instruct her beforehand to try to remember as much as possible without rereading.

When she has read the paragraph, have her tell you what she remembers in *as much detail as she can* without looking back. Then go over the paragraph in detail together, giving your student feedback at the same time you teach visualization and grouping.

After this exercise, have the student practice on other textbook material until she is able to use the visualization and grouping techniques on her own. (A more detailed script follows the reading.)

Mesolithic people invented pottery and fishing equipment

One very important Mesolithic advance was the first crude pottery. Pots made of sun-baked clay were used to store food. By about 7000 B.C., oven-fired clay bowls and jars were used to store water. Since many Mesolithic peoples lived along shores of water, fish and shellfish were their main foods. Mesolithic people invented the fishhook and many types of nets, and they learned to hollow out logs to make boats. They also invented the bow and arrow and made fine stone spearheads. (Wallbank, et al. 1990, 11)

Ask the student to tell back everything she remembers of the paragraph. Keep score, one point for each fact remembered, a minus for anything important omitted. Compare how your student did with the following scores. There are roughly 10 pieces of information in the paragraph, so a score of 8 to 10 points is excellent, 7 is good, and 6 is fair. Anything below 6 definitely needs work. Using these numbers, let the student know how she did.

Looking at the book, go over the above paragraph with your student to demonstrate grouping and visualizing. This script includes explanations that may be useful but need not be followed exactly.

You did pretty well (or had some trouble) on this.

We're going to go over it right now, and I'll show you how to remember close to 100 percent of what you read in a paragraph. Not that it's important to always get 100 percent, but it *is* important to be able to do it when you choose to.

It's harder to remember factual material than it is a story because it is often less interesting and it is also harder to visualize: For instance, it's harder to see 'the exports of Brazil' in your mind's eye than 'the coffin stood in the middle of the room.'

Because it's harder to remember factual material, it takes a conscious effort to master it. Here's a way that works for most people. It's based on the idea that you can usually remember what you see in your mind's eye and that if you mentally place information into groups you can remember it better. Grouping is really simple. You do it in real life all the time. For example, when you go to the store to buy several items without a list, you try to put all the dairy items in one (mental) group, all the meat together in another, and so on. We're going to mentally group the items in the paragraph the same way.

You know what a diorama is, right? Three-dimensional figures in a museum display. They might represent native people going about their lives, for example, or animals in their natural environment.

I like to imagine that the material in the book is a *moving* diorama. (Kids usually like this last concept.)

Then I alternately read aloud from the paragraph and explain what I see in my mind's eye:

In the diorama, imagine where the people are and what they're doing.

A group of people is over here making pottery out of clay.

They are putting the pottery out in the sun to dry, and then they are able put food in it. You got (or didn't get) this part.

About when was this? 7500 B.C., the book says. What does B.C. mean? Imagining the date on a timeline can help you remember it.

Demonstrate by drawing a rough timeline.

The women put the pots in the fire. I've done this myself. You put the pots on the ground and build the fire over them. When they're done, you can put water in them without "melting" them. (Keep commenting on whether the student remembered or missed each piece of information in her tellback.)

Now it says something about the type of area where they lived. Where was it? The fact that they lived on shore, if you'll picture it, gives you enough information to get the next few points.

They developed fishing equipment. Imagine a group of people near the shore using their boats, nets, and hooks. Imagine where the potters and fishermen are standing in relation to each other. This is part of the grouping. The paragraph mentions spears, bows, and arrows. Who would have been using those tools and where were they? Men hunting, maybe going into the forest.

So now we have a moving diorama, kind of a short documentary, showing three groups going about their business. It's not hard to see the potters, the fishermen, and the hunters, and it's not hard to follow the action of the potters, first making the sun-dried and then the kiln-baked pottery. In other words, you've got the whole paragraph, with 10 or 12 facts, pinned on those three pictures, or groups. It's a lot easier to remember the three pictures than 12 facts. That's the point—you can easily call up the facts from the pictures.

Have the student do the tellback again from memory using visualization. Practice on other passages using the moving diorama technique.

The gift of boring material

Some students think that if an activity is not interesting to them they are *incapable* of understanding or remembering it. Counter this notion by telling the student she may still find material dull, but by using the following exercises, she will be able to understand and remember it.

Point out that being able to remember something because you *choose* to is a big advantage. You might say, "Being able to direct your attention gives you control. It gives you power you didn't have before. You may very much need and want to understand something you find deadly dull." If you have not already done so, see if the student can come up with some examples from real life in which this might be the case—for example, directions, tax information, driver's test booklets, laws.

"On the other hand, just because you *can* read carefully and remember most of what you read, it doesn't mean you *have* to. It's a choice. Maybe you just need to get the general idea of a passage, and that's fine. The point is, if you can choose, you are in charge of the situation." Putting it this way seems to give resistant teens permission to succeed because it frees them of fear of being locked into what they might see, not without reason, as a trap.

Several years back, I decided to set up a homeschool program for teens. Kids who were unable to attend school because of physical or emotional problems would be able to come study basic subjects for school credit, with good teachers, as part of a small group of other students. Before I set up my program, however, I needed to find out if what I was proposing was legal. I also needed to find out if my students would actually be able to earn credits that would count toward high school graduation. The program did eventually fly, and continued for several years, but before I opened the door for business, I spent six months researching the idea. For one thing, I had to know all the state laws and local policies that might affect my project. And that meant reading every single piece of paper written on homeschooling policy and law, either by the state legislature or the school district.

I use some of these legal documents to illustrate for students the necessity of being able to read material they may not find interesting.

Do you think this looks interesting? But do you see that I had a strong motive to read it anyway? And that I needed to understand and remember it? So, you see you can have a need and a desire to read something you might not actually find *interesting*.

Fortunately, there are some techniques you can learn that will help you read and remember almost anything. I can teach you those. After you start using some of these techniques, you may find that material that was previously not very interesting to you, can be—if not exactly interesting—at least tolerable.

Most young people have the belief that "if it's not fun, I can't, and shouldn't, be expected to do it." Boring material gives us an opportunity as teachers to poke holes in that mistaken idea. Since teens find much of their assigned reading boring anyway, there is no lack of material on which to practice.

Exercises for remembering factual detail

Count facts on fingers

Is your student doing well with factual recall, or is her memory still "iffy"? If she needs a boost, teach her to "count facts" on her fingers. Start by explaining that using physical cues can help people remember. You may have noticed that if you are driving and listening to the radio, you often remember exactly where you were when you heard a certain song or story."

By the same token, ancient people imagined placing the facts they wished to remember in various locations around a room. For them, recalling the facts was as easy as looking around the room. The next exercise helps us remember by associating something we want to learn with a physical action or location.

Explain to the student that the more senses she can bring into play, the more likely she is to remember.

When you read, if you use your sense of touch, recite aloud and write down what you wish to recall, you are more apt to remember than if you do only one of these things. Then teach her to "count facts on her fingers" as follows:

As you read, find key words, or 'trigger words', that will help you recall the rest of the information in a passage. You pretend that you are physically placing each fact, or key word, on a finger. It will look as if you are counting on your fingers. Whisper each key word to yourself as you "place" it on your finger. When you are done with the passage, look away from the book and review by "retrieving" the key words off your fingers. As you touch each finger, you will be reminded of the word you placed there. And, if you can recall a key word, you are also likely to be able to come up with the ideas surrounding it, and then the whole paragraph.

At the beginning, try to remember only three or four key words at a time. Then through practice, gradually increase the number of facts you can recall. Try to remember nine or ten key words from a paragraph. To do this you'll need a textbook that is packed with information.

Remember, try to fill in the entire passage from memory if you are able. If you forgot what you read, simply reread and try again. It may come to you right away, or it may take several practice sessions to be able to recall an entire passage. It helps to combine this exercise on counting facts with the previous work you did on visualization.

As with the other exercises in this book, counting facts on fingers helps many, but not all, students. Some people do better just aiming to get the main "drift," and focusing on key words only confuses them. So introduce the exercise and have your student try it for two or three weeks, but drop it if it's not helping. For the majority of your students, however, it will be a valuable learning exercise so ask them to give it an honest try.

"Weird words"

Here's a technique for the students who are able to remember everything in a passage *except* for all those "weird" names of people and places found in textbooks. You'll find that many youngsters simply skip unfamiliar words, and some even fill in with their own inventions.

Tell the student it's a very common and understandable mistake to overlook all those odd names, but it's a habit that won't do her a lot of good in the long run. Names are crucial in class discussions and tests. Besides, I say, remembering what a person did isn't much use if you can't remember his name.

Here's how to remember "weird words." First, sound the word out as best you can, and then say it *out loud* three times, even if you have been reading silently. (Books may provide phonetic spellings of difficult words, but students often skip them. Have the student practice using the phonetic spellings, but be prepared—kids may need help even with these.)

If you are in school or at the library, you can mutter the words under your breath, but you still need to say them to remember.

After the student reads a paragraph saying all of the unfamiliar words aloud, she then does a tellback, recalling those tricky words first so she won't forget them. When she gets better at remembering them, she can integrate the new words into the paragraph, and say everything aloud in the normal order. Most students find this skill difficult, but practicing it usually helps.

Many students ask if they can take notes to help them remember these unfamiliar words (and the key words in the previous exercise), but it's best to avoid note-taking at this point. The goal here is to help students develop their reading memory, and taking notes would slow down the process. Kids seem to understand the rationale.

As you teach students to tell back what they've read, you may notice that many readers ignore visual cues such as pictures or diagrams that could give them pertinent information about the written material. By drawing your students' attention to these sources of information you will give them new resources for understanding their reading. (See Appendix F, Maps and Timelines, for effective ways to use these resources.)

Summary of Key Points

- The ability to read, understand and remember textbooks and other nonfiction material does not come automatically. It has to be developed through instruction and practice.
- Help students understand how skills in reading nonfiction will be useful to them in school and in life.
- Teach students to read for detail by showing them how to "take a paragraph apart" and analyze it. This type of focused attention

gives them an alternative to the unfocused reading for general impression that is common among inexperienced readers.

- In teaching nonfiction reading, a step-by-step approach translates into student achievement.
- Key strategies for improving comprehension and memory of factual materials include:
  o grouping information
  o combining visualization with tellbacks
  o counting facts on fingers
  o attending to unfamiliar terms
- Using stories, anecdotes and pictures can add interest to a lesson and build a framework of understanding for students.

If students are able to read for detail, visualize, and tell what they've read, they have made a strong start in becoming skilled nonfiction readers. But it is only a start. Without the next steps—predicting, identifying main idea and taking notes—students will have only a snail's eye view of their reading. They still need to be able to register the big picture, to answer *why* and *what next* about their reading, and to commit their learning to long-term memory. The activities presented in Chapter 8 will help them accomplish these goals.

8 | Paraphrasing, Predicting, and Identifying Main Idea

THE EXERCISES IN THIS CHAPTER—paraphrasing, predicting, identifying main idea, note-taking, and anticipating test questions—help students read nonfiction material precisely, interpret insightfully, and recall accurately. They have the added purpose of preparing students to arrive at an overview, or to see the big picture in their nonfiction reading. Thus, this chapter marks a transition from concrete to abstract thinking in reading nonfiction. This will be an important turning point for many students, who may be ready to graduate from tutoring when they have completed the work in this chapter.

If all goes well, they will have mastered the basics of fiction and nonfiction reading and will be able to read for both detail and main idea. True, some students will want to remain in tutoring for more advanced work, and others will need continuing support to master the basics, but the majority will be ready to face school on their own by the time they have worked their way through these exercises.

In the first exercise, *paraphrasing*, the student simply puts what he's read in his own words. Paraphrasing doesn't require much teaching so it makes a good first activity in learning to gain an overview. However, to do it adequately, kids do need to be freed up and turned loose to put things in their own words without worrying too much about the results. Suggestions for helping students cut through the mental barriers that prevent them from paraphrasing are included in this chapter.

People who are adept readers naturally practice *predicting*, or educated guessing about what's ahead in a passage, even if they are not aware of doing so. If we can help less skilled readers get into the habit of predicting, we will go far in helping them gain an overview of their reading. Teaching predicting includes helping students see what clues to pay attention to, giving them time to practice this skill, and helping them learn from the results.

The process of predicting can be taught through a series of questions and answers: "What do you think the rest of this paragraph (section, article) is going to be about?" "Were you right?" And, "How did you know?"

Reading for *main idea* is crucial to gaining an overview. Ability to identify the main idea of a passage is the foundation for effective summarizing, note-taking, and even writing. Knowing the main idea allows students to remember what they read and to understand the author's purpose.

Moving from main idea into *note-taking* is relatively simple, since notes are essentially a list of main ideas supported by selected details. I've included work on *anticipating test questions* in this chapter because a student who reads with a questioning frame of mind, as the activity requires, will be likely to see the big picture.

Paraphrasing

Paraphrasing is the "free rendering or rewording of a passage" (DK Illustrated Oxford Dictionary 1998). Paraphrasing factual material builds on tellbacks and on the fiction techniques you've already used. Teaching paraphrasing before predicting gives you a chance to begin in an open-ended way and then move into relatively more structured work. Paraphrasing can be a little looser, making it easier to teach. For example, in paraphrasing you might ask the student to "tell what you think this means in your own words," rather than, "what do you think the rest of the paragraph is about?" (predicting) or "what is a word or phrase that covers the entire paragraph?" (main idea). Here's a paragraph from *History and Life* to use for practice.

> Each [ancient Sumerian] city-state had its own local gods who, the Sumerians believed, had the power to destroy their city through floods. To please and calm the gods, the Sumerians built a splendid temple in the center of each city. By 2000 B.C. the temple had become a ziggurat, a massive stepped tower that dominated the city. It was the first monumental architecture in Mesopotamia. (Wallbank 1990, 22)

To *paraphrase* this paragraph a student might say, "The Sumerians were afraid of floods so they had a lot of gods and goddesses and temples to protect them." Main idea would be a little more concise: "the religion of the Sumerians."

All good teachers understand the importance of having students put ideas into their own words, or paraphrase, and you would begin by asking the student to do just that. What should you do, though, when a student is unable to make the switch to paraphrasing and insists on merely parroting back everything he has read, word for word? First, realize that rote memory is OK, even good, at the outset. After he's had some practice with what may seem like meaningless regurgitation, *then* start asking, "In your own words, what does this sentence (or paragraph) mean?"

Students who aren't able to paraphrase or interpret are rarely incapable; instead, they block themselves. Often, the reason they can't tell you what they've read is that they think that you, the tutor, understand the passage completely and that their answer is both inadequate and unnecessary. After all, *why explain something to someone who already knows it?* Talking directly to the student about this problem, even explaining it the way it's stated here, often helps.

Another way around "fear of paraphrasing" is for the tutor to "shrink" a little, in a manner of speaking. Thus, if the student can't tell you the meaning of a passage, switch roles. Have him pretend he's the tutor and you're the student, then ask him to explain it to you.

ROLE REVERSAL

Brett, age 17, was able to read for detail, but anything the least bit abstract seemed impossible. I explained the importance of reading for meaning and not just for facts, and we tried various exercises without much success. Finally, I began asking him to explain the material, not to me, since I already understood it, but to an imaginary 12-year-old. We did some role reversal, with myself as a normally curious but confused child. I asked questions and misinterpreted in ways I thought a child might. My questions were not just for dramatic effect. They were meant to help him sharpen his thinking. Brett, like many other students, benefited greatly from this exercise. And I had fun being the kid for a change.

If the student is still unable to tell about his reading and you think he might be blocking himself, ask him to use his imagination: "Why *might* it be that way? *You don't need to be right, you just need to try.* There's no way of telling for sure, so just guess." These words can cut through years of tuning out. Accept what your student tells you, pointing out what is right or at least reasonable about his answer. If possible, help him discover his mistakes by focusing on the material itself: "Was your answer right? How do you know?" Switch to easier material if your student still isn't able to paraphrase.

Predicting

By the questions we ask, we encourage students to predict the outcome of a story when they read fiction: "What do you think is going to happen next?

How do you think the story will end?" Yet how often do we ask students to predict what will come next when they read nonfiction? Probably not often enough, yet being able to predict—to see the trend of a paragraph or a textbook section and guess its direction—will help readers save time and energy and allow them to become more active readers.

We can help haphazard readers improve their reading by teaching them to become better "guessers" and engage in prediction just as more skillful readers do. Here's a suggestion. Next time you read a magazine article, stop once or twice in a paragraph to ask yourself what will come next. Were you able to predict fairly accurately? If so, how did you do it? Small clues in your reading probably allowed you to trace a trajectory. In other words, you predicted based on the available evidence in the article.

How predicting helps

Being able to predict is an important reading skill for a number of reasons. A reader who easily and accurately predicts the direction of a passage is ahead of the game since he will not be continually surprised by unpredictable twists and turns. Unpredictability is fun in a mystery novel but disconcerting in a textbook for several reasons.

First, readers who do not rely on prediction must expend a much greater amount of energy to remember what they've read than do those who easily see and follow the patterns in their reading. The nonpredictors must resort to rote learning and memorization of many separate facts and ideas to do well on quizzes and discussions. If they could see patterns emerging, however, they might merely mark the turns of the path rather than have to remember every single rock and tree along the way. So the first reason to predict is that it saves time and energy.

Second, a student who is able to predict the topic of the next sentence or paragraph does so as a result of making educated guesses based on significant information. This information is often in the form of key words and phrases found in topic sentences and transitions. If the student is paying attention to these elements, he will be reading well generally. In other words, skillful predicting produces skillful reading.

A lesson on predicting

GOOD AT FICTION, POOR AT FACTS

Jane was a 12-year-old with a bright smile, a winning manner, and a thick mop of brown curls. She was a voracious reader, going through a new fantasy fiction novel every week with good understanding. She could also relate a few random details from her history text, but that's where her reading skills ended. Jane was unable to remember what she had read or to identify the main idea in a passage, and her score on the Reading Drills exercise was low, at 40 percent. There was definitely a piece missing in Jane's textbook reading skills.

This was a puzzle, though. How could a student be performing so poorly on factual material when she was doing such a good job with fiction? I wasn't sure exactly what the missing piece was but decided to teach predicting with the following activity on the chance it might help. It turned out to be just what was needed, and the results were even better than I had hoped.

Jane's first lesson on predicting was a revelation for her. She was amazed that we were able to find clues that would allow us to guess what was coming next in a passage, and there was many a happy "Oh, yeah!" as she saw her predictions "come true."

Predicting is a relatively easy skill to teach and learn. Some reading materials are better than others for practicing this activity. Obviously, you want to try to find material that is predictable but not too transparent.

Begin teaching by reading aloud one sentence at a time from the passage. Cover up everything below where you are reading so the student can't see ahead. As you proceed, ask the student to guess what the next part of the article is likely to be about. If he is unsure, point out key words that might provide clues. Explain to the student that these words are often in topic sentences and transitions, then make sure he can recognize those elements.

If your student is unfamiliar with the terms *topic sentence* and *transition*, explain this way. *Topic sentence*: the sentence that contains the main idea of the paragraph; it usually comes first in the paragraph. *Transition*: the bridge between two topics, A and B. It usually contains an element of each, A plus B.

For practice, the left column of Table 8.1 on the next page contains excerpts from "Glass," an article in *Reading Drills* (Fry 1975, 23). Corresponding discussions with the student are provided in the right column. It may take a few repetitions doing passages like this, but before long the student likely will be picking out key words and making accurate predictions on his own. When questioned, some students say they don't know what is coming next in the passage when what they really mean is they don't know for sure and don't think they should hazard a guess. You can reassure a shy student that this activity is not about being right—all he's doing is giving his opinion.

Table 8.1. An exercise in predicting using the article "Glass."	
Glass Article Excerpts	**Questions**
For thousands of years, people thought of glass as something beautiful to look *at*. Only recently have they come to think of it . . .	After you read this paragraph: What do you think is coming next? What's something different from looking *at* glass? Answer: looking *through* it. A clue that you're looking for a difference is the phrase "only recently," meaning something has changed from how it used to be.
. . . as something to look *through*. Stores display their goods in large glass windows.	Here's our answer. Were you right? What could come after this part? A: Maybe more examples of glass to look through.
Glass bottles and jars that hold food and drink allow us to see the contents.	Were you correct? A: Yes, these are things in glass containers to look through.)
Glass is used to make spectacles, microscopes, telescopes, and many other extremely useful and necessary objects. Spectacles, or glasses are used by people who cannot see perfectly or by people who want to protect their eyes from bright light.	Notice the three items just listed. What was the first one? A: Spectacles. See it repeated again, with more detail in the second sentence? Using this pattern, what two topics will be discussed next? A: Microscopes and telescopes.
Microscopes make tiny things larger so that we can examine them. Telescopes make objects that are far away appear much closer to us . . .	Were you correct?

Main Idea

The main idea of a passage is its topic expressed in a short sentence or phrase. Teaching students to identify main idea in expository writing will be easier if they have practiced on fiction first, but it will still take some effort. The rewards make it worthwhile, however. When you teach your students to identify the main idea in reading, it is a good deed in the same way as promoting honesty and hard work—you know it's going to help them go far.

In identifying main idea, your student will start with one paragraph at a time, move to doing several paragraphs, then find the theme of entire passages. Later he will learn to take notes on whole chapters and will learn to see how themes or opinions build and are expressed over the course of a book. But it all starts with one paragraph.

Students must attain a certain level of abstract thinking to identify the main idea consistently. If they are not yet able to tackle main idea they can be helped to reach this point by using the exercises for building abstract thinking described in Chapter 6. Learning to identify main idea is a good brain exercise in itself, and consistent practice with main idea can go a long way in helping students improve their abstract thinking.

Introducing main idea

Discuss with the student why it is helpful to know the main idea of a nonfiction passage. You may be surprised at how little most teenagers understand of this concept. Ask, "What good will it do you to learn to identify main idea as you read?" and then bring out the following points.

- Understanding the main idea helps you discuss better in class and do a better job taking tests, because teachers often want to know what the ideas are, not just the facts.
- If you read only for details but don't think about the main ideas, you probably won't remember much of what you read. Knowing the main ideas gives you a "skeleton" to "pin" the facts on so you can remember them.
- On tests like the PSAT and SAT, you'll be asked what a good *title* for a passage would be, or what the *author's purpose* was. That's really a way of asking for the main idea.
- If you don't recognize the main idea, it's difficult to take notes—both reading and lecture notes.
- Outlining and writing a term paper would be a lot harder, even impossible, if you just had facts and details but no overview, so being able to find the main idea is a skill that can really help your reading and other classwork.

Using pictures to teach main idea

Some students have trouble identifying main idea if they start directly with textbook reading without any preliminaries. For these students, begin with pictures instead. Using pictures to introduce main idea has several things to recommend it, the most important being interest. Some students who have done main idea worksheets in school may come into tutoring thinking that identifying main idea is just busywork, so using pictures will catch their attention and give you an "in" to re-teach the material. Starting with pictures is also good for students who are visual learners, and it sparks an interest that can carry over into textbook reading.

Using a children's illustrated history encyclopedia with colorful, panoramic pictures, I start out by showing the student a picture and asking, "What is this a picture of, generally?" If the student can't tell what the picture is about in one short sentence, do it for him, explain how you did it, and then have him try on another picture.

The following discussion is based on a picture titled "Life in the Stone Age" (Rand McNally 1985, 14):

"This picture is of a family in cave times going about their daily activities." That's the main idea. When asked what the picture is about, however, some students will start by talking about each separate activity: "Making arrows, bringing in animals they've killed," etc. Redirect the student by saying, "But what's the *whole* picture about?" It helps to tell the student to "pretend I can't see the picture and you have to explain it so I'll have a mental image of what you're talking about." The next exercise fits in here and simply adds a helpful element to teaching about main idea.

The inverted pyramid

A graphic organizer, the *inverted pyramid*, can be used as to call attention to main ideas and details. When you were in school, you might have learned that newspaper articles are often organized using the inverted pyramid construction. News articles, of course, usually start with the most important facts—the answers to all the "w" questions—"who, what, why, where, and when." The beginning of the article is heavy on main ideas since the author usually tries to give an overview in the first few paragraphs. As you continue through a news article, the material ordinarily becomes more detailed and less important.

Arranging news articles in this way got started in the days before computer layout when journalists did not want to put important information at the end where it might be chopped off to make the article fit the newspaper space available.

Use the inverted pyramid diagram in Figure 8.1 to help a student who is slow to understand the distinction between overview and detail. The concept works well with both pictures and text, and can also be used to teach topic sentence in writing. First draw a downward-pointing triangle and say, "We can arrange information, from general to specific, in other words, main idea to detail, by writing it on this triangle." Put a one-phrase description of the picture (main idea) on the top where the pyramid is broadest. Jot down more and more specific details as you move toward the narrow bottom of the triangle.

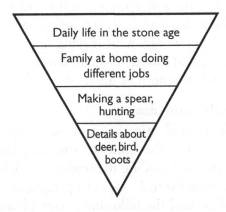

Figure 8.1. Inverted pyramid.

Here is a description of the exercise in detail for anyone who needs it. Using the picture from the previous section, write "Daily Life in the Stone Age" at the top of your triangle. That's the main idea. Then, continuing downward and with as much input from the student as you can elicit, comment and write in abbreviated form inside the triangle, "Family at home doing different jobs. Old man (grandfather?) making a spear." Point out that it's OK to guess if those guesses are based directly on observation.

Then discuss and list the other activities shown in the picture. "This man who has just gone hunting is coming home with the animals he's killed." And then, going into detail even more, "It looks like he's got a deer. And this bird hanging from his belt could be a pigeon." And then "super-detailed," written at the bottom tip of the triangle. Explain that it usually would be ridiculous to go into this much detail and that you are just doing it here to teach the process. "The pigeon is gray. The man wears boots made of strips of hide tied to his feet."

End the activity this way. "This upside-down triangle is a picture of the way our paragraph is organized. If the main idea were at the *end* of the paragraph, what would the triangle look like? If there were no main idea stated in a paragraph, but you had to read the whole thing and put two and two together to figure out the main idea, how could you draw it?" (Answers: A triangle with the tip pointing up; a rectangle.) When the student understands the activity, have him interpret several more pictures, while you jot down what he says in pyramid form.

Finally, select some pictures that show stages in a process—for example, various steps in harvesting grain, or building a bridge—and see if the student can come up with a description on his own that explains the sequence in which things happened. The triangle diagram wouldn't be used for these subjects. All you need is a list moving from first to last.

You may wish to spread this exercise out, having the student work with one or two pictures a lesson until he has mastered the activity.

Using text to identify main idea

When the student can identify the main idea using pictures, introduce text with the next exercise. This exercise introduces the concepts of "too general" and "too specific," guiding the student to pick an answer that is just right when choosing the main idea of a paragraph.

Have your student read the following paragraph and choose the best main idea from the multiple choice answers:

Paula's day at the circus

Paula waited expectantly for her older brother, Joe, to take her to the circus performance in town. When they arrived she quickly found her seat. She tapped her foot to the music of the circus band. She sat at the edge of the seat as she watched the animal trainer putting wild tigers through their performance. She gaped with open mouth at the trapeze artists. She laughed with glee as the clowns put on their acts. Joe brought her a hot dog and she munched on it delightedly. (Joffe 1980, 73)

Which of these sentences represents the main idea of the paragraph?

a. Paula went to the circus.
b. Paula enjoyed watching the clowns at the circus.
c. The circus comes to town once a year.
d. The circus band did not play.
e. Paula enjoyed her day at the circus.

The correct answer is *e*, "Paula enjoyed her day at the circus." If the student picked that answer, ask what the second best answer was and what was wrong with each of the other answers. It helps to draw a simple diagram to illustrate.

The second best answer is *a*, "Paula went to the circus." Let's look at why it's not the first choice, though. The story talks about all the things Paula enjoyed doing. Draw some X's to represent the things she enjoyed, and say:

X . . . she enjoyed this,

X . . . she enjoyed that,

X . . . and she enjoyed the other thing.

But "Paula went to the circus" (*a*) is such a broad idea that it sounds as if the *paragraph* should also include other things such as how much the circus cost, where it was, etc. So *a* is . . . *too general.*

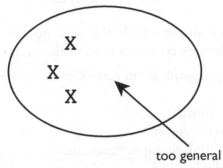

too general

On the other hand, "Paula enjoyed watching the clowns at the circus" (*b*) is too _____(what)?

(*b*) is too specific, because it mentions only the clowns, and that's just one little part of the paragraph. The main idea has to be as specific as possible and still cover the whole paragraph.

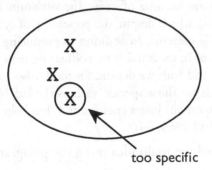

too specific

"The circus comes to town once a year" (*c*) is _____?

(*c*) is not mentioned in the paragraph.

"The circus band did not play" (*d*) is_____?

(*d*) is false.

So *e* is the best answer because it covers the whole paragraph but is still as specific as possible.

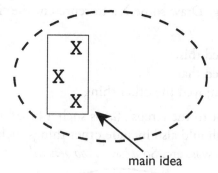

main idea

Here's a *formula*, almost a trick, that students can use for finding the main idea. Write the answers as you proceed through the discussion.

Q: What's the paragraph about generally, in one word?
A: "Paula"
Q: What about Paula?
A: "She went to the circus."
Q: What about Paula going to the circus?
A: "She enjoyed it."

So now, putting the answers together, we have the main idea: "Paula went to the circus and enjoyed it" or, to rephrase it, "Paula enjoyed her day at the circus."

Here is another paragraph for practice:

> Not all insects are enemies of man. The silkworm (Order Lepidoptera) spins threads of silk, which despite the popularity of synthetic fabrics is still an important textile material. In addition to producing beeswax and honey, the honeybee aids us immeasurably by pollinating many of the angiosperms upon whose seeds and fruit we depend for food. Also to be included among man's insect friends are those species, such as the ladybird beetle and many others, that prey upon our insect enemies and thus help us to keep them under control. (Kimball 1965, 64)

Here's a script for teaching main idea using the paragraph on insects:

> You know that the main idea is often in the first sentence of the paragraph. Be careful here, though. The first sentence only hints at the main idea, and you have to change the wording some to come up with the main idea.
>
> It isn't necessary to know the meanings of all the big words in this paragraph to figure out what the main idea is. Even if you don't know all the

words, you can still figure out the main idea. To do this, you do need to think about *what all the sentences have in common.* If you can answer that question you'll have the main idea.

Young people may understand the word theme better than they do main idea. If your student is still at a loss, ask for the "opinion that runs through all the sentences."

Jot down the student's answers as you go, and say, "OK, using our formula, let's go over why you're right (or what the answer should be)."

Q: In one word, what is this paragraph about?"
A: "Insects."
Q: "What about these insects?"
A: "They are friendly, or they help people."

So, put those together and you have: "Some insects are helpful to people," which can be shortened to "helpful insects," the main idea.

This series of questions forms a guide for identifying main idea and can be applied to almost any paragraph. It's good to use when the student seems stuck or confused in textbook reading. Additional questions to get students thinking about main idea (and author's purpose) are: "What is this paragraph doing in the book? Why did the author put it here? What ideas would be missing without it?"

As implied earlier, students may need to be weaned away from the notion that the main idea of a paragraph is stated explicitly in the first sentence. Students may be surprised to find that sometimes none of the words used to express the main idea is found in the paragraph. Unfortunately, students who do not move beyond formulistic thinking will continue to do a shallow job of interpreting their reading. It is difficult if they have been allowed to use such oversimplifications at school. Counter sloppy thinking by continuing to ask for the overview.

Move to a textbook

Start with headings

Introduce textbook reading by drawing the student's attention to the chapter titles and subheadings. If he isn't outlining yet, help him see how the headings relate to each other and that a similar type font indicates a similar rank of ideas. The information contained in headings is quite useful in determining the main ideas that will be covered in the text, but students often skip them, depriving themselves of information they need to form an overview. Read some headings aloud and discuss their meanings with your student. If he already knows how to outline, help him discover that the headings could form an outline. Ask which headings are parallel and which are subordinate.

Try the main idea of a textbook paragraph

Have the student read a paragraph and do a tellback of the kind he's been doing all along, aiming only for details. After he has done a tellback, ask for the main idea of the paragraph. Since determining the main idea is actually a stepping stone to note-taking, it helps to link the two. Teaching students to determine main ideas as one step in note-taking will simplify the task and eliminate much unnecessary instruction.

Try this. Tell the student you want him to list the main idea of each paragraph as if he were writing headings for some imaginary notes. Point out that if he were taking notes, he would be able to add details under the headings, so the heading could be fairly short, but would need to contain enough information to be meaningful when he rereads his notes to study for a test. For example, in the textbook paragraph from Chapter 3, "Sumerians" would be too brief for a heading, and "The Sumerians moved into Mesopotamia from the Southeast in about 3500 B.C." would probably be too long. A happy medium, and the correct main idea, might be "Ancient Sumerians entered Mesopotamia."

At first, the student may find it impossible to give you the main idea without reciting all the details first. Just let him do it that way at the beginning, then gradually have him switch to *thinking the details, but telling the main idea*. Some students pick this up immediately but for others it may take weeks. Don't worry if your student isn't catching on right away.

In over 40 years of teaching, I've hardly ever had a student who wasn't able to do a good job on this task eventually, regardless of how hopeless the situation looked at first. It may take four to six months of weekly practice for some students to master the skill of identifying the main idea.

Even college students can be helped by learning the essentials of main idea. You simply have to choose reading material that's on their level. For instance, I've recently been working with a college student on identifying the main ideas in Joseph Campbell's *The Hero with a Thousand Faces*. The book is challenging, but the principles are the same regardless of the difficulty of the material.

Handle the process of correcting the student's responses to the main idea tellbacks the same way you have done with all the other exercises—by acknowledging parts he got right, telling him the answer, and explaining how you came up with your own idea. In this exercise, as with others, your critique should be positive but it doesn't have to indicate that work was excellent; the student may be "close," "pretty good," or you might ask him to try again. Continue by having your student identify the main idea of several textbook paragraphs.

Review the formula and the purpose for main idea

You might review the formula for finding main idea introduced in the above lesson on "Paula" and "insects" to show how it works with the paragraphs you've just done. Also, if needed, review the purpose of your work with main idea to help the student see where you are headed: "Knowing how to come up with main idea will help in the future with note-taking, will make reading easier, and will allow you to mentally keep track of longer sections and understand more complex ideas. And that will allow you to read more interesting material and make better grades."

The phrases or sentences used to express the main idea can be expanded or contracted as desired. Doing the main idea like this is similar to the way we had students expand and contract section summaries when they did fiction reading. In case you need more, here are some paragraphs with the main ideas noted.

> If no other knowledge deserves to be called useful but that which helps to enlarge our possessions or to raise our station in society, then mythology has no claim to the appellation. But if that which tends to make us happier and better can be called useful then we claim that epithet for our subject. For mythology is the handmaid of literature; and literature is one of the best allies of virtue and promoters of happiness. (Bulfinch 1913, v)

Main idea: The study of mythology is useful because it adds to our happiness and virtue.

> In sixteenth-century Europe . . . folk wisdom . . . obstructed [man's] vision of himself, and his exploration of the human body. . . . In Europe the knowledge of the human body had been codified and put in the custody of a powerful, exclusive, and respected profession. Stored in learned languages (Greek, Latin, Arabic, and Hebrew), such knowledge was the preserve of monopolists who called themselves Doctors of Physick. Handling the body, for treatment or dissection, was the province of another group more akin to butchers and sometimes called barber-surgeons. (Boorstin 1983, 338)

Main idea: In the 1500s, learning about anatomy was difficult because the "experts" had no direct scientific observation or experience of the human body.

> While the young ladies of genteel families were immured in the school-room their brothers were enjoying the freer life of Eton or Harrow or some other scholastic establishment; and at sixteen to eighteen, the age when their sisters 'came out,' the young gentlemen went to the university, which in those days meant Oxford or Cambridge. The young ladies looked forward to two or three years of parties, admiration, strict chaperonage, and Minerva novels, to be followed by a handsome bridegroom, a fashionable wedding, and an adequate establishment. The young gentlemen saw before them a pleasant life in a community without the restrictions of school, freedom and independence, as much study as they chose, and a chance of gaining distinction through the high degree which they (most of them) meant to take at the end of their course. (Cruse 1930, 108)

Main idea: Unlike their sisters of the same age, young English gentlemen enjoyed freedom and independence when they entered university.

> About 300 years ago a German scientist sent word to his emperor that he wished to show him an experiment. The scientist was Otto von Guericke. . . . A big hollow [metal] ball was made in two halves that were not fastened together. With an air pump he had invented, von Guericke pumped out most of the air from inside the ball. Then the air on the outside held the two halves together. It pushed on them with so much force that strong horses could not pull them apart. (Parker 1960, 612)

Main idea: von Guericke did early experiments with a vacuum.

Home practice

It may be necessary to have the parents and student work at home on main idea, just as you did with fiction tellbacks. If so, ask them to work on several paragraphs a day, concentrating on main idea tellbacks. As before, have the parent and student jot down the dates practiced, the page and paragraphs studied, and include the student's notes on the main idea of each paragraph. Ask the student to bring in both the notes and the book. Do a quick check at the beginning to see that both the student and parent are on track.

Note-taking

Your student is ready for note-taking if he is able to recall details and identify the main idea in nonfiction material successfully. And if a student is able to read a textbook with understanding and take good notes, he has cleared a major hurdle on the way to academic self-sufficiency.

Introduce note-taking in the same way you've introduced other skills, by discussing the purpose of the activity, in this case by asking what notes are good for. Students may not understand how helpful notes can be, and I've met high school students who literally believe that the sole purpose of taking notes is to prove to the teacher that they have read the material.

Students should use notes to:

- study for tests
- prepare for class discussions
- move material from short- to long-term memory in the mental "filing cabinet"
- *understand* information
- keep mentally alert during reading and lectures

This experience at a college preparatory high school where I used to tutor emphasizes the need for good note-taking. I was working with a group of ninth-graders who had received A's and B's in public school, but were floundering after they switched to a more difficult private school and were now getting D's and F's in their science and history classes. The students' idea of taking notes was to highlight everything in their texts with yellow markers. I mean they were highlighting *everything*, whether they understood it or not (which they usually didn't), and whether or not it was important (hard to tell if it's important when you don't understand it).

These students explained that since they really didn't know what they were reading in the first place, they were taking no chances so they highlighted everything. And how did they use their notes to study for tests? They didn't, of course. It was impossible.

My current students who hear this story understand the caution it implies (understand what you read and take notes selectively), and it makes a good entrée into teaching note-taking.

Note-taking tips

Begin by going over the following note-taking tips with your student. Then dictate the important points for him to write down and use as a reference sheet. He should familiarize himself with these points, and then the two of you can use the list as a guide as you teach each step. Have him keep this sheet of note-taking tips in his folder, along with other "how to study" sheets he'll be receiving from you in the future, and bring them to tutoring each week.

- Notes don't have to be beautiful but they should be clear enough for you to read when you return to them to study for the test in a few weeks.

- Important: When you take notes, don't copy out of the book. In fact, don't look at the book at all when you write your notes. Instead, read a paragraph, then:
  o Look away and summarize aloud in your own words. This is a tellback just like the ones you've been doing.
  o Write a summary of your tellback from memory, including the main idea and selected details.
  o Use a "modified outline form" with dashes and dots to make notes visually clear. (Using the numbers and letters of a formal outline slows the process, and random notes are too disorganized, so compromise by using dashes for main ideas and dots for details.) Arrange them to indicate priority, dashes flush with the margin, dots underneath and a little to the right for details.
  o Check your notes against the book if you need to, but make it a quick check and try to wean yourself away from looking back. Taking notes this way is a memory-building exercise.
- Write only material that you don't know or couldn't figure out on your own.
- Write anything that you think would be important to the teacher, or to the author, or that is important or interesting to you personally. For example,
  o To determine what the teacher thinks is important, look at what type of tests he gives and at the points he wants to discuss in class. Pay attention to the teacher's body language.
  o To find out what the textbook author thinks is important, notice the use of boldface, italics, and the amount of space devoted to a particular subject in the book.
  o Include what you personally think is important. Put down information you think might help clarify material yet to come. Let your own interests figure in.
- Take notes on your notes, meaning reread your notes and underline or otherwise mark parts that are important.
  o Don't overdo it. Underlining an entire page defeats the purpose.
  o Using colored pencils to underline makes the finished product visually clear, and besides, it looks cool.
  o Other useful marks:
    ▪ Stars or brackets in the margins call attention to important information.

- Arrows can show cause and effect.
- Number items in a list.
- Equal signs indicate definitions.
- Asterisks can flag related information.

- Abbreviate. Expand your knowledge of standard abbreviations and then make up your own. Later you can use these abbreviations in your lecture notes.
- Number the pages of your notes and include page numbers from the book. (What if you drop your notes or lend them? What if you want to check your notes against the book?)
- When you have finished "taking notes on your notes," come up with key words or study questions that summarize or ask about the material in your notes. Write these study questions in the margin, then quiz yourself by covering up your notes and answering the questions aloud. This tip is adapted from the Cornell Notetaking System; see Pauk and Owens (2013).
- Write key words and study questions in the margin. They will allow you to quiz yourself so you won't need others (like your mom) to help you study, and that equals more independence.
  o Study questions or key words could be things such as, "List the steps in the scientific process," "three agents of erosion," or "Where and when did the Proto-Indo-Europeans live?"
  o You may wish to draw a wider margin on your paper to make room for your study questions.
  o As you work aloud, try to come up with substantive answers to your questions. Regard the questions as memory prompts to help you tell as much as you can remember of your notes.
  o If you work aloud you will remember better.
  o For difficult classes, cover your notes then say and write them from memory, using the questions in the margin as guides. Check what you have written against your notes. If you make a mistake, no reason to feel badly, just notice what you did wrong and say the correct answer a time or two.
- Review your notes once right after you take them, again about 10 minutes later, once the next day, and at least once more before the test.
  o You start to forget right after you learn something, thus the 10-minute review (Pauk and Owens 2013). The other two

reviews cut down on how much you forget, which can be a quite a bit without them.

- o Adding 15 minutes of review time quadruples the amount you can remember from an hour of study.
- o Plan ahead so that you can include this review time in your study sessions.

Following through on note-taking

Remember to have your student write down the main points from these note-taking tips. It's best if he brings these notes to each lesson. That way he'll have them at home to use and you can also refer to them in the tutoring session.

Show your student a few pages of good reading notes he can use as a model. They could be your own notes or those of another student. Point out that even if the student never looks at his notes again, just the act of writing them will help him remember what he has read.

Go through each note-taking step, demonstrate, and have the student practice it until he becomes proficient. Explain to the student that he won't have to take notes one paragraph at a time forever. "Do it this way until you're good at it, and after a few months' time, you can switch to any style of note-taking you like."

Check to be sure that your student is not copying from the book. This is a big step for many teens. If he's stuck in copy mode, work with him to break the habit. Kids may resist, so you may need to be fairly directive, but remember that doing notes this way will help their thinking skills in the long run.

Look over your student's notes for the common problems of over-detailing and its opposite, skipping important information. The only way to teach students how to get the right amount of detail is to show them how you would do it yourself. Explain your reasons for including or leaving out material, and have your student continue practicing until he gets it right.

When your student understands the basics, assign note-taking homework. Have him take reading notes at home or at school—three to five pages a week—until you think he has the hang of it. If he has textbook reading assignments at school, so much the better, but if not, have him read and take notes on whatever is being discussed in class. Kids will try to bypass this assignment, so be insistent, and don't be afraid to keep him at it for several weeks if needed. This note-taking assignment alone can dramatically raise a student's social studies and science grades, and that applies even to classes in which the teacher does not hand out the textbooks, much less give reading assignments.

Test Questions

It's a common problem: A student tests poorly on material he believes he has studied well and then is puzzled by the outcome. Of course there are many reasons a student might get poor grades on a test, but one of the most common is that he does not anticipate what kinds of questions he will encounter on the test. He can learn to "think more like a teacher" by coming up with mock test questions and then answering them himself. Your guidance in this process is important.

Ask your student to read a section from a science or social studies text, take notes or do a tellback, then write and answer his own questions about the reading. He should try to make these questions like the ones from class as much as possible. Of course, having old tests from the class can be a big help. Teens have a tendency to make up superficial questions based simply on facts—and not even the most important facts—so your input is important here. Guide your student to come up with test questions that are both realistic and thought-provoking, and supervise to make sure his answers are clear and thorough.

READING IN A QUESTIONING FRAME OF MIND

George was a high school junior. He was a bright, hard-working young man, but he was failing his advanced chemistry class. By making up his own tests, studying for these tests and taking them in writing, George went from getting D's and F's to receiving straight A's in a few weeks' time. Of course, it helped that we spent quite a bit of time studying his old tests to see what kinds of questions his teacher asked and what errors George had made. So that helped, but it wasn't all. The real change took place in George's reading. Knowing that he would be asked for questions at the end of a section or chapter reading put him in a questioning frame of mind as he read. Reading was no longer a passive procedure filled with unconnected facts, but an active question and answer session that helped him prioritize and group the information he read.

Putting It All Together

It is useful to use the *whole-part-whole* approach in planning for new learning. In this method, the learner first experiences whatever it is he is learning in its entirety, then practices its separate skills or components, and finally puts them together again into a cohesive whole. For instance, after a minimum of instruction, a young skier might begin on some gentle slopes, then practice turns and stops until he has mastered these components, and finally combine and apply his new skills to real downhill skiing.

In the terminology of the whole-part-whole method of instruction, we could say that your reading student has been practicing the turns and stops—the separate components of nonfiction reading—and that now it is time to complete the experience by putting the separate skills together. So far, the student has worked on tellbacks, paraphrasing, identifying main idea, and note-taking. Now it's time to return to textbook reading, not to practice separate skills as before, but with an eye to combining and applying the skills the student has already learned.

To do this, have the student read an entire chapter in a social studies or science textbook. This time he will not be as focused on single paragraphs, but will aim for more overall understanding, taking the book a section at a time, paraphrasing and explaining as he goes. At this point you are asking your student to read then teach you the content of the chapter as if he were the instructor. He should include information from pictures, maps, and diagrams in his explanation, and should focus on finding the main ideas of entire sections, rather than separate paragraphs. Adding note-taking will help the student gain an overview.

Finally, if your student has been successful so far, have him read another textbook chapter in its entirety and take a test on it. Let him know beforehand only that you will be testing him and that he is to use everything he's learned so far to aid his understanding and memory. You may wish to write the test yourself or use one from a teacher's guide to the textbook you are using. Whatever your source for the test, try to keep it fairly close to what the student might encounter in the classroom.

Use the test results to re-teach any skills that are lacking. There will be another "final" at the end of Chapter 9, so although this test isn't an end point, it serves as an interim task that says, "This is what you have learned so far, and this is what we still need to work on."

Asking students to read at this level of understanding is a tall order, and not all will succeed at this time. The next chapters provide more opportunities for mastery of higher-level reading.

Summary of Key Points

- Students can build skills in reading factual material through:
    o paraphrasing
    o predicting

- o identifying main idea
- o note-taking
- o creating test questions
- The exercises in this chapter all have the goal of allowing students to read nonfiction precisely, to interpret with insight, and to recall accurately.
- Learning to predict—to see a trend in a paragraph and guess its direction—will help students save time and energy and allow them to become more active readers.
- Have students paraphrase nonfiction material, or put it in their own words, as a step toward identifying main idea.
- Students who have trouble paraphrasing may be helped to trust their own ideas through role playing.
- Workbook exercises can lend structure to teaching reasoning skills and may be very effective. Exercises may include work on sentence completion, figurative language, categorization, analogies, and cause and effect.
- It is essential for students to be able to identify the main idea of a passage since it is the foundation for effective note-taking, summarizing and even writing. Knowing the main idea allows students to remember what they read and to understand the author's purpose.
- Teaching main idea through pictures before starting on text can help students begin working on higher-level thinking skills in an engaging way.
- The main idea of a paragraph must be as specific as possible and still cover the entire paragraph. Try the "Paula" method of teaching main idea.
- Go over note-taking tips with the student, work on having the student make up test questions, and then put all the previous skills together and test your student's ability to understand an entire textbook chapter.

The completion of this chapter marks a turning point. Some students will now be ready to graduate from tutoring, and for them it marks a closure. For others, this is the threshold between intermediate and advanced work in reading—between competence and mastery. For a third group, those for whom understanding has been slow in coming, the following chapters offer another chance at success.

9 | Branching Out: Higher-level Nonfiction Reading

Until this point, the amount and type of reading material you've used with your student has been somewhat limited. Since the purpose was to make sure the student succeeded by keeping the teaching steps small and orderly, it made sense not to offer a lot of distracting choices. You don't want your students' reading to be limited forever, however. Now is the time to make the switch from doing primarily academic reading to using a variety of interesting factual materials, including newspaper and magazine editorials for older students, sports and outdoors magazines, how-to books, self-help, psychology, and spiritual development books—depending on your students' tastes and your own.

For a few students, branching out will mean remaining at their current reading levels but simply using a wider variety of materials. For the majority, however, this is a time for learning to read more challenging and thought-provoking material—in other words, to read critically at higher levels.

Next Step: Mastery

If your student is now able to read mid-high school level novels and textbooks with understanding and is taking useful notes, you have reached an important milestone. You may have spent weeks or months getting to this point. Until now you have been warping the loom and sharpening the axe. Now the tools for understanding that you and your student have so painstakingly constructed are ready for use. The student has developed the background and skills to move beyond easier novels and textbooks into more difficult and challenging material, including books and articles written on a college or adult level. This new stage of learning can bring both joy and frustration: joy at discovering a fascinating world of new ideas but frustration with material that may be elusive and difficult to interpret.

This is the time to help students move from the surface understanding typical of beginners to the depth and insight of more mature thinkers. The majority of students (and many adults) never make the transition to higher-level reading, and it is unlikely that your student will make the jump on her own. Your student needs your guidance in this process now more than ever. If you are in any doubt about how unusual it is for people to read well at these higher levels, ask around and see how many people in the general public read and understand the editorial page of the newspaper, for example, or are science literate.

According to the ACT, Inc., Executive Summary on college readiness, students' ability to read and understand complex texts is the most important predictor of college success, yet only about half of students taking the ACT were able to read complex texts successfully (Act 2006, 2), when judged against ACT's "benchmark" scores. Complex texts contain multiple layers of meaning, and a single superficial reading will not be enough to grasp them fully. Students must call on sophisticated reading skills and strategies to unlock their meaning.

Most educators don't even attempt to teach students to read for mastery at levels above the average, or mid-range, high school level. They may *want* students to read better and ask them to do it, but teaching them *how* is another matter. For instance, a high school language arts teacher might assign students a challenging novel and then spoon feed the material to get them through the book rather than teaching them the reading principles they need to do it on their own.

There are several reasons classroom teachers do not offer instruction in higher-level reading at school: Guiding students to achieve at higher levels is very time-consuming, and it may be necessary to go through months of practice that looks and feels like failure, both to the student and to the teacher. Furthermore, the teacher must be reading and thinking at the advanced level. The student may be doing pretty well anyway, so "why bother?" And most important, the task often looks impossible at the outset. No wonder teachers don't often take this step. In tutoring, it may sometimes seem cruel to the kids and a waste of parents' money to keep students working on something that shows no promise of success for long periods of time.

It was only the result of a quirky, counterintuitive discovery that convinced me teaching higher-level reading skills to remedial students was feasible. I liken this discovery to one of my favorite science reading passages in which Charles Goodyear found the process of vulcanization to make tires usable when he accidentally dropped a chunk of rubber into a pan of hot sulfur. I discovered that if I could keep students plugging away at the more difficult reading for about six to eight weeks, they would eventually experience a breakthrough in which the material became clear. Vulcanization had occurred! This was true in almost every case, even if there were no signs of success early on.

Needless to say, keeping students from giving up and parents from balking during this process takes some doing. After several years' practice, however, I can predict a little more comfortably that the breakthrough *will* happen, and I find people are usually willing to trust me, trust the process, and stick with it until the student becomes an adept college-level reader. I recommend this endeavor—or rather, this experiment—to try with your own students.

Use a Variety of Factual Reading Materials

The first step will be to find some good materials to practice on. Some students enjoy bringing their own materials to tutoring, but others will gladly leave the selection up to you. Either is all right. You might put it this way: "If you bring in your own book or magazine, we'll use it. But if you forget, don't worry; we'll just use mine." That way there's an incentive for the student to bring a book, but no need to apologize if she forgets.

There's no substitute for capitalizing on kids' interests when it comes to teaching higher levels of nonfiction reading. Over the years I have learned a lot more than I wanted to know about subjects in which I initially had no interest, but that was part of the fun. My students and I have studied mountaineering, famous ballerinas, race car driving, and biographies of astronauts and sports greats.

Besides the materials that students bring in, I collect well-written history and science articles from magazines such as *Smithsonian Magazine*, *Natural History*, and *Discover* for high school students to use for practice. Most teens are interested in the content, and the articles are an excellent way to take reading beyond the textbook format. Enjoy starting your own collection of reference articles. You'll have more fun teaching if you're working with material you find interesting yourself, and your students will pick up on your enthusiasm.

These articles lend themselves to working on critical thinking, so you can use them to question, reflect, speculate, and predict with your student.

An example is provided in Appendix G, "Human 'moms' teach chimps it's all in the family" (Rock 1995, 70), an excerpt with comments and discussion questions.

From Paragraph to Overview

Teaching higher-level reading may seem quite different from working with easier material since it requires greater abstract abilities and more background knowledge. The idea of incremental learning still applies, however, so we'll approach the advanced work as we did simpler skills, breaking the material into exercises and activities and moving through the process one step at a time. All the exercises in this chapter can be used to help students achieve greater skill and understanding in reading nonfiction.

Following the example in Appendix G, in-depth reading can be taught step-by-step as follows. Begin by introducing the idea of overall theme and author's purpose. Ask your student to look for the main point of the entire article, not just of individual paragraphs.

- Have the student read the title.
- Start on familiar ground by having her do a regular tellback for the first paragraph (main idea and detail.) Ask what the purpose of the paragraph is.
- Continue tellbacks one paragraph at a time.
- Ask for predictions.
- After a few paragraphs, introduce the new question: What is the point of the entire article, in one sentence, based on what you know so far?
- Continue asking this same question periodically as the student reads through the article and notice how the answer changes as she gains more information.
- Refer back to the title to see how the ideas in the current paragraph relate to it.
- Ask how each paragraph
  - o relates to the one before it
  - o relates to the one that follows it
  - o repeats, adds information, or introduces a new idea
- Have the student identify transitions in the article and note
  - o what subjects are bridged by each transition. (What falls before and after it?)
  - o how the transition is constructed. (Does it contain elements of

what comes before and what follows? If so, have the student locate these parts.)
- What was the author's purpose in writing the article?

As you work your way through the magazine articles, it can make sense to begin SAT test preparation since it entails similar types of reading. SAT reading is covered in detail in Chapter 11.

The next section, SQ3R, brings us back to textbook reading, and gives us tools to help students understand the material in more depth by analyzing its structure.

SQ3R: Reading a Textbook Chapter Step-by-Step

SQ3R (survey, question, read, recite, and review) is a study technique used to enhance understanding and memory of factual material. It is particularly useful for reading and studying chapters in social studies and science textbooks, and in the long run, SQ3R can also make studying faster, though it takes several practice sessions to reach that point.

The idea behind SQ3R is that people understand and remember better if they have some idea of what they'll be reading (the survey) and have some way of relating it to what they already know or hope to find out (question). Your students are already practiced at the "read" part of SQ3R. The "recite" and "review" steps are additions that will help them study for tests.

A few years ago, students learned SQ3R regularly in school, but they hardly ever made use of it. Teaching this technique one-to-one as you are doing here gives you a chance to provide the follow-up that was missing in school. As a result, your students are more likely to see the value of the technique and actually get into the habit of using it.

The SQ3R process is outlined below. It is a condensed version of what is usually taught in schools and should be easier for students to use and remember. Have the student write these steps and keep them handy in her tutoring folder.

Survey and question. Starting with one section of a chapter, look over the material you are going to read. Ask a question about each heading. Glance over the other sections in the chapter.

Read first sentences. Read the first sentence of each paragraph in the section.

Read a section. Read the section your regular way and take notes.

Recite and Review. Review out loud either from your notes or from the textbook.

Now let's go over the steps in more detail.

The following lesson on the SQ3R method is written as a script. While the script material is aimed at the student, it also contains enough information to help you learn to use SQ3R yourself. Locate a textbook with headings and subheadings, and proceed as follows:

SQ3R is a way to read and remember a chapter in your textbook. You've worked on separate paragraphs before but not an entire chapter. We're starting on some more advanced material here, and that's good. After you use the SQ3R method on about six or seven chapters, you'll find that it will actually take you less time using this technique than without it. Also, after you learn to do all the steps in the SQ3R method, you can decide which ones you want to use in any given situation. You don't have to go through the entire process, but can pick and choose.

Survey and Question

One reason many people don't know what they've read when they finish a textbook chapter is that their brains weren't engaged to begin with. When you do the first two steps, survey and question, and when you read the first sentences, you are previewing—that is, getting an overview. Getting an overview is a way to get your brain working well before you start reading so you don't miss anything important.

To *survey*, look over all these features in your textbook: pictures, captions, maps, graphs, chapter summaries, introductions if informative, and study questions. When you read the study questions at the end of the textbook sections, you aren't trying to answer them. You are simply putting them in the back of your mind to guide your reading.

Another way to engage the brain is to get into a *questioning* state of mind. To do this, look over the headings and subheadings and ask questions—out loud, if possible. Focusing on the headings will give you a good overview, something that's lacking with much textbook reading. Taking note of the headings also provides a framework for storing further information from your reading.

Asking questions can also spark your curiosity. See if you can find answers as you read. If you can't, that's OK. Just asking the questions is the important part.

Another purpose of questioning is to tie new material in with what you already know. If you know something about the topic of the heading, then stating a fact rather than asking a question will help you "firm up" the connection between old and new. If you are unfamiliar with a word in the heading, you should ask about the meaning of that word. In your questions, it is helpful to repeat words and phrases from the heading, since part of the reason for doing this exercise is to draw your attention to the headings and help you remember them.

Here are some sample questions to aid you in forming your own. The headings are from an American History textbook section on labor unions in the late 1800s (Cayton 1999, 402).

Section title: "The Great Strikes: A Turning Point in History"

Your question: "In what way were the strikes a turning point in history?"

Heading: "The Widening Gulf Between Rich and Poor"

Q: "How big was the difference between the rich and poor?" Or, "What was causing the rift?"

Heading: "Socialism in the Industrial Age"

Q: If you don't know what Socialism is, your question would naturally be, "What is Socialism?" If you are familiar with the term, however, you might ask, "Was Socialism big in the United States before the turn of the century?"

Heading: "The Return of Labor Unions

Q: "When did the earlier labor unions exist?"

Read first sentences

In a textbook, four-fifths of the main ideas are in the first sentences of the paragraphs. In addition, we remember most what we read first and last, but less of what we read in the middle of any study session, so *if we read main ideas first, we will remember them best*. If a textbook is well-organized, reading the first sentences and putting them together in your mind can be almost like reading a good summary paragraph. The parts often fit together surprisingly well. If the first sentence is very long, read only the first part of it. If the first sentence doesn't say much, but it looks as though the second one does, read the second one. Some study skills teachers now recommend reading the first and *last* sentences as part of the preview.

Read a section

Now that you're finished previewing, read your normal way and take notes, using the long smooth underline. If you keep your pencil in hand while you do the LSU, you can use it to underline (without marking). That will keep the pencil handy so you don't have to keep picking it up and setting it down when you take notes. Doing the LSU with a pencil may become a habit that helps you focus automatically, definitely a plus.

Recite and review

A student who does not review material can forget 80 percent of what has been learned in only two weeks! The first review should come very shortly after the material was first presented and studied. Reviewing early acts as a safeguard against forgetting and helps you remember far longer. Frequent reviews throughout the course will bring rewards at test time and will alleviate pre-test anxiety (Chadron State College).

This section goes over what you've already learned about note-taking, but with a bit more explanation. As before, put key words or study questions in the left-hand margin of your notes, cover up the body of the notes, and answer your questions in the margin out loud. Writing your own questions helps to clarify meanings, reveal relationships, establish continuity and strengthen memory. Also, writing questions sets up a perfect stage to study for exams later (Pauk and Owens 2013).

Reciting, or saying out loud what you want to remember, will help you recall much more than simply rereading silently. Reciting helps move material from short- to long-term memory, and according to study experts, will allow you to remember about 80 percent of what you learn (Pauk and Owens 2013, 147). Uncover your notes as you recite, checking to see if you made any errors or missed important information. If you did make a mistake, simply repeat the material aloud correctly to help it stick in your mind.

When you are finished with this part of your review, include one extra step: *reflect*. That is, ask yourself the significance of the facts you have just learned. How do they relate to each other and what comes after? How can you apply the ideas or principles from the reading? How do they fit in with what you already know?

There may be difficult courses such as physics and chemistry for which an oral review is just not enough. That's the time for a written review. When you cover up your notes and try to recall them from your study questions and notes in the margins, do it in writing rather than out loud, then compare what you wrote with your original notes. In some cases, you will want to reproduce in writing everything that is in your notes, but sometimes it's OK just to get the "important stuff." Knowing what kind of test questions the teacher asks can help you judge that.

Doing a review is easy, but here are a couple of points to help you master the process. Aim for 15 minutes of review for every hour of study. Since you start forgetting within just a few minutes of the time you stop studying, the best times to review are right after you read, once the next day, and a time or two before the test. You will find that you forget less and less after each succeeding review, and you will forget less rapidly with each review. On the other hand, it will take less and less review time for you to remember much more, a great payoff!

You can review from the textbook as well as from your notes. To do that, cover up everything but the first sentence of the paragraph, recite what you think is in the rest of the paragraph, then reread the passage quickly to check yourself.

This marks the end of the script for teaching SQ3R.

Test on SQ3R

After a student understands the steps of the SQ3R technique and can do them separately, test her skills by having her do a whole section, using SQ3R. It will help you track her progress if you can have her explain what she is doing each step of the way. For example, "Now I am going to read the first sentences." Or, "Now I'm reviewing from my notes." You can even have the student do an entire chapter and then give her a written test on it, with the explanation that it will help with her schoolwork.

I often use the SQ3R method myself, and can really see the difference it makes. One of the things that will make your students more willing to use the techniques you are teaching is your own personal testimonial. When you, the tutor, have learned and used these techniques yourself, you will be able to talk them up convincingly.

Outlining

Outlining is another method of helping students understand and work with the organization of nonfiction reading material.

What do we need outlining for? Teachers don't often have students outline in class any more. I still teach students this skill, however, as a way to help them organize their thinking about their reading and writing. Students often become aware of the structure of an article for the first time after they learn to outline. Indeed, some may become aware for the first time that articles even *have* structures. Also, although outlining is not essential for note-taking, it does help.

To learn to outline, students must first be able to group ideas into categories, then name the categories. They've practiced on this thinking skill in *Reasoning and Reading* and in working on the concept of "group" and "members of a group" concept in determining main idea, as in the paragraph we worked on earlier, "Paula's day at the circus." So our students have had some experience with grouping ideas. Outlining is an opportunity to carry this skill one step further.

Here are some activities to help students learn to outline. The first is one of my favorite tutoring activities, an introduction to outlining using file cards to sort and put in order. The final product is an outline, but it's the process, not the product, that's important here. Teens may really enjoy this hands-on activity. You can spread the cards out on the floor, a good way to involve a standoffish teen. Seeing how the student deals with grouping the cards can provide important information about his conceptual skills.

To do the exercise, find a well-organized, simple article in a children's encyclopedia and outline it yourself. Take each entry from your outline and write it separately on a 3x5 note card. Headings and details will be on separate cards but there will be no clues on the cards to help students group them except by ideas. Mix the cards up and have the student put them in outline order again.

Urge your student to start by finding just a few cards that go together. She can add to that group and find other groups, then add titles and subtitles. When she has all the cards grouped, she can put them in outline order, complete with "indentations" by aligning the cards either to the left or right. Demonstrate that parallel ideas line up vertically, more general ideas go to the left, and more specific ones are indented to the right.

When the student understands the outlining process, have her practice by outlining some children's encyclopedia articles as she reads.

Finally, have her outline a topic you suggest. This is not an article she has read—you simply give her the topic and she must come up with the outline. For instance, you might ask her to outline "dogs" or "nineteenth century art" or "Wyoming." Tell her to pretend she is making an outline for a short talk or magazine article she will present to other students her age. Go through the process with her once or twice to demonstrate, then have her outline a topic on her own.

It may take several weeks for a student to master outlining. That's because you are not simply teaching a technique, but a new way of thinking. While outlining is certainly a helpful skill, for most students it is not an essential one. This gives the tutor some choice concerning whether or not to teach it and what level of mastery to expect.

When your student is adept at using SQ3R and outlining, decide whether she needs further instruction in working with the organization of nonfiction material. She may simply need to read to gain confidence and skill, but if she needs more work on predicting, the following exercise on identifying paragraph structure will be helpful.

Paragraph Structure

Learning the various ways that paragraphs can be organized helps students know what to expect in their reading and allows them to read faster and with less effort. If students will learn to identify types of paragraphs—cause and effect, or time order, for example—they will be able to see them coming as they read. This is an easy way to take some of the mystery out of reading since it encourages readers to predict what a paragraph will be like based on the first few sentences.

For older students, try the chapter titled "Analyzing Patterns and Organization" in *Active Reading in the Arts and Sciences* by Shirley Quinn and Susan Irvings (1991, 189-203). Decide how much of the book to use, though, since you may find some parts overly detailed.

Some examples of paragraph types are given below. I've used sentences instead of paragraphs for brevity, but you can come up with your own practice paragraphs based on these. Notice that there are specific words that act as clues to the type of sentence or paragraph structure to expect.

Cause and effect

Something makes something else happen. "The girl hurt her friend's feelings, so the friend refused to walk home from school with her." Or, "Spain's economy went into a depression as the result of large amounts of gold from the New World flooding its markets." Or, "Babies who are never held often do not bond with their parents."

Time order

First something happens and then something else happens. "John got married. He and his wife had five boys, and then a girl. After that, they had no more children." (Maybe there is some cause and effect here, but it's also time order. There can be overlap.) "Ancient Sumerians first believed in goddesses, then in gods and goddesses who shared power equally, and finally they worshipped male gods exclusively."

Compare and contrast

Similarities and differences: "My father is Australian. My mother is a Texan. They share a love of travel and classical music."

Definition

"Democracy is government of the people, by the people, and for the people."

Explanation

Explanation overlaps with both cause and effect and definition. "We have a juvenile justice system in part to keep from housing youthful offenders with hardened criminals." "The light rail system in this city has not taken people out of their cars, only switched bus riders to train riders."

Enumeration

"There are five things to look for in buying a used car. First, what is the mileage? Second, . . . etc."

Transition

Transition is the bridge between two thoughts—how you switch from one subject to another. "Now that we've looked at how to divide your back-yard into high water and low water zones, let's talk about how to choose plants for the dry area of your garden."

Practice

Based on the above categories, have your student practice identifying sentences and paragraphs from her reading using these categories. It is easy to incorporate this paragraph analysis exercise into other work such as an-alyzing a magazine article or SAT readings. Learning about the paragraph types is also a good lead-in for writing instruction.

The end of this section on paragraph structure concludes the work we began back in Chapter 7 on the subject of factual reading step-by-step. All that's left now is for us to evaluate how well the student has learned to read factual material and whether or not she is able to use her new skills in real life. That's the purpose of the final exam.

Final Exam

The final exam is straightforward. Simply ask the student to read a text-book chapter then test her on it. You might use an old test from her school as a model. Don't ask or even remind her to use any of the skills and tech-niques she's already worked on. It's up to her to decide how to study for the test. To save time you can have her read a chapter at home, but she should take the test during the tutoring session. Problems with the test may point to areas that need to be re-taught.

Summary of Key Points

- Encouraging students to read a wide variety of materials will help them move from instruction based on drill to a richer, more fulfill-ing reading experience.
- Begin working on college or adult level reading with students who are ready.

- Some students may require several weeks of instruction before they can apply higher-level reading skills, so don't give up too soon.
- The SQ3R method will help students read and remember textbook material significantly better.
- Outlining can help readers organize thoughts as well as notes.
- Understanding paragraph structure can make predicting, and thus all nonfiction reading, easier.

This is a good time to take stock. What can your student do now that she could not do, or was not willing to do, before? Unless something unforeseen has taken place, she is better able to focus, is now in the habit of preparing for class, has a good grasp of what she has read, and shows an understanding that extends to ideas and concepts as well as facts. Any initial resistance to reading has decreased, even evaporated, and her enjoyment and enthusiasm have grown, not through any direct effort on your part to promote reading, but for the simple reason that people like to do the things they are good at. You have helped your student become proficient at the rewarding but sometimes difficult and challenging tasks required to become a literate adult. Part IV on reading speed adds the final touch to our mix of strategies and skills.

Part IV: Reading Speed

PART IV PRESENTS A COMPLETE speed reading course for adolescent readers. Chapter 10, "Reading Speed with Comprehension," introduces reading speed and teaches techniques that will allow students to increase their reading speed. Techniques presented in Chapter 11, "Higher-level Reading Speed," will help students double or triple their reading speed while maintaining their level of comprehension.

10 | Reading Speed with Comprehension

WHAT IS SPEED READING? Does it mean speeding through books at three or four thousand words a minute? Trading comprehension for speed, or giving up enjoyment? No, no, and no. Speed reading as it's presented here is a way to increase speed in a realistic way while maintaining or improving comprehension and enjoyment. In talking to families about speed instruction we should point out that their students will be learning reading speed *with* comprehension.

Unfortunately, some types of learning disabilities can make it difficult or impossible for a student to learn speed reading. Individuals who *must* murmur to themselves to understand what they read are not good candidates. In addition, students whose native language is not English can also have problems learning to read faster. So when you speak with parents before beginning a course of speed reading, you want to be optimistic and encouraging, but if you have any doubts, acknowledge that there are some students who will not benefit, and that the only way to tell for sure if speed-reading instruction is right for a particular individual is to try it.

Introduction to Reading Speed

Why read faster?

It might seem at first glance that teaching speed reading is a luxury or maybe even a gimmick—certainly not a necessity in the same way comprehension instruction or phonics is. However, for a student who needs to read faster, it *is* a necessity. Students who read slowly often become bogged down in their work. This state can lead to "overwhelm" and make it more likely they will give up. They lose sight of the overview, have trouble remembering what they've read since the end is so far removed from the beginning, and may blame books, teachers, or reading itself for their problems, not realizing that the culprit is their slow reading speed. Learning to read faster has turned the tide for many, many students, moving them from apathetic to willing readers when nothing else could.

Most students find speed reading highly motivating. It has an aura of sophistication. Students know it's not remedial work, and yet it is easy to learn. Also, since it is motivating, most students are willing to practice speed reading even if they aren't agreeable to doing any other type of reading practice and even if previously they haven't been willing to read anything at all.

Beyond the beginning practice stages, speed reading helps students become more enthusiastic readers by making it easier and less time-consuming for them to get through their books and helping them feel more "on top of things." It also allows students to gain an overview of their reading rather than becoming bogged down in the details. Finally, learning to read faster may actually improve recall.

Speed reading is relatively easy to teach. Many of the techniques used to aid comprehension can be put to work again with slight variations to teach reading speed. Because the techniques are dual-purpose, students can improve their comprehension as they work on reading speed. Finally, learning the basics of speed reading paves the way for skimming and scanning, both essential skills for proficient reading.

What students can expect from their speed-reading course

Here's how a typical speed-reading course might be described to the student.

- You will be able to increase your reading speed by 50 percent. Some students double or even triple their rates.
- The course takes about six weeks if you have adequate comprehension to start with.
- You will need to practice 45 minutes a day, five days a week.
- You will end the course with better or at least the same level of comprehension than when you started. Your comprehension will go down temporarily when you begin working on your speed, but will come back up quickly.
- For the most part, you can practice on books you enjoy. At the beginning you will need to read books that are fairly easy for you, but as your speed improves, you can practice on your school books. Even so, there are some books—your chemistry text, for instance—that you will always have to read slowly.
- The average reading speed for eighth graders is 225 words per minute, and that's roughly what you need to be reading in order to get through

your schoolwork comfortably in grades seven through nine. We'll talk about goals for other grades later.

- You will probably feel more like doing your schoolwork when you can read faster.
- Using speed-reading techniques will help your concentration and may make your reading more enjoyable.
- You will learn and practice three or four different speed-reading techniques that can be used to suit your purpose and desired speed.
- Once you learn the speed-reading techniques, your reading speed will keep improving for up to a year if you continue to practice, even if you are not receiving any instruction.
- Learning the techniques and using them will improve all your reading. You will actually develop better eye and brain habits that will rub off on your reading even when you are not actively using speed techniques.
- In a manner of speaking, *your eye trains your brain*, and simply working on visual tracking can help in unexpected ways.
- Even though learning speed reading can be a breakthrough for you, it's not magic, and for it to work, you must have the desire to read faster. *It's also necessary for you to practice for the required amount of time exactly the way I ask you to do it.*

How much of the above information you tell your student depends on the student, of course. You'll find you can get away with a little bit more talking with girls, older students, and more highly motivated kids. With younger children or those with attention deficit disorder (ADD) you'll want to keep the explanations to a minimum and just launch into the exercises.

When to start speed reading

With some students it makes sense to start teaching reading speed very early in the tutoring process, even before you introduce reading comprehension, and sometimes even before the evaluation is completed. Students who have motivational or behavior problems may need the boost that speed reading can provide. In that case, start speed-reading instruction with the LSU right after you test the student's speed and comprehension in the evaluation. Doing this can give immediate help to a teen who is discouraged about school and may quickly get a resistant student on your side.

READING SPEED: AN ANTIDEPRESSANT

Rachael, a high school student, was angry and depressed about being brought to a tutor and wanted nothing more than to walk out of her first session. I found out that she didn't like reading because it was tedious for her, so I started her on reading speed right away. Although she had barely read one book in her life, Rachael rapidly went from sullen to enthusiastic in her first hour when she saw how much faster she could read using the speed-reading techniques she learned. We continued speed reading and homework help for the first few weeks. Then I introduced comprehension instruction, which she badly needed but would not have tolerated earlier.

On the other hand, there are some learning disabled students who need a great deal of work on comprehension before they try to speed up, and starting them on speed reading too soon might have the effect of slowing them down in the long run.

Why people read slowly

The following script can be used to introduce speed reading to your students. I've included quite a bit of detail, but as always, adjust what you say to the age and maturity of the student.

Back in the thirties and forties, reading experts wanted to see if they could help people read faster. To do this, they needed to know why some people read more slowly and why some read faster. They found out some interesting things. First of all, they noticed that intelligence didn't seem to have much to do with reading speed.

The next step was to study the eye movements of people while they were reading. To do this, researchers drilled a small hole completely through a book from cover to cover, put a movie camera under the book, aimed it through the hole, and took pictures of people's eyes as they read. They noticed that fast readers read in phrases, or groups of words, and people who read slowly read one word at a time.

At this point I show by moving my hand on the page how it would look if a person were reading in phrases rather than one word at a time, how faster readers might pause briefly at the end of each phrase but slower readers pause for each word.

The pauses that the eye makes on the page are called eye fixations. The eye takes in material only when it is still—during the fixations. Fewer fixations mean faster reading.

In the studies, the fast readers were able to keep their eyes moving steadily from left to right, focusing on three or four words at a time. The slow readers, on the other hand, did a lot of rereading and backtracking because they hadn't taken in what they read in the first place. I show with my hand what backtracking would look like, reading a sentence and then going back over it once or twice.

Obviously, continual re-reading slows people down. The experts say that when a slow reader finishes reading a page, he has actually read it about five times because of these repetitions. Sometimes the reader was aware of going back over material but it can also happen that the reader has random eye movements he isn't aware of. I show with my hand how a person might be reading along, and then, for no good reason might momentarily skip to another location on the page and back.

Also, when the slower reader gets to the beginning of a line, he sometimes loses his place and ends up searching for the correct line. This might take only a split-second, but it could still slow the reader down because it would break his concentration. You can show this by moving your hand around uncertainly at the beginning of the line.

Another possible cause of slow reading is trouble focusing the eyes. Difficulty getting the eyes to focus on the same spot at the same time can take up energy and time. It would also take a lot of the fun out of reading. People with serious focusing, or visual tracking problems, might need to go to an optometrist who specializes in reading difficulties, and get special glasses and do eye exercises. But, short of that, we can do a lot in tutoring to help with tracking, and that in turn will improve reading speed.

Slow reading, then, usually is caused by poor visual or mental habits, and like most habits, can be corrected through practice with the right techniques. All that's needed is the desire to improve reading speed and a willingness to practice.

Students are usually surprised and relieved to hear that slow reading can be overcome. They may have thought of it as a character defect, a view perhaps reinforced by parents and teachers who tell them "of course you don't read well, because you never read," which may be true, but still isn't very helpful. The look of relief on the student's face when he learns about the causes of slow reading will encourage the teacher and may even be an informal indicator of the success of the speed-reading course to come.

In addition to having difficulties with visual tracking, some people move their mouths as they read, either making audible sounds or doing so silently. These movements, known as *vocalizing* and *subvocalizing*, may stand in the way of increasing reading speed. When readers who vocalize try to keep their mouths still, however, they may lose comprehension. To help students who vocalize speed up, teach the speed-reading techniques described here, but don't try to make a student quit moving his mouth until he is ready to do so. Students often automatically drop the vocalization as their reading speed increases. If a student is still vocalizing after a few weeks of speed-reading practice, you can help him break the habit simply by having him keep his mouth closed tight as he reads. On the other hand, if a student who mutters is reading faster than 250 words per minute, the muttering probably isn't doing any harm.

Most people can overcome their tendency to vocalize, but there are others who cannot. Some individuals with learning disabilities *must* subvocalize to understand what they are reading. Even though it slows them down to subvocalize, it doesn't work to try to take the crutch away since no amount of practice removes the need for subvocalization. Only experimentation over time will tell if that's the case.

Using the Long Smooth Underline (LSU) to Increase Reading Speed

I introduce the LSU this way:

> The experts who studied reading speed devised a reading technique that can help smooth out eye movements and make it easier for you to keep your place as you read. Obviously that could help you speed up. It's a technique you already know because you've been using it to help with concentration, only now you're going to use it to increase your reading speed. Here I demonstrate, moving my hand along smoothly, fingers curved, half-way down the space under the line.

> The LSU is very versatile, and can be used both for helping you concentrate and for helping you read faster. You are the one who decides which way you use it. If you want to concentrate, for example on a textbook, use the LSU more slowly. If you want to read fast, maybe on a novel, move your hand faster, and your eyes will be pulled along by the motion of your hand. Of course, as before, you don't want to look straight at your hand, or it will confuse you. You just see your hand moving out of the corner of your eye, and that is what "pulls you along." You don't even have to try to read faster. You just move your hand and it happens automatically.

Calculating baseline reading speed

Before you have the student practice the LSU, do a timed reading to determine a base rate to help you track future improvement. You may have a timing from the initial evaluation (Chapter 3) if you had your student do a *Reading Drill*, but it's likely that your student's speed has improved since then as a result of working on comprehension. So you will probably want to do another timed reading now. To do a timing from an article or book:

1. Have the student read for two minutes and mark his beginning and ending points in the book. (Yellow post-it notes are handy markers.)

2. As a comprehension check, have him tell you what he's read. In all speed timings, the student's comprehension score should be 70 percent or higher. There's no use charting the reading speed if comprehension falls below that.

3. Then calculate his speed as follows.

4. Determine the average number of words per line in the reading selection. You don't need to find the mathematical average, just the median. To do this, count all the words except for *a* and *the* in each of five lines and estimate the number that would fall in the middle by crossing off the lowest and highest figures.

5. After you have a figure for the average words per line, count the total number of lines the student read. Put partial lines together to count as whole lines.

6. Divide the number of lines read by two since this was a two minute timing.

7. Multiply the number of lines read in one minute by the average words per line. This is the student's reading speed, expressed in words per minute.

8. If you wish to time the student's reading of an entire article, rather than for two minutes, count the total lines read and multiply by the average words per line. The result equals the total number of words read. Then divide the total words read by the time it took to read them. Express the number of minutes and seconds in decimal form—for example, one minute and 15 seconds equals 1.25. Dividing the total number of words read by the time it took to read the article equals the student's reading speed, expressed in words per minute.

9. Show your student how to figure his own reading speed and begin a chart for him to record his improvement (Figure 10.1, discussed in the next section).

Speed goals by grade

We all know it is easier to improve if we have a goal to aim for, and this is particularly true in speed reading. The figures below are a general guide to appropriate speed goals for students. These are goals for a hypothetical student who is reading material a little below his "challenge" level. "Below challenge level" means that the material is easy enough for the student to be familiar with almost all the words in the passage and to have a good understanding of the content, provided he reads with moderate care.

Grade 6   180 to 225 words per minute
Grade 7   200 to 225 wpm
Grade 8   225 to 250 wpm
Grade 9   225 to 275 wpm
Grade 10 250 to 300 wpm
Grade 11 275 to 350 wpm
Grade 12 300 to 400 wpm

Some teachers may think these goals are too high, too low, or simply too arbitrary, but it's necessary to come up with some sort of guide and then adjust it to fit the individual. The best way to develop a clear idea of realistic goals is to take several students through the course and keep track of their progress.

When presented a goal at the outset, most teens will work hard to reach it *if* they understand they will be given the tools to do so. After doing the two-minute timing, you might present the goal to the student like this: "Here's where you are now and here's where you need to be. It may look like a big jump, but it's not going to be that hard. You just have to work on it, and you'll be learning some techniques that will really help you pick up your speed."

So far, you've gone over what to expect of the speed-reading course with your student, explained why people read slowly, and introduced the idea of using the LSU for increasing reading speed. You've done a timing to determine your student's current speed, you've shown the student how to time his own reading, and you've discussed possible speed goals. Now it's time to have your student actually start using the LSU to increase his reading speed.

Script for teaching the LSU

This script for teaching the LSU builds on what your student has already learned about the technique.

As you learned before with the LSU, if you move your hand faster, you will read faster automatically. You don't have to *try* to read faster. Your eyes will be pulled along by the movement of your hand. When you start, don't try to read super-fast; just read a little faster than you usually do. You can gradually increase your speed as you go along. It's all right for your comprehension to go down a little when you first start reading faster; in fact, it's normal. Don't slow down. Your comprehension will come back up after a few pages of practice. If you slow back down every time you don't understand something, you'll never increase your speed.

I know I'm switching rules on you here. Before, I always wanted you to know exactly what you were reading, even if you had to slow down or reread to get it. But now that you are able to do that, we need to move to this next stage. In this type of reading, it's as if your eyes start out by going fast, but your brain is lagging behind, and then, after a few pages, your brain catches up with your eyes. So even though it's a little uncomfortable not to understand what you're reading at first, stick with the process, because it really does work, and the feeling of discomfort goes away quickly.

Even so, you may have to go through the same discomfort every time you practice, or at least every time you increase your speed, but just remember it's temporary. It is best not to practice on a book that you need to read for school unless you are planning on re-reading.

Have your student try the LSU in the tutoring session. First, make sure he is doing the technique correctly physically, then ask him to read a few paragraphs to see if he comprehends what he is reading. If he does, he is ready to start practicing at home on his own.

Students do best when they have practice sessions laid out for them. Here's a plan that works well for most students:

Read for 10 minutes using the LSU then do a two minute timing and enter your speed on your graph. Note your comprehension. This is for you to judge yourself.

Read 20 minutes your regular way, meaning without the LSU. (Ten minutes for a middle school student.) The LSU can become tedious, and practicing without it lets your hand rest.

Read 10 more minutes using the LSU and time yourself again at the end of your practice session. Graph your timing, as before. Bring your graph and the book you are reading to each tutoring session.

If the student does not understand what he is reading, however, keep practicing in class to see if you can help him gain the understanding he needs. You might assign the technique for a week of home practice to see if his comprehension kicks in. If not, you may wish to jump ahead and teach him phrasing as a speed technique to use instead of the LSU, or you may temporarily discontinue the speed-reading instruction, wait until he has developed more readiness for it, and try again later.

I require students to time and graph their readings during their home practice sessions. One way for them to record their progress is by using a reading graph like the one in Figure 10.1.

If the student is practicing the LSU at home, it is important to check frequently to find out how the technique is working for him and how he feels his speed and comprehension are progressing. Ask him to be specific regarding what is working or what "speed bumps" he may have hit. Only intuition and experience can teach you how to help him through all the difficulties, but some of the possibilities are covered next.

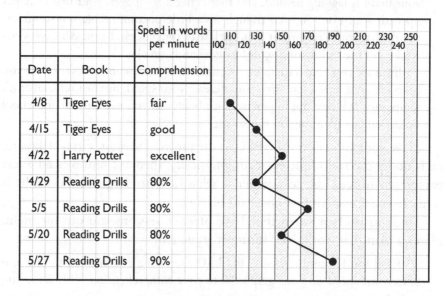

Figure 10.1. Graph of speed-reading progress.

Troubleshooting

For some students who are studying speed reading, it's smooth sailing from here on out, but for others there will be setbacks. The following section addresses ways of helping students find solutions to their most common reading and study problems.

To understand this section, imagine a student and tutor discussing the student's complaints. The tutor's possible responses are set down in script form. The tutor's questions and comments would not be a running stream of talk as it appears here, however, but a two-way conversation dependent for direction on the student's responses.

Can't concentrate

Do you have a quiet place to work at home? Can you get one? Do you have something on your mind, either good or bad that could be distracting you? Would you like to talk about it? Is the book you're reading interesting to you? Do you want to switch books? Is it too quiet in my office? Do you want the radio on? (Some kids *need* noise.)

Suggestion: Introduce more comprehension checks for yourself. For instance, during your home practice keep using the LSU to gain speed, but continue doing tellbacks, too, the way you used to. You could do a one-minute timing, then a tellback, another timing, another tellback. Or speed read a chapter or a section, and go back to doing a written summary for each one. Knowing you will need to remember what you are reading will help you focus. Work with your parents if you need to.

Can't speed up

You may have the feeling you are doing something wrong by speeding up and losing comprehension. Or you may be "stuck in a rut." In either case, a speed-reading technique called "pacing" will almost certainly help. (Pacing is covered in Chapter 11.)

The LSU bothers me

Try it for a week, and if you still don't like it, don't use it. Try phrasing instead. Or try using a card or bookmark to keep your place. A small card you can move from side to side works best.

I'm bored

If you have a good book and you're still bored, it probably means you're not reading fast enough or concentrating hard enough. *Nothing is more boring than not paying attention.* If you were moving faster, you probably wouldn't be bored.

I can't find a book I like

Ask your friends and your parents what books they're reading and try those books. Keep trying. The first three or four chapters in a book are often boring, difficult, or both, even for people who like to read. You just have to keep reading and push through the boring parts. Reading faster will help you do that. What kind of TV shows do you like? You might look for books with similar themes. Go to the school or public library or a bookstore and browse.

I don't like to read

You may not really enjoy reading during the first few months of tutoring. This is not due to a character flaw. It just may take that long for you to develop the skills and attitudes needed to enjoy reading. Some students have told me they didn't really start to enjoy reading until they had read 10 or 12 books. Hang in there, and don't blame yourself, me, or the books if you're not enjoying reading. It'll come.

Reading flexibility

Now that we've talked about reading speed, and looked at solutions to some potential reading problems, let's talk about balancing the demands and needs associated with reading.

ENCOURAGING READING FLEXIBILITY

Robert was an adult student, a Ph. D. clinical psychologist who wanted to improve his reading speed. He had a great deal of professional material that he needed to get through for his job but he also had a backlog of recreational reading he wanted to tackle. The words "get through" and "tackle" describe his attitude toward reading. I learned that Robert approached all reading with the same deliberate care. For instance, it took him more than an hour to get through the morning paper because he read it the same way he read professional journal articles—as if he were going to be questioned on them by a doctoral committee. And talk about tellbacks! He could tell me almost verbatim what he had read in any given book or article. So Robert had thoroughness and he had recall, but he was lacking flexibility. He did not distinguish among the different types of reading he had to do, and he read newspapers, journals, and novels all the same way.

The key for Robert was to identify his purpose for reading each book or article and vary his speed and style accordingly. After some instruction in reading speed and skimming, he was able to speed up his recreational reading (when he wanted to—some novels still merited a slow, enjoyable reading), he learned to skim the newspaper, and he read journal articles and professional books carefully in places and more quickly in others. Now he categorized his reading "for fun," "of passing interest," and "to remember," and read accordingly. He had gained reading flexibility.

Many teens lack reading flexibility simply because they are inexperienced readers. I introduce the concept of flexibility to them with Robert's story and explain that of my students, doctors and lawyers have the most trouble with flexibility because they read everything as if a life or a court case depends on their reading. This introduction helps teens understand the problem, and it also puts them in good company. Later, as we proceed through the speed-reading course, I can point out the need for reading flexibility again.

Summary of Key Points

- Slow reading is a habit that can be reversed.
- Learning to read faster will help students complete their school

assignments more easily, boosting their confidence and making reading more enjoyable.

- Techniques that aid concentration and comprehension also can be used to increase speed.
- Students often double or even triple their reading speed after six weeks' practice using the techniques described here.
- The LSU technique improves visual tracking, increases reading speed, and even enhances cognitive abilities.
- Reading growth is marked by flexibility, and not speed alone.

The **LSU** can be very helpful, but sometimes more is needed. People also have their own best method of reading, and the LSU is not everyone's favorite speed technique. The techniques discussed in the next chapter—pacing, phrasing, skimming, and scanning—may be used to solve reading problems or provide further opportunities for faster reading.

11 | Higher-level Reading Speed

MANY STUDENTS WILL WISH TO ACHIEVE higher speeds than is possible with the LSU alone. In addition, they will need to be able to find answers to questions in a textbook quickly or gain an overview of a reading selection without reading the entire piece. For students who are stuck at a particular speed or who need more advanced work on textbook reading, the techniques of pacing, phrasing, skimming, and scanning will offer opportunity and relief.

Pacing

Pacing is for people who are stuck in a rut. They've been reading at the same slow speed for several weeks and don't show much sign of budging. Pacing is a great way to get "un-stuck."

The basic idea of pacing is that you set a speed goal for your student and tell her how fast she needs to be reading each page. Then, as she reads, you'll ask her to hurry up or slow down depending on how fast she's reading compared with the goal.

After you read through this explanation and have tried pacing for yourself, go over the purpose of pacing with your student and show her how it's done. You don't want her to feel she is being hurried through her reading by a bossy adult. You want her to recognize that pacing is a tool that will help her feel less stressed about her reading load at school, that will help her on the reading sections of the SAT and ACT, and that might even allow her to have more free time. Here is an analogy:

Imagine you are on the highway driving along at 55 miles an hour, which feels fast, but then you decide you'd like to get to your destination sooner, so you speed up to 75. At first 75 seems impossibly fast, and you feel a little unsure of yourself, but then you find you are totally alert—you have to be at that speed—and you are able to see clearly everything that is happening around you. You begin to relax but maintain your mental alertness, and that's the key here—to be physically relaxed but mentally alert.

Then you slow down. Maybe you entered a section of the highway with a lower speed limit, so you back your speed down to 55 again—but now, 55 seems slow! Why is that? It's only slow by comparison.

This analogy applies to the pacing technique in several ways:

Slow and *fast* are relative ideas that can be changed more easily than we might think.

When you are reading fast, like driving at high speeds, you need to be mentally alert but physically relaxed. So aim for a state in which you feel totally in control, and no matter how fast you're going remember to keep breathing.

You will feel more comfortable at 55 after you've been going at a much faster speed—say 75. And that's the point of the pacing: to help wake up some brain cells you haven't been using and teach them to process at higher speeds. After that, regular speeds are a piece of cake.

Introducing pacing

To introduce pacing you might say: "It looks like you actually have the ability to read quite a bit faster than you are reading now. You're in the habit of reading slowly, but that's a habit that can be changed, like any other. I'm going to show you a fairly painless way of improving your reading speed right away. It's called *pacing*. You might find it slightly stressful at first, but you won't be doing it for more than a few pages at a time, so it shouldn't be too bad."

Setting the target speed for pacing

In preparation for pacing you'll need a stopwatch and an interesting, moderately easy book to practice on. A novel such as *Two Old Women* by Velma Wallis will do well. Before you start, pick a target speed for your student that is about 25 to 50 words faster than she is currently reading.

To determine how many seconds it will take to read one page at the desired speed, follow these steps:

1. Find the average number of *words per line*, as you did for speed timings. (Count the number of words on each of four or five lines and pick the median.)
2. Find the average *lines per page*. To do that, simply find an average looking page and count the lines.

3. Multiply these two figures together: average *words per line* X average *lines per page* = average *words per page*.

4. Divide the number of words per page by the target speed you have chosen for your student.

5. When you divide the words per page by the target speed, the answer will be in minutes and some decimal fraction of a minute, which you then convert to minutes and seconds.

The result is the time it should take your student to read one page for the pacing exercise. A good goal is the student's current reading rate plus 25 or 50 words.

SETTING THE TARGET SPEED: AN EXAMPLE

Say there are 250 words on a page, and you want your student to be reading 225 words a minute. 250 (words per page) divided by 225 (words per minute) is 1.11, or one minute and 11 hundredths. To convert the 11 hundredths of a minute to seconds, multiply the decimal 0.11 by 60. The result is 7 seconds. Put the number of seconds together with the one minute, and you will have your target speed for one page: 1 minute and 7 seconds. Thus, it should take the student 1 minute and 7 seconds to read a page if the goal is 225 wpm and there are 250 words per page.

Now that you have a target speed in mind and know how many seconds it should take your student to read one page, calculate her target speed for a quarter, half, and three-quarters of a page, and jot the figures down to use during the pacing exercise. Here's the math for the example we've been using:

To get the speed for half a page, divide 1:07 (67 seconds) by 2 = 34 seconds (rounded up). Then divide in half again to get the desired speed for one-fourth page =17 seconds. For three-fourths of a page, add the target speeds for one-fourth and one-half page.

Make a graph like this for yourself to use during the exercise:
Target speeds, in seconds, for reading one page
¼ page: 0:17
½ page: 0:34
¾ page: 0:51
1 page: 1:07

Finally, using your hand, demonstrate for the student approximately how fast she'll need to read to reach the target speed. Obviously, you'd want to practice with a timer before showing your student.

The pacing process

To do the pacing, time the student as she reads, telling her to speed up or slow down to meet the target speed you have chosen. It's probably best to wait a page or two before asking her to speed up, though, just to give her a chance to settle in. Of course, if the student is reading at the desired speed, you don't need to say anything. Here's how the pacing process can be explained to the student:

I'll tell you when to start, and I'll tell you when you should be a quarter of the way done, half done, three quarters, and at the bottom of the page. If you're going too fast, which is usually what happens, I may tell you to slow down. On the other hand, if it looks like you're on a roll, I may not say anything, and will just let you keep reading even if you're going faster than the goal. If you're behind where you should be, I'll tell you where on the page you ought to be. For instance, if you're supposed to be three-fourths of the way through but you're only half done, I'll say "three-fourths," and you'll just need to read faster to catch up. When you're supposed to be done, I'll say "bottom of the page." Again, if you're not there, you just need to read as fast as you can to get there, and don't worry about comprehension. If I don't say anything, it means you're going the right speed, and you can just keep going. You might read several pages without my saying anything.

It may seem surprising that I might want you to slow down. Though higher speeds sometimes feel too fast, it can also happen that when people speed up, they may not be aware of how much faster they're reading than usual. They might be reading 50 or even 75 words a minute faster than they ordinarily do, but they aren't even aware they have speeded up. The goal is to speed up gradually over a period of weeks, and not to make a huge jump all at once. An increase of 10-25 words a week is plenty.

That's about it for speed. But what about comprehension? The idea here is that when you first start, you don't need to worry at all about comprehension. You may read two or three pages with little idea of what you've read, but as you go along, your comprehension will kick in. Your brain will catch up with your eyes. It may take a little while for this to happen, but it almost certainly will. It may take six to eight pages of pacing before you have any level of understanding. If you continue not understanding for more than a few days, we'll simply lower the target speed for a while.

Now go ahead and start pacing. Stop every few pages and ask your student how she's doing. Is she comfortable? How's her comprehension? Give her lots of praise if she's able to keep up and even more if she understands what she's reading. Some people have no drop in comprehension at all, which is nice. Others understand nothing. If that's the case, keep trying unless you see no progress at all after several 10- to 20-minute practice sessions.

After all these "how-to's," you might still be wondering if pacing really works. Definitely! I rarely get a student who does not benefit from pacing, as long as the target speed is reasonable and we keep at it persistently. Moreover, it sometimes happens that a student goes beyond expectations to make a huge breakthrough as soon as she tries pacing, increasing her speed 50 or even 100 words a minute right away, and only has to practice pacing occasionally after that to keep from falling back into old habits. So it's definitely worth trying. As with other techniques you've learned, it's not necessary to do this exercise constantly to maintain higher reading speeds. The mental and visual skills learned from pacing will transfer onto other reading tasks, and after that, all of the student's reading will become faster as a result of doing pacing occasionally.

On the other hand, what should you do in the unlikely, but possible, event that pacing isn't helping, and your student is still stuck? At that point it's time to become a bit more assertive. Warn the student first, then move a card down the page at the estimated target speed, covering up everything the student should already have read, essentially giving her no choice but to read at the target speed.

Practicing pacing at home

About 10 minutes of pacing at one time is enough. It's a demanding practice and can be quite tiring mentally. Sometimes you might want to ask students to practice pacing at home with a parent, at least if the student and parent work well together. If you do this, you'll want to have the parent come in to a session so you can teach him or her how to do the exercise. Allow plenty of time to go over it to make sure the parent understands the rationale for the exercise, just as the student does.

Some students either can't or won't work with their parents on reading speed, but they are still able to do pacing on their own, though they'll need to do it in a slightly different form. Tell your student to use a timer that beeps, pick a target speed, determine the amount of time required to read at that speed, and set the clock to sound after the correct number of seconds. To the student: "Try to reach the end of the page by the time you hear the beep. Keep reading until this speed feels comfortable, or until you're sick of it, whichever comes first." This method is not quite as good as the actual pacing exercise, since pacing works partly because of the feedback and expectations from the other person, but the do-it-yourself exercise can still help.

Phrasing for Higher Speeds

The next technique, *phrasing*, is one you have encountered before in this book. Phrasing is a versatile actor. It appeared in a bit part early on, where it assisted in oral reading. Now it has returned as the star in a technique for helping students gain higher reading speeds. Here's a script for teaching phrasing to increase reading speed. The intended audience is a student who has not previously used the phrasing technique.

Phrasing step by step

You can teach phrasing using these steps, beginning with an introduction to the technique. This teaching script explains the process.

Your speed has improved enough that you are now ready for the next speed-reading technique. So in a way, you've graduated. This technique, called *phrasing*, is to help you gain speeds that are higher than you'd be able to reach using the LSU. Some people swear by it, but others prefer to stick with the LSU, probably just because they're used to it. Both are valuable techniques and can be used in different circumstances, but the only way you'll know which you want to use is to learn phrasing and practice it, then decide.

Now that you've been using the LSU for a while, you may have noticed that the faster you read the more tiresome the process becomes. Your hand gets tired, your brain and eyes may resist, and yet when you quit using the LSU, your speed may taper off. Phrasing is the solution to these problems.

Phrasing is a hand technique like the LSU that is primarily used for speeds above 250 words per minute. A phrase should be somewhere between one and four words in length. The words in the phrase should make sense together and should *sound* like a unit.

Start phrasing by marking words in your book into phrases with a pencil. At the beginning, say each phrase aloud and put a slash after it. When you can do this easily, quit marking, but still touch each phrase with your hand and read it out loud. (Reading out loud is just a temporary step when you're first learning phrasing.) When you "touch" the phrase, you actually are only putting your fingers under it, holding your hand in the same position as you do for the LSU, with the fingers curved, together, and below the line.

Practice until you are comfortable with oral phrasing then switch to silent reading.

Continue reading silently. Move from reading in phrases that are based on meaning into a more regular rhythm of touching down three times per line, then gradually decrease the touchdowns to two per line. You will automatically speed up as you do this. When you are able to read consistently with only two touchdowns per line, you'll find that you are no longer actually dividing the text into phrases according to which words make sense together. (This is good, not something to be avoided.) Instead, you'll be touching in a regular pattern with the first pause about one-third of the way along the line, and the second pause about two-thirds of the way. This should be a quick, automatic movement. Don't spend time looking and trying to figure out where to touch down—just do it. Something interesting happens at this point. Even though you are no longer dividing sentences into phrases with your hand, your eyes and brain will continue to read in phrases.

Your speed will keep improving as you practice phrasing, although the phrasing technique can still be used to read slowly and with greater attention to detail if you choose to do that.

Aim for 10 minutes of practice twice a day. You may find phrasing so helpful you'll want to use it all the time.

To reach higher speeds, keep moving your hand at a consistent speed. Force yourself to keep going. Try to think in phrases rather than in individual words, and join those phrases together in your mind to make whole images and ideas.

Phrasing and affirmations

Some students find that use of affirmations can help them read better. Affirmations are repeated positive statements people tell themselves with the goal of changing their psychological and emotional reality. If you think your student might be receptive, you could introduce affirmations as follows. "Tell yourself that the 'ideas on the page will simply flow off the page and into my mind.' And that 'the ideas will automatically enter my head, all with no conscious effort on my part.'" Add that this is to happen without your having to concentrate on individual words—that's the connection with phrasing and the reason I've included affirmations here. Affirmations really can help some people, so it's worth a try, but it's sort of like Tinker Bell, the fairy in *Peter Pan*: for it to work, you have to believe in it.

When to use phrasing

How will your student know when to use the LSU and when to do phrasing instead? Some people choose to use one technique or the other exclusively, and that's fine. But for people who use both, the LSU may be the best technique to use at the beginning of a book since it's a painless way to get started on material that can sometimes be hard to get into. Then, after the first few pages, the reader can switch to phrasing to gain higher speeds. If the student comes to difficult material and needs to slow down, she can still keep using the phrasing technique. While it may seem like a contradiction, phrasing is good for the two opposite ends of the spectrum: slow reading that calls for serious concentration and faster reading that will allow the student to move into a groove.

Throughout the pacing and phrasing exercises, it is still necessary for the student to keep visualizing as she reads. Also, she should still be encouraged to stop for mental tellbacks.

At this point, as always after a block of new learning, show your student what she's accomplished, and tell her how it's going to help her, not just in school, but for the rest of her life. It is also worth noting that if the student has become fairly skillful at phrasing but is still not achieving speeds higher than about 250 words per minute, the remedy is to combine phrasing with pacing.

The LSU, pacing, and phrasing techniques may each require several weeks, or even months, of practice before they become automatic. However, mastery of these skills can open up a new world of reading enjoyment for your students, as well as the power, control and efficiency that come with good reading.

Scanning and Skimming

Scanning and skimming are methods of finding main ideas or specific pieces of information in a hurry. Scanning means glossing over a passage to locate a phrase or a particular piece of information; skimming means reading quickly to find the main idea, or merely to get the gist, of a passage.

Not everyone can learn the high-speed skills of scanning and skimming, but they are highly rewarding for those who do. Ask yourself what an ability to find facts or main ideas quickly could do for you, and then put the same question to your student. Though you as an adult can see the benefits, a teenager may not. Convincing students of the benefits of scanning and skimming can be as easy as simply giving a demonstration, however.

Start with scanning

Scanning, or picking a piece of information off a page quickly, is the easier of the two high-speed techniques to teach, so let's start with it. As preparation, explain the "grocery store method" of scanning:

> If you are looking for information about a particular business in the yellow pages, and you know the street it's on, you don't have to read all of each listing to find the address you are looking for. All you have to do is pick one word, in this case the name of the street, form a strong mental image of the word, and start looking for something that matches that image in your head.

This analogy explains how to do that and why it works.

If you were to go into a grocery store looking for hamburger you wouldn't have to look at each item you saw in the store and name it for yourself—bread, milk, pickles—to figure out if it was the thing you were looking for. All you have to do is have a mental image of ground meat, and you can easily discard everything that doesn't match. That's a much more efficient way to find things than having to look at each item you see and identify it.

By the same token, the key to successful scanning is to have a clear mental image of the word or phrase you are searching for, then pull your hand down the page of listings quickly looking for something that matches your image. Say you are looking for a motorcycle dealer in the yellow pages. You don't have to read all the listings. Just glance through them quickly, as if you were walking through the grocery store in a hurry. You don't even have to form a mental image of the entire address. You just look for part of it: the street name or the first number in the address, for instance, and then scan for anything that matches the picture you've placed in your mind.

Using a phone book to demonstrate, have your student pick an item for *you* to find—a phone number, address, or phrase. As you look for that piece of information, explain your own mental process—what you are looking for, and what you're ignoring. (Naturally, you'd want to become fairly skilled at scanning before putting yourself to the test.)

Now have the student try. Without revealing to her what you are looking at, pick a topic from the yellow pages you think she might be interested in—let's say, sports equipment. Pick some piece of information that would be fairly easy for her to find such as a particular address. Have the student go through the drill several more times, finding prices, services, etc., that you ask her to locate.

Finally, try the white pages. This exercise can be turned into a game. How fast can your student locate key words? Can she shave a few seconds off her time?

I tell students how I once avoided missing an airplane at the airport because I was able to skim the departure listings quickly, allowing me to get to the gate on time.

After the phonebook search, which most students find fairly easy, try scanning using a textbook. Start by asking your student to find a particular phrase on a given page. The principle here is the same as with the phone book exercise, meaning the student must visualize and search for a key word, but now she must also decide on which key word from the phrase she should use to find the pertinent information.

When your student is able to locate simple facts, broaden the task by having her find the answers to study questions. This requires her to pick a phrase from the question and narrow it to a key word. If she is successful at finding the answers to study questions in a textbook, she is ready to start skimming.

Try skimming

People often skim at two or three times their normal reading rate. Skimming isn't meant to be an in-depth reading, but it can help your student get an overview, find the answer to a question, or decide whether a section or a whole book is worth returning to later for a more careful reading. Skimming is a very useful, even essential, skill for college-bound students.

Even so, I've met quite a few bright college seniors who have never learned to skim. When they pick up skimming in a speed-reading class they are astounded. "Why didn't I know this before?! This makes all the difference in the world!"

Not everyone is capable of learning to skim, however. People with learning disabilities, ADD, or dyslexia, for example, are the most likely to have trouble with skimming. That's probably not something you'd want to mention to a student who's having trouble, but keep it in mind as you set your own teaching goals. Even though learning to skim is not particularly easy—it can take several months—it's so helpful for those who do succeed at it, it's worth trying with everyone.

Introduce skimming with this overview:

> When you were scanning, you were merely looking for a piece of information. Skimming, on the other hand, means finding the main idea of a passage. To skim, read the first sentence of the paragraph at your normal speed, then pull your hand down quickly over the rest of the paragraph, mentally picking out five or six key words as you go. Visually, you'll see all the words, but your mind registers only the most important ones.
>
> Reading the first sentence helps you focus on the main idea, which is likely to be found there. Picking out the most important, or key, words from the rest of the paragraph gives you a summary that's a bit more in-depth than the main idea alone, but still a very quick overview. Attempt to find three to six key words from a paragraph in three or four seconds.

Some people find it difficult to pick out key words in this way but are able to get a general idea of the subject anyway, so finding the key words should be optional.

Read the following suggestions, try them yourself, then give your student the opportunity to learn them. You may have to teach the material several times over a period of months before it "takes." Your student has already had some practice finding answers to study questions, but this exercise carries the activity a bit further. For a first skimming exercise, use a book that is written on an easy high school level with clear factual articles accompanied by study questions. *Reading Drills* works well for this purpose. Have your student look over the study questions in the book, then without reading the article, skim to find the answers, one question at a time. Here's how I introduce and teach the task.

Pretend you were supposed to read this article for school and answer the study questions. But what if you ran out of time and couldn't get it done? That could happen to anyone. What could you do to answer the study questions on material you hadn't read if you were given only a few minutes? Skim, of course! Don't take this as permission not to read the textbook. This is just to show you how handy skimming can be.

Take a study question from the book, single out a key word or phrase to concentrate on, and skim to find the answer to the question. To skim, read the first sentence of each paragraph until you find a part of the article that seems likely to contain the information you are looking for, then pull your hand down the page quickly, looking for key words to tell you if you are in the right spot.

Here's the rationale for doing it this way: You've already have some clue as to the main idea of the paragraph from the first sentence, and when you pick out the key words later on in the paragraph, you are just seeing whether you actually guessed right in the first place. You are also checking to see if the subject changed unexpectedly part way through the paragraph.

Note to the tutor: If you can do this (and not all even skilled readers can), demonstrate to the student how to find pertinent key words by skimming a paragraph *aloud*. Don't be discouraged if you are not able to do this exercise aloud right away. It may take a few weeks for you to gain proficiency at saying the key words aloud as you read. Even if you can't do the demonstration this way, you can still teach your students to locate key words. Just underline them as you read, either with a pencil or by hand, instead of saying them.

The main pitfall in skimming, other than simply not understanding, is that students can get so engrossed in their reading that they slow down and end up reading the entire section at their regular rate, which defeats the purpose. You can help correct this problem by again using a card to pull down over the page at the desired speed, in effect giving the student no choice but to skim.

Some students will pick out all the wrong words, choosing irrelevant ones and skipping important ones, so work to help them see where they are on track or off, even to the point of discussing the relative importance of individual words. Reassure the student beforehand that it may take several tries, even several months, to become adept at skimming, but that the only way to learn it is to practice.

Finally, have your student read from an ordinary textbook or factual article using the same techniques she's been practicing all along, skimming at speeds of 500 to 700 words per minute, and identifying main ideas as she goes. After you have practiced skimming for main idea, have your student try doing some tellbacks from her skimming. To do this, she will simply skim a paragraph, look away and tell what she got out of it. People are often able to absorb a surprising amount of the material even though they are not doing a thorough reading. Give lots of encouragement and praise for anything your student accomplishes in the way of skimming. This is a challenging area, and *any* progress is an accomplishment.

Are Other Speed-reading Books Necessary?

At this point, you may wish to purchase some books on speed reading to become familiar with methods other than the ones you've learned here. It can't hurt, and it might help you with your own skills. However, I don't recommend teaching teens any methods other than the ones described in this book. In my experience, middle school and high school students usually end up confused and frustrated by them.

For instance, one common speed-reading exercise asks students to avoid saying words mentally as they read. Instead, readers are supposed to lift whole ideas from the book without voicing the words mentally. Exercises that try to stop readers from thinking the words hardly ever work, and they can be frustrating. A better alternative is to ask the student to pretend he has a "radio in his head" and to simply turn the volume down a little. And instead of skipping everything that's not a "key word," as some books advise, you can tell students they'll still *see* all the words in a sentence or a paragraph, but that they shouldn't focus on the unimportant words.

By using tellbacks, the LSU, phrasing, pacing, and skimming, students will automatically decrease their mental vocalizations, shift focus away from nonessential words, read in units of thought, and zero in on key concepts. If they've succeeded with the exercises presented here, they have already accomplished what's taught in most speed-reading books.

SAT/ACT Vocabulary and Reading

Parents may want private tutoring instead of a commercial SAT/ACT test preparation course for their college-bound offspring, especially for students with weaknesses in reading comprehension, speed or vocabulary. If students have issues with skills, beginning to prepare for the SAT/ACT can be a moment of truth. Teens who have never been serious before about improving their reading may suddenly see that it is in their best interests to do so. Thus, between eager parents and kids who have sudden-onset motivation, you are likely to have an earnest, cooperative clientele if you decide to offer SAT/ACT preparation. If you can teach math as well, so much the better.

It is helpful to talk with your student about the relative importance (or unimportance) of the test. Teens and parents alike can go to extremes, either ignoring the test altogether or attributing almost magical powers to it. To help the student put things in perspective, emphasize that the test is not an evaluation of a person's worth and that, though "you want to work hard and do your best, the purpose of doing well on the test is to open up as many options for yourself as possible, not to prove anything."

The beauty of tutoring is that you can work individually and over a prolonged period to identify and remediate a student's educational deficiencies. Commercial test preparation classes, on the other hand, are good primarily for teaching test-taking tips and strategies to people who already have the basics. They usually do a good job teaching these tricks and tips, but parents shouldn't expect a commercial course to improve their student's basic reading skills—that's your forte, or will be as you develop your expertise as a college prep tutor.

As tutors, our focus is on the type of test preparation we do best—that is, a long-term, in-depth course in reading improvement. We're not trying to substitute for a Princeton Review or a Kaplan course. Through this division of labor, private tutors and commercial test preparation courses can complement each other in helping students succeed on the college entrance exams.

Over and above the reading improvement methods we've discussed so far, what are the skills you can teach your college-bound and college-hopeful students to help them succeed on the SAT and ACT? First, let's broaden the discussion to include other college entrance exams, for example, preliminary tests such as the PSAT and the PLAN. (The PSAT is the preliminary SAT, and PLAN is a pre-ACT test.) Now, what pointers and what kinds of practice can we give students to help them on their college entrance exams?

Vocabulary

One of the most important things you can do to prepare students for the SAT/ACT is help them build vocabulary. Vocabulary isn't a quick fix, however. It can take from six months to a year of daily work for a student to increase her vocabulary appreciably. I would estimate that students must learn about 500 new words for the gains to make a difference on the test. Vocabulary building does work, however, so it is definitely worth trying.

Few students or parents understand how much time is required for real vocabulary improvement (as opposed to simply memorizing a list of words that appear frequently on the SAT), so some education is in order. Explain to the student and parents beforehand that working on vocabulary takes time but will help with all schoolwork, not just the SAT. And even though it can take many months to build vocabulary, it requires only a few minutes a day. To learn 500 words the student will only need to learn four or five words a day (school days only) for six months. Most kids can do that in 10-15 minutes a day, review included. That seems to cut the task down into manageable parts and yet emphasize its seriousness. If the student agrees, proceed with a vocabulary course similar to the one described below.

Many students who "study" vocabulary in English classes at school have little to show for their efforts. That's because they merely memorize definitions for the test and then promptly forget them as soon as the test is over. Before you begin to work on vocabulary with your student, explain that you want her to be able to actually use the words she is learning. That means she should aim for mastery, learning the words thoroughly enough that she will not forget them.

The goal is to be able to recognize and use the words in her reading, speaking, listening and writing. Remind the student that if she's going to put the time in on learning these words, she'll want to make sure her investment counts. If she finishes this vocabulary course and still doesn't know how to use these words, she will feel she's wasted her time. Here are some suggested SAT vocabulary activities:

Have the student learn Greek and Latin prefixes and roots. Look online to find a good list of prefixes and roots. If she's done something similar at school, make sure she actually knows the material. (See "Memorization

Tips" in Chapter 12.) Explain that learning this material can help her learn many new words and correctly guess the meanings of many more. It will also allow her to use a process of elimination on the vocabulary section of the test even though she may not know the exact meaning of a word.

Have the student memorize the list, and check her ability to apply what she's learned by giving her new words with the same prefixes. Teach her to memorize using a study sheet with the prefixes or words on the left half and definitions on the right, covering or revealing words as needed. Many students don't know how to memorize, so observe by having the student teach herself a few prefixes in the tutoring session before sending the sheet home.

- Have the student learn three words at a time, review, do the next three and review again, on up to nine words at a sitting. More than that may not stick.
- Go over the vocabulary section of a sample SAT, showing the student how to use logic to answer questions when she doesn't know all the words. The sentence completion part of the test lends itself to this logical approach; look for ideas that are the same or opposite of what is in the question stem.
- Have your student read books with challenging vocabulary and jot down three to five words a day to look up and learn. If she won't or can't do this, at least have her mark the words in the book then bring the book to work on with you in class.
- Use vocabulary workbooks. *Sadlier Oxford Vocabulary Workshop* (Sadlier 2001) is excellent.
- Have your student learn the words by making and memorizing flash cards and doing the lessons in the book.
- See if you can get the parents involved in discussing the week's words over the dinner table. (This activity is usually popular with both teens and parents.)
- For flash cards, the student should put words on one side and the definitions on the other. It is important to have her include sentences of her own on the cards. Allow plenty of time for review to make sure the student has the words entered into long-term memory.

With all vocabulary activities, after the student gets the knack of learning the words, have her do the time-consuming work of memorizing them at home and save your class time for reviewing any words she is unsure of.

Make sure she is learning to pronounce the words correctly, then have fun making up sentences and stories using the words.

On the vocabulary section of the SAT, ask your student to think of an easy word that makes sense in the blank before she looks at the actual choices provided by the test. Coming up with answers of her own will help her think more proactively.

Reading

Is there anything else that can be done to teach reading speed and comprehension for the SAT and ACT tests? Although you and your student have already done the major work, you can take some additional steps to make sure she will do her best on the test.

Have your student take one or more sample SAT tests. You should be able to obtain the sample SAT I test booklet at the counseling department of your local high school. Though you might want a commercial test preparation book later, the sample booklet from the school is free, and it's a good way to get started. The tests are real, not made up as in some preparation books, so that's a plus.

To prepare your student for the task, go through the booklet yourself and mark the parts in the "test-taking tips" section that you want her to pay special attention to. Take the test yourself first, complete with timing and scoring as directed in the test booklet to see exactly what you are asking your student to do.

Next, before your student takes the sample test, explain some of the highlights and have her do some sample questions of each type from the front section of the booklet. On the reading selections, explain that she can go back and forth between the questions and the article and that she can mark on the test booklet. Don't show her the test yet, and ask her not to look at it until she is ready to take it.

Have the student take the test home, read the preliminary material herself, and schedule about a three-hour block of undisturbed time to take the test. She should time herself as if it were a real test, *score it*, and look over anything she missed before the next lesson. (Students often miss these steps.) If the student doesn't understand why a particular answer is wrong, ask her to flag it to go over with you in class.

Students like to know what the scores mean, so after your student has taken the test and brought in her scores, you can use a college guide book such as *Peterson's Four-Year Colleges* (updated each year) to show how her scores would compare with those of other incoming freshmen who were accepted at various colleges. Far from being discouraging, these comparisons are viewed by most teens as something that helps them define their goals, including how much they'd like to improve their test scores.

After your student has taken the practice test and gone over any puzzling questions with you, you may see she needs additional work on the readings. If you haven't already done so, go over several reading selections in detail, one paragraph or even one sentence at a time, having her interpret when she can, with you filling in the rest. Do the questions for the passages the same way. Use your tried and true methods of helping students dig into the meaning of a reading, asking "what does this mean in simple language?" after anything that might possibly be puzzling.

Explain to the student that although it takes a long time to discuss the readings in this way, using a "fine tooth comb" now will help her do the test more quickly in the future. The type of careful reading that's required for the SAT and ACT will not be anything new for a student who's already had the experience of working on tellbacks and main idea, although you could imagine what a shock it might be for a student who doesn't have that background.

If your student needs even more practice, you will probably want her to purchase SAT preparation materials. *Official SAT Questions* and *Study Guides* put out by the College Board are best since they feature actual SATs. The College Board website (http://sat.collegeboard.org/home) provides several important resources for students, including an online practice course, test dates, registration, and scores.

Sometimes parents want to get involved in administering the sample test to their teen, but it's best if they don't. Like driving, taking the SAT or ACT is a kind of rite of passage, and it's best for the student to do it—or not do it—on her own.

For one last major push, if the test date is approaching fast and your student is serious about improving her scores, have her read several hours a day during the weeks leading up to the test (I suggest 2-4 hours). This kind of intensive brain work is excellent preparation. Not all students will be able to follow through on this activity, but for the ones who do, the benefits are dramatic. Suggest literary works, but also emphasize well-written, adult level books on science and history, for example, *The Discoverers*, a history textbook by Daniel Boorstin, or anything by Rachel Carson, known for her seminal work *Silent Spring*. I especially recommend Carson's book *The*

Sea Around Us. National Geographic magazine is a reliable source of informative and interesting articles, many with a scientific bent.

Have the student underline key phrases in these books and put summary notes in the margins, as she will do on the real test. (If needed, make a photocopy to mark up for this exercise.) She should also stop to paraphrase from memory every page or two, aiming not only for an overview, but for as much supporting detail as possible. This exercise is really just a longer tellback. To gain skill in doing tellbacks without the tutor's help, the student may jot notes from memory as she does a tellback, then reread to check her memory. Continue to encourage her to ask how each paragraph fits into the overall theme of the work. (See "Helping Students Get the Point" in Chapter 18 for more on SAT reading.)

Summary of Key Points

- The goal of speed-reading instruction should be to increase both speed and comprehension.
- Speed-reading instruction builds on skills taught previously such as tellbacks.
- Students can achieve higher reading speeds by using pacing, phrasing, scanning, and skimming techniques.
- In pacing, the teacher sets a speed goal for a student. The reader then slows down or speeds up as directed to meet that goal.
- Phrasing helps students read words in groups rather than one at a time for increased understanding and speed.
- Scanning and skimming are high-speed methods for finding specific pieces of information or main ideas.
- Tutoring offers an ideal setting for SAT and ACT preparation.
- Extended vocabulary practice and an intensive reading program will prepare students most thoroughly for the tests.

With luck and persistence, now you have shepherded, guided, cajoled, or even pushed your student into that state of grace known as the mastery of higher-level reading skills. You have helped her succeed in the areas of reading comprehension and memory, abstract thinking and reading speed. You yourself have succeeded because you've chosen exercises, activities, and materials commensurate with your student's age, abilities, and interests.

At this point, using the suggestions and learning activities provided so far, most students will be ready to graduate from tutoring. Not that they've learned everything they need to, but they are prepared to work more or less independently and are also willing and able to use the resources available to them at school, at home, and in the community. There will still be some students, however, who need more than what's already been presented.

Chapters 5 through 11 were arranged so they could be followed from beginning to end as a chronological, step-by-step guide to teaching reading. The final sections of this book, Part V on phonics and Part VI on emotional aspects of learning, are meant to supply the missing pieces. They are not about what to do next.

In Part V, Chapters 12 and 13 cover phonics and can be incorporated as needed into the reading program. Chapters 14 through 18 in Part VI provide a theoretical basis for emotional learning that reveals the inner workings of student behavior and helps tutors deal insightfully with difficulties that may arise in the teacher-student relationship. These areas of study will also allow you to go the next step in sharpening your own teaching skills, even putting you in a position to help students other teachers may have given up on.

Part V: Phonics and Word Recognition

Part V contains a step-by-step course in phonics for students who have fallen behind because of an inability to decode unfamiliar words. A guide to when (or whether) to introduce phonics instruction is provided. Chapter 12, "Phonics: Teaching the Basics," describes problems with phonics instruction as well as its benefits. Using the material presented here, tutors will be able to teach teens to use phonetic cues to improve their reading. Chapter 13, "Syllables and Phonics Practice," continues phonics teaching at a more advanced level. These two chapters on phonics instruction could be inserted anywhere into the teaching process, as needed.

12 | Phonics: Teaching the Basics

THIS CHAPTER ON PHONICS and word recognition is placed after the chapters about comprehension and reading speed for a couple of reasons. First, the majority of students do not need phonics instruction, so you won't use it frequently. In addition, there's a great variation among students as to the best time to introduce phonics for those who can benefit from it, and there is no hard and fast rule in this regard.

When *should* phonics be introduced? As noted in Chapter 4, a good time to start phonics instruction is when the student has gained some degree of confidence as a reader and when the lack of phonics skills has become the weakest link in that student's chain of abilities. Thus, phonics might be introduced within the first few weeks to as long as several months after tutoring begins. Whenever it's introduced, however, phonics should not be taught in isolation, but should be part of a broader effort to help students build word recognition and fluency.

Word Recognition

Word recognition is the ability to read individual words correctly, through familiarity (sight recognition), phonics (using the sounds of the letters to decode a word), and context (use of surrounding words to determine the meaning of an unknown word). Understandably, a student who has problems at the word recognition level will have problems in all other areas of reading. It's difficult to miss several key words in a paragraph and still be able to do higher-level reading tasks such as understanding the point or predicting outcome, yet this is what students who cannot sound out words are asked to do in school every day. This chapter shows you how to teach secondary students to use phonics, or the sounds of the letters, to read unfamiliar words. The next chapter covers syllables and context. Taken together, these skills will go far in helping students with problems in word recognition gain accuracy and fluency in their reading.

In the elementary grades, phonics teaching varies greatly from school to school and even from teacher to teacher within schools. Some children have received excellent early instruction while others have no background in the subject at all. Furthermore, phonics is usually not taught in any systematic way beyond the early grades. As a result, you will be confronted sooner or later with students who either have not been exposed to, or have not benefited from, the study of phonics. For these students, you will need to teach the subject from the ground up. The ideas outlined here, although not an entire course in phonics, will at least help you get started.

It is difficult to teach a thorough phonics course to adolescents in school. Tutoring presents a different situation, however, so if you have tried teaching phonics in a classroom and failed, try again. You may be surprised at the success you and your student can achieve with phonics in tutoring.

Why Teens Don't Learn Phonics at School

If a teen is stumbling over familiar words and seems unable or unwilling to sound them out, what's the reasonable thing for a reading teacher to do? The obvious response would be to determine whether the student needs phonics instruction, and if he does, to provide it. Unfortunately, though, that's not usually how it works. If a 15- or 16-year-old is having reading problems in school, he may be assigned to easy history and science classes, not to mention language arts, so that the work is "within his reach"! What about helping him *extend* his reach?

Teachers may wrongly assume that if a young person isn't adept at using phonics by the middle teen years, the situation is a lost cause—that "the student doesn't know phonics because he wasn't capable of learning it." This misguided thinking does a great disservice to young readers. It is never too late to need phonics and it's never too late to learn it. Some kids with poor phonics skills can read fairly decently, but they can read only words with which they are already familiar through repetition or from context. For people to have flexibility and control of their reading, they obviously need to have a system for decoding unfamiliar words, and that's what skill with phonics provides.

What holds schools back from teaching phonics? First, students themselves fight it. They don't want to learn a subject they associate with beginning reading in a classroom. (Tutoring is another matter.) Second, phonics is (or was recently) a politically charged issue. For one camp of educators, phonics instruction has come to symbolize everything that is mechanistic, rigid and joyless about education. For others, the opposite is true. For them, phonics means an orderly, disciplined, and even morally correct approach to learning. Even talking about phonics can get educators upset and trigger a bombastic exchange. It is hard for schools to plan and maintain sensible programs in an atmosphere that encourages opinion at the expense of observation and common sense.

Other reasons schools don't teach phonics to teens are lack of time, training, and money. But beyond these, there's an even more pressing reason phonics skills get short shrift in school: It is much harder to teach phonics in a classroom than in a one-on-one setting. So, for want of better solutions, tutors are often "it" when it comes to helping teens learn the phonics skills they need to read fluently.

Benefits of Phonics Instruction

In our work on phonics we're using some rather ordinary, mundane-looking tools (a lot of phonics work hinges on syllables and vowel sounds) so phonics instruction is not exactly glamorous compared with, say, literature, but when a student learns to apply phonics skills in his reading, it can be life-changing.

MAKING UP FOR LOST TIME

Nguyen at 17 didn't read much and didn't like to read. As a result he often failed at his schoolwork, though he was a curious and imaginative young man with a desire to help others. He came to this country at age five speaking no English, and to complicate matters, he had correctable but undiagnosed deafness for several years in the early grades. By the time his hearing was corrected, he had already lost several years of reading and language instruction at school. He poured his efforts into sports and became a stellar soccer player by his mid-teens. A trip to his home country touched his heart and convinced him that he wanted to do more with his life than he had previously aimed for.

Nguyen came into tutoring wanting to learn but with no foundation in the basics. Where to start? Since he was already in his late teens I tried to bypass phonics instruction as nice but nonessential and head straight for the pay dirt of reading comprehension, hoping some enjoyment would come out of it. Our efforts were frustrating. Nguyen was in the habit of ignoring everything he didn't understand in his reading, and although six months of instruction brought some valuable changes in learning style and attitude, his reading skill did not develop along with them.

Finally, I got what most teachers only dream of. His parents asked me to homeschool him, so I had the opportunity to go back to the beginning and fill in much that he had missed. Nguyen studied English and History with me for high school credit in the morning, but attended his regular school in the afternoon for electives and sports. This worked well, and without the time pressure I had felt previously to keep him afloat in his academic subjects at school, we could now do a complete phonics course. Within a couple of days after we started I got a thrilled phone call from his mom. She reported that she saw some big changes in his reading. "He has quit skipping the words he doesn't know. He can actually sound them out now. His reading makes so much more sense to him. What did you do?"

All I had done was show him how to divide words into syllables and teach him how the vowels would sound based on those divisions. There were more successes to come, and soon we returned to our original goal, comprehension and enjoyment, but this time the higher-level reading skills were based on a firm foundation and they "took" better.

Multisensory Language Programs

Some individuals have difficulty with *phonemic awareness*—that is, with hearing, remembering, or blending sounds, problems commonly associated with dyslexia. (See "Fluency" in Chapter 18.) Individuals with difficulties in phonemic awareness may need instruction beyond what you can provide in tutoring. If you work hard with a student for several weeks but find phonics instruction is not having the desired effect, discontinue phonics and concentrate instead on areas that may yield better results, such as memorization of sight words, use of context to identify unfamiliar words, and instruction in comprehension at a level appropriate for the student. At the same time, consider referring the student to a practitioner trained in a specialized, intensive phonemic awareness program, or multisensory language program. The best of such programs can cut through years of reading failure associated with the inability to distinguish and manipulate sounds.

For children and teens with dyslexia, specialized approaches to phonics instruction may be successful, so even though students might not succeed with phonics in tutoring, there is still a good chance for them to learn the necessary skills using another approach. Such multisensory language programs are taught in clinics and independent schools, and offered by private practitioners (Appendix H).

Identifying Phonics Problems

Not all poor readers need to learn phonics, but if your student paused frequently, stumbled, or misread words in the oral reading section of the evaluation, there's a strong likelihood he would benefit from phonics instruction.

Phonics pretest

First use the short phonics pretest provided below to learn something about your student's phonics skills. This pretest is fairly easy, and it is quite possible that someone might do well on the test but still have trouble sounding out multisyllable words. Explain that the words are nonsense syllables that aren't supposed to mean anything (except maybe in Martian). You want to see how the student does at sounding out unfamiliar words, and the only way to make sure the words are really unfamiliar is to use ones that are made up or are very uncommon. Have the student tell you how he thinks the words should be pronounced. It's all right to correct him as you go along since you want to see not only what he doesn't know, but how easily he can pick up on the phonics instruction he does receive. Mark any errors, then see the points below for a discussion of phonics errors.

The phonics pretest:

vim	*het*	*mab*	*zing*	*foss*
puce	*yuck*	*plete*	*clunshatted*	*bargle*
prelation	*glazer*	*thexcot*	*storious*	*crile*
wuggy	*krink*			

Notes: *vim*, *het*, *mab*, *foss*, *wuggy*, and *yuck* all have short vowels. So do *clunshatted* and *thexcot*. In *puce*, *plete*, *prelation*, *glazer*, *storious*, and *crile* at least the first vowel is long. (Consult Appendix I for an explanation of long and short vowel sounds.) *Puce* rhymes with *spruce*, *storious* with *glorious*. *Zing* and *bargle* rhyme with *ring* and *gargle*. *Krink* rhymes with *think*.

Some students read words better in isolation and some do better with words in context, so it's necessary to check both. Observe your student's applied phonics skills by having him read a few paragraphs aloud from a challenging book. For this purpose, I like Armstrong Sperry's *Call It Courage* or *The Incredible Journey* by Sheila Burnford. If those books are too easy but you still suspect the student is missing unfamiliar words, try using *1491* by Charles C. Mann or even *Frankenstein* by Mary Shelley. As the student reads orally, observe and take notes on his ability to read unfamiliar words. Does he try to sound out words he doesn't know or merely skip them? When he sounds out words, notice whether he divides longer words into syllables and whether he knows how to pronounce the vowels when he does. Some students only sound out words when you are checking on them but skip over anything unfamiliar when they're reading on their own. Ask your student if this is the case.

You can tell a lot from mistakes. Phonics errors come in several categories. Watch for the following. The student:

- does not know the sounds of some letters or letter combinations such as *au*, *tion*, or *ous*
- knows letter sounds but cannot blend (combine) them to make whole words
- adds sounds that are not in the word ("*preach*" for "*peach*")
- omits or changes syllables (*accompany* for *occupy*)

Does the student know when vowels should be short or long, including long vowels before a silent *e*? In what part of the word does the student makes most of his errors: at the beginning, middle, or end?

All these errors might call for a little different instructional approach, so you will have a better chance of picking the approach needed to remedy the problem if you can break phonics problems down into patterns. If you're not sure what's needed, though, try all the exercises presented in this chapter in order and let your student either "test out" of them or demonstrate by his errors that he needs to work on those particular skills.

Explaining phonics instruction

At this point, if you have decided that your student does indeed need phonics instruction, you still have to sell it. It is necessary to introduce the idea of phonics instruction to your student in a positive way. If you merely start in with no preparation, you probably will be met with an unengaged teenager who goes through the motions but doesn't use what he is learning because he doesn't see the need for it. Or worse, an offended teen who thinks you are forcing baby work on him. You might start out this way:

> I've noticed that if you have seen a word before, you usually know what it is, but if a word is unfamiliar to you, it's hard for you to figure it out. (Give examples from the student's work.) Doing some work on sounding out words could definitely help you. When people ask you to sound out a word, they mean to use the sounds of the letters to figure out the word. That's the same thing as decoding, or phonics. You might have learned phonics when you were younger, but we're working on a whole different level here.

When you feel the time is right, explain to your student that you want to show him how to use the sounds of the letters to figure out "weird" or difficult words—the kind that are in his science, geography, or history textbooks. I might say, "Imagine how much better you could do on class discussions if you knew how to pronounce the terms in your textbook."

And, if you sense resistance:

> Phonics may not be the most fascinating thing we could work on, but it's one of the things that will help you improve your reading the most, and do it the most quickly. A lot of adults haven't learned phonics, and when they come in to improve their reading or spelling, they need to learn phonics first if they're going to get anywhere, so in one way you are getting a head start. It's something you won't need to do as a grownup.

Some younger teens like to earn points by reading words correctly from the following phonics lists then cashing in their points for a game or story. For the past year I have been teaching phonics to a second grade girl with moderate dyslexia. I require lots of phonics drill, but she never objects because she knows her payoff is a story at the end of each lesson. So many words correct equal a minute of story time. We've had the same story running for the past year with a new installment each week. It's a wonderful activity. The story is a collaborative effort, and my student has become a great story-teller, too. Plus she works hard on her phonics lessons without too much urging.

Reassure the student that he won't be inundated with demands to sound out every strange word he meets. Ask, for example, "What do you do when you're reading a novel and you come to a word you don't know how to pronounce? Try to sound it out? Ask someone what it is? Skip it? Look it up in the dictionary?" Explain that flexible readers use a mix of approaches, and depending on the circumstances, any of these tactics might be appropriate. For instance, if the student is reading material he needs to get through as quickly as possible, maybe a novel for English class that's due in a week, it would be impractical to stop and sound out every word he doesn't know. The same is true for highly challenging books with many unfamiliar words. In both cases, he might decide to plow ahead, simply ignoring unfamiliar words.

There are other situations, though, in which it is desirable to sound out every word. For example, similar to vocabulary practice, when the reader has gained the necessary skills, he might choose a challenging but interesting novel and sound out every unfamiliar word he comes to within a certain number of pages.

Remind the student that just because you *can* do something doesn't mean you *have* to do it. This important idea not only applies to phonics practice, but to any situation in which it's possible for perfectionism to become incapacitating. Give your student permission to learn a new skill (sounding out words, for instance) but to decide for himself when he will use his new knowledge.

Steps in phonics instruction

One of the main criticisms of phonics instruction, or with any teaching that breaks skills up into their smallest components, is that students never get the big picture. They never learn to apply their new skills and they don't see that what they've learned is *for* anything. So it's important to balance the detailed view and the overview when we teach phonics. For example, after a lesson on dividing words into syllables, you could read a story or article that provides practice in that skill.

Phonics instruction should be stepwise, progressing from phonetic elements to whole words to words in a passage. Here are the basic steps in teaching phonics. Syllables and other aspects of phonics are discussed in greater detail in Chapter 13, while sounds are detailed in Appendix I.

Sounds. First identify the sounds and combinations that your student needs to learn and teach those. These may include short and long vowels, vowel combinations, and consonant combinations.

Syllables. Next teach syllable division and show how the vowel sounds are affected by these divisions.

Practice. Give lots of opportunity to practice on real words (and nonsense) both in isolation and in context.

Review.

Dictation. Provide practice in dictation (spelling) of sounds and syllables.

Applied phonics. Shift to more difficult reading material to teach applied phonics.

Dictionary work. Practice reading dictionary entries. Go over diacritical marks.

Ongoing. Finally, use the student's own reading and writing as an ongoing resource for phonics learning even when you are no longer doing any formal phonics instruction.

Fitting in Phonics

To keep the student's interest and provide a balanced lesson, spend only about 15 to 30 minutes at a time on phonics and fill out the rest of the lesson with other activities such as reading speed, comprehension, and vocabulary. You might change activities every 15 minutes for younger students or those with ADD, every 20 to 30 minutes for older ones.

Memorization Tips

Don't shy away from memorization. To help students memorize, teach them to *overlearn*. Overlearning means continuing to practice on something beyond the point when one first knows it correctly. For example, if your student makes a mistake on something he's memorizing, he should repeat the process until he gets the entire list right three times in a row. The purpose of overlearning is to move material from short-term into long-term memory. You probably intuitively understand the value of overlearning, but many students have a tendency to quit working on something as soon as they get it right once. Your student is likely to resist or misunderstand overlearning at first, but keep at it until he masters the material—and the concept of overlearning.

In addition, use the "rule of three" to teach your student to memorize. This concept will be familiar from our work on vocabulary. The "rule of three" says that if you memorize three items at a time (in this case, phonics flash cards) and review those before you go on to the next set of three, you will learn faster and remember more. The student reviews all the cards after learning each set of three. Don't teach more than nine cards in one sitting or confusion will set in.

Research shows that students remember better when they work out loud to memorize, especially when learning sounds. If students resist, I might say, "I want to hear you muttering over there." For some kids, though, working out loud is nearly impossible, so if you've given it several good tries with no results, the best course is simply to drop it.

Summary of Key Points

- Students who have problems with word recognition will have problems in all other areas of reading. Learning to use the sounds of the letters to identify unfamiliar words can boost students' overall accuracy and fluency in reading.
- In school, phonics instruction may be inconsistent in the early grades and nearly nonexistent in later grades, so the only opportunity a teen may have to receive phonics instruction could be in tutoring.
- Students who stumble over words or skip them entirely will likely benefit from phonics instruction.
- The need for phonics instruction should be explained with care.
- Phonics instruction should be approached in a stepwise fashion with adequate practice both on isolated elements (sounds and

syllables) and real words. Teaching progresses from phonetic elements to whole words, and then to words in a passage.

- Phonetic elements include:
  - o short vowels
  - o long vowels
  - o digraphs and diphthongs
  - o consonant blends

This chapter (along with the Appendix) has taken us through the basics of phonics instruction, including long and short vowel sounds and letter combinations. In the next chapter we go beyond the basics to work on syllables and then whole words. We also discuss using context to aid in word recognition and revisit oral reading to round out the process.

13 | Syllables and Phonics Practice

KNOWING THE SOUNDS of the letters may be a crucial part of word recognition, but it is only a first step. To decode longer words students must also have a knowledge of syllables. When faced with an unfamiliar word of several syllables, your student can make sense of it easily only if she knows where to divide the word and how the vowels will likely sound based on those divisions. It is estimated that 80 percent of the language is phonetically regular, so even when a word contains irregular elements, a reader who is able to divide the word and decode most of its parts can often guess the entire word correctly.

One flaw of school phonics programs is that there isn't enough carryover from phonics teaching to actual reading. The only way to achieve this transfer of learning is through targeted, supervised practice. This chapter covers both syllables and phonics practice.

Introducing and Teaching Syllables

Learning about syllables can help some students immensely. Even students who readily use letter sounds to decipher unfamiliar words can benefit from work on syllabication. Prime candidates are students who sound out shorter words correctly but have trouble with longer ones. Sometimes just one or two lessons on syllables can produce noticeable results.

Here is an overview of rules for syllable division, followed by a series of lessons designed to help students understand and use syllables to decode unfamiliar words. (These rules are for the tutor's use only.) Rules 1 and 2 below use the slash mark to separate the syllables in the sample words. Ask your students to use the slash mark to separate syllables in their exercises. Rule 3 shows the use of hyphens for the same purpose. Because hyphens are more easily identified in type, especially italics, they are used in this chapter to separate syllables from the examples in Rule 3 forward.

1. *If there are two consonants together* in the middle of the word, divide between them as in *tăb/let*. The vowel preceding them will be short. In a two syllable word, the second vowel may be irregular, as in *rĭb/bon*.

2. *If there are not two consonants together*, divide right after the first vowel in the word, and mark that vowel long, *hō/tel*. (This is the same as dividing before a single consonant.)

3. Continue to follow these two rules for the rest of the word, either dividing between double consonants or before single consonants, *ac-cu-mu-late*.

Using syllables in decoding

The object of this lesson is to show students that words can be divided according to simple rules depending on where the consonants occur in the word, and the vowels can be sounded based on where they are located in the syllable. After you are familiar with these rules yourself, you might introduce syllables by saying, "I'll be showing you how to sound out longer words so that you will be able to read the 'weird' words and harder words that are in your science and history textbooks." Then show the value of dividing words into syllables using the following steps and exercises.

Whenever you can, guide students to discover the syllable rules themselves rather than always teaching them directly.

Introducing syllables

Here's a script for a playful approach to introducing syllables.

This is the longest word in the English language. Write *antidisestablishmentarianism*. (Don't pronounce it. Just write it.) Have you seen this word before? Do you think you would be able to read it? It looks hard, but if you know where to divide words into parts, or syllables, you could probably figure it out on your own.

If you know where to divide the word, you'll also know what sounds the vowels will take—not 100 percent of the time, but about eight out of 10 times. So it's not foolproof, but it's worth learning. I'm just using this word to show you what I'm talking about—it's not really important whether you can actually read this particular word or not. I'll show you how vowels sound depending on where they are in a syllable, and then we'll sound out the word together.

Vowels at the end of a word or syllable. Write:

he   so   we

What are these words? Pretty hard, huh? How do the vowels in these words sound? *Where* is the vowel in the word? (Answer: The vowels are long and they're at the end of the word.) The vowels are long *because* they're at the end of the word.

Vowels in the middle of the syllable. Change the words you've written by adding these ending letters:

hen   sod   web

Now what do these words say? How does the vowel sound now? Where is the vowel? The vowel is short *because* it's in the middle. Now tell me the rule you've just learned about vowel sounds. (Answer: When the vowel is at the end of a word it's long, but in the middle of the word it's short.)

What you just learned is true of short words with only one vowel, and it's also true of syllables—parts of words. Syllables are sounded out just like short words.

Put a vowel at the end of one of the sample words to demonstrate the sound change.

Now watch as I add an *a* to make *sod* into *soda*. What just happened to the *o*? (A: It's long again.) What made it long? (A: It's at the end of the syllable.)

Show the syllable division with a hyphen after the *o: so-da*.

If you haven't done so already, teach the terms *vowel, consonant,* and *syllable.* Explain that the vowel is where you open your mouth, and the consonants are where you close your mouth. Have some fun showing your student how words might sound with no vowels (this requires clenching the teeth).

Every syllable has to have at least one vowel so that you can open your mouth.

It is also important for students to learn the following two rules for dividing words into syllables. They will have plenty of opportunity to practice and perfect their knowledge of these rules later; right now you are simply introducing the concepts.

First, divide a word into syllables by splitting it between two consonants (*rib-bon*) and second, if there are not two consonants together, divide after the first vowel (*ho-tel*).

These rules are oversimplified, and there are many "if's and but's" to qualify them, but there's no harm in starting out simply then augmenting them, as we do here. After you've explained these two rules, proceed as follows.

Now let's use the rules you just learned to divide and read the word *anti-disestablishmentarianism*.

Don't pronounce the word yet, just point to it on the page. You want the student to have the fun of discovering the pronunciation on her own. This exercise is not meant as a serious teaching activity, but as a playful way to arouse the student's interest in the subject.

Remember that if you know where to divide the word, you can make a pretty good guess at how the vowels sound. Then you sound out the word, one syllable at a time, with some help from the student, marking syllable divisions and vowels as you go. The result will be:

ē
ăntī-dĭs-ĕs-tăb-lĭsh-mĕn-tār-i-ąn-ĭsm

You and your student may notice that some of the syllables in this word do not follow the two rules you've just taught. This is because prefixes (such as *dis-*) and some other syllables in this word are exempt from the rules.

Dividing a word between two consonants

Re-teach the rules for syllable division you just introduced and have the student apply what she's learned by reading words from a list like the ones in this section (after Kottmeyer 1989, 104-112). I might introduce the task this way:

Let's try it with some real words. We're going to start easy and get harder. Please don't be insulted by the easy work. I know you're way above this reading level, but it's better to learn the rules using easy words, then you can move on to the harder ones.

Explain that in two-syllable words that divide between double consonants, the first syllable is usually regular (sounds the way you think it would) and the first vowel is short because it's in the middle (or the beginning) of the syllable. Remember *hen, sod, wet*?

But the second syllable is often irregular, and the vowel could have a long, short, or schwa (ə, indistinct "uh") sound.

Even if the word is not completely regular, you can usually guess what the rest of the word is from the part you do know. So mark the first vowel short according to the rule, then see what makes sense for the pronunciation of the second vowel.

Using the list of words below, demonstrate dividing between the two middle consonants, then have the student do some. Have the student mark the syllable divisions, mark the vowels with diacritical marks, and then pronounce the words. Although dictionaries usually mark the schwa sound with an upside down backward *e* (ə), a letter with the schwa sound can be marked easily by putting a dot under it, as in this example:

rĭb-bọn, sĕl-dọm, tăb-lĕt

ribbon	*seldom*	*tablet*	*object*	*rescue*
letter	*master*	*supper*	*thunder*	*splinter*
goblin	*bandit*	*stampede*	*umpire*	*velvet*
trigger	*admit*	*traffic*	*candy*	*circus*

Have the student work on phonics drills each week until she can easily mark the syllable divisions and vowels and pronounce the words. Include a review of words missed from previous lessons each time before moving on to a different set of words. In doing this and all phonics exercises, make sure the student knows the meanings of the words she is reading.

The words in the preceding double consonant exercise are quite easy, and most students would be able to read them without marking them, but the important part of the exercise isn't reading the words so much as it is learning the rules for marking the syllables and vowels correctly. Many students have a tendency to mark the words carelessly as they rush ahead, so insist on care in this task.

In addition, students are often confused about the terms we use in teaching phonics. Ask questions to help them master the terminology. Here are some sample questions to help students become adept with syllables as well as with the vocabulary of phonics. These are only examples, and you may think of others.

Each time the student marks and identifies a word, try asking *one* of these questions:

- How many syllables are in the word?
- How is the first vowel pronounced?
- How is the first syllable pronounced?
- How is the second syllable pronounced?
- How many consonants are there in the second syllable?
- How many vowels are in the whole word?
- Why was this vowel long (or short, or a schwa)?

This next step is an important one. After the student can mark syllables and read the words correctly, have her read words from the list without marking them. Tell her, though, that she must continue to divide the words into syllables *mentally* or she will miss them. Work on each type of word only until the student is proficient at it, but also review the next week. Use the same steps for the syllable exercises that follow.

Dividing before a single consonant

Explain that if there are not two consonants together in the middle of the word, you divide right after the first vowel. Example: hō-tel.

The *o* in the first syllable is long because it's at the end of the syllable. Remember the *he, so, we* words we talked about before? Even though those were whole words and this is a syllable, you still sound them the same way.

Again, have your student mark the syllables, sound out each syllable, and then read the entire word. Ask her to pronounce each syllable separately and distinctly. Some students may prefer to tell you what the whole word is first and then sound out the syllables, and that's fine, but don't skip the step of sounding out syllables until you are certain your student has mastered it.

The following words contain a single consonant in the middle. Explain that a syllable may consist of just one letter if that letter is a vowel, as in *ē-vil* or *ō-mit*. Add that the number of vowels in a word gives an idea of how many syllables there are in a word (not containing silent *e* or two vowels together). That's because each syllable has to have a vowel (so you can open your mouth):

tū-lĭp, hō-tĕl

tulip	*hotel*	*final*	*rumor*	*evil*
recent	*decay*	*Kodak*	*fiber*	*virus*
radar	*sinus*	*clover*	*vibrate*	*music*
flavor	*cider*	*vacant*	*evade*	

Practice with mixed double- and single-consonant words

gossip	*humor*	*tunnel*	*pilot*	*omit*
whisper	*local*	*motel*	*member*	*hero*
tiger	*rascal*	*clover*	*napkin*	*fever*
digest	*total*	*stampede*	*cotton*	*vocal*
miser				

Practice with longer words

When the student can do the preceding types of words easily and quickly, it's time to tackle longer words. Here's how to divide and mark the first three words in the list:

ăb-sō-lūte, ăc-cŏm-mō-dāte, ăc-cū-mū-lāte

absolute	accommodate	accumulate	advantage	surrender
impolite	porcupine	corporal	tomato	professor
torpedo	comprehend	admittance	ambulance	bulletin
independent	circulate	incubator	elastic	indignant
lumbago	pendulum	tornado	gymnastics	harmonize
volcano	romantic	dynamite	calculate	democracy
hibernate	dictator	horizon	innocent	sarcastic
inspector	tonsillitis			

When the student marks these longer words she will have to use both the double consonant and single consonant rules, often in the same word. You will almost certainly have to do a review of the rules when you get to this last exercise because students often become confused at this point, but it shouldn't take too long to clarify. To make sure the student knows the rules, have her explain them back to you rather than repeating them numerous times yourself.

At 15 to 30 minutes per lesson, it can take between three sessions and several weeks of practice to complete all the syllable lists. Limiting work on syllables to a weekly lesson may be enough practice for most students, but if the student seems to need more drill, have her practice at home with a parent. This requires some explanation for parents, since most people can read the word lists without a problem but don't know the rules for dividing words into syllables.

Parents can usually learn the rules quickly so they can help their teen divide words on the practice sheet at home, but they may also need to be reassured that it's okay if they don't know the rules. I explain that most people don't *need* to know the rules for syllable division, and it's only when kids are having trouble learning to pronounce unfamiliar words that they need to learn the rules. Also, help parents see how to correct students without trying to teach them. "If your child makes a mistake, just tell her the correct answer and circle the word for us to go over in tutoring."

Advanced Dictation

You may have already been doing dictation of real or nonsense words. If your student has the basic phonics skills down, now is a good time to do more advanced dictation using real words to teach specific spelling rules—doubling or not doubling consonants, for instance.

Read words aloud from the preceding syllable practice lists and have the student write them without showing her the words first. Another great way to practice is to pick longer words from the dictionary and ask the student to write them from dictation without allowing her to look at the words beforehand.

Even though it would be nice to have the student write the whole word correctly, that's often an unrealistic goal, so I've narrowed the task down a little. She doesn't have to write the words correctly, only phonetically. The important parts of this task are that the student marks the vowels using the diacritical marks for long, short, and irregular (schwa) sounds and that she doubles the middle consonants correctly, depending on the sound of the preceding vowel.

Here's an example. In writing the word *trigger* from dictation, you double the *g* because it follows a short *i*. In the word *tiger* a single *g* follows the long *i*. These are the same rules the student learned for reading but now she's applying them to spelling. I explain it this way. "If you hear a short vowel, it has to have two consonants after it. If you only *hear* one consonant, that means you have to double that letter." If your student needs an extra step in learning this rule, dictate words and just have her tell you whether the vowels she hears are long or short.

Many students leave sounds or even whole syllables out when they read and write, a possible indication of dyslexia. If this is so, work with the student to help her hear all the sounds. Say the word out loud, emphasizing each sound as you write it down, then have her do the same.

Learning correct, or at least phonetic, spelling can help your student grasp sound-letter correspondence at a basic level, giving her a foundation for phonetic skills she can utilize in her reading. If you will call attention to the shape the mouth takes when you pronounce certain sounds, it may help the student become aware of those sounds in spelling and reading.

Accented and unaccented syllables

Work on teaching accented and unaccented syllables. In my experience, this is not a skill all students are able to learn, so it's all right to drop it if your student doesn't pick it up easily. It's useful but not essential.

As before, use the dictionary to choose words for practice. Show how accented and unaccented syllables are marked in the dictionary. As a playful way to show how the accent changes the way a word sounds, pronounce some words incorrectly, accenting each syllable in turn.

Use your hand to indicate accented and unaccented syllables, as if you were directing music—up for an accent, down for a syllable with no accent. Have the student do the same and explain that "accent," when we are talking about syllables, is similar to stressing or accenting musical notes. Show that your voice is not only louder on the accent but often higher pitched, as well.

Dictionary work

This is a good time to show how diacritical marks are used in the dictionary and to begin having the student look up words. Almost all teachers would agree that being able to use a dictionary (and actually doing it) is essential for academic independence. But using diacritical marks to pronounce words from the dictionary can be daunting for students with decoding problems. Provide practice with pronouncing words from the dictionary, but don't expect overnight success, and don't get bogged down trying to force the student to use the dictionary. A hand-held electronic dictionary may be very helpful for some dyslexic teens and is more likely to be used than the standard model.

Some teens with learning problems have trouble finding words in the dictionary because they only know the alphabet as a song, which makes it difficult to alphabetize. The alphabet song is too rote, or automatic, to be useful. If this is the case, you must re-teach the alphabet in a way that is more accessible. To do this, have the student learn the letters in groups of three, three groups to a row, totaling three rows for the entire alphabet. Have the student practice saying the alphabet with pauses between the groups of letters, then write the alphabet from memory in this form:

abc	*def*	*ghi*
jkl	*mno*	*pqr*
stu	*vw*	*xyz*

She should try to visualize the alphabet in this form, then answer questions such as what letter comes before (or after) another, all the while focusing on her mental image of the alphabet. After some practice looking up words, have the student find (and perhaps write) definitions as she reads.

Word origins

Some teens are fascinated by word origins, so talking about the history of the language fits in here. The differences between Anglo-Saxon and Latin words can be intriguing. If you'd like more information on the subject for yourself, I recommend the DVD course *The History of the English Language* (Lerer 1998). The DVD is for sale through The Great Courses online catalog, but you may be able to obtain it free through your local library's interlibrary loan service. Also, try using an etymological dictionary to trace word origins, such as the one at http://www.etymonline.com/.

Combine phonics and SAT preparation

If your student is in tenth grade or higher, you may wish to combine work on phonics (specifically dictionary notation) and SAT vocabulary. You might want to use a PSAT list or a set of SAT vocabulary flash cards to do this. Test prep books, the internet, and the school counselor's office are all resources for good word lists. Have the student learn a few words a day and be able to use them in sentences of her own, taking care to pronounce them correctly. Ordinarily, students and tutors both like vocabulary work because it gives the two of you a chance to make up interesting, and sometimes funny, sentences together and learn more about each other as individuals.

Since you are only spending between 15 and 30 minutes a week on phonics instruction, the entire process may take several weeks. It's actually preferable to spread it out this way and do frequent reviews, as this helps the student retain the learning better in the long run. And, of course, when you have finished with the steps described above, it doesn't mean you drop phonics altogether. Instead, you draw on the student's own reading and writing as a source of further phonics practice.

Context

In the "bad old days," children were taught to use phonics, and only phonics, to determine the meaning of unfamiliar words. One of the criticisms of phonics instruction is that it ignored context—that is, deriving meaning from the surrounding words. Modern phonics instruction is more balanced and teaches students to pay attention not just to letter sounds, but to what would make sense in a given passage.

Some students seem to have a natural inclination to use context and don't need to be taught much about it. Others, however, need practice on this skill, which you can provide for them.

The Cloze technique

Students will pay more attention to context if they receive directed practice in this activity. Exercises in which students fill in words that have been omitted from a reading passage are called "cloze" exercises. Cloze exercises are a good way to get students thinking about context.

For middle school students, use exercises like this one: Read out loud to the student from a book she finds interesting and leave a key word out every once in a while. Have the student, who is simply listening, supply the missing word without looking at the book. The words you leave out should be fairly easy to guess from context. Of course, if the word she supplies makes sense but isn't the same as what's in the book, you accept it. An alternative is to give a student a copy of an article with some words "whited out" and have her fill in the blanks. *Reading Drills* has good cloze exercises for more advanced students.

There are a number of sites on the internet that allow teachers to construct cloze exercises using their own material, but I don't recommend these because they simply let you type in the text and then omit every *N*th word, an exercise that's probably too arbitrary to help students learn to use context.

CONTEXT FOR COMPREHENSION

Carly was a sixth-grade girl with poor reading comprehension and next to no knowledge of sounds and syllables. She was cooperative and well-behaved but had no love of reading, which to her was only an unpleasant chore. Then I discovered an odd thing about her reading. When Carly was familiar with all the words in a passage, she was able to understand the entire passage well, but if she missed only one or two words in the passage, it threw her comprehension completely off and she wasn't able to tell me a single thing she had read. This happened not once, but over and over. Carly's case was fairly extreme, but I had seen other children with similar problems so at least I had some clue about how to proceed.

I reasoned that Carly needed to work on phonics to enable her to decode the words she was missing, but beyond that, decoding aside, she needed to pay attention to, and make sense of, what she *was* able to read. But how to get her to do that? I was trying to solve a mystery and felt the missing piece had to do with context. On a hunch I read a paragraph aloud to Carly, leaving out the words I thought she might not know. I would just say "blank" when I came to a difficult word.

At first Carly didn't have much understanding of what I had read to her. It seemed she needed everything to be there for her to get any part of it. But with some practice and discussion—"What does this part mean? What do we know so far?"—she began to understand more. We also discussed not shutting down mentally just because she didn't know something. And I gave her a booklet of cloze exercises to do. She disliked doing them, but they seemed to help her anyway, and after a couple of weeks she was understanding and remembering more of her reading. Soon I allowed her to quit doing the cloze exercises and simply read from her book. What had been a serious-looking problem at the beginning was remedied fairly easily with exercises that required her to use context to make sense of her reading.

Strengthening context use through oral reading

Some secondary students who start with poor phonics skills but receive no remediation still may become accurate, skillful readers through intensive reading practice. This is the exception rather than the rule, however. In my experience, these are the students who are expected to read a great deal at school and who keep up their intensive reading practice for a year or two. They are usually under intense pressure from both parents and teachers to achieve. Needless to say, this cure doesn't work for all teens; it can be highly stressful, and it's hard to administer.

Let's look at the teens who don't have a pressure cooker to mold them. I have in mind the students who learn phonics skills and who are quite able to read words off a list or spell from dictation but do not apply what they know to their actual reading. Their oral reading is poor, and they do not use context to determine word meanings. For these students, the solution to their reading problems is consistent, structured practice in both oral and silent reading using challenging but not frustrating material. In these structured reading activities, timely feedback to correct errors is important for success. Here are some suggestions.

As a first step, read with your student in tutoring sessions to help her see how to use context to determine the pronunciation and meaning of unknown words. When students run into words they are unable to sound out quickly, they need a procedure to follow. Here's what I recommend:

> Try to sound out the word once or twice, but if you can't get it, go ahead and read the rest of the sentence. You will often be able to figure out the meaning of the unknown word from what comes after it. If this doesn't work, ask a grown-up or at least mark the word to ask about later. Yellow stickies are handy for flagging words in books you don't want to write in.

Beyond reading in the tutoring sessions, having a student read aloud daily at home over a period of several weeks can really make a difference in her general reading level. If you assigned oral reading before, this is nothing new. The only difference is that now the student will be more skillful at sounding out unfamiliar words. This oral reading can be done alone or with a parent. Ask your student what she thinks she should do at home to find out the meanings of words she doesn't know. Through discussion, you might come up with a rule of thumb similar to this: "To figure out the words you don't know, you use phonics, context, and the dictionary. If all else fails, ask your parents."

Reading aloud draws together the separate skills a student has learned and provides invaluable real life practice, making oral reading a great way to finish off the phonics program.

Summary of Key Points

- Decoding longer words requires a knowledge of syllables. Knowing where to break a word into syllables provides a key to how the entire word, including the vowels, will be pronounced.

- To teach syllable division, explain the phonics pattern you wish the student to understand, provide examples, have the student mark words to indicate syllable divisions and vowel sounds, and have the student read words from a list without marking them.

- Having students spell words phonetically from dictation reinforces phonics skills in reading.

- Learning about diacritical marks and becoming adept at finding words in the dictionary add to a student's independence as a reader, but dictionary work may require a special approach for students with dyslexia.

- SAT work may be combined with learning about diacritical marks, syllables, and pronunciation.

- Help students learn to use context through discussion, Cloze exercises, and oral reading.

Although we have talked about students' behavior, motivation, and emotional reactions, we have not looked into these matters in much depth. As tutors we need ways to cut through the mind games students play, bring out the best in our students, and allow our *own* true natures to shine through in our work.

Part VI, Chapters 14 through 18, covers the emotions, attitudes, and aptitude that play into the psychological and physiological aspects of learning. This information can be used at any time to help tutors understand that extremely important part of the tutoring process, student behavior. Before proceeding to Part VI, you may wish to review the section on "Troubleshooting Motivational Problems" in Chapter 4.

Part VI: Psychological and Physiological Aspects of Learning

PART VI COVERS THE INTERNAL WORLD of the learner. It presents a structure for teaching about internal dialog, discusses the hidden aspects of the teacher-student relationship, and talks about how to avoid manipulations. Here you will find ways to reach students whose behavior may have marked them as "difficult" or "problem students" in the past. Teens who are withdrawn and anxious also need understanding.

The basic principles explained here can help, not so much by proposing specific solutions to problems, but by creating a framework of understanding that will allow tutors to cut through a wide variety of difficulties by recognizing their common causes.

Many of the ideas in Part VI come from Transactional Analysis (TA), a psychological theory originated by psychiatrist Eric Berne in the 1960s. Other concepts are taken from general psychology or from Jungian psychology. Chapter 14, "Ego States and Inner Dialog," gives teachers a useful resource for understanding and shaping student behavior, as well as a way to help students learn about their own inner dynamics. This information can be a real gift at a time when teens are grappling with problems of identity and self-control.

Chapter 15, "Contracts, Transference, and Strokes," discusses the agreements and relationships between tutors, students and parents, how communications can go wrong and how to keep them clear. Chapter 16, "The Drama Triangle," shows a simple but ingenious way to avoid emotional entanglements. Chapter 17, "Character and Temperament Types," helps tutors direct lessons more precisely to students' interests and needs based on their temperament types.

Chapter 18, "Helping Students Build Attention and Fluency," offers practical suggestions for tutoring students with dyslexia and ADD. It includes sections on helping students arrive for a tutoring session prepared to learn, teaching listening skills, and helping students with attention problems get the point of what they read. Physical aspects of learning such as exercise and nutrition also are considered.

The material in Part VI is not intended to be a scientific or even particularly thorough examination of these topics. Rather, the intent is to explain and discuss a framework that has worked well for many teachers, therapists, and others in the helping professions over a period of several decades. It is also an approach that I hope will help you in your own tutoring.

14 | Ego States and Inner Dialog

DURING THE COURSE OF TUTORING, it is likely that you and your students have established a good working relationship, one that has ripened into mutual trust and perhaps even friendship. Things don't always go as planned, however, even with the best teaching methods and greatest care on the teacher's part. Students can be balky and uncooperative, even manipulative or downright rebellious.

In this chapter on ego states and inner dialog we'll consider how to help students gain more control of their behavior by increasing their self-understanding. Anyone can benefit from these ideas, however, not just those with behavior problems. The following material is about both motivation—the desire to accomplish—and motivations—the reasons behind people's actions. Almost all students are interested in learning about why people act as they do, and many teens will be enthusiastic about using the concepts presented here as a means of self-discovery.

Only a brief introduction to Transactional Analysis (TA) is provided here, and it is naturally geared toward tutoring. When I teach TA to students in tutoring my purpose is not to present a complete course, but to do the least amount of teaching that still will produce the desired changes in attitude and behavior. For a more complete picture, in addition to Eric Berne's books, I highly recommend *Born to Win: Transactional Analysis with Gestalt Experiments* by Muriel James and Dorothy Jongeward, and *Raising Kids O.K.: Transactional Analysis in Human Growth and Development* by Dorothy E. Babcock and Terry D. Keepers. *The People Book*, also by James and Jongeward, is written for teenagers, and if you read this book with students in the tutoring session, you can teach TA at the same time you teach reading. These books may seem dated to some students, but the material itself is fresh as ever, so use the basic ideas but avoid having the students use the books if that's a problem.

An Educational Approach to Motivation

Taking an educational approach to address motivational and behavior issues, as we will be doing here, has several advantages. Teaching about behavior is straightforward and direct (unlike psychotherapy, which is non-directive by definition), so it can be tailored to the individual, and it grows naturally out of the tutoring relationship. As a low-key, nonjudgmental form of intervention, it is likely to be accepted by students. Above all, teaching and learning about behavior *works*.

Students who learn the concepts presented here and have a chance to talk them over with a sympathetic adult frequently make striking, positive changes in their lives and their commitment to learning. Moreover, combining psychological learning with the academic techniques outlined in this book can help students progress in ways neither tutoring nor psychotherapy alone could accomplish. I have this on good authority. My husband, Terry, a child clinical psychologist for 30 years, often commented that I could do things in tutoring that would be impossible in psychotherapy. So I'm a strong believer in the therapeutic potential of tutoring.

To teach about behavior, tutors might use the following activities:

- choose a TA topic that might help the student overcome a particular problem
- find out what the student knows or feels about his current situation
- explain the TA concept (often with diagrams)
- give examples from real life
- ask the student how the idea might apply to his own life
- assign the student to observe or work on changing certain behaviors
- check on the student's progress periodically

The concepts in this chapter are presented in lesson form to help you see how to introduce them to your students as you learn them yourself. Though the first topic, "brain-building," is not a TA concept, it makes sense to begin with it since students who understand something about the physical nature of learning may become more engaged in the process themselves.

Brain-building

Brain-building refers to the physiological development of learning ability. For students who have not had much previous academic success, learning about the remarkable powers of the brain can offer inspiration. To introduce the subject, you could explain that the simple act of learning something—a skill or a fact—physically builds brain cells and connections, and even makes the neurons more complex and better able to carry messages. Perhaps you've seen those time-lapse photographs of live animal brain cells that are viewed with optical fibers. As the animal learns to run a maze, the cells grow and develop root-like nerve endings called *dendrites*. It's quite miraculous.

One way of explaining brain-building to the student is that "anything you learn today is actually helping your brain become physically more capable of learning tomorrow." It's not too far-fetched to say "you build your own brain." Have you personally ever had to learn to do an extremely difficult task—something so difficult that it seemed impossible at the beginning, yet ended in success? Most adults have, but to young people, this may be a novel experience, and one your student would probably appreciate hearing about. Examples could be learning a foreign language or just working up to lifting increasingly heavy weights in weight-lifting workouts. The whole concept of building the brain by learning encourages kids in the face of what must seem a daunting, even at times impossible, task.

BRAIN-BUILDING AS MOTIVATOR

Ace was an intelligent but "squirrelly" 12-year-old who produced an almost constant stream-of-consciousness monologue. Unfortunately, he could barely stand to listen to anyone else talk, especially to explain a subject, and most especially not when that subject was reading improvement. He did want to do better in school, however, and perhaps deep down wanted to *be smarter*—something that appeals to many children even before the concepts of paying attention and working hard have entered their minds.

After several months of gradual progress during which Ace was given time to talk about himself and ask questions, I found that there were some things he *would* sit still for. One of them was an explanation of how learning produces "brain-building," which in turn enables one to learn more. He was fascinated, and he now began to comment at the end of each lesson, "Well, I wonder how many brain cells I built today." This was a turning point for Ace in becoming a more engaged learner.

Students appreciate knowing that the mere *effort* of learning, even when they get the answer wrong or have not yet mastered a skill, has the effect of brain-building. In other words, we grow brain connections, in the form of axons and dendrites, just through trying. People find it comforting to know that when they make an effort, "they're getting smarter even if they get it wrong," and that practice makes it more likely that they'll get it right next time.

Introducing Ego States

Amy was 23, a late-blooming college student who came to me for help with organizational and study skills. After checking out her academic skills—making sure she could read, understand, take notes, and review—we tackled her organizational problems. Amy was extremely bright and picked up the academic work quickly, but she was quite immature when it came to managing a schedule and directing her own learning. She had difficulty turning the TV off when it was time to study, and as a result, she often stayed up late and skipped classes the next day. Furthermore, she did not exercise and she ate mostly junk food.

I began by helping Amy improve her study skills through a problem-solving process based on questions and discussion, a technique that might be called "directed discussion." We started with her study area and moved on to her schedule, exercise and food.

I asked questions, then listened carefully to Amy's answers. "Where do you study?" "How does that work for you?" "What would work better?" "How could you set that up?"

"What is your school schedule? When do you study now? Is that adequate? How much time should you be putting in, ideally? Would it be possible for you to do that? How do you feel emotionally when you are studying? Do you have trouble getting started? What would make it easier to start studying?"

Amy responded well to this directed discussion, and with a little prompting, she came up with a color-coded schedule, a welcoming study area, and the idea of having certain snacks only when she was studying. The ideas were largely hers, and I made suggestions only when she was stumped. I also provided general tips on time management and study skills, which I had her write down and keep in a notebook for future reference. In a few weeks I could see that she had a good system set up for herself, but I also knew from experience that once the "new" wore off she would falter. It was time to begin teaching ego states.

I pulled out a piece of paper and wrote "Transactional Analysis" and "Ego States" at the top. After explaining that Transactional Analysis is a type of psychology started by Eric Berne in the 1960s, I said that we were going to be using some ideas from TA to understand more about why people act and feel as they do.

According to Eric Berne, ego states are consistent patterns of feeling and experience and their related behaviors. This is the official definition for your information, but not one to use with students. Here is how I introduced the idea to Amy:

It's possible to take people's behavior, anyone's behavior, and sort it into categories. Here's one way to do it. In TA, categories of behavior are called ego states. Besides being simply categories of behavior, though, ego states can also be thought of as parts of the personality. (I drew a circle.) When babies are born, and for the first few months, they are mostly little bundles of needs, feelings, and wants. They register physical perceptions and experience the primary emotions—fear, happiness, anger. As they get a little older, curiosity comes into play. (I jotted the words *feelings* and *curiosity* beside the circle.) The first part of the personality to develop is called the Child ego state. (I labeled the circle *Child* as in Figure 14.1).

Figure 14.1. The Child ego state.

The Child ego state, like a real child, likes to have fun. She also "wants what she wants when she wants it." She's impulsive and spontaneous. Sometimes the Child wants to please, but she can also be rebellious. Just because you grow up, your Child ego state doesn't go away. You keep it but add other parts of the personality as you grow.

The next part of the personality to develop is the Adult ego state. (I drew another circle above the first one, as in Figure 14.2. The Adult is the computer part of the personality. It deals with information. It is observant and objective. It uses logic and deals with information.

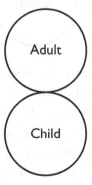

Figure 14.2. The Adult ego state.

You can see the first glimmerings of the Adult ego state when a baby is about nine months old and first puts together the idea that the light switch makes the light go on. The Adult continues to develop, gathering information and learning to think.

No matter what your age is, for you to learn, it is essential for the Child and the Adult to work together. The Child is curious, so that's where the energy or the driving force for learning comes from, and the Adult's job is to observe, to analyze, and to find answers. The Child and Adult are a team, and one without the other would not accomplish much, whether it's learning about life and surviving in the real world, or learning in school.

The Parent ego state develops last. (To show the Parent, I draw a third circle above the other two.) Now all three ego states are represented as shown in Figure 14.3, which also provides one example of an inner dialog between Parent and Child. The Parent is the part of the personality that takes care of the individual internally and also cares for others, externally. In many ways the Parent is like a real parent, concerned about right and wrong, good and bad. In TA, the Parent is the source of a person's values and conscience.

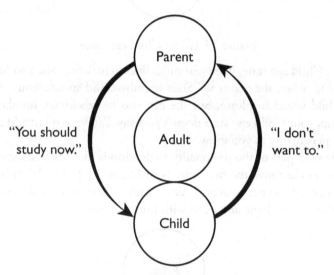

Figure 14.3. The three ego states with an example of
inner dialog between Parent and Child
(adapted from Babcock and Keepers 1976, 40).

Besides being our moral compass, the Parent ego state is also the part that cares for us internally. We use the Parent to encourage and comfort ourselves. The opposite is also true—the Parent is the source of the cranky voice that sometimes tells us we are to blame for whatever's wrong.

The Parent ego state develops gradually in childhood. We're not born with a Parent—the ability to care for ourselves and to tell right from wrong—but by the time we reach adulthood, most of us have a functioning Parent. Here is a diagnostic milestone in the development of the Parent ego state. You've seen young children with dogs. So you know that young kids, three or four years old, are not able to make a dog do what they want it to do, and that it's not just because of the child's small size. Children don't have the authority, and the dog knows it. That authority comes from the Parent ego state, so when a child of eight or nine is finally able to give the dog a command it obeys, that shows the child now has a functioning, though not yet fully mature, Parent ego state.

We talked about the Child's curiosity and the desire to learn and the Adult's ability to take in and process information. But where does the Parent fit in terms of learning? The Parent is the boss—the job supervisor. If there is work we know we ought to do but we don't particularly want to do it, the Parent becomes involved, either persuading us to do the things we know we should do or, on the other hand, being overridden, usually by the Child. I explained to Amy that being able to plan and follow through successfully with schoolwork requires being able to get yourself to do what you know needs to be done, and that requires an operational Parent ego state.

The development of a strong inner Parent can be an ongoing undertaking. As Thomas Huxley wrote in his *Collected Essays*:

Perhaps the most valuable result of all education is the ability to make yourself do the thing you have to do, when it ought to be done, whether you like it or not; it is the first lesson that ought to be learned; and however early a man's training begins, it is probably the last lesson that he learns thoroughly. (Huxley 1877, 404)

This was a good time to take a break from teaching and ask Amy about her own Parent, Adult, and Child. I used these questions to guide the discussion: "What do you enjoy doing? In other words, what makes your Child happy?" For Amy, it was watching NASCAR racing on TV. "What is your Adult good at?" In Amy's case, it was chemistry. "What have you done in the past week that showed self-discipline? This is your Parent at work." To this, Amy answered, "I watched less TV and spent more time at the gym." These questions helped Amy become more aware of her own ego states, and this awareness gave her more feeling of control over her own balky Child.

This information about ego states is just a beginning. James and Jongeward's *Born to Win* and *The People Book* are full of great activities and exercises to help students learn more about ego states in general and the content of their own ego states in particular.

Inner Dialog

Far from being static, our ego states relate and even "talk" to one another. In fact, we're constantly having conversations in our heads between our different ego states, whether we are aware of it or not. Our ego states do not always see eye to eye, though, as evidenced by the saying, "I'm of two minds about that." Here is an example of inner dialog having to do with a fairly common school situation.

> To continue Amy's TA instruction, I pointed to the appropriate circles in Figure 14.3 to show who's talking, and said, "Imagine that you look in your planner and Your Adult notices that a big reading assignment is due tomorrow. The Child says 'Oh, poop,' or some equivalent. The Parent might come back with, 'You'd better get on it.' The Child could object to the Parent, 'No, I don't want to.'" Here I drew arrows from Child to Parent and back from Parent to Child to show this transaction. "The Adult might get involved, too, and say to the Child, 'If you do the assigned work, such and such is likely to happen, but if you don't do it, this other thing might happen.'"
>
> "Like you could get a bad grade or feel embarrassed," Amy puts in, nodding. The internal struggle is familiar to her.
>
> I explained that it's important for the Parent to win this argument often enough that the person is successful in meeting her own goals, but it's also important for the Adult to keep the Parent informed about reality and mediate so that the Parent's demands don't get out of control. For example, during a heavy study session, the Adult might say to the Parent, "A 15-minute break isn't going to sink the study schedule."

Though there are bound to be disagreements among the ego states, when things are working well, the conflicts are resolved in a way that furthers the individual as a whole. Truly successful people, termed "winners" in TA, are ambitious and also have a life; they know how to work hard *and* have fun. They are able to do that because they have a strong, sensible Parent, a well-informed Adult, and a fun-loving Child. In other words, all three ego states are fully operational and work together.

The Child

Now that we've talked about some of the basics of ego states, let's go back and look in more detail at how the internal Child responds to the Parent. In life, if a parent asks a child to do something, the child may act one of two ways. If the mother says, "Come here and put your toys away," the child could respond obediently and put the toys away. That's called *Adapted Child*. Adapted Child simply tries to obey. Or the child could refuse: "I don't want to and you can't make me." That's *Rebellious Child*. If, on the other hand, the parent has not yet asked the child to pick up the toys, and the child simply plays with them, having fun, she is operating out of *Natural Child*. The Adapted Child, Rebellious Child, and Natural Child are all subcategories of the *Child ego state* (Figure 14.4).

The Natural Child is the original and spontaneous part of the personality that every person is born with. Natural Child is what we have and what we are before society intervenes. The Natural Child is fun-loving, curious, and emotionally genuine. He is unspoiled, but also uncivilized. For you to succeed at schoolwork, or almost any other undertaking, the Child must be on board. The Child is a powerful player, and the success or failure of your plans will depend on him.

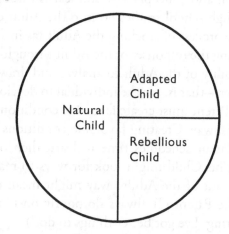

Figure 14.4. Divisions of the Child ego state.

Allowed free rein, the Adapted Child and Rebellious Child do not serve the individual well. The Adapted Child may be obedient but is also unthinking; imagine a well-meaning bureaucrat holding up a project because he has no vision or motivation of his own. And to understand what it would mean for the Rebellious Child to be in charge, imagine an angry two-year-old calling the shots. The Adapted Child and Rebellious Child are flip sides of the same coin since they are both responses to what someone else wants (either an authority figure in the real world or else a person's internal Parent) rather than what we ourselves want. A person who obeys unthinkingly, or struggles against authority just because he doesn't want to be told what to do, ignores the real needs and wants of his Natural Child. The solution is to focus more on what we truly want for ourselves and to concentrate on our goals.

The Parent

The Parent ego state, like the Child, is made up of more than one part. The *Nurturing Parent* is the caring aspect of the Parent. It is concerned for our safety and happiness and wants only the best for us. The *Critical Parent*, on the other hand, can be very stern and demanding, often under the guise of doing things "for our own good." Poor self-esteem often has its root in negative self-talk from the Critical Parent to its captive audience, the Child.

The Adult

The information and concepts a person learns through observation in daily life and through school studies go into the Adult ego state. Getting an education is the process of stocking the Adult (as in stocking a store or a pantry), sharpening the responses of the Adult through practice and drill, and refining the ability of the Adult to analyze and draw conclusions. For the Adult to prosper—that is, for the individual to develop intellectually—the Child and the Parent must create favorable conditions for learning and then stay out of the way. Creating favorable conditions for an individual might mean his Parent schedules time to learn then offers praise when he succeeds, while his Child might look for ways to make learning more enjoyable. Staying out of the Adult's way might mean omitting negative comments from the Parent ("I always do poorly on tests") and from the Child ("This is boring. I've got better things to do.")

Real-world Applications

We all come with a fairly standard set of ego states; it's when we look at the *content* of those ego states that things get interesting. Beyond the basic explanations, the real value of working with ego states comes from helping students examine the content of their own Parent, Adult, and Child, particularly as it relates to school work.

BEYOND THE REBELLIOUS CHILD

"Now that you know more about ego states," I said to Amy, "let's look at how you could use these ideas in your own life. Let's take a situation that's troubled you in the past. You told me that it was very difficult for you to start studying. After you got started you were OK, but you might not study for days because you were not able to make that first step."

"Yeah," said Amy, chagrined.

"I'm not trying to put you on the spot. We're just exploring the problem right now." (In TA terms, "I'm not going to use my Parent to put you down about not studying. Instead, we'll both use our Adults to investigate why you're not doing it.")

"So, you're sitting looking at your books on one side of the room and the TV on the other side. What do you say to yourself?"

"I say, 'I can watch TV for a little while, and I can stop any time I want and study.'"

"Is that true? Can you stop any time?"

"No. I kind of lie to myself."

"Yes. What else do you say to yourself to explain why it's OK to watch TV?"

"That I've been so stressed I need it and deserve it."

"Then how do you answer yourself?"

"I don't really answer. I just go ahead and watch TV."

"In its own way that *is* the answer. Let's look at who's been talking so far. It's the Child who is 'stressed,' then 'needs and deserves' a treat. Those are things the Child would say. Imagine a real kid complaining about having too much work, feeling overwhelmed, and needing a reward to cheer her up."

"You're telling me that's juvenile?"

"No. It's understandable your Child would feel that way, but when you stay in those feelings it doesn't give you control over your own behavior. Your Child feels justified in wheedling rewards out of the Parent, but there is a repetitive cycle of feeling stressed, watching TV, missing school, then feeling more stressed. The Child always ends up feeling badly in this cycle." (In TA, repetitive behavior that ends in bad feelings is known as a "racket" or a "game.")

"Also, your Parent almost always gives in—pretty easily, from the sound of it."

"Yeah. My Parent needs more backbone."

"Yes, but that's only part of it. Your Child is also looking over her shoulder at your real parents. How do they fit in here?"

After some discussion, I found out that Amy's mother and father were still paying all of her school and living expenses, even though she had been taking community college classes for more than four years. "How would the conversation about the TV go if you were talking to your real parents?"

"They'd say, 'After all we're paying, we are in charge of things, so turn the TV off.'"

"They feel that if they are paying, they get to decide."

"Yes. But that just makes me want to watch TV."

"Who just said that?"

"Child."

"What part of the Child?"

"Rebellious?"

"Yes."

"Are you saying I should just do what my parents want?"

"If you did do what they want, what ego state would you be in?"

"Adapted Child."

"I'm not asking you to either obey or disobey your parents. I'm asking you to get out of that box and think about what you want for yourself. And that doesn't mean little treats that end up making you feel bad."

"OK," said Amy after some thought. "I want to graduate from college. I want to study something I'm interested in, not what my folks are asking me to study. And I want to have fun."

"What you just said is extremely important. Let's start with the last one. What would you enjoy doing that wouldn't dig you further into a hole?"

"Going out with my friend Joe for pizza and a beer on the weekend. I'd like to do it on a weeknight but I'm starting to think that might not be a good idea."

"Your Parent is wising up."

"Yeah. Kind of like I'm onto myself."

Exactly!

As we continued talking, Amy realized that much of her nonadaptive behavior was a Rebellious Child reaction to her real life parents' micromanagement. She saw that she needed to substitute her own Parent for theirs, and that failing to do so would invite them into her life at a time when she passionately wanted to be her own person. I explained that the advantage of using her own Parent was that she could be more flexible than her actual parents in the way she parented herself. (It turns out that they had forbidden her to have a TV.) Amy decided on some rules for herself regarding the TV, and as far as I can tell she has kept them.

Amy had made some important decisions, but in TA, when a person comes up with plans for solving problems in his life, the teacher or therapist asks that person how he might possibly sabotage his own plans. In other words, "How could your sneaky Child undermine your decisions?" When I asked Amy how she might sabotage her own study plans, she saw right away that having the TV next to her study area was asking for trouble. She decided to move her furniture to make it much more difficult to watch TV when she was studying.

When I asked Amy what the downside of not following through with her plans would be, she answered, "Being a child forever." When I asked her what the rewards were that had kept her trapped in her present dilemma, she answered with the same phrase: "Being a child forever." She understood that her addictive behavior was a double-edged sword.

Over the next few weeks we discussed every aspect of her academic life from the viewpoint of ego states and transactions. Amy had already made many positive changes in her life, but now she understood how to maintain them.

A semester later, Amy was making good grades, had signed up for the school courses she wanted (criminology and forensics rather than the business courses her parents wanted her to take), and for the first time in her life, she felt self-motivated rather than pushed around by others.

Amy is obviously insightful and highly intelligent, but even young teens whose verbal skills are not well developed can benefit from learning about ego states. The presentation and analysis would have to be simpler, of course, but even developmentally disabled students can often understand fairly complex ideas if the concepts are expressed in simple terms, are accompanied by concrete examples, and are taught in small steps.

Engaging the Student's Adult

Earlier, when I was talking with Amy about her study habits, our discussion took on a question and answer format. When one person asks a question and the other responds with the appropriate information, it is usually a sign that an Adult/Adult exchange has taken place. One goal of these conversations, aside from the obvious one of my gathering of information, was to help her look at her study habits from an Adult perspective. It was clear, based on how much she had sabotaged her own schooling, that she had a fairly Rebellious Child lurking just under the surface, and I strongly wanted to avoid a Parent/Child showdown in tutoring (with me in the Parent role), so I tried to engage her Adult ego state early on in the process. I believed that if she could stay in Adult until she understood ego states, we could then examine her Rebellious Child reactions together, Adult to Adult.

It did turn out that shining a light on Amy's rebellious behavior helped her avoid it. This was a highly positive development, since previously her rebellious gestures had backfired and usually ended up hurting her. The goal was not to get her to be overly docile or obedient in tutoring, which would have been Adapted Child. Instead, I wanted her to think clearly about her study habits (Adult) and how those fit into her life goals (Parent, since goals reflect values). Having a little fun (Natural Child) wouldn't hurt either and would even make it less likely for a bored kid to undermine the whole endeavor.

Interestingly, besides discussing ego states, one way to encourage more Adult behavior is to teach students to use "Adult" posture in their tutoring sessions. The idea is that the way we hold our bodies affects how we think—that we can actually "get ourselves into" different attitudes by using different postures. You can demonstrate Adult posture by sitting straight but not rigidly and focusing on a book or another person with a steady gaze. In Adult posture, the mouth is closed but not clenched shut and feet are placed lightly on the floor. Needless to say, a student "messing with stuff" in the tutoring room, as sometimes happens, is not Adult. But then neither is a command from the tutor to "quit messing with stuff!" A lesson on ego states could bypass both. Thus, instead of saying, "Sit up and pay attention!" the tutor would teach Adult posture and say, "You can help your brain process better by sitting this way."

The Tutor's Ego States

Different parts of this book are aimed at the tutor's various ego states. For instance, in the interview, when tutors were encouraged to take the attitude of an interested bystander, they were being advised to use their Adult ego state. When a sympathetic approach was recommended, that was a call for a Nurturing Parent response. And using Mad Libs or other fun activities was an invitation for a Child-to-Child interaction.

As a general goal, it is desirable for both the student and the teacher to have all three ego states accessible. A teacher might use his or her Adult to give information, enlivened by a Child who's ready to laugh, backed up by a Parent standing in the wings for authority. And even though it is desirable for all of the teacher's ego states to be available, the Parent should be used with caution since Parent, either Nurturing or Critical, tends to elicit Child responses in others.

Reaching the Adult

If the goal is to encourage students to think, it makes sense to aim our teaching at their Adult ego states. Reaching the Adult can sometimes be tricky, though.

BYPASSING AN OBSTRUCTIONIST CHILD

Linda was a 12-year-old seventh-grader who had just started receiving tutoring to improve her reading, writing, and study skills. For the first lesson or two she was on her good behavior, but then she began to show an annoying pattern. Every time I tried to teach her anything, she would argue. It really didn't matter what the subject was, she always had a querulous response. Either my information was wrong, or that wasn't what she was supposed to be learning, or the teacher at school had said something different. She seemed stuck in a whiny Rebellious Child state. There were several choices open to me. I might use my Parent and simply tell her to quit arguing, I might use my Child to find more playful or interesting ways to learn, or I could continue trying to teach with my Adult, even though that wasn't working well. There was another way, however, and as it turns out, it was the right one. I used my Adult, not to continue teaching, but to help her look at her own behavior.

During a troublesome spate of arguing, I set aside the geography book and said, "Let's stop for a minute. I want to talk to you about something. This isn't about geography. I notice that you argue a lot." ("Notice" is an Adult word, and when I said this I aimed for an Adult tone, interested but nonjudgmental.) Of course, she started to argue.

"I wasn't really arguing," she said. "It's just that what it says here in the book is . . ."

"OK. I'm not talking about this particular case. I'm talking about generally. You do often search out what's wrong with the book or with what I say."

Linda drew a deep breath, but I cut her off before she had a chance to continue. "It's not you arguing against me that's the problem. That part doesn't bother me. If you think I'm wrong I want to hear about it." (As a teacher, if you are going to say this you have to mean it.) "Here's the problem: when you argue, you focus on everything that is wrong and on how things don't make sense, and that keeps you from learning about the way things really are. So when you argue, you put a roadblock in the way of your own learning."

"Imagine this," I told her. "You've just spent an hour in your lesson, and you're in the car going home. How would you feel if you knew you had learned something you wanted to know?" Linda said that would feel good. "But on the other hand, imagine how you would feel if you hadn't learned anything at all. Wouldn't that make you feel like you'd wasted your time in tutoring? You might feel annoyed or frustrated about it. Now think about what happens when you argue. You look for and point out everything you can find that's wrong with what I say or with the book, but that kind of negative searching isn't going to help you learn."

Linda quit sputtering, and I saw her expression change to one of recognition. I went on to assure her that she could still question and point out errors as long as she did it respectfully, but that she should argue only if the subject meant something to her personally, and not simply out of habit.

This approach worked well, and now, a year later, Linda is getting straight A's in school. The trick was to bypass her obstructionist Child and appeal directly to her Adult with something that concerned her self-interest. Of course, not all students would care whether or not they learned anything in their tutoring sessions, but in Linda's case I guessed correctly that she didn't want to waste time or end up feeling stupid.

Linda's story illustrates the value of recognizing your student's ego states. In addition, working skillfully with ego states and internal dialog may turn tutoring into a process of self-discovery for both the student and teacher.

Summary of Key Points

- Tutors can help teens gain more control of their behavior and increase self-understanding by teaching the TA concepts of ego states and internal dialog.

- In brain-building, the physiological development of learning ability, anything a person learns today helps the brain become physically more capable of learning tomorrow. Students may be inspired by the idea that they have a hand in constructing their own brains.

- Ego states are consistent patterns of feeling, experience, and behavior. Understanding the idea of ego states gives students a framework to think about their own internal lives.

- Each person has three ego states which are separate and distinct sources of behavior: Child, Adult, and Parent. Ego states are parts of the personality that may be used or held in check depending on upbringing, habit and choice.

- For us to learn effectively, our ego states must act as a team. The Child supplies the curiosity and energy, the Adult handles intellectual content, and the Parent supplies direction and self-discipline.

- Our ego states relate internally and even talk to one another. Tracking internal dialog can help students better monitor and control their own motivations and behavior.

- Recognizing your students' ego states and using your own ego states strategically will go far in reducing distractions and discipline problems in tutoring. In addition, it may begin a process of self-discovery for both the student and teacher.

In Chapter 15 we discuss *contracts*, the social and educational agreements we make in tutoring; *transference*, the special bond that facilitates the identification of one person with another; and *strokes*, attention, and how attention shapes behavior. Our understanding of these concepts can help us avoid confusion in the tutoring relationship and create a clearer, more nurturing environment for ourselves and our students.

15 | Contracts, Transference, and Strokes

TUTORING CAN BE UNPREDICTABLE. Students and parents may act in ways we find puzzling, and we ourselves occasionally have personal reactions we wish we understood better. Learning about the concepts of contracts, transference, and strokes will shed some light on the human aspect of tutoring. Though you may still be surprised by what takes place in tutoring, studying these topics can lead to an awareness that will prevent you from being blindsided. In learning about contracts, transference, and strokes, we will explore how our agreements with, and our imaginings about, our students affect the tutoring relationship and ultimately the outcome of tutoring.

Let's return to Amy, the late-blooming college student who came for help with organizational and study skills. After a successful semester at the four-year college she now attended, Amy no longer needed tutoring. When I proposed ending our sessions, though, she was distressed. "Can't I stay in tutoring and just tell you my troubles?" she asked. Yes, of course she could, but some adjustments would have to be made since we were moving into new territory, passing from education into therapy.

In TA terms, we needed to "renegotiate our contract." We were doing something she had not originally signed on for, and it kept things clear to acknowledge the change. It was also important for me to be aware of transference, a special kind of bonding that had taken place in our relationship. Let's see how contracts and transference work generally, and then examine them in the context of tutoring. After that, we will look at the way attention, or strokes, determine behavior.

Contracts

In the tutoring situation, or indeed any setting in which one person has agreed to provide services to another, there is a contract of sorts, though it is often an unspoken one. What were you hired to do? How will you know when you have done it? Do you and your clients agree both on the general goals and the particulars of tutoring? As teachers, our job is to be clear in our own minds about what our responsibilities are (and are not), and to communicate our understanding of those guidelines and boundaries to our clients when it is appropriate. In TA, an understanding about shared responsibilities is called a *contract*.

The contract we are talking about is not a legal arrangement, of course, but a social agreement. When a patient enters therapy or a student signs up for tutoring, there is a certain understanding about each party's rights and responsibilities. In addition, there is some mutual agreement about the purpose of the undertaking. So if Mr. and Mrs. Jones bring Suzy in and ask the tutor to teach her spelling, and if the tutor agrees, then the contract is to work on spelling. If, at some point down the line, however, the tutor discovers that besides not being able to spell, Suzy doesn't read very well either, the tutor will need to "renegotiate the contract," or seek a new agreement with the parents regarding the changing focus of the sessions.

In Amy's case, when we moved from study skills to "therapy mode," I needed to let her parents know that our sessions had changed direction. Her parents were paying for my tutoring, and the original contract was between three parties—me, Amy, and her parents—so it made sense to include them. Fortunately they were agreeable.

STUDENTS' PRIVACY

Jeremy was 17. He did the least amount of work possible, instead depending on his mother's strong ambition to carry him along. One Saturday he came to my tutoring office to take a sample SAT test, but half-way through the test, after a 10-minute break, he returned to my office bleary-eyed and reeking of marijuana smoke. This was a dilemma for me. Should I tell his mother or not? Here's what I did. I said, "Jeremy, if you will come to tutoring sober, I won't say anything to your mother." No preamble and no explanation. He knew what I meant, and he did come sober to the rest of his lessons as far as I could tell. I suppose technically it was blackmail, but looking back on it, I think it paid to keep Jeremy's secret.

The point is not that we must reveal everything about the goals and methods we employ in tutoring. However, we ourselves must be aware of our ends and means and share them with parents and students, but only when doing so would further the student's overall development. That means we sometimes need to keep secrets. For Amy, privacy meant that though I had told her parents we were no longer doing tutoring, there was no reason to explain exactly what subjects Amy and I discussed as she "told me her troubles." I kept my contract, and Amy kept her privacy.

Transference

Transference is a psychotherapy concept with a useful place in tutoring. Sigmund Freud originated the term *transference* to explain what occurs in psychotherapy when a patient has strong positive or negative feelings about the therapist that are not justified by the current reality but are based instead on the patient's past emotional experiences. In transference, the patient reacts to the therapist in terms of what she needs to see (positive transference) or is afraid of seeing (negative transference). Transference is a kind of "ink blot test" in which a patient attributes all sorts of imagined qualities and motives to the therapist, about whom she actually knows very little, all the while believing she is simply responding to reality.

In transference, people see what they expect to see, not what actually is there. A patient with a rejecting father may expect the therapist to be rejecting as well or, just the opposite, may believe she has found her "savior," someone who approaches saint-like status and is filled with understanding and love. In psychotherapy, the therapist analyzes and uses the transference to reveal to the patient the unrealized and unresolved issues from the past that color the present.

Transference and projection

Transference is a type of *projection*. To *project* means to deny one's own personal qualities and instead imagine them embodied by another. Thus, the unfaithful husband believes (with no evidence) that his wife is cheating on him, and the honest person assumes others will be honest. A patient who sees her therapist as highly intelligent and powerful while she believes herself to be just the opposite may be projecting. She denies her own intelligence and potential power, placing them instead on the therapist.

Transference in education

Transference and projection also take place in education. We've all heard of the grade-school boy who falls in love with a pretty teacher or the college student who hero-worships a charismatic professor. These are instances of transference, a student seeing what he or she desires to see. Of course, transference isn't always as positive as an innocent crush. Teachers come in for a lot of resentment, too, and if it is undeserved, this negative reaction is also transference.

Transference works both ways, and it's not just students who have unrealistic images of their teachers. The teacher can have a positive or negative projection on students, idealizing students or needlessly suspecting the worst of them. The chief problem with projections, of course, is that they are illusions, which means that if we believe in them they can cause us to act in ways that are detached from reality. A positive projection can allow a teacher's pet to get away with mischief unnoticed, and a negative projection often causes a teacher to blame a student unfairly.

Clearly, projections can create problems, but are projections and transference always bad? Let's ask the question differently: What good, if any, is transference in an educational setting? And how do we handle transference to do the least harm and the most good for students? It may sound strange to ask what good it does for students to delude themselves regarding their teachers. From my perspective, though, this "delusion" is often a positive, even essential, component in learning.

Before thinking about how to use projection positively, we must understand the damage that can be caused by unexamined projections.

A NICE BOY WHO DIDN'T LOOK THE PART

Alan was a third-grader who was deaf until his hearing problem was corrected at age five. Even though his hearing was fine at the time I started with him, he was still behind in his reading and other verbal skills. Alan was a sweet-natured, sensitive child with a handicap. No, not his hearing—his appearance. He was big for his age and lived in a body that in no way reflected the sweet child within. To put it bluntly, he was ugly. He had low, protruding brows, small eyes, short arms and a layer of body fat that gave him the look of an overweight adult. In addition, he was shy, perhaps because of his earlier deafness. He was a nice boy who didn't look the part.

In my conversations with Alan he related some disturbing news. He was the brunt of much unkindness as school, not just from other students but from the teachers! He was often punished unfairly and accused of not trying even when he was doing his best. But surely they could see what a nice person he was—couldn't they? No, apparently they couldn't see past his unattractive exterior. To them, his quiet ways must have seemed sullen and his ungainly body indicated a character flaw. Why? Projection, of course. The teachers imagined he was a certain way, so to them he must be that way.

The real tragedy occurs when the mistaken notion becomes true through the power of suggestion. Then the unattractive child becomes uncaring and unthinking because that is what is expected of him. I have no indication that happened to Alan, but it is a common risk with projections.

What should teachers do, then? How can we be fair when projections may intrude to cloud our vision? In my experience, if we simply *aim for awareness, fairness usually follows.* This means that we should examine our reactions to students carefully and compare our gut reactions with reality as best we can. And, in the words of the bumper sticker, "Don't believe everything you think." Sometimes a reality check from a clear-sighted colleague can help. Also, remember it is not necessary for teachers to rid themselves of all projections. As stated earlier, some positive projections can be useful.

Transference and the tutoring process

Not all student-teacher relationships entail transference, nor should they. Relationships without idealization and fantasy are straightforward, serviceable, and work perfectly well to accomplish a goal. They are "bread and butter" relationships based on a mutual interest, need (information and skills on the one hand and a pay check on the other), and shared responsibility.

But here's how transference furthers the tutoring process when it does occur. The teacher believes in the student, and the student trusts the teacher in return. An element of idealization enters in. The teacher may think, "This girl could be a fine student. She's smart and she has such a good imagination. She just needs encouragement." Now, the child may not have demonstrated any of these qualities, but the teacher is sure they're there and it's just a matter of time before they are revealed.

On the other hand, the student may feel, "The teacher is so nice. She really likes me. She thinks I'm smart. I'm not sure about that, but she must see something in me I don't know about yet. Plus, I think she'd like me even if I messed up. That shows she likes me for who I am and that I'm not 'buying' her good opinion of me. So I want to try even harder." The student and the teacher are not necessarily wrong about each other. In fact, their beliefs, though as yet unproven, help create the reality.

Transference can move beyond positive personal regard and enter into fantasy. With some care, however, even that is not necessarily a bad thing. Several years ago I started working with a new student, a 12-year-old Latino boy who had no interest in school and very little patience with tutoring. To him, formal learning was irrelevant, or worse, a wedge to separate him from his friends who thought book learning was un-cool. What I saw in my tutoring room was a sullen, unresponsive boy who resisted all my efforts to interest him in reading. But when I looked at his handsome brown face, I imagined him as an Aztec angel. In the end, the tutoring turned out well, though I don't remember exactly what methods led to that result. I do know that the actual interventions mattered less than the positive, though fanciful, image I held of the boy. This mental image predisposed me to like him, and it set the emotional tone of our work together.

But can't fantasizing about students be dangerous? It certainly can. That's why awareness of our own inner workings is essential. A teacher who imagined a hoodlum instead of an angel would have drastically different results. And, of course, in the rare instance when a teacher acts out sexually with a student, the situation must have started with a fantasy that was not only inappropriate but remained unconscious and unexamined. In those unfortunate examples, the problem is not just that the teacher "thought bad thoughts" but that she did not see her thoughts as projections—in other words, she didn't understand that they weren't "true." Projections, by definition, are not about the other but about ourselves.

Here's transference in a nutshell: First, it's not about you. And, second, the illusion can be useful if it serves the student's needs in the long run and as long as you remain aware that it *is* an illusion.

Using metaphor to define the tutoring situation

Sometimes transference, in the form of fantasy about a student, gives rise to a metaphor we can use consciously as an image to guide and sustain our work. Imagine you are starting work with an angry, resistant teen. This kid does not want to be in your office. He wants nothing to do with you. How can you reach him? Regardless of how you end up handling the problem, regardless of what you do or say, the crux of the matter comes before that, in the image you make for yourself to understand the problem on an emotional level. For instance, in taming a resistant teen, I might imagine my interactions with that individual as a kind of dance. The images of fishing or horse training also come to mind.

In the fishing image, I am reeling in a large and powerful fish. I know if I haul this big fish in too fast, he will thrash about and pull loose from the hook. But I can't be too timid, either. I have to play the line in and out just right to bring in my catch.

With horse training it's the same thing. A beautiful, wild creature needs to be gentled and tamed, but I do not wish to break the animal's spirit. To bring this horse around, I must gauge the amount of "play" correctly. That calls for good timing and gentle insistence, not brute force. Holding these images will guide my actions. Metaphor, in a nutshell: To influence reality, we begin with our own thoughts.

Rather than deciding on what thoughts to entertain, however, we find an image that tells the truth and sustains on an emotional level.

Positive uses of transference

Now that we have a definition of transference and some examples, let's return to Amy. She had finished a round of academic tutoring and asked if she could continue on "just to talk about her problems." It was evident that to propose this arrangement, Amy must trust me, but it went beyond that. She had developed a bond—transference—that would allow her to work with me in what was essentially a therapeutic relationship. I realized this was a serious undertaking. My task was to be aware of the special bond that had been created and to honor Amy's trust by being trustworthy.

Amy is progressing well in therapy, though we don't call it that. We both think of it as "emotional tutoring." Mostly she talks and I listen, though I do some teaching as well. The important aspect here is that I understand the transformative power of her belief in me, yet know it for what it is, and that though I'm a very nice person, I am not the idealized teacher she imagines me to be.

That leads back to the question of how we handle transference in a way that is most helpful to students. Now we're ready for some answers.

- Enjoy, but don't necessarily believe, all the good things that your students or their parents say about you.
- The same is true for anything negative—it's not usually about you. Do examine criticism, however, to see if there is any truth to it, and try to use mistakes as aids to "teacher education" rather than as ammunition for your critical inner Parent to use against your helpless Child (Chapter 14).
- Transference can guide you in dealing with a student's unresolved issues centered around past learning experiences.
- Be aware of students' crushes and resentments, but take care not to encourage either.

A note on handling crushes

For reasons already mentioned, it's common for students to develop crushes on teachers. When that happens, remain friendly but professional, and dress modestly. Sometimes young women are unaware of the effect their dress can have on their male students. And for both males and females, be conservative about how close you sit or how long you look into a student's face. As for touching, some teachers are naturally "hands on" and others keep their distance. Do what's natural for yourself, but keep close track of your students' reactions: a cringe or an open smile will tell you volumes.

Strokes

You will remember that in TA, strokes are units of attention and that everyone is born needing strokes (Chapter 1). You may also remember the phrase, "What you stroke is what you get." Now we'll build on this introduction to discuss how you can teach students about strokes in ways that will help them understand and better control their own behavior.

Let's start with the basics:

- Strokes are basic units of attention. They can be words, touches, or gestures.
- Everyone needs strokes. People are born needing and wanting attention, and that need remains throughout life.
- We respond to strokes with all three ego states, but it's our Child that experiences the need for strokes most.
- Some strokes are positive, some negative. A positive stroke might be a word of praise, a smile, a good grade. A negative stroke could be a scolding from the teacher or a nagging reminder from a parent.
- "What you stroke is what you get" means that as teachers we train students to act in certain ways through what we choose to stroke or ignore. A tutor who comments on writing that is clear and well-organized is likely to receive more such writing. "You just can't sit still, can you?" will produce a chuckle and, likely as not, more wiggling.
- Strokes can be thought of as a kind of currency, and as the basis of a "stroke economy." Strokes may be given, received, and exchanged in ways that bear a similarity to money. In groups, noticing who is giving and who is receiving strokes, as well as what kind and how many, allows us to track the flow of stokes and shows us the inner workings of the stroke economy.
- People will do what it takes to receive strokes, and if no positive stokes are forthcoming they often seek negative strokes instead.
- People learn to value the kinds of strokes they are accustomed to. That means the class clown would probably consider derisive laughter satisfying but might dismiss, even avoid, praise as being the incorrect "currency."

Those are the basics. Now let's look at strokes more closely.

- Students themselves can learn to shape others' behavior positively through conscious use of strokes. Tutors can help students gain positive attention at school by teaching behaviors that net them better quality strokes. It doesn't hurt to be obvious about this.

- One of the best strokes—best because it is easily accepted and has the potential to change student behavior quickly—is the "Look at what you did!" kind of stroke. For example, "That's great! Last week you didn't even know what a clause was, and this week you're punctuating them correctly."
- Though generosity with strokes is usually a good thing, avoid over-stroking. Praising people for meeting simple, routine expectations has actually been shown to decrease the desired behavior. For instance, you probably would not want to say, "That's so good! You did your reading assignment." You *expect* the student to do his assignment. Instead, praise him for *understanding* it.
- "Keep up the good work" is one of the most effective strokes you can give a student.

Being aware of strokes—and teaching students about them—can help solve a variety of teaching problems. For instance, developmentally delayed individuals often do not receive adequate strokes for their accomplishments because teachers and parents may not realize how difficult a particular activity might be for them. Knowing each student's "challenge level" allows you to respond appropriately.

If you have a student who needs more help to understand and control his own behavior, and if you have already taught ego states, try teaching about strokes. Then when trouble arises, you can raise the student's awareness about his own stroke needs and the kinds of strokes he invites.

For an unresponsive, apathetic youngster, try explaining that everyone needs strokes, including the teacher, and that one reason you teach is that you like to receive strokes from your students. You could even demonstrate through role-playing what kind of strokes you'd like to receive. Say how you feel when you receive strokes you want and the opposite, how it feels to receive no response. This tactic, done well, usually produces good results.

HOW STROKES MADE A DIFFERENCE

Rita was a 14-year-old Latina girl. The main strokes in her family came in the form of teasing, and parents and siblings often attempted to keep others in line through embarrassment. Rita's response was to avoid standing out. She was shy and reluctant to take risks. There was also an undertone of "you can't make me" in her attitude. "You can't make me think, work, enjoy, or imagine anything."

I had just learned about strokes in my TA studies and was eager to put my knowledge to work. How could I help Rita open up and be willing to take risks? I felt that strokes must be the key. So I set aside some time in each lesson just for strokes. I taught Rita about strokes and I asked her to tell me something she had done during the week that she was proud of. "You're supposed to brag," I told her. This concept was foreign to her, but with some coaching she came up with something to brag about. Her first brag was that she had read the funny papers to her younger siblings. I told her that was a nice thing to do and that I bet her brothers and sisters would remember it.

I explained that people needed to know how to both accept and give strokes. She had just accepted a stroke, and now I would like her to find something about me that she could comment on positively. She sat with her head down for a while. This was clearly embarrassing for her. But after a minute she looked up and said, "You have a nice smile." That comment did indeed bring a warm smile to my face. "Thanks, Rita," I responded. I explained that we should acknowledge strokes, and that usually a simple thank you was enough. This was definitely a "basics" course.

Each week, as Rita thought of more "brags," her pride in her accomplishments grew. Gradually her attitude changed for the better, and she even learned to give a compliment without embarrassment. Looking back on it, I see that focusing exclusively on strokes in this way was a little contrived, but it did work. As I continued teaching, I no longer set aside time especially for strokes but incorporated them into the lesson, an approach that seemed more natural. At that time, though, I was learning along with Rita.

Summary of Key Points

- In tutoring, a contract is an agreement, spoken or unspoken, between the teacher, student, and parent about the responsibilities and rights of all concerned.
- Transference, or projecting an unrealistic image onto others, occurs in education as well as in therapy.
- In tutoring, transference that goes unrecognized often causes serious interpersonal difficulty.
- Not all transference is negative, and positive transference can be a valuable component of tutoring.
- A successful tutor understands the art of using attention strategically.
- In TA, strokes are units of attention. Strokes include praise, rewards, or simply being noticed.
- Everyone needs strokes, and people will do what it takes to get them, so if no strokes are forthcoming, people often seek negative strokes.

- "What you stroke is what you get" means that, as teachers, we train students to act in certain ways through what we choose to stroke or ignore.
- Stroking students for meeting routine expectations can backfire.
- Teaching about strokes can break through student apathy.

For many students, learning about ego states, inner dialog and strokes will be all that's needed for them to let go of behaviors that stand in the way of their learning. If this is not enough, however, and students continue to engage in aggressive or self-defeating behaviors, learning about the drama triangle (Chapter 16)—in which the roles of *persecutor*, *rescuer* and *victim* are used to manipulate others—may help the teacher to break the cycle.

The tutor may choose to teach these ideas to the student or not, depending on the circumstances, but either way, the tutor's awareness and conscious avoidance of the drama triangle in tutoring will set a clear, unambiguous tone that will go a long way in directing energy toward learning rather than game playing.

16 | The Drama Triangle

TUTORING IS NO DIFFERENT from the wider world in the way it provides a stage for manipulative behavior. No one is exempt from acting in ways that stir up relationships, complicate communications, and undermine learning. For instance, a parent may criticize a tutor without knowing the whole story. A student may report that a teacher is always being "mean" to her, when a closer look reveals only reasonable requests. The tutor may feel compelled to do too much for students, completing their homework assignments for them and continually letting them off the hook. These behaviors are all examples of life in the drama triangle.

Manipulation is an emotionally dishonest attempt, usually originating in an individual's Child ego state, for the Child to get its needs and desires met by maneuvering others into acting certain ways. Though the individual's original needs may be legitimate, the devious attempts at control are not. If manipulative behavior from parents, students, or teachers is interfering with students' learning at school or in tutoring, and if we can identify and counter those behaviors, we can clear the way for much more effective learning and more satisfying relationships all around. The first step in dealing with manipulative behavior is to become aware of it. Learning about the *drama triangle*, as it is known in TA, is a good place to start.

Drama Triangle Roles

In their attempts to control others, people often take on certain predictable roles. They can manipulate either from a blaming, helping, or helpless position. These three common manipulative *game* roles, as they are called in TA, are the *Persecutor*, the *Victim*, and the *Rescuer*. If each of three players takes one of these prescribed parts, and if the players then switch roles, considerable drama and excitement ensues. This setup, complete with role switches, is known as the *drama triangle* (Figure 16.1). Learning to spot and head off drama triangle entanglements can improve the emotional climate, enhance communications, and free students to learn.

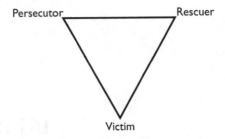

Figure 16.1. The drama triangle.

Legitimate roles and drama triangle positions are different from each other. There are appropriate times to scold and blame (persecute), and there are many cases in which we are called to give real help (rescue). People may truly be victims as well, suffering because of circumstances beyond their control. These are legitimate roles. But when people play out roles in repetitive ways, and when their actions lead to negative outcomes, they are probably acting out parts in the drama triangle.

A Persecutor (the capital denotes the drama triangle role) blames, criticizes, and demands. He or she may lie in wait for another person to do something wrong and then pounce. In school, this person is the teacher who seems to enjoy punishing students. Not that the Persecutor is consistent, though. He or she may be lax at times and punitive at others. That is part of the drama. Teachers are not the only Persecutors, of course. Students often persecute as well when they bait teachers with provocative behavior.

Victims, on the other hand, have a way of inviting others to take advantage of them (Persecute) and then bemoaning their fate. Or they may act helpless, thus inviting others to Rescue them. Their invitations may be covert or quite direct. One common characteristic of Victims is that they unconsciously try to make others more uncomfortable about their problems than they are. That is how they maneuver others into Persecuting or Rescuing them. As might be expected, Victims frequently get in trouble in school since they are likely to be disorganized and poorly prepared. When a teacher or another student tries to help a Victim, this help rarely has the desired effect. Seeing whether the help offered actually does any good is one way of assessing whether a person is in the Victim role. Victims may promise themselves and others they will do better, but not much changes because either they don't believe anything can be done to improve their situation or they would rather play Victim than do anything effective.

Rescuers, on the other hand, try to "help" people in ways that do not really help. They give unnecessary advice and do things for people the recipients could do for themselves. They jump in too fast to think and talk for others. Rescuers end up making (or trying to make) others dependent on them. Rescuers are plentiful in school settings.

In tutoring, drama triangle roles show up in several different ways. The Persecutor might be a parent who wants the student to raise her work to a certain grade level and then is critical of the tutor when the student falls short of achieving that goal. A Persecutor could also be a student who teases the tutor from a one-up position, making it clear he or she is too good to follow the tutor's silly rules. On the other hand, a student who repeatedly shows up half-asleep and late is likely in the Victim position. And I have to stop and wonder if I have been Rescuing in my tutoring when I find myself repeating advice that should be obvious or when my proffered help does not have the desired effect.

One of the main reasons to steer clear of the drama roles in an educational setting is that when people are engaged in the drama triangle they do not solve problems effectively. If a student is not learning well, we should look for possible drama triangle involvement on the part of the student, parent, teacher, or all three.

When one person assumes a role in the drama triangle, others will be tempted to follow suit. Thus, when a student acts the helpless Victim, the tutor may be under pressure either to Persecute or to Rescue, and the parent may be tempted to take the third, unoccupied, role.

For example, let's say Suzy comes in with a poorly done homework assignment. If the tutor says, "This paper is terrible. What's the matter with you?" then he or she is Persecuting. The parent may then defend Suzy, becoming the Rescuer. However, if the tutor takes pity and rewrites Suzy's homework for her, the tutor has just moved into the Rescuer position. And in this case the parent may counter by "cracking down" and Persecuting Suzy—and maybe even Persecuting the tutor to boot. To add to the drama, Suzy may switch from hapless Victim to one of the other two roles, either defending the tutor and blaming the parent or vice versa. This unpredictability adds to the drama. It is that drama, or excitement, unpleasant as it may be, that provides the impetus for people to play out the drama roles.

Avoiding Drama Triangle Entanglements

One value of knowing about the drama triangle is that when we observe people engaged in blaming, overhelping, or unnecessary suffering, we can predict and prepare for the switch of drama roles before it happens. For instance, if a mother comes into tutoring complaining loudly from a "put upon" Victim position that the school system has done wrong by her child, it's probably just a matter of time before she switches to Persecutor and that the tutor is likely to be her next target. Prediction is one thing, but what can a tutor do to circumvent such criticism before it occurs? Here's a way that usually works. The tutor could sympathize briefly with the mother and then move on quickly to discussing goals and ways to reach those goals—in other words, get the Persecutor thinking and engaged in problem solving. The goal of this intervention is to get the Critical Parent to switch to Adult.

PREEMPTING THE PERSECUTOR: FROM CRITICAL PARENT TO ADULT

Mother (outraged): "They started Tina in AP English but then they took her out without telling me and put her into a regular English class. I don't think she's learned any grammar (phonics, handwriting, etc.) at all. When I was in school . . ."

Tutor: "That's a shame. None of that should have happened. Is there anything you could do? What have you tried?" (Short discussion takes place.) "We can discuss the school situation in more detail later. For right now, I'd like you to look at this (reading, grammar/book, worksheet) I'm thinking of using with Tina." (The tutor can then bring up other activities he or she hopes to use with the student.) "It would be helpful if you could come in each session. Let's talk about her progress, and I'll let you know if there's anything you can do at home to help her. And be sure and let me know if you have any concerns or questions."

This reply, though not guaranteed to prevent Persecution, should go a long way toward decreasing its likelihood. The tutor did not ignore the mother's concerns about the school but did not dwell on them, either. Instead, the tutor discussed solutions, enlisted the mother's cooperation, and invited the mother to air her concerns before they grew out of proportion. Thinking (Adult behavior) was encouraged. Hopefully, in this transaction and others, the tutor came across as a kind person, but one who will not be bullied. Confident body language and tone of voice are strong deterrents for bullies and wheedlers (Persecutors and Victims).

Keeping communications straightforward and simple can help circumvent the drama triangle. That's easier said than done, of course, but here are a couple of tips, both learned the hard way. First, don't talk about anything of an emotional or personal nature on the telephone. If you have bad news or must ask a personal question, have the parent come in to your office to meet face to face. You need all the information you can pick up from facial expression, tone of voice, and body language, and the phone leaves out too much. People will understand that you care about them and their child if they can see it in your face, but caring is easy to miss on the telephone. *People are more likely to stay away from the drama triangle if they feel they are truly heard and seen.*

Second, keep interactions simple and private. For instance, it's best not to have parents in the tutoring room for the student's lesson because it changes the dynamic. Also, if you need to ask parents to change their own behavior, you'd want to avoid holding that conversation in the student's hearing. By the same token, if you have to scold a student, you don't do it in front of the parent. You may even choose not to tell the parent about a student's misbehavior. The key is to keep the social dynamic simple and allow people their privacy.

Any time someone approaches us from a manipulative "game" position, it is important to be aware of, and think about, the role we are being invited to play and to decline it clearly.

REFUSING TO PLAY

Rolf was a sophomore at a private high school. The boy never completed his homework and was temporarily suspended from school until he could show he was willing and able to do his work consistently. Rolf was extremely creative with words and was probably more intelligent than most of his teachers, a gift he used not to learn but to show off, obfuscate, puzzle, and put down—in short, to manipulate. Rolf started working with me on a home-school course to help him improve his study skills to the point he could be readmitted to the school. He liked the school and wanted to return, so that gave me some leverage.

During our work together I discovered that despite Rolf's considerable verbal talents, his reading comprehension was somewhat lower than I had anticipated. All of Rolf's bluster had been aimed at keeping anyone from knowing he was behind in his reading. He misinterpreted fiction passages, for instance, reading too much into them and imagining that objects and actions were symbolic of things they had nothing to do with. Rolf arrived at overly broad and imprecise interpretations in his textbook reading, as well. Rolf himself wasn't aware of the problem, however. He had concealed the difficulty so thoroughly that no one had ever noticed it, much less pointed it out to him. The standardized tests he had taken in school were no help either, since their multiple guess questions did not expose the more subtle problems he was experiencing.

When I first tried to explain to Rolf that we needed to work on his reading comprehension, he was incredulous. His reactions swung from Persecutor to Victim and back again several times. He was sure I was the one who had misunderstood the novel he was reading. He tried ridiculing my interpretations from the Persecutor position, then switched to Victim to explain sadly about how he couldn't stick with any reading he wasn't interested in, and how stressed he was, and how unfair it was he had been asked to leave the school. Indeed, I did feel intimidated by this intelligent young man who was using all of his skill to make me feel wrong; there was real pressure for me to take the Victim position.

Rolf's "poor me" talk, on the other hand, was an invitation to Rescue him, and the temptation, known in TA as a "game invitation," was to sympathize but not to do anything effective to help him. I knew it was very important for Rolf not to "win" this struggle. I must let him know I was on his side, but I also had to decline to play the drama triangle roles he was proposing. Not that Rolf was aware of any of this. Part of the "cure" was to raise his consciousness about what was going on. In the end, after several fairly intense sessions, Rolf did quit manipulating. Then he improved his reading, began doing his work, and returned to school.

But how did all this happen? The first thing I did was have Rolf quit reading the book we were arguing over and start on something less open to misinterpretation. Then I sat down with him and had a talk.

"I am guessing you are used to being treated one of two ways when you fail to do your work. Either people become angry with you and blame you for being lazy, or else they feel sorry for you and let you get away with things they shouldn't. Either way, they are not helping you." Rolf looked riveted, so I knew I'd hit on something. "I won't do either of those things," I assured him. I continued, explaining how I thought he probably reacted to being either blamed or babied. "If people are angry, my guess is you become angry yourself and use that as an excuse not to work. If they feel sorry for you, you agree with them that you can't do the job." He nodded in agreement. Then he listened as I laid out my expectations for our course of work together.

The purpose of this exchange was to expose the maladaptive drama triangle positions he was addicted to playing and for him to hear what I thought we should do instead. Though it is usually a gradual process to confront and change "gamey," manipulative behavior, in this case the breakthrough came suddenly. There was a moment of revelation when Rolf heard the ways in which he was shortchanging himself named and acknowledged. He agreed almost in spite of himself and was captivated (or stunned) enough to sit still and listen to my ideas for his tutoring course.

There was more to the story, and this was not the only time I confronted Rolf's argumentative and lazy ways. I also explained to Rolf that he must make an important decision about how he was going to use his talents and that the decision point was "now or never," that there really *is* such a thing as "too late," and he was fast approaching it.

Rolf worked with me a semester and then was readmitted to the school he wished to attend. During the time he studied with me, Rolf put his talents into real learning and developed his abilities to read, write, and study, not just effectively, but with outstanding results. His energies, which had previously been tied up in defending his position, were now set free to use productively, which he did with ambition, kindness, and humor.

What Roles Do We Play?

We've talked some about ways to deal with others in our lives who are playing drama roles, but how can we stay out of the drama triangle ourselves? The answer is that we probably can't, entirely, but with awareness of the "hooks," or temptations, that get us involved, we can greatly reduce the likelihood. Here are some questions to ask ourselves. What actions and feelings do we lean toward? Righteous anger (Persecutor)? Overhelping (Rescuer)? Being overworked and underpaid (Victim)?

What behaviors of other people "hook" us? A rude or impertinent student? Someone who looks pathetic? A parent who seems uncaring? When we see clearly what our sensitivities and resulting habits of behavior are, we can consciously set out to change them.

We can often identify drama triangle roles most clearly in hindsight by examining the results of our actions. For instance, if the tutor either punishes or helps the student, but the student continues to respond from a Victim position with whining, guilt, or overdependence, that may indicate that the tutor's interventions were initiated from a drama triangle position.

My favored role is that of Rescuer. If I am not careful I can fall into doing more for students than is good for them. I may answer my own questions without giving students enough time to think, and I sometimes excuse absences and homework lapses too easily. When I went through a TA training program, one of my assignments was not to help anyone unless they directly requested help. Of course, it is not possible to do this all the time with everyone, but the exercise was revealing. As a result of that exercise I worked hard to teach my students to ask for help, and that in itself cut down on Victim behavior. And I became much more aware of my own tendency to give unneeded help and advice. That awareness allows me to counter the tendency, though not without lapses.

Interventions

Here are more examples of interventions that may be used to circumvent drama triangle behaviors.

Persecutor

Mary's mom says to the tutor, "So what *are* you doing in class these days? We haven't seen much improvement." Stay confident but receptive.

Provide a reasonable amount of information. Involve the person in problem-solving. Apologize if you have actually contributed to some problem for which you are being blamed, though it's best to avoid abject apologies. Use humor if appropriate.

Victim

Alexa looks browbeaten and always sounds unsure and apologetic even when she is answering a question correctly. Ask her to "*act as if.*" That means she should *act as if* she *is* right even if she is not sure of the answer.

Nguyen is late again, his papers are flying from his notebook, and he looks as if he has a hangover. Put the responsibility directly on the student. He should pay for missed sessions himself, stay late to make up lost work, and come up with a plan to get on track. The cure is to *make sure the student is more uncomfortable about the situation than you are.*

Teach your students to ask for help, encourage parents to voice concerns earlier rather than later, and whenever you can, build independence by getting kids to act and think for themselves. For instance, don't accept "I don't know" for an answer unless you think it's genuine. Require kids to "repeat back to me" or even "fake the answer" to break through passivity. And have students put as much effort as you do into solving their educational problems.

Rescuer

You find yourself bending over backwards for a family but have nothing to show for it. You allowed them to pay less, but now they show up with an expensive new car. Renegotiate at the first sign you have been taken advantage of, preferably before you get angry and switch into Persecutor. Again, keep others more uncomfortable about the problem than you are.

To avoid Rescuing, keep advice, warnings, and scoldings brief and to the point. Avoid repeating. And, most important, give your student time to try things on his own and to think things through. Most Rescuing takes place when teachers lack patience and jump in with answers or solutions before kids have had time to thoroughly process their own thoughts and feelings.

Summary of Key Points

- People sometimes take on predictable roles in attempts to control and manipulate others.
- Common roles are those of Persecutor, Victim, and Rescuer, also referred to as drama triangle roles.

- Learning to spot and head off drama triangle entanglements in tutoring will clarify communications, enhance learning and improve the emotional climate.
- Persecutors try to intimidate by blaming, criticizing, and demanding.
- Victims manage to be blamed or taken advantage of repeatedly and may rely on others to bail them out.
- Rescuers "help" people in ways that do not really help. They give unnecessary advice and do things for people they could do for themselves.
- It is important to steer clear of drama roles in educational settings since people do not think clearly when they are engaged in the drama positions.
- Drama triangle roles are most clearly identified in hindsight, and looking at the results of our actions will help us see if we have been operating from drama triangle positions.
- To avoid Persecution, make it clear you wish to cooperate but cannot be bullied.
- To minimize Victim behavior, make the Victim more uncomfortable about a given problem than you are, and encourage students to ask directly for help.
- To avoid Rescuing, keep advice and warnings brief and to the point.

Until now, our attention has been taken up largely with what to do about particular situations. How to target an ego state, clarify a contract, make positive use of transference, or avoid the drama triangle. Now, though, we are moving into territory where we're not required to do much other than understand.

We are going to be looking at introversion, extraversion, and character and temperament types. These are not qualities or characteristics to be changed, but simply ones to be understood and appreciated. We can help our students understand their own temperament types, since typology affects learning style, and we can make variations in our tutoring approach to accommodate the different types, but the purpose of the next chapter is primarily to understand student behavior, not change it.

17 | Character and Temperament Types

*If I do not want what you want, please try not to tell me that my want
is wrong.*

Or if I believe other than you, at least pause before you correct my view.

*Or if my emotion is less than yours, or more, given the same circum-
stances, try not to ask me to feel more strongly or weakly.*

*Or yet if I act, or fail to act, in the manner of your design for action,
let me be.*

*I do not, for the moment at least, ask you to understand me. That will
come only when you are willing to give up changing me into a copy of you.*

*I may be your spouse, your parent, your offspring, your friend, or your
colleague. If you will allow me any of my own wants, or emotions, or beliefs, or actions, then you open yourself, so that some day these ways of mine
might not seem so wrong, and might finally appear to you as right—for me
. . . [Eventually] you might come to prize my differences.*

—Keirsey and Bates (1984, 1)

THE MAIN ADVANTAGE OF TUTORING is that it's not a one-size-fits-all prop-
osition, but a highly individualized undertaking. Academically, at least,
we take into account our students' individual interests and their varying
levels of skill and understanding. But what about the side of tutoring that
is concerned with the *personality* of the learner, with the subtle (and sometimes not-so-subtle) differences that distinguish people from one another
in terms of character and temperament? These fundamental differences
determine how individuals experience and respond to life. They also influence learning style, not so much in terms of sorting people into "visual" or
"auditory" learners, but by shaping their whole emotional and psychological approach to learning.

Most teachers intuitively understand and respond to their students' individual differences, at least to some extent, but taking the next

step—deepening our understanding of temperament and character—can lead to a richer and more nuanced approach in our own teaching and an increased level of awareness and learning for our students.

INDIVIDUAL DIFFERENCES: BRODI AND KASEY

Brodi and Kasey came for tutoring last semester in adjacent time slots, and I couldn't have asked for a more striking demonstration of individual differences. Both enjoyed their tutoring sessions and were getting a lot out of tutoring, but for very different reasons.

Brodi was extremely shy when he started tutoring and hated being put on the spot. He liked to hear my ideas about the novels he was reading and was quite happy doing the vocabulary exercises out of his workbook, but he didn't particularly like being asked about himself. He blushed if I even asked his opinion, and he would never make a guess if he wasn't sure of the answer. I tried to stay in Brodi's comfort zone at first then gradually guide him into being more willing "put himself out there" and take some risks.

Kasey, on the other hand, loved having the chance to express her opinions and was supremely confident even when she was wrong, but she needed to be told (nicely) to think about what she was doing and to be more observant. Just as Brodi got what he wanted (not to be put on the spot), Kasey also got her wish (her turn in the spotlight).

It's possible I would have known intuitively how to handle these two very different individuals, but learning about introverts like Brodi and extraverts like Kasey when I studied typology made it easier for me to choose the best way to teach them. For one thing, it helped me be more patient with them, because I saw them simply living out their natural differences rather than exhibiting character flaws.

Typology: The Study of Character Types

Many people take the view that "everyone is pretty much the same," but common sense and psychological theory both show us this is not the case. The study of typology is about the differences between people, and this section is about how awareness of these differences can enhance our relationships with students.

Let's start with a look at individual differences as described in *Please Understand Me: Character and Temperament Types* by David Keirsey and Marilyn Bates, which is the source of much of the material on typology in this chapter. I encourage you to read (or reread) this book, especially the chapter entitled "Temperament in Children" (Keirsey and Bates 1984, 97).

Keirsey and Bates refer to character and temperament types that are based on the Myers-Briggs test (Myers-Briggs Type Indicator, MBTI). This test is designed to assist in identifying important personal "preferences," or differences. MBTI criteria are derived from the "function types" described by Swiss psychiatrist Carl Jung (1976).

Many people in the general population are familiar with Myers-Briggs work on character types, or typology, and may even have taken the test themselves. Therefore, other than providing a quick summary for those unfamiliar with the basics, the purpose here is to look at how students with these character types might function in an educational setting and some ways to accommodate them. That includes points on choosing books and educational strategies with the types in mind.

Keirsey uses four pairs of types to describe character and temperament: *introversion* and *extraversion*, *intuition* and *sensation*, *thinking* and *feeling*, and *judging* and *perceiving*. Familiarity with the types will allow us greater flexibility in teaching to our student's inclinations rather than automatically using our own types as templates. Without this awareness, our own differences may bias us unfairly for or against certain differences in our students. It would be helpful to find out about your own type before introducing the subject to students. A short test for this purpose is provided in Keirsey and Bates (1984, 5).

The types are also sometimes referred to as "preferences" since people exercise at least some degree of personal choice in their use. In the Myers-Briggs system, one word from each of the four pairs mentioned above is used to describe an individual's personality. So for instance, a person might be an extraverted, intuitive, feeling, perceiving type (ENFP). In the next section, we begin with introversion and extraversion, followed by the three remaining pairs. Teaching suggestions follow.

Introversion and Extraversion

In our society it is commonly believed that all people are motivated by the same basic desires and motives. According to Keirsey, the belief that people are fundamentally alike appears to be a twentieth-century notion that is related to the growth of democracy. "If we are equals, then we must be alike." Obviously, if I believe everyone is fundamentally like me, then I will be inclined to think a person who acts and feels differently is in need of correction. Keirsey, however, believes people's temperament and behavior "may be just as inborn as their body build" (Keirsey and Bates 1984, 4). If this is so, differences in character type need to be understood and respected rather than changed. *Introversion* and *extraversion* are prime examples.

People have very different desires and needs when it comes to socializing. Those who gain energy from being around others prefer extraversion. Those who prefer solitude to recover energy may tend toward introversion. These terms frequently are misunderstood. Extraversion doesn't necessarily mean friendliness and concern for others, and introversion does not always mean shyness or lack of social skills. Instead, these two categories of feeling and behavior have to do with the way people choose to "recharge their batteries."

Extraverts feel lonely when they are not in contact with people, but introverts are more likely to experience loneliness in a crowd. Though introverts may enjoy interacting with people, it eventually drains their energy to be around others and they will seek time alone to recharge. With extraverts, it's just the opposite. Socializing renews and invigorates them. They must exercise self-control to do solitary work and are often tempted to socialize when faced with tasks that must be done alone.

Think about what these differences would mean for school kids. The extraverts would have to struggle to make themselves study, and the introverts would be worn out at the end of the school day simply from being around other people. Then there's the social stigma associated with being an introvert.

Keirsey explains it this way: Western culture sanctions the outgoing, sociable, and gregarious temperament. The notion of anyone wanting or needing much solitude is often viewed as reflecting an unfriendly attitude. Introverts are often the ugly ducklings in a society where the majority enjoy sociability. One mother was heard to protest loudly, "My daughter is not an introvert. She is a lovely girl!" (Keirsey and Bates 1984, 16.)

One of my chief goals in working with children and teens is not to turn them into something they're not, but to help them "become who they really are." That means giving them freedom to be themselves despite societal pressure to the contrary. Those pressures are described in "Understanding Introverted Kids," an article by Linda Kreger Silverman, Ph.D.

> The American dream is to be extraverted. We want our children to be "people who need people." We want them to have lots of friends, to like parties, to prefer to play outside with their buddies rather than retire with a good book, to make friends easily, to greet new experiences enthusiastically, to be good risk takers, to be open about their feelings, to be trusting. We regard anyone who doesn't fit this pattern with some concern. We call them "withdrawn," "aloof," "shy," "secretive," and "loners." These pejorative terms show the extent to which we misunderstand introverts. . . .

. . . Introversion is a perfectly normal personality type identified by Carl Jung. It is actually healthy to be an introvert. The only unhealthy part of it is denying your true self and trying to disguise yourself as an extravert.

Introverts need to learn about the positive benefits of their personality type. They need to be taught that reflection is a good quality, that the most creative individuals sought solitude, and that leaders in academic, aesthetic and technical fields are often introverts. . . . (Silverman 1991)

It is clear that introverts need some special care and consideration, but what about extraverts? Talk with your extraverted students to find out what is most troublesome for them regarding their school experience and their studies. Many teens, especially boys, say they don't like to read or study because it makes them feel lonely. Teens who have trouble sitting and studying alone can try the following.

- Play the radio *softly* in the background.
- Chew gum. (Studies have shown chewing gum helps people think. Really.)
- Set aside special snacks to have only at study time.
- Decorate your study area to make it cheerful.
- Reward yourself with a call to a friend after a set amount of study time, but only if you think you can limit your time on the phone.
- Don't study where you will be tempted by the phone or by instant messaging. It may be necessary to turn the phone ringer off and avoid studying alone in your room with the computer.
- If you study with others, choose study buddies who have more self-control than you do.
- Keep a log of what, when, and how long you study, and bring it to tutoring.

In addition, particularly sociable students should ask *not* to be seated near their friends in class. (This step takes some gumption, but kids will do it when they see the need for it.)

Although we've been speaking of introversion and extraversion as if they were two separate categories, with people falling clearly into one or the other, that's not always the case. It's probably more accurate to think of introversion and extraversion as the opposite ends of a continuum. Some people might be extreme introverts or extraverts, but many will fall somewhere in the middle, introverted in some circumstances and extraverted in others. These preferences—or functions, as Keirsey calls them—may also change over time, so they should not be considered static.

Introversion and extraversion may be a source of misunderstanding and intolerance among students themselves. Extraverts may think the introverts are socially inept "nerds," while the introverts may regard the extraverts as "plastic" and shallow. Discussing introversion and extraversion with teens can further both self-understanding and the appreciation of others. For some students, learning about their own and their opposite functions can be a life-changing first step in self-forgiveness and compassion.

Since tutoring is usually conducted quietly and one-on-one, introverts may shine in tutoring. In fact, tutoring may give a shy, insecure introvert her first taste of academic success, and that confidence may subsequently carry over into other areas. A bookish and isolated teen may also find life-changing help in tutoring through the supportive relationship with a sympathetic tutor. In fact, some bookish teens will only accept a literary companion as a life guide, and the tutor will occasionally find him or herself in the strange position of being more trusted than the student's therapist. ("Why is this kid telling *me* all of this stuff?")

Extraverted teens also benefit from tutoring, though for the opposite reason. Instead of drawing them out, the quiet one-on-one exchange of tutoring helps them calm down and focus. A chatterbox, a social butterfly, or an athlete with little experience in introspection may discover aspects of themselves they didn't know existed.

For further reading, see the excellent chapter in *Please Understand Me* on temperament in children(Keirsey and Bates 1984, 97-128). The section on introversion and extraversion in children is particularly informative.

Sensation and Intuition

Sensation types are "sensible." They are grounded, down to earth and practical. They are interested in facts and are more concerned with reality than possibility. For this reason, the past and present are more compelling to them than the future. They value perspiration over inspiration. When it comes to reading, they would probably enjoy nonfiction and might find history and "how-to" books appealing. Sensation types know their world through their physical senses more than intuitive types do. According to Keirsey and Bates, sensation types make up 75 percent of the adult population (1984, 25).

Intuitive types, on the other hand, are dreamers and daydreamers. They are interested in what might be: "Whatever is can be better." They work from hunches and may receive "brainstorms" in which complex ideas come to them all at once. Even though they can be hard workers, they value inspiration over perspiration. They love metaphor and vivid imagery. Their reading tastes might tend toward fiction and poetry. Fantasy fans are likely to be intuitive types. Twenty-five percent of adults are intuitive types (Keirsey and Bates 1984, 25).

As to reading tastes in children, the intuitive child is apt to ask for a repetition of stories and likes to hear stories of fantasy and metaphor. The sensation type child, on the other hand, is likely to enjoy sequential adventure stories about familiar and factual subjects. She wants the story to have action and to make sense. The sensation child likes detailed stories and usually prefers a new story to a familiar tale. Also, the sensation type child may prefer playing games or some type of other activity to hearing stories.

Keirsey and Bates say that intuitive children may be hard to handle since they have a core of "being their own person," which adults sometimes find objectionable and offensive (1984, 103). Intuitive types may seem willfully opinionated to others since they know what they know but cannot justify their convictions. They are given both to strong dislikes and crushes, and may put teachers on a pedestal (if they do not hate them). They often "space out" and daydream when they are supposed to be working. Compared with sensation types, they are the most likely to seem different in a way that is unacceptable to adults. Here are some tutoring suggestions for both types.

For sensation types

- Emphasize information.
- Provide reasons.
- Don't be concerned if their writing is not highly imaginative. Simply help them be clear.
- Emphasize skills. They want to know how to do things. Cue cards explaining the sequential steps in a process, SQ3R, for example, would be appreciated.
- Try to come up with simply stated principles, procedures, or rules to guide them through tasks. The "Paula" method of determining main idea is a good example (Chapter 8).
- There's no need to avoid assigning detailed or routine tasks. For instance, students might enjoy diagramming sentences once they've learned parts of speech, and even taking science or history notes might appeal to them.

- If sensation type teens read novels at all they will probably like action/adventure or historical novels.
- Some sensation type boys are willing to read adult level history books about subjects that interest them. For instance, some high school boys will gladly read quite detailed books on WWII and Nazi Germany. Biographies of sports or music greats are also popular.
- Stand by to help when rules or procedures become complicated. A sensation type might write a perfectly acceptable report only to stall out on the conclusion.
- Though working with symbolic language and abstraction is not their forte, sensation types can gain skills through practice, so don't avoid symbolic literature and poetry, but do provide a scaffold for understanding literature. A list of themes in literature might help, as would a study of idioms.
- For intuitive tutors, be patient with your more pedestrian students, and enjoy them for what they are, even as you encourage them to imagine.
- For sensation type teachers, challenge your like-minded students to join you in unaccustomed flights of fancy.

A SENSATION TYPE STUDENT

Ted, a ninth-grader, was a math whiz who enjoyed his science classes. Because of his interests and intelligence (he wanted to be an engineer), the grownups in his life thought he ought to excel at school. Instead, he was failing almost everything. What could be done to help this young man fulfill his promise?

I determined that the reason Ted was doing poorly in the subjects that interested him (math and science) was that he didn't listen to the lectures or class discussion. He was too busy drawing doodles in his notebook to pay attention. I thought he was probably a sensation type and that he would probably respond well to learning some procedures he could use to focus his attention. Therefore, I taught note-taking and asked him to substitute taking notes for doodling in his classes. Then I asked him to bring the notes to his lesson each week. Another boy might have rebelled, but for this sensation type, the assignment was fine.

When Ted's grades improved in the classes he liked, we moved on to English and history. I taught the basics of reading comprehension, then introduced SQ3R. Ted liked the how-to sheet we made together that listed the steps of the SQ3R method, and he used it in his history reading.

The last big gap was writing. I believe Ted had dysgraphia (a disability that affects writing similarly to the way dyslexia does reading). A third grader could have done better. Ted's writing was not only incorrect, it was filled with fuzzy assertions and vague generalities. (Just because Ted was a sensation type, it didn't necessarily follow that he would be good at the practical aspects of writing.) We worked hard on writing essays, using all the rules and procedures I could come up with. ("This is your task in the introductory paragraph," etc.) After some success at essay writing, we started on creative writing, a consciousness-raising experience for both of us.

The work Ted and I did on using description, examples, and dialog in his writing was a turning point. This work pushed Ted to think in specifics as well as globally and to rely on his imagination as he never had before. The combination of the down-to-earth and the imaginative clarified both his writing and his thinking.

Ted wrote a story about a drunken, lazy college student who was kidnapped and held for ransom. During his captivity the boy sobered up and started rethinking his values. The boy in the story had turned over a new leaf by the time he was released, and Ted had a new outlook, too.

For intuitive type students

- Feed intuitives' imaginations through creative writing and verbal prewriting activities. "Let's role-play and make up dialog for our characters. Then we can write it down."
- The goal is to help teens *develop both roots and wings*. Point out that attention to details and routine can lay the groundwork for real freedom, not destroy it. "Learning correct spelling and punctuation will not compromise your creativity. Imagine the dynamite combination of your creativity *plus* correct mechanics."
- A good way to get ideas across to intuitives is through parables and anecdotes.
- It is very important to teach intuitives to use their strengths, particularly their superior imaginations, to overcome their weaknesses— for instance, their intolerance for repetitive detail.
  - o Teach the concept contained in this metaphor: "When you empty the trash, you can focus on the trash or you can look up at the sky."
  - o An example of getting through a dull task by exercising creativity is to use vocabulary words to make an interesting story.
  - o Waldorf education is a rich source of ideas on the subject of creative learning. For a basic explanation of Waldorf education, see the Association of Waldorf Schools of North America (AWSNA) website, www.awsna.org. The Waldorf Library Online, www.waldorfonline.org, has a list of books on Waldorf methods.

- Ask intuitive teens themselves how they can best get through the academic drudgery that is required of them and still keep their souls alive. (The wording of this question will resonate with the intuitive student.) These students often have answers for themselves, but will need you to draw them out through questions and discussion.
- Poetry by teens is often highly subjective and overemotional. It may be cathartic, but it is not good poetry. Teens need to express themselves, though, so teach them to substitute metaphor and image for intellectual concepts and overwrought feelings.
- Show your intuitive students the value of their own gifts. They may feel that since "imagining things" or being able to draw, or being insightful about people comes easily to them, those things couldn't possibly be very important. Gently point out (perhaps through a parable) how unfair that attitude is to themselves.
- Intuitives form strong transferences. Be prepared.

An intuitive type student

Helen was a pretty, vivacious 15-year-old who came to me to make up a social studies class she had failed in school the previous semester. We did plenty of work on maps, of course, and I made sure she could read the geography text and take notes, but I also (intuitively) threw in a novel and a couple of movies. Helen was geographically challenged (it took her several weeks just to learn the cardinal directions on a map), but she did a remarkable job of understanding and explaining the complex human relations depicted in the novel and the movies. She insightfully explained the inner workings of the characters in the novel, yet when I asked her to read and explain an article about the economics of world poverty, a subject in which she was actually quite interested, she looked anxious and sad. Despite her intuitive gifts, it appeared she thought of herself as dumb when it came to schoolwork. She certainly did not shine in the subjects she was expected to do well in at school.

For Helen to do her best at both her strong and weak subjects, it was important for her to value her strengths, but she was going to need some help to do that. I put it to her this way: "You have a wonderful ability to look below the surface to see why people feel and act as they do. You have excellent people skills and you are very insightful. Knowing map directions or remembering facts about foreign countries is a different matter. Those things are harder for you. Look at it this way, though. In real life, as an adult, how important is it going to be for you to know how to read a map? Sometimes it might be handy, but it's not crucial. On the other hand, how important is it to be able to 'read' people? That *is* important. That skill in itself will take you far in life. So you're already good at the most important stuff. Of course we still need to work on geography, and you will get better at it, but I'd rather have you start out good with people and poor at geography than the other way around."

Helen beamed, and she seemed to try harder at geography after that. I was also glad to note that she no longer took her difficulties with the subject personally. Realizing the value of her intuitive nature helped Helen gain new confidence, and having a teacher who put things in perspective for her helped her make the connection.

Another Intuitive Type Student

Anna was a wonderful actress and talented singer, and she excelled in drama at the small private high school she attended. She, too, had failed a social studies class and came to me to make up a semester's credit in geography. Regarding Anna's tutoring, two aspects stand out.

First, Anna was an intuitive, and I knew I had to work with, not against, her creativity if I wanted to bring out her best. Academic work didn't hold much importance for her. Art, along with listening to and caring for her friends, was her life. When I learned this about Anna, I thought of Tosca's aria, "Vissi d'arte, vissi d'amore," "I have lived for art and for love."

Our discussions revealed that Anna dreamed of becoming a "musical ambassador." She would travel to other countries to bring a message of love and good will from the American people. What a wonderful idea! How could I encourage her dreams? And how could I design a geography course to make the most of her interests?

Lofty as these goals sounded, meeting them turned out to be both entertaining and surprisingly easy. With Anna's interest in drama, a good part of the course consisted of watching films set in other countries, then studying those countries and reporting on them in creative ways. Of course I did the usual lessons on how to read a textbook and how to take notes, but these cut-and-dried tasks were always balanced with ones that involved some drama, in this case dramatic films to teach about a foreign country. Anna loved the films and she understood the terms of our deal—she needed to do well on the mundane tasks before she could spend much time on the more interesting ones (see "Grandma's Rule," Chapter 1).

To find good films, I consulted my next door neighbor, a filmmaker and world traveler, and I even got Anna and the neighbor together for a visit. I believe Anna came to understand that the way to her goals was not to fight against academic requirements but to accept them and use them for her own ends—exactly what intuitives, the dreamers of the world, need to do if they are to use the system and not be crushed by it.

Aside from how we ourselves relate to an intuitive student, another issue that may emerge is the parents' response to their teen's creativity. How do the parents deal with the teen's sometimes irresponsible-looking passions and hobbies when these interests do not fit into the parents' desires for the student? (The movie Dead Poets' Society explores this problem.) Anna's parents were happy their daughter was learning good study skills and work habits in her tutoring. That meant she could go to the rigorous four-year college they had in mind for her. But Anna had other plans. She wanted to major in drama at a school other than the one her parents favored. Anna was a bundle of mixed feelings. She had new confidence in herself as a student, but now she was afraid her parents would mismanage her new skills and try to shape her into something she didn't want to be. And what a dilemma for me! Should I sit back and watch the train wreck happen, or should I intervene, with the possible result of being seen as interfering and unprofessional? True, I was hired to be Anna's advocate, but it was the parents who were paying me, so this was tricky. I chose to intervene, and looking back on it that was probably the right decision.

I explained to Anna's rather mainstream (probably sensation type) mother that it is very important for creative kids to be able to pursue their artistic dreams. "Art is like food and water to these kids. For a creative person, the creative urge is a force that builds up, like water in a fire hose. You can't just block it without creating problems other places in their lives. It's reasonable to ask her to do well academically, but she'll probably still get the academic subjects she needs even if she's in drama school. I've heard they read a lot of Shakespeare."

The day after my talk with her mom, I got a grateful call from Anna. The parents were allowing her to be in the school play, something that had been off limits "until she got her grades up." And she would not be applying to the college with the business program her parents wished her to attend. All I needed to do now was make sure Anna understood how important it was to balance her schedule so she could keep up with school *and* do rehearsals, too. Things seem to have worked out. She's a senior this year, and when I see her in the halls at school, she's beaming.

Thinking and Feeling

Thinking types tend to make decisions based on impersonal, objective judgments. They are likely to be logical and objective—or at least they value these attributes far more than feeling types do. Thinking and feeling types are distributed about equally in the population, though there is more societal permission for women to be feeling and men to be thinking types. Thinking types like to think for fun and may enjoy intellectual puzzles. They may feel deeply but do not often show their emotions outwardly.

Feeling types are more likely to rely on the "personal basis" for making decisions, meaning it is important for them to know how their decisions will affect others. How they feel personally also carries a lot of weight when making decisions. They are comfortable with making value judgments. The feeling type values feelings, of course (his or her own, and perhaps other people's), and tends to be emotionally expressive. Knowing that people are feeling types says little or nothing about their intelligence, however; it only indicates their favored mode. In fact, I once tutored a developmentally disabled young man who was a thinking type. Both types can choose to make decisions in the opposite style. The difference is how comfortable they feel doing so; a person's "default" style will simply feel more natural.

How do these types get along in school? School is designed for thinking types but this circumstance may not always be in their best long-term interests. Keirsey and Bates write:

> People with the F [feeling] preference may have an advantage over those with the T [thinking] preference for developing the less-desired preference. Formal schooling addresses the T areas far more than the F. Thus, those with a natural preference for F also tend to develop their T, while those with a natural preference for T do not have an equal opportunity to develop their F side, which may remain relatively primitive. (1984, 21)

For example, drama majors are expected to know their multiplication table, but how many engineering majors could be expected to deliver a soliloquy?

Carl Jung wrote that it is desirable for people to explore and develop the qualities that represent their less developed, or "off side" (1966, par. 86). If that is true, the thinking type's task might be to develop warmth, while the feeling type student should work on logic and sequential thinking. Thus, in tutoring, we might help thinking types learn better "greeting behavior," which we could teach under the heading of learning about strokes. Feeling types, on the other hand, are already disposed to spend the entire hour being warm, gracious, and helping us decorate our offices. For these students, lessons in logic would be helpful. Both approaches are necessary and valuable.

Although thinking and feeling types are capable of complementing each other well, misunderstanding and intolerance can develop between them. Feeling types may be put off by school rules, which they see as too impersonal, and they may regard thinking types as cold and heartless. Thinking types may see feeling types as "too soft-hearted" or "fuzzy thinkers."

In tutoring, thinking types might find SAT and ACT preparation rewarding, while feeling types would be apt to enjoy novels and poetry. Often the same destination can be reached by either route. Teachers might require all their students to do both SAT and novel reading in school, but we can modify our expectations slightly in tutoring, allowing students to follow their own interests within reason, and we can soften the impact of academic demands by teaching students about typology.

Teachers should not just assume that students will automatically prefer reading fiction to fact. Many young people would actually rather read nonfiction, and tutors can help students develop their own interests by encouraging them to sample a variety of reading materials. Some thinking type kids find it exhilarating to read books and articles that are rich in ideas and concepts. For them, political and social commentary, as well as scientific writing can be good choices. Avoid "dumbed down" textbooks, and as soon as their skills are up to it, let them try editorials and articles from the *New York Times* and *Atlantic Monthly*. Some feeling-type girls will favor whatever sentimental novel is currently at the top of the bestseller list. Of course, there are no hard and fast rules about which type of student will like what reading material, but typology offers a place to start.

In my experience, intelligent feeling types process information and come to conclusions much differently than intelligent thinking types, though their conclusions may be similar. Nina and I have been close friends for more than 20 years, and we take pleasure in seeing how similar and yet how different we are from one another. Nina is highly intuitive and is also a thorough-going feeling type. Drama, beauty, and art are predominant in her life.

Over the years I've been intrigued by the way Nina makes important life decisions because her process is so much different from mine. As a thinking type, I'm fairly linear. I go from A to B to C, or at least I try to. Nina is much more of a "global" thinker. Instead of going from A to B to anywhere else, she seems to "sit in the middle" of the choices and imagine how she would feel under this circumstance or that, then make a decision based on those feelings. She might also check out the "vibes."

When Nina chose a private school for her daughter she "felt" that one school in particular was right based on a simple act of kindness when a teacher came and took her daughter's hand to show her around the school. When I chose a school for my daughter I checked their "stats"—percentage of students who went on to college, the endowment, etc. Yes, I wanted to see if the kids looked happy in the hall, but that was frosting on the cake.

I am always amazed at the depth of Nina's intuition and insight, and she seems to admire my steadiness and ability to persevere. Neither of us would trade places, though. We're just fine as we are.

The point? Just because a teen uses a different path from the teacher's, it does not necessarily mean the student is headed in the wrong direction. Wait and see—and guide gently.

Judging and Perceiving

The terms *judging* and *perceiving* are somewhat misleading, since there is very little about either judging or perceiving in their functions. Instead, the judging type values closure while the perceiving type desires more open-endedness in making decisions and settling matters. Judging types (J's) feel good about making definite decisions, while perceiving types (P's) are likely to feel uncomfortable about having their "options cut off" when matters become finalized. According to Keirsey and Bates, judging and perceiving types each make up about 50 percent of the population (1984, 25).

Judging types take deadlines seriously and try their best to meet them. In contrast, perceiving types may regard a deadline merely as a signal to start a project, not finish it. Judging types have a strong work ethic, while perceiving types seem to operate from a "play" ethic. Judging types will do what it takes to complete their work, even if it means forgoing play and rest. They will plan, maintain, and clean up afterward to make sure their work is done right. For perceiving types, though, work doesn't have to be done before play begins. Keirsey notes:

> And if the process of work is not directly instrumental (is mere preparation, maintenance or clean up), then the perceiving individual may balk at doing it or find something else to do. P's are much more insistent than J's that the work process is enjoyable. One might say that P's are process-oriented while J's are outcome-oriented. (1998, 24)

P's and J's are apt to criticize each others' work style. J's may describe P's as indecisive, foot-dragging or aimless, while P's may talk about J's as being as driven, rigid, arbitrary, and too task-oriented. Though J's and P's can irritate each other, when they learn more about the others' type, they often respond with interest. As they gain understanding, they can learn to make allowances for the others' differences.

What would J and P teens look like in school, and what would help them most in tutoring? Imagine two students, one a goal-oriented J, the other a P out to have a good time, and suppose they are equally intelligent. In fact, let's make all the other variables the same. They are both extraverted, sensation, thinking types, and they are both boys.

One of the big problems for the P will be meeting deadlines for papers and projects at school. Being ready for tests will also be an issue. Many kids have these problems simply because they have not learned time-management skills yet, but the cure is the same whether the student is exhibiting a personality trait or simply needs help organizing. Show your student how to plan ahead for papers, projects, and tests by marking the due date in his planner and then working backward to the present, deciding what he should do when. For a paper, the planner would have entries showing when the student would go to the library, have his reading and note cards completed, have a rough draft, and have a final draft. He should leave a couple of days free at the end "just in case."

Then ask the student how he should organize his time on a daily basis to meet these deadlines. Have him write out a daily schedule for himself and talk about how he can keep himself on task. (Kids know most of this organization and self-discipline stuff. They just need us to ask them so they can say it aloud in front of a witness.) Later, the student will note on his planner what he *actually* did for each step.

The J student might not need much help, or if he does, it would be of an entirely different nature. He might benefit from having a teacher's permission to plan some "down time" and schedule in some fun. Chances are he will skip anything that is not work related unless it's in the schedule.

The goal in all of this is not to remake kids but to help them see ways to succeed without giving up who they are. Telling them just that would be a good first step.

If you wish to continue your study of character and temperament, you can read a second book by David Keirsey, *Please Understand Me II*. Beyond that, I recommend Gordon Lawrence's (2009) *People Types and Tiger Stripes*, which contains much valuable information and insight concerning young people, types, and education.

Summary of Key Points

- Individual differences that are based on typology need to be understood and respected rather than regarded as characteristics to be changed.
- Familiarity with character types will allow us greater flexibility in teaching to our student's inclinations rather than automatically using our own types as templates.
- The Myers-Briggs Type Indicator (MBTI) uses four pairs of terms to describe temperament and character: introversion and extraversion, intuition and sensation, thinking and feeling, and judging and perceiving.

- In tutoring, extraverts often benefit from guidance on how to get themselves to do the solitary work of studying.
- Introverts may shine in tutoring, and the confidence they gain from the one-on-one relationship with the tutor may carry over into other areas of their lives.
- For sensation types, provide reasons, emphasize information, and come up with simply stated principles and procedures to guide them through reading tasks.
- Intuitive type students are likely to be creative dreamers. They will benefit from learning to value their own gifts and finding ways to deal with drudgery. Allow for creative expression and teach through parable and anecdote.
- Thinking types are likely to be intrigued by complex ideas and concepts in their reading.
- Feeling types may look for emotional intensity in reading material.
- Character type can only offer a rough guide. Have students sample a wide variety of reading subjects and styles, and don't automatically assume that students will favor fiction over nonfiction.
- Judging and perceiving types operate differently in how they meet deadlines.

Many parents and teachers have asked me about how to work with children and teens who have learning problems. Chapter 18 addresses this topic and will give you some insights and ideas about how to help students with ADD and dyslexia. I'm hoping it will do more than that, though. I'd like to think of it as a troubleshooting chapter, one to use before the problem has a chance to get out of hand. In deciding what to include, this was my guide: "What do I need to do as a tutor to make sure that every student who shows up for his or her lesson is ready to learn?"

18 | Helping Students Build Attention and Fluency

No education guide would be complete without a section on learning difficulties that are physiologically based: learning disabilities (LD), dyslexia, attention deficit disorder (ADD), and attention deficit hyperactivity disorder (ADHD). So much has been written about these problems, however, and there is so much differing opinion, that I propose to take a different approach. Instead of discussing possible causes, diagnosis, and plans for remediation, I'm going to make an end run and talk about what tutors can do to help students who exhibit various learning problems, regardless of their origins. That should help avoid the difficulties associated with labeling and philosophical debates. With the exception of some discussion on the causes of dyslexia, the focus will be on the positive—how to strengthen *abilities*—rather than on *disabilities*.

For teens with ADD and ADHD, *attention* is naturally a major issue, and for those with dyslexia, *fluency* is key. However, all students who have trouble listening, sitting still, or maintaining reading accuracy and speed can benefit from the exercises and activities in this chapter.

This approach is admittedly incomplete. To fill in the gaps, you may wish to do some further reading. For insights into ADD and for an introduction to a variety of valuable resources, see *Driven to Distraction* by Edward Hallowell and John Ratey. To learn more about dyslexia and teaching dyslexics, read *Overcoming Dyslexia* by Sally Shaywitz, M.D., which combines cutting-edge research with sound practical advice.

In this chapter, we begin by looking at changes that could be made in students' internal and external environment that would help them arrive in tutoring better prepared to learn. Next we go over ways to help students improve their listening skills. After an overview of dyslexia, we talk about the usefulness of timings, drills, and other methods of building fluency. We look at how to help teens who have learning problems focus better and "get the point" from their reading. Finally, we discuss the value of students becoming accustomed to work.

Helping Students Arrive Prepared to Learn

Here we look at factors that may affect a student's preparation for learning. These include rest and relaxation, nutrition, medication effects, and vision.

THE CULPRIT WAS THE ICE CREAM!

A friend of mine tutors reading to a very fidgety and distractible young teenager. The boy wants to succeed but struggles visibly just to sit still for a few minutes. I received a call from her recently exclaiming over how differently her student acted in his lesson today. "He was sort of like a little Buddha," she said. "He seemed almost contemplative. He was concentrating deeply and was not at all distractible."

"How could this be?" I wondered. My friend explained. It seems the boy's father had withheld the son's usual after school snack of chocolate ice cream. "It made all the difference in the world," added the tutor. "I'm thinking of asking his father to get rid of the ice cream altogether."

The point is not that chocolate ice cream is bad—sometimes it is, sometimes it isn't—but that making a small physical change in a student's environment, internal or external, can at times result in a big difference in an individual's attention level. Consider rest and relaxation, for example.

Rest and relaxation

In tutoring, we recognize the blatant problems concerning rest or lack of it—teens who show up for lessons with only four hours' sleep, for instance. But there are more subtle problems as well. I once saw a 16-year-old change overnight from a "dunce" to a smart girl when I moved her lesson from an after school time, when she was exhausted, to before school. Any student can suffer from being tired and stressed, but kids with learning problems seem particularly vulnerable when their rest is disturbed. Because of this, they have much to gain from being rested and relaxed.

Sometimes there is nothing a tutor can do about teens who are burning the candle at both ends other than wait a few years for them to grow out of it, but it's still worth making an effort. Surprisingly, it often helps to ask the parents to intervene. A phone call from the tutor may be just the excuse parents are looking for to set an earlier curfew or insist that their teen simplify his schedule. Also, incredible as it may sound, it often works simply to "assign" students to get more sleep. "All right, Nguyen, for the next lesson I want you to be here rested and organized. Write that in your planner."

Teens who have trouble concentrating because of stress may benefit from relaxation exercises they can do in the tutoring session. (See "Relaxation improves concentration" later in this chapter.) In addition, relaxation tapes, a class in stress management, or meditation instruction may help more than you might think.

Nutrition

Good nutrition may be vital for good concentration, particularly for teens with learning problems, but I've found that people are easily offended by even the most tactful suggestions about their eating habits or those of their children. As a result, I usually steer clear of the subject unless invited to give my opinion. In addition, most teens who make poor food choices report that they are knowledgeable about good nutrition but don't have time to eat right. Maybe a key to good nutrition is for teens to simplify and organize their schedules.

Observing the effects of medication

As a tutor you are in a position to see things others might miss, and with no particular vested interest other than wanting to help the child, you can be an unbiased observer. Parents realize this as well, or at least most of them do. For instance, to find out whether a particular medication is working for a child, parents may ask you to keep track of the student's behavior and report back to them. Naturally, when you do this, you will want to talk with the student about his own experience.

THE OBSERVANT TUTOR

When Jeff's mother started him on a new medication prescribed by the boy's psychiatrist, Jeff began having headaches. I didn't know whether the medication was causing the headaches, but I did know the timing was suspicious. Poor Jeff moaned and groaned his way through his lessons, and of course learned next to nothing. I called his mom and voiced my concerns, pointing out that the headaches started right after Jeff began the new med. No, it was OK. She was sure. "The psychiatrist says this is the medication with the least side effects. The alternative is worse. Besides, he has headaches all the time anyway."

I was incredulous. "He has headaches all the time?" Why hadn't I noticed?

Jeff came to his lesson with no headache the next week. When I asked why, he answered, "Oh, I forgot to take my ADD pill." Ah-hah!

I called Jeff's mom again. And again. After our fourth conversation, she called me back and said that she had insisted on a change in Jeff's medication. Jeff was now taking the so-called "worse" medication with no perceptible side effects and with good results in controlling his ADD. Bingo.

Jeff's mom was not stupid or negligent and neither was the psychiatrist. (I know the doctor.) What they lacked was perspective, and because of my special vantage point, neither too close to the situation nor too removed to see what was happening, that is what I was able to bring to bear. Jeff's headache days were over, and so were mine, at least for then.

Vision and vision therapy

Naturally, one of the first things parents should do when they suspect a reading problem is to have their child's vision checked. By the time a teen with reading problems arrives at tutoring, chances are he has been tested and re-tested for vision problems. Chances are also good that if the teen has reading glasses, he doesn't wear them consistently. Not only do teens not want to look "dorky" wearing glasses, but many adolescents with reading problems have organizational problems as well and may leave their glasses at home frequently—that is, if they haven't lost them.

So what's a tutor to do? First, check with the student to see if he is experiencing fatigue, eye strain, or headaches while reading. If so, find out whether he's had his eyes checked recently and whether he has glasses. If he has them but is not wearing them, why not? After some discussion, you may be able to make a deal for the student to wear the glasses, at least to tutoring, and preferably whenever he needs them.

Many parents ask whether vision exercises prescribed by a developmental optometrist can help their son or daughter read better. Vision therapy seems to be a mixed bag. Some kids don't seem to benefit at all from months of eye exercises, while for others it can be a major turning point. Maybe it depends on exactly what was wrong in the first place and who the doctor is.

In some cases, simply participating in a good tutoring program can allow students to achieve the same positive results as vision therapy for much less money. For instance, if an individual needs help with visual tracking, using the long smooth underline (LSU, Chapter 5) is often enough to correct the problem if the exercise is done correctly and over a long enough period of time.

Why does vision therapy have such mixed results? This is conjecture on my part, but perhaps vision therapy treats some kinds of reading problems well but other problems poorly. For example, what if vision therapy successfully treats tracking problems but not dyslexia, and what if optometrists aren't distinguishing between the two? The matter needs to be studied, but the studies should be done by unbiased observers, not vision therapists, as is the case now.

It's true that some students benefit from vision therapy even without tutoring, but this is unusual, and vision therapy alone is usually not enough to bring students up to their highest level of proficiency. That is because when teens have experienced visual tracking problems serious enough to hold their reading back for several years, they also have missed out on important stages of reading growth, as well as, presumably, cognitive development. In that case, vision therapy could remedy the immediate visual problem but leave residual reading problems unaddressed. For example, a teen might be able to read more smoothly after vision therapy, but what if he is still unable to identify unfamiliar words or understand idiomatic speech? For this reason, I believe it is best to combine vision therapy with tutoring.

Daily Drill

Daily drill is important for kids with learning difficulties, whether or not they have dyslexia. But if kids or parents aren't able to work at home every day, one possible alternative is for the parents to hire a study helper to work with the student several times a week. As a tutor, you may wish to help parents locate a qualified helper. I've found it works well to place a job notice on the bulletin board at the university that serves our area. Education majors often make excellent study helpers. I interview the applicants myself, then send a short list to the parents. The parent hires the study helper, but I orient the person and provide any training needed.

So far we've talked about ways to help students arrive at their lessons prepared to learn. Now let's turn to the lessons themselves.

Lessons in Listening

Learning disabilities—brain-based problems of perception and processing—can cause poor auditory perception and memory, which translate into poor listening. Kids with perceptual problems aren't the only ones who have trouble understanding and remembering what they hear, however. Teens with ADD or ADHD may also have difficulty listening, not because of perceptual problems, but because they have trouble paying attention.

Auditory problems are complex, and causes can be hard to pin down. Many educators blame excessive TV for children's listening problems. I certainly have noticed a decline in children's, teens', and even adults' listening skills during the past fifty years. It's hard to believe TV and other electronics have had nothing to do with this trend.

Regardless of the cause, teens who listen poorly often can be helped greatly by a long-term, consistent program to teach good listening. Expecting kids to listen well is a good first step. Though teens with perceptual deficits or ADD may still have to contend with their underlying physiological problems even after remediation, good instruction can help them change their listening behavior in positive ways.

Do you have a student who consistently misinterprets or ignores your instructions? This is the kid who, when you say, "Read this paragraph silently and tell me what you read," immediately asks, "Should I read it out loud?" If so, do two things. First, listen to yourself, preferably with the help of a tape recorder or video camera. How do you sound when you give instructions? Are you clear? Friendly? Do you sound as if you expect the student to listen? And what do you do when you must repeat directions for a student who isn't paying attention? Ignore the problem? Sound exasperated? (Neither is particularly helpful.) Imagine being a student under the direction of the teacher you hear on the tape recorder, and if needed, work to develop a friendly but firm tone of voice. Use the tape recorder to guide your progress.

Second, discuss the problem of inattention with the student and explain that practice can help him improve his listening skills. Briefly call the student's attention to those listening behaviors you believe are not serving him well. Explain that there is a natural inclination for people to ignore instructions—after all, as you're growing up, instructions are likely to be things you don't want to hear like "eat your spinach" or "make your bed." So it's natural to get in the habit of not listening to directions, but in the long run it's not helpful. Point out that good listening can help in a variety of areas, not just with directions. After all, many jobs and relationships run aground on poor listening.

Next, find out how your student does with taking lecture notes. Lecture notes are a big concern for most kids with learning problems, at least for classes in which the teacher does not provide notes on the board or from an overhead projector. Reassure your student that although taking notes from a fast-moving lecture can be difficult, it is something he can learn to do with practice.

After you've talked with your student, embark on a series of exercises to help him improve his listening skills. Though it may take several weeks to notice much progress, a consistent program, even if it's only one session a week, can often make quite a difference in the long run.

Read and repeat

Begin with this exercise. Read an interesting novel aloud, one sentence at a time, and have the student repeat each line back to you clearly from memory. Begin with short phrases and proceed to longer and longer portions as your student becomes better able to remember what he has heard. (Avoid having the student look at the book other than to enjoy the pictures.) I like to use *Matthew and the Sea Singer* by Jill Paton Walsh. It is the story of a boy with a magical voice and of his friend who saves him from the seal people who kidnap him to hear him sing. Though the book is written for younger children, most high school students respond to it readily, and the subject matter fits in with the theme of listening. The language of *Matthew and the Sea Singer* is just quirky enough to require careful listening. Insist on clear diction and good expression, modeling them yourself. Plan to devote 10 to 20 minutes a session to this exercise for a period of several weeks.

This read-and-repeat exercise may be simple, but it can be highly effective in helping students who have difficulty listening, whether because of a learning disability, ADD, or just too much TV. It has even helped students with Asperger's Syndrome, an autism spectrum disorder that affects a person's ability to relate to others. For kids with Asperger's, repeating what they hear read from a book may be a low-stress way of learning to relate.

For students who need more than the read-and-repeat exercise, using audio books can be a wonderful way to experience great stories while improving listening skills. Have students follow along in their own books to exercise their reading muscles. Some students have greatly improved their listening and reading skills by using audio books, which also can be a lifesaver for students who need help getting through reading assignments in English class. Sources of audio books include online Books on Tape, Audible.com, The Audio Bookstore, Recorded Books, and many public libraries.

Following oral directions

After the student has finished the read-and-repeat exercise, have him do some exercises that require following oral directions. One excellent activity is to ask the student to draw an object, one line at a time, entirely by following your verbal directions. Part of the fun of this exercise is that it involves drawing a mystery object. The student is in the dark about what he is drawing, at least at the beginning. Then, as he follows each of your directions accurately, he will begin to see a pattern take shape and eventually will be able to guess what you are having him draw. Start with simple objects, such as a toothbrush, snowman, or umbrella, and work up to more complicated ones.

Here are the steps of the drawing exercise in more detail. Beforehand, if needed, review the cardinal directions on a map and how to measure out an inch using the thumb. Then, draw a picture to use as a reference for yourself. This is your "secret picture." Give directions for your student to reproduce this picture without having seen it. Give more than one direction at a time so the student has to remember them, and don't let him pick up the pencil to draw until you have finished the last direction in a series. Try to work up to giving three or four directions in a row.

Directions for drawing an ice cream cone might be, "Draw a triangle that has two-inch sides, with the point facing south. On the north side of the triangle, and touching it, draw a semi-circle. The round part will be to the north. Make the semicircle as wide as the triangle."

To succeed at this exercise, it will be necessary for the student to form a mental image of what he hears; it's nearly impossible simply to remember the words of the oral directions. When the student is finished with the drawing, show him your picture to compare with his own and discuss any errors. Trade places sometimes so that the student gets to be the "teacher," drawing the original picture himself and giving you directions on how to reproduce it.

When students can draw objects fairly well, move on to maps. To do this, have the student draw a fictitious map from oral directions you provide. Try the following example from Carlisle (1987, 44), then make up your own.

> Follow this set of directions. Draw a map.
> Mr. Smarty is a detective. Ralph the Robber has hidden money he stole from the bank. Help Mr. Smarty find the money by drawing him a map to go with these directions. (North is toward the top of your paper.)
> Draw the bank in the bottom left corner [of your paper]. Go north from the bank three blocks on Ocean Rd.
> Turn right on East Street. At the second stop light turn left on Trapp Street.
> You will pass two large pine trees on the left. Then go over the railroad tracks. Take your next right turn.

On the left you'll see the town's baseball field. Home plate is nearest the road. Walk to second base. Examine the bag used to mark the base. Put an X on this spot to mark the hidden money.

After some practice, your student might like to make up his own maps for you to draw according to his directions. This is a good exercise for kids who can't seem to put two words together. As with the previous object drawing exercise, the person who is giving the directions, in this case the student, constructs a map which he keeps secret until the end of the game. His map could contain streets, mountains, lakes, bridges, and whatever else he wants. Then, without showing you the map, he tells you how to draw a duplicate of it one step at a time. For instance, he might say, "Go three miles (inches) north. Turn east. Go over a bridge and continue east a mile."

You "travel" by drawing a road as you go. All the time the student is giving you directions, he's also consulting his own map. At the end of the game you compare your two maps. If they are similar it means you both did well. Did the student explain clearly what he wanted you to draw? Discussing differences between the two may help him see how to clarify his own directions.

It is also possible to have students do science experiments from oral directions. There are many guides to simple, interesting science experiments kids can do at home, and it's often fun to do them together in the tutoring session. Again, work up to a series of directions and have students try to visualize the steps before he does them.

Tuning in at school

Help your student learn to listen better in class. Many students tune out at school because lectures are boring (or so they think), and it seems a waste of their time to listen. Lectures and class discussions *can* be repetitive or juvenile (even for kids). As a result, many students develop poor listening habits simply out of self-preservation. Unfortunately, they usually go too far, missing interesting or informative parts because they are too busy daydreaming, doodling, or even sleeping. The key is not to insist they pay attention to everything—probably an impossible goal—but to teach them to be selective.

You can start by breaking them of the habit of doodling in your tutoring sessions, and then make sure you keep the pace of learning moving along at a steady clip so that it pays them not to tune out. Ask them how much they doodle in class and make an agreement with them either not to doodle at all or only to doodle when they are sure of the material being discussed. Follow up on the agreement: "How are you doing about cutting down on the doodling? How well do you think you're listening?" In some situations, you can help kids tune in by requiring class notes from them even if their instructors don't.

Talk to students about the "cues and triggers" that indicate a speaker is about to say something worth listening to. "It's not necessary to listen all the time, but it is important to know *when to start listening.* To do that, you have to keep some key words and phrases to look for, along with some examples of body language, in the back of your mind." Then brainstorm with your student. What are some of the words, intonations, and gestures teachers use to introduce or stress a point that is important to them? List them and tell kids it's possible to stay on "autopilot" until they hear them, then that's their cue to sit up and take notice. Examples might be that the teacher walks toward the students, repeats a point, speaks louder or with more emphasis, gestures broadly, or writes on the board. In *Learning to Learn: Strengthening Study Skills and Brain Power,* Gloria Frender offers more advice for students on "reading" teachers (Frender 2013, 106-108). The problem with many students is not that they can't listen but that their "on/off switch" doesn't work very well. Discussing and practicing it in this way can help.

Taking lecture notes

After completing the exercises described above, your student will probably be ready to start taking lecture notes. It is quite difficult for kids with auditory processing problems to take lecture notes, so while this is an important learning activity, it should wait until the student has had plenty of practice with other types of reading and listening activities.

Show your student how to take notes when the lecturer is going faster than the student is able to write. You do this by abbreviating—jotting down the first letter or two of each important word—and leaving space to fill in complete words and thoughts later. Whole lines can be left blank for this purpose. To demonstrate, have your student give you a short talk on a topic of interest to him while you take notes. Then give a short lecture yourself with your student taking notes in this abbreviated form. Have him fill in his notes with whole words and sentences as soon as he's able, perhaps during a lull in the lecture.

Explain that most lecturers present their information in bursts, alternating a few minutes of fact—or concept-filled material with a period of "down time." The down time is usually a digression, such as what the teacher did over the weekend. This "human interest stuff" is what most people perk up and listen to, but your student should be encouraged to do the opposite—tune out the digression and use the down time to fill in and complete any unfinished words and thoughts in his notes. It will take several weeks for your student to become adept at taking lecture notes. In the meantime, ask him to bring in his class notes from school so you can go over them together.

When students have the basics down, you can ask them to take notes from radio news programs such as NPR (National Public Radio), first in the tutoring section and then independently. Take some time to go over the structure and content of the news articles you hear, especially the introduction and conclusion, from a writer's point of view. You can gain some excellent material for lessons on essay and report writing in this way.

Another good activity to teach more advanced note taking is to have students listen to and take notes from a *Great Courses* lecture. *Great Courses* are recordings of some of the best college lecturers in the country. You can get a copy of the *Great Courses* catalog by mail (www.thegreatcourses.com). Many *Great Courses* offerings are available free through interlibrary loan.

Paying Attention

By definition, kids with ADD and ADHD have difficulty directing and maintaining their attention. They may find it difficult or impossible to stick with one activity or even with one thought for very long. Sitting still and paying attention for an hour's tutoring session can be very challenging. This is not a reason to scrap the expectations, but to help the student adapt as much as possible to meet expectations. (Refer to "Troubleshooting motivational problems" at the end of Chapter 4.)

Actively directing student attention

Kids with attention problems need to learn that even though sitting still and concentrating are difficult, it won't hurt them to do it, and with practice it will become easier. In working with students who have severe ADHD, I sometimes use a method I call "directed attention." I keep up a line of patter, encouraging students to "keep looking and keep focusing," then praise and reward them when they do. Often, I'll sit shoulder-to-shoulder with a student, a book or piece of paper on the desk in front of us, and physically point out what I want the student to be focusing on, all the while talking the kid through the task. I'm insistent, sometimes pushy, not allowing the student's attention to wander for a moment. This process of "directed attention" might sound like nagging, but it's different in a couple of ways: It's short term, it's goal-directed, and I convey an expectation of change.

Directed attention still might seem like hectoring to the student, but it does have the desired effect of helping students break through whatever mental barriers keep them from immersing themselves in a task. Needless to say, this only works if you have already established a good relationship with a student. You also have to know how far to push. Some kids can tolerate only a few minutes of focused attention to begin with, so an important part of the plan is to work incrementally to build students' tolerance and ability to focus. Three minutes at a time this lesson, five minutes next lesson, fifteen minutes next month.

Surprisingly, most teens don't respond with anger to these demands and, in fact, will usually try to do what is asked of them. Maybe that's because the teacher's voice urging them to "keep focused" delivers a message they know they need to hear, but are not able to provide for themselves, at least in the beginning. In psychological terms, this makes sense. Developmentally, children first hear an important "Parent message" externally, then internalize it and make it their own. After that, according to TA theory, they would be able to draw on the new content of their Parent ego state to direct their own attention.

I don't mean to imply that ADHD or other problems that have to do with ability to focus are entirely a matter of discipline or will. There are strong neurological components to ADHD. But it's also true that assertive direction from a respected adult often does help children and teens learn to Parent themselves and direct their own attention in a purposeful way.

Relaxation improves concentration

Having students relax at the beginning of a tutoring session can help them concentrate. The goal is to have an alert mind but a relaxed body. Ask students to breathe deeply and put their minds in neutral. You can do a simple relaxation exercise by having the student tense each muscle group as much as possible then let go. If you tense as much as possible, hold it, tense even more, hold that, and then tense even more, you'll get the full effect. If you are tensing your arms, for instance, they should be shaking from tension before you let go. When you relax, do so three times in succession. "Relax as much as you can, hold it, relax even more, finally let go of any remaining tension." I find it works best for the tutor to do this exercise along with the student. Most people are less self-conscious if they do the exercise with their eyes closed. Yoga exercises for the head, neck, and eyes can also help kids whose distractibility is due to stress-related tension. Of course, a little friendly conversation can set a relaxing tone as well.

Exercise and attention

Everyone agrees that people need exercise to do their best, but do we really follow up on this idea? Adequate exercise is particularly important for children and teens with attention or perceptual problems. Exercise before a tutoring session may help a hyperactive child sit still or wake up a groggy one. I have a tutor friend who keeps an exercycle in the tutoring room for just that purpose. She calls it the ADD bike. We all know that exercise can brighten people's moods, but did you know there's evidence that exercise actually aids physically in brain development? Movement is an indispensable part of learning and thinking. I sometimes "assign" kids to run in the park before their lessons. Being physically tired helps some hyperactive kids concentrate, but this only works if the tiredness is a result of exercise and not stress.

Helping students pay attention

"PULLING YOURSELF BACK": LEARNING TO REDIRECT ATTENTION

Sam was 11 and in the sixth grade. He was seriously ADHD and even with medication was often bouncing off the walls. He talked with machine-gun speed, and his eyes darted around the room, seemingly unable to light and rest. I wondered if his thoughts did the same.

Sam and I had been working on his writing for about three months when I realized I was directing him to pay attention much more than was good for either of us. My frequent reminders to "look here" and "keep watching" had crossed over into Rescuing. The reminders might have been appropriate during the first few weeks of tutoring when I was still "breaking Sam in." In fact, early on, they were essential. At some point, though, I had to shift the responsibility to Sam for his own learning. Specifically, he had to start monitoring and directing his own attention. It helped that Sam liked me. "He thinks you're a divinity," his mother commented. (She wondered if I could also get him to clean up his room.)

In TA, when we wish to help another person change his behavior, we first describe the behavior (it helps to do it from Adult ego state), say how we think the behavior is a problem, explain what we want the person to do instead, and find out whether he is willing to do it. It's not necessary to follow the formula exactly, but just knowing the structure can be helpful.

Even behaviors that appear to be ingrained and involuntary can sometimes be changed more easily than one might expect. Not always, of course. But in Sam's case the results were quick and satisfying. It took just one interchange. We were working on punctuating a story he had written. For what must have been the tenth time that lesson, I directed his attention to the paper between us on the desk. He looked at it for a few seconds before his eyes slid away again. "Sam, I've asked you over and over today to focus on what we're doing. That was OK back at the beginning of tutoring because you were just learning to pay attention. But you're old enough now that you can tell yourself to pay attention."

I pointed out that he wouldn't always have a grownup around to remind him to pay attention and that the goal was for him to be independent and not need grown-ups so much to regulate his life. I emphasized that he had more control than he might think. "If you can pay attention when *I* ask you to do it, you can also tell *yourself* to pay attention. I know you have ADHD and that makes it hard for you to focus sometimes, but you can do better than this. You may not be able to pay attention 100 percent of the time, but," and here I gestured around the room, "if your attention goes off somewhere, you can pull your eyes and your mind back here to the page." I explained that he might need a mental rest every once in a while, and that was OK, but it was still up to him to bring himself back into focus after the rest.

Sam nodded in agreement, and that was the end of that. I never had to ask him to focus again. Not that he is always focused, but I can depend on him to pull himself back in when he wanders off.

Using an "attention meter"

Paying attention is not always that easy, of course. And sometimes nothing helps. But occasionally approaching a child or a problem just a little differently can turn the tide. For instance, it may help young teens to see a visual rating of how they're doing rather than having you tell them. For this exercise, start by making sure your student knows you consider working on "attention" and "organization" as important as doing schoolwork. Then, as an alternative to telling him to pay attention, which can get old fast, try this. On a piece of paper, use colored pencils or crayons to draw a colored strip, one end green and the other red, with yellow and orange blending into one another in the middle. Put a "man" or marker on the colored strip and move the marker back and forth from red to green, depending on how well your student is paying attention at any given time. Red, bad; green, good.

Telling whether a student is "paying attention" is highly subjective, of course, and kids may not look like they are paying attention when they actually are, so be clear with the student about what you're judging on. It's probably best not even to emphasize the term "paying attention." Instead, simply look for "sitting upright," "looking in the right direction," "speaking clearly," or "not interrupting." Also, it helps to pare down expectations and focus on just one or two behaviors to change at a time. Make sure students understand that these are not, strictly speaking, virtues in themselves, but methods of directing attention. Most kids will go along with the game, especially if there is some payoff for them in the end.

Sometimes the chart isn't necessary at all. Simply using an egg timer works for some kids. "If you do X for the next five minutes, we'll have some talking time."

Interruption tickets

Here's a great technique to cut down on distracting interruptions using what I call "interruption tickets."

INTERRUPTIONS HAVE A PRICE!

Twelve-year-old Ari had Asperger's, a physiologically based disorder that affects social functioning. He had a habit of interrupting me often—it seemed like every few seconds—and of changing the subject away from whatever we were studying to what he wanted to talk about. A lot of these interruptions came under the guise of joking. It seemed I couldn't say anything without Ari making a joke about it.

Ari wasn't aware of how his interrupting was affecting his lesson or how I might feel about it. He wasn't even aware he was doing it. If I scolded Ari or explained to him repeatedly he would feel ashamed, and that would not make it any easier for him to change his habits. Individuals with Asperger's can be extremely "locked in" to a behavior, however, and a weak intervention would fail to have any effect. The solution was "interruption tickets."

I gave Ari five pieces of colored paper, each about the size of a dollar bill. On the front of each one I had written, "Good for one interruption," along with a little design to make it look somewhat like money. I gave the five tickets to Ari and set the timer for 15 minutes. "You can interrupt or change the subject five times in 15 minutes, but you have to pay me one ticket each time you do. When your tickets are used up you can't interrupt at all."

"Oh, no," Ari said as we got started, "I feel really guilty now. Like I don't think I can say anything without interrupting and that interrupting is really bad."

"No, I don't feel that way. I want you to be able to say a few things that are not directly on the subject. Everyone needs the freedom to say what comes into their heads *every once in a while*. You have a lot of funny and interesting things to say. The problem is with how *often* you interrupt. I just want you to cut down on it."

We proceeded with the lesson: "You just interrupted. Give me a ticket."

"Uh-oh, I didn't even know I was doing it. Is joking always an interruption?"

"Yes, usually. You just have to think about what you're saying before you say it."

"That's hard."

I knew it was. Ari almost *never* thought about what he was saying. That seemed about to change, though.

After the 15 minutes were up I gave Ari the tickets back and set the timer again. Eventually, Ari got the hang of rationing his wisecracks and was able to get through half an hour with five tickets, then an hour. We were able to discontinue the activity in a few weeks, and Ari seemed happy to focus on what we were doing rather than chasing his random thoughts.

Plugged in and tuned out

Have you worked with kids who are so "plugged in" they can't focus on any one thing? Between their cell phones, iPods, and text messaging, these kids are both victims and generators of electronic sensory overload. In a world of gadgets, they learn to multitask but not to focus. Though there's not much any one person can do about the wider problem, there are ways we can help our own students slow down and tune in.

TIME TO UNPLUG AND TUNE IN

Haley, a high school sophomore, was making up some geography credits for a class she had failed. As part of her homeschool program with me, she was to study at my office several times a week after her regular lessons. That way her homework for me was sure to be done, and I could keep an eye on its quality. The setup sounded perfect, and in the end, it did turn out to be just right, but there were some bumps along the way.

First, even though Haley did well in her lessons with me, when she studied on her own she didn't seem to be learning anything. Second, and I suspected the two were related, she always had a music player plugged into her ears when she studied. At the beginning, I gave her the benefit of the doubt. Maybe it wasn't the music that was distracting her. Maybe she just didn't know how to study. So during her regular lessons, we had a quick study skills course, including how to memorize flash cards. I taught her the rule of three, asked her to work aloud when learning unfamiliar terms, and explained the importance of review.

Haley seemed to be trying, but she still wasn't learning much. Could she really be that slow mentally? When it came to the music, I naively assumed that if it were distracting her, she would simply turn it off. If she was listening to the music, it must be OK, right? After one disappointing study session, however, I realized a change was needed. I wasn't quite ready to take the bull by the horns, though. Interfering with a teen's music felt a little presumptuous to me—like telling her how to dress or criticizing her posture. So I said, "Haley, I'd like you to try an experiment. I want you to turn off your music the next time you study and just see if it makes any difference in how well you learn." I reiterated that it was just an experiment and that she should try another session after that with the music on to compare. The "experimental" approach seemed to work. I don't know if any comparison was done, since I never saw her listening to the iPod again, but she seemed to be satisfied studying without it. I can't say her study skills improved greatly overnight, but they did get better gradually. Maybe kids need time to learn to concentrate, and unplugging is just the first step. The need to unplug is greater than ever: It now appears that frequent computer use decreases our ability to focus on book reading.

"Don't bother me now"

Sometimes simply asking a student to report on his concentration can provide keys for helping him pay better attention. Asking questions like these can help start the discussion: "What are you good at concentrating on? How long can you concentrate when you're interested in something? If you're reading and lose your focus, what is the likely cause? What do you think you could do about it?" Some students, mostly girls, say thinking about the social problems and complications of their lives distracts them from their reading.

One solution that works well for many people is to have them stop and jot down distracting thoughts as they occur, then mentally set the problems aside. It's like saying to the problems, "Don't bother me now. I'll pay attention to you later."

Fluency

As noted, fluency refers to the ability to read smoothly, accurately, and with adequate speed. Children who have ADD, learning disabilities, or dyslexia may read slowly and haltingly, and their reading may be marked by frequent errors. In other words, they lack fluency. Dyslexia in particular is associated with lack of fluency. Children and teens with dyslexia often have trouble sounding out words. They sometimes read longer words correctly but make seemingly careless mistakes on shorter words, and they may know a word on one page but miss it on the next. (See "Multisensory Language Programs" in Chapter 12 and Appendix H.)

Of course, not all fluency problems can be attributed to disability. Foreign speakers or individuals who lack experience with standard English may lack fluency because of cultural differences. Students may also lack fluency because of poor or lacking instruction, emotional and motivational difficulties, or delayed language acquisition due to deafness or institutionalization in early childhood. Within limits, however, and given enough time with a student, a common tutoring approach can work to help all students gain fluency, regardless of the problem's cause.

About Dyslexia

Dyslexia is "a reading difficulty in a child or adult who otherwise has good intelligence, strong motivation, and adequate schooling" (Shaywitz 2003, 132).

ENCOUNTERING DYSLEXIA

Early in my teaching career I worked as a resource room aid in an elementary school. One of my students was a sixth-grade boy who was reading on a first-grade level. Billy was a pale, thin boy with hunched shoulders and a hesitant manner. When I was assigned to tutor him, I knew one of my first tasks ought to be increasing his sight word vocabulary. This was easier said than done, however. As I soon discovered, it took between fifty and a hundred tries for Billy to commit a word to memory. No wonder the child hadn't learned to read!

At that time I didn't know much about helping children with problems like Billy's, and there wasn't much knowledge in general circulation that could assist me. Billy's reading did improve somewhat, but my tutoring wasn't notable because of any great success. On the other hand, working with Billy did start me thinking and asking questions, and afterward it opened my mind to the problem of dyslexia, which I now see must have been the cause of Billy's difficulties. We know more about dyslexia than we did then, partly due to advances in brain science.

Following is the research definition of dyslexia adopted by the International Dyslexia Association Board in 2002 and used by the National Institute of Child Health and Human Development:

Dyslexia is a specific learning disability that is neurological in origin. It is characterized by difficulties with accurate and/or fluent word recognition, and by poor spelling and decoding abilities. These difficulties typically result from a deficit in the phonological component of language that is often unexpected in relation to other cognitive abilities and the provision of effective classroom instruction. Secondary consequences may include problems in reading comprehension and reduced reading experience that can impede growth of vocabulary and background knowledge. (Shaywitz 2003, 132)

Recent studies, including research based on brain imaging, make the following points about dyslexia:

- In some people, dyslexia affects only the ability to read. They may have a normal ability to speak, listen, and do math. For others, several areas may be affected. (Personal observations)
- Important recent neuroimaging findings indicate that dyslexia is not related to intelligence, so IQ should not be taken into

consideration when diagnosing dyslexia. Thus, a child with reading difficulties, "regardless of his general level of cognitive abilities (IQ) should be encouraged to seek reading intervention" (Tanaka, et al. 2011, 1442).

- A defining characteristic is that individuals with dyslexia almost always have trouble remembering sounds and connecting speech sounds with letters (Shaywitz 2003, 55-57).
- Brain scans done with functional magnetic resonance imaging (f/MRI) suggest that dyslexics have trouble with rapid sensory input in any form (Temple, et al. 2000).
- Sound/letter confusion can result in difficulties with word recognition, poor spelling, slow reading speed, and general lack of fluency (Personal observations; International Dyslexia Association, FAQ).
- In turn, these problems can all affect reading comprehension. (Personal observations)
- Dyslexics often experience fatigue from reading. f/MRIs suggest that dyslexics must perform more mental steps to read than do others (Sherman 2009; and Yale Center for Dyslexia and Creativity).
- There's even evidence that dyslexics make use of a different area of the brain when they read than nonimpaired readers do. Effective remediation actually can change which part of the brain dyslexics use for reading so that it matches that of nonimpaired readers on an f/MRI (Shaywitz 2003, 76-86).
- Studies show that dyslexic children who receive intensive, targeted instruction in the first three grades can largely overcome their reading problems (Shaywitz 2003, 257-258).
- Successful instruction for young children with dyslexia includes systematic work on phonological awareness, vocabulary and fluency (Shaywitz 2003, 262).
- Brain scans done before and after one year of intensive, targeted instruction show that at the outset brains of dyslexic children process reading differently (and less efficiently) than normal brains but "light up" like the brains of skillful readers by the end of the year (Shaywitz 2003, 85-86; and Simos, et al. 2002, 1203-1213).

Remediation for teens with dyslexia

What can we do to help our dyslexic students read more fluently? Though the best time to remediate dyslexia is clearly in the early grades, it is my experience that teens who receive intensive help can make surprising transformations even as late as high school. Transformations can't always be counted on, but they do happen.

Improving Fluency

Regular use of the LSU, phrasing, pacing, and timings can all work to help older students gain fluency. Daily oral reading is helpful, and intensive work on phonics and spelling is crucial. Phonics instruction should include phonemic awareness, which means not simply teaching students to sound out words but helping them hear, recognize, and remember speech sounds and connect those sounds with words and their correct spellings.

Timing a student's reading or writing and graphing the results can be extremely helpful in working with dyslexic students if the timings are done consistently over a period of several months. Timings work this way: At the level of brain function, individuals with dyslexia do not process what they see on the page as quickly or efficiently as other readers. To develop fluency they must learn to see and think faster and more accurately. However, ordinary reading practice will not help them do this. With no intervention, dyslexic children could work for years reading in the same halting, inaccurate way. They need a nudge, and that nudge can best be provided by timing and graphing. (See "Planning lessons and exercises" below for more on speed of processing.)

Here are some exercises that can be used to help teens build fluency:

- Do daily timed readings using short passages with questions.
- Graph the student's reading speed and comprehension.
- Note comprehension and discard timings if comprehension is less than 60 percent.
- Have students aim to improve their scores from week to week.
- Encourage students to choose their own target scores.
- Use the LSU to strengthen visual skills. Students with dyslexia may feel uncomfortable using the LSU and resist it. Whether you push it or let it slide depends on the student.
- Use the phrasing technique (Chapters 5 and 11), which is like the LSU except that the reader points out phrases—words that make sense together—as he reads. Like the LSU, dyslexic students may resist phrasing, but if you can get them to use it consistently it has a good chance of helping them improve their speed and fluency.
- Pacing, with or without the LSU, is crucial for anyone with fluency problems. Students should practice pacing at home daily.

- Teach oral reading as explained in Chapters 5 and 13.
  - o For students who make mistakes frequently in their reading, have them read orally and tally errors on one side of the page and sentences read correctly on the other. This simple exercise is one of the most powerful tools available in promoting reading accuracy.
  - o This exercise is similar to the earlier scorekeeping exercise for reading comprehension, but now we're tracking accuracy rather than memory.
  - o Have students set goals for accuracy and then try to better their scores.
  - o Turn it into a game or contest, perhaps between tutor and student. The tutor receives points when the student makes errors and the kid gets the points for each sentence (or paragraph) read correctly.
  - o Younger students may wish to use points they earn in this exercise to "buy" talking time or a story.
  - o For a student who reads haphazardly, try sounding a bell or buzzer the student finds unpleasant whenever he makes a mistake. This only works if the kid doesn't take offense, so discuss it first.

Could LSU improve speed of mental processing in dyslexics? Though unproven, this would be a useful research topic. It would also be fascinating to see if there are brain changes over time in areas used for processing as a result of using the LSU. An f/MRI could be used to determine this.

Promoting Accuracy

If students read words from a practice list, introduce a scorekeeping element. For instance, have students read a certain number of words in a row correctly before moving to a harder list or stopping for the day.

Large print books (like the ones for the vision impaired) are great for teens with dyslexia. Students will read surprisingly difficult material if it is in large print.

Phonics instruction for dyslexic teens needs to be intensive, focused, and specialized. If you need to teach phonics in tutoring, start by using the exercises in Chapters 12 and 13, and Appendix I.

If students need more than you can provide, refer them to programs that use the Orton-Gillingham or Lindamood methods to teach phonemic awareness. The Wilson and particularly the Hill schools have developed highly effective versions of these methods. (See "Multisensory Language Programs" in Chapter 12 and Appendix H.)

As an alternative kind of graph, some young teens may enjoy keeping track of their progress on a chart made to look like a path or road. The student earns points by reading sentences, paragraphs, or pages correctly, by reading words off a list, or by memorizing phonics flash cards. Each sentence (or other item) counts as one point, and he shows his progress by moving a game piece along the path on an imaginary journey.

Here's a handy way to make a journey chart. Inside a manila folder, draw an outdoor scene with a path running through it, then mark numbers along the path to indicate the number of points the student has earned by doing various reading tasks. To use the chart, move a marker along the path from start to finish to reflect the student's progress. The journey could be finished in one lesson, or it might take several sessions for the student to reach the final goal.

Here is one idea for a journey chart that most young teens are sure to like. Draw a mountain with a trail going up one side and down the other. Next to the trail draw a tree with a picnic laid out under it. You could have a bridge crossing a stream, and there might be a cave along the way. Put in some traps such as boulder fields and avalanches. Counting by tens, write numbers from 1 to 100 or 200 on signs that you draw at regular intervals along the side of the trail. The journey chart is simply a fun way to keep track of how many points the student has earned. The pictures are motivating, and kids have fun pretending they are on a real trip. Other charts could feature a boat crossing a lake or a hero escaping lava and monsters, all laid out with a path and points. These charts are reusable for other students if you don't write on them.

Planning lessons and exercises

Timing, graphing, and other activities help students develop reading fluency, but how and why do they work? First some background. What we call fluency is really the ease and speed with which readers take in new information and put it together with what they already know. The process of accessing existing information is known as retrieval. Dyslexics seem to have a built-in "speed barrier" that slows their retrieval time, particularly when it comes to recognizing phonemic elements, the sounds and the letters that spell words. The key to overcoming dyslexia lies in cutting through the speed barrier to decrease retrieval time.

In talking about decreasing retrieval time, though, we really need to talk about what happens in the brain. This is a crucial piece: The new nerve connections needed for the brain to process more quickly develop only when the brain is pushed to work at its highest level of challenge. In other words, the brain develops only when it is stressed. I'm referring not to emotional stress but to neurological stress, in which nerve synapses develop new pathways and connections in the presence of "stress chemicals" that are produced when the brain is intensely challenged.

Unsupervised, people do not ordinarily subject themselves to this level of mental work, since it is usually experienced as "too hard." Still, working at one's edge is the only way to gain faster retrieval time and thus fluency. The tutor's job, then, is to set up a program of exercises and activities that will present students with the needed "brain stress," but do it in a way that's emotionally supportive. If you've done the pacing exercise with students, you'll understand this combination of pushing students as far as they can go and still being there for backup.

The drills, exercises, or activities we use to remediate dyslexia must be done frequently enough and continued over an adequate length of time to break through the barrier. As with other exercises in this book, students should understand that these activities are "brain exercises." One important element in building fluency is to set achievement goals and have clear ways of tracking progress toward those goals. Again, students should be encouraged to set their own goals daily and try to better their old records for speed and/or accuracy. This is where timing and graphing come in. Another important (and familiar) element is to have students move up to a harder task when they show mastery of the task at hand. In other words, to work incrementally.

Helping Students Get the Point

Though ADD and dyslexia do not specifically affect higher-level reading skills, you can understand how trouble attending to details because of ADD or with recognizing words because of dyslexia could affect students' ability to see the big picture and get the point of what they read.

Here are the stories of how three kids learned to "get the point" of their reading. Though they were very different people with differing reading problems, the strategies that helped them overcome their reading problems were similar. All were bright kids with learning difficulties, and all were in tutoring to work on reading comprehension. They were cooperative but felt frustrated and seemed to be "spinning their wheels" when they read.

JACK

Jack was 12. He had been diagnosed with a learning disability, and I guessed he might be dyslexic. We worked for months on his reading, and he seemed to be catching on, but when he was asked to read a rather difficult and (to his mind) boring book for school, he failed miserably. I had him read several pages and do a tellback but he could remember only peripheral information and had no idea of the main points. I did my usual pep talk on visualizing and looking for key phrases, but nothing did any good.

I began probing to find out what was going wrong. Finally, I discovered the problem. Jack was unfamiliar with many of the words in the book. Both his teacher at school and I wanted him to work on his vocabulary and had said so. As a result, Jack was paying a lot of attention to the words he didn't know, trying to figure out their meaning from context and also trying to remember them so he could look them up later. However, he was paying so much attention to vocabulary that he had no energy left over for understanding. This was quite a problem! When I saw what was happening, Jack and I talked about putting the meaning first and setting the vocabulary on the "back burner" temporarily. "Don't pay attention to what you *don't* know. Pay attention to what you *do* know, or could easily figure out," I told him. He was able to shift focus and did much better with his new goal of reading to understand.

JENNY

Jenny was 15 and a student to warm any teacher's heart. She tried her best and took all my suggestions very earnestly. She was in a biology class that used a rather difficult and detailed textbook, one I thought would be at home in a college classroom. Jenny was getting D's in the class since she didn't understand the reading and the tests were taken straight from the book.

As with Jack, we worked for several months and Jenny's reading improved a lot, but the biology text still stumped her. Again, I wanted to find out why. I asked questions about what she understood or did not understand as she read, as well as how she felt about the book. Her answers were revealing. Not only was the book puzzling to her, it was annoying. "Why do they have to put in all that stuff nobody understands?" she complained. "What difference does it make? Look at this. It's just pages and pages of details. What's the point?"

Though Jenny's complaint might have seemed generic, it turned out to be the key to what was tripping her up. I read a few sections in the book myself and discovered that each main topic was covered in a similar pattern. First, a great deal of seemingly unrelated background information was given, and then, at the end of the section, the various loose ends were tied together and all was explained—how a muscle moves or how a neural tube becomes a living being. Suddenly I understood Jenny's problem. The main ideas were at the ends of the sections, but to understand them one had to "slog through" a swamp of tedious facts. Also, it wasn't enough just to read casually: The reader was being asked to remember a mass of seemingly unrelated information. With no clue as to the importance or meaning of any of these details, they did indeed seem like a meaningless jumble. Jenny was tuning out before she got to "the good part," and no wonder.

I explained how the book was organized and showed Jenny how to pre-read, starting with first and last sentences, so she could look for main points before she became bogged down in the details. I also had her make simple drawings as she went along to illustrate whatever process or structure she was reading about—cell structure or the steps in nerve firing, for example. This was simply a visualizing exercise (seeing what she read in her mind's eye), but with drawing added to help her understand the technical material. The pre-reading and drawing allowed her to tune into the details without becoming overwhelmed. Along with this, I insisted that Jenny be able to explain everything she read clearly and in detail—kind of a glorified tellback. She gradually learned to do both the drawings and tellbacks quite well. When she read alone at home, she was supposed to continue drawing the pictures and explaining out loud. Jenny practiced reading her science book daily, whether she had an assignment or not, and she did actually succeed, not just in the course, but at a reading task most adults would find daunting.

What do Jack and Jenny's tutoring have in common? It is that they were missing the point because they were sidetracked (or swamped) by irrelevant details. Having them focus and prioritize was important, but first I had to know what the problem was, and that took some detective work.

Tina

In Tina's tutoring we tackled a similar problem, but on a different level. Tina was preparing for the SAT. Her thinking was quite advanced in some areas (her favorite book was *Jane Eyre*), but the SAT readings were tripping her up for the same reason Jack and Jenny had trouble with their reading: she couldn't see the forest for the trees. The solution was fairly simple. I explained that the writers of the SAT try to throw people off by including a lot of irrelevant details, and that it is really important to read for the main points. "There is going to be one opinion or thought that's the key to the whole thing. You should be able to state that thought in two or three sentences. The details are just window dressing."

To practice, I had Tina jot notes in the margin of the SAT booklet—short phrases summing up the main points of the passage—and when she could, simply underline key ideas in the text. Then, at the end of each reading, she was to write a three-sentence summary. This may not sound like much, but it worked. Tina and I had been working together for a couple of years, and she had had plenty of practice working on all kinds of reading material, so this was simply a reminder to use what she already knew. The SAT looked hard, but she just needed to know how to approach it.

The strategy that worked for all the kids was a simple one. They needed a reminder that details in a passage are usually included to back up a point. They are examples. The question is, "Examples of *what?*" All readers can get lost in difficult or overly detailed explanations, but kids with learning disabilities, ADD, and dyslexia need particular guidance to help them through what can sometimes seem like a maze of random facts.

Even in reading a novel, the tutor can help students keep their focus. We might ask them to look for anything in the next section that indicates what kind of person the main character is, or phrases that clue them in to the emotional climate or to the political situation. These are ideas kids often miss because they don't realize they should look for them. This type of guided reading in the tutoring session helps students know what to look for when they read on their own.

Becoming Accustomed to Work

A disability doesn't mean we should baby kids or let them get away with things. It means we have to make some accommodations and then expect them to do their best. But they may not know what their best is until we draw it out of them and show them what they are able to do if they try.

The all-out approach

Edward was a tall, spindly 15-year-old who attended a local Christian high school. I doubted if he had ever done even an hour's work in his life. He reminded me of a long slender water plant waving languidly in the current. According to his mother, he never, ever did any of his homework assignments from school, and even avoided classwork.

I remembered my psychologist husband mentioning that in the mental health field, when previously unemployed people start work, they must become "work-hardened," or accustomed to work. The idea caught my imagination, and I thought of schizophrenics whose mental illnesses had been brought under control with medication for the first time in their lives and who were now learning to make it in the real world. A scenario full of drama and pathos filled my head.

The previously homeless or hospitalized would have to get used to working. It would be hard for them at first. They'd need toughening up. They might have to move into it gradually. The boss would have to be tough, too—kindhearted but tough. They'd want to quit, but they couldn't. They might try to smoke on the job or go in the back room to listen to the voices in their heads, but you couldn't let them. Their feet would hurt, they'd cry, but they'd stick with it. And in a few weeks, they'd join the work world and the human race. They'd be able to work like the rest of us. The first paycheck. The hugs. The tears of joy.

This fantasy, farfetched as it was, offered a spark of off-beat inspiration as I began to work with Edward. Not that he was mentally ill. He was just soft, though it was a softness he had cultivated assiduously. He would need to become work-hardened. But how to begin? I opted for the "kill or cure" approach.

Kill or cure

This all-out approach is not recommended for everyone, but my intuition told me it was right for Edward. I asked him to study at my house every Saturday morning for three hours. He was to bring assignments from school to work on, but lacking that, I would provide work. (Yes, indeed.) "You aren't used to working, and I want you to see that you can do it," I explained.

I don't know if this cure had a lasting effect, but I do know that Edward surprised himself by his efforts. He was able to concentrate pretty well for the three hours, and got better as he went along. I was careful not to frame the activity as a punishment, and I tried to bring an element of fun into it. Edward was studying ancient history, so I had him turn his lesson into a "dungeon" for a "Dungeons and Dragons" game, building passageways for his heroes through the ancient city of Ur. We didn't call it Dungeons and Dragons, because the traditionalists at his school wouldn't have liked that, but Edward still managed to plan a game and learn some history in the process. He also learned that studying wouldn't kill him. Not all assignments would be as entertaining, but starting with some fun seemed the right approach.

What to do about whining

Becoming work-hardened might require quite a bit less than sitting and studying for three hours. Some kids simply need to quit whining. Though there's no evidence that children with learning problems complain more than others, it would stand to reason they would. People tend to avoid what they're not good at, and griping and shirking are time-honored ways of responding to unwelcome demands. Some students who have been in special education classes at school for years develop a pattern of learned helplessness that has been referred to as "resource room syndrome."

In tutoring, kids may whine about their teachers, their parents, and about anything you might ask them to do in tutoring. It's "too hard" or "too boring" or "too long," or they already know how to do it, or they haven't learned to do it yet. They have a sore or writer's cramp. Opportunities abound for a determined whiner.

The question is how to handle these complaints without either Rescuing or Persecuting. My approach is two-pronged. I offer a little aid and solace, and then I suggest they get over it. Example:

Step 1. "Would you like a . . . drink of water, few minutes to collect yourself, some help getting started?"

Step 2. "I know it's bothering you, but try to ignore . . . your mosquito bite, the fight with your girlfriend, the fact that you only had four hours sleep."

I tell these students that although the problem is not going to just go away, they can still put it on the back burner for the duration of the tutoring session. If the problem is at school or at home, the lesson itself will provide a good opportunity for them to set their troubles aside for a little while.

If the "problem" turns out to be something I'm requiring the student to do in tutoring, I try to talk him through it. For a lesson that's "too hard" from the kid's point of view, talking him through a task might include a brief pep talk with some phrases like these: "I think you can do this," "I think you can do better," "I wouldn't ask you to do something I didn't think you could do," "You'll have to be kind of strict with yourself about this work," or "You're used to giving up, but you need to push through this."

For a youngster who can't quit picking at a sore or worrying about some minor injury, I'll usually say, "Be brave!" with just enough of a smile that they don't quite know whether I'm making fun of them or just being cheerful.

Working with the upsets of everyday life

For students who actually do have serious problems, find out if they want to talk about what's wrong, sympathize when appropriate, then continue with the lesson. Being a kid is no picnic, as most of us probably recall. It only looks that way to adults who don't remember. Kids can be betrayed by their friends, they worry about each other, they may have to deal with mean or irrational adults, and they can suffer depression or anxiety without the perspective of experience. Adolescents experience crises of faith and identity, almost by definition. Yet these troubles are usually beyond our scope as tutors. Unless a teen chooses to bring up a situation to discuss in tutoring, all we can do is be there, be open, and do our best to teach reading.

Once, just before I was to begin a tutoring session, I received a phone call from the police saying that my 17-year-old daughter had totaled our car, and though she didn't seem to have any serious injuries, she was in the hospital for observation. I was told I wouldn't be able to see her for an hour or two, and since I was not needed at the hospital for a while, I could wait at home if I wished. I was shaking with fear when I hung up the phone.

My student's father naturally offered to take his son home when he learned what had happened, but I thought that since there was nothing to do but wait anyway, I might as well do something to keep my mind off my troubles. Our subject for the day, parts of speech, was the farthest thing in the world from broken bones and concussion, and that was just fine. I taught the lesson, and my fear subsided as we worked through the orderly task of diagramming sentences. It was just what I needed. After the lesson, I went to the hospital to be with my daughter, who only had a sprained ankle, and I gave thanks for the relatively minor nature of her injury and the calming effect of work.

My adolescent students almost always understand the point of this story. They see it's not about denial. Rather, it's that our minds can be channeled and focused in ways that may surprise us. And though they wouldn't put it this way, we can use this suppleness of mind to our advantage. They see that it's possible to set aside a problem for an hour's lesson and that the difficulty, whatever it is, may be more tractable when they return to it.

Responsibilities that Promote Learning

It's a good idea for all young people to have responsibilities, but it's especially important for teens with disabilities to have responsibilities at home besides their schoolwork. Physical work, like play, can help remediate sensory integration problems in addition to improving attention and patience. Participating in the life of the family through work also gives kids a sense of purpose and belonging.

Parents should not confine kids' jobs to "scut" work such as emptying the trash or putting the clean dishes away. Parents can also teach their teens how to do some of the more complex tasks of running a household. The object is to give kids work that will help them grow. So, for instance, instead of having teens empty the trash, parents could show them how to plan a week's menu and shop for the necessary ingredients. In assigning chores, parents should sometimes ask themselves, "Will doing this job well make him feel proud?" Using this standard, emptying the trash could probably be skipped.

Both boys and girls can learn to plan meals, shop, cook, clean, do laundry, sew, garden, and help with repairs. Some jobs give teens practice working with others and planning ahead when it really matters, such as putting a meal on the table in time. Other tasks improve eye-hand coordination (folding clothes and mending) and attention to detail (cleaning the car). Writing out checks to pay household bills is a good job for a responsible older teen because it gives him a preview of his own finances.

Summary of Key Points

- We can help students arrive at tutoring better prepared to learn by paying attention to matters of rest and relaxation, nutrition, and effects of medication.
- Teens with poor listening skills can learn to listen more effectively by reading and repeating from a book and by following oral directions.
- Students can improve their note-taking and listening skills with structured practice during the tutoring session.
- To aid concentration, aim for an alert mind and a relaxed body. Some students find relaxation exercises and tapes helpful.
- Use creative scorekeeping methods to help students pay attention.
- Fluency refers to the ability to read smoothly, accurately, and with adequate speed. ADD and dyslexia can interfere with fluency, though not all problems with fluency can be attributed to a disability.
- Brain scans done before and after one year of targeted instruction show that at the outset, the brain of a dyslexic processes reading differently (and less efficiently) than a normal brain, but "lights up" like the brains of good readers by the end of the year.
- Though the best time to remediate dyslexia is clearly in the early grades, teens who receive intensive help can make surprising transformations as late as high school.
- Timed daily readings, the LSU, pacing, and phrasing all help dyslexic teens and others develop fluency.
- Phonics instruction that emphasizes phonemic awareness, or awareness of sounds, is crucial for students with dyslexia.
- Pushing students with dyslexia beyond their comfort zone allows them to experience levels of "brain stress" necessary to develop fluency.

- Students with learning problems need extra help to keep from becoming bogged down in the details while reading.
- Students who are unused to applying themselves need to become accustomed to work.

We've looked at ways to help students gain the attentional skills they need to succeed, including listening, focusing, and becoming work ready. Finally, we conclude with a review of some general principles for building a successful tutoring program.

A Final Note

HERE IS A REVIEW OF THE GENERAL PRINCIPLES that go into constructing a successful tutoring program for all students.

Goals: Set Clear Expectations

1. First see what the student is able to do and calibrate your expectations based on that starting point.
2. Set goals based on your intuition about what your student can accomplish, but don't be afraid to set expectations your student will have to work hard to meet. True pride comes from rising to meet a challenge.
3. Besides working to meet your goals, encourage your student to set goals for himself.

In goal setting, it works best to have both long- and short-term goals. Short-term goals should be seen as "mileposts" by which we can mark our progress, and meeting them will eventually lead us to our long-term goals. As the student gains experience, help him redefine his goals more realistically and specifically: "I want to get a good enough score on my SAT to go to CU," or "I aim to learn five new vocabulary words a day."

Charts and graphs are highly motivating methods of helping people track their progress. Kids like colorful, artistic charts and may want to make their own. Students often respond with enthusiasm to speed-reading charts, and reading accuracy can also be charted with good results.

Provide Worthwhile Activities at Which Students Can Succeed

1. Assuming you've read *SMART! A Reading Tutor's Guide*, you will have a variety of activities to choose from by now.
2. One key to a successful tutoring program is timing: using the right

activities at the right time and in the right order. Rely on your own intuition to find that order.

3. Intuition comes from good instincts, experience and self-aware observation. You can further your own intuition by building awareness of your own ego states and internal dialog.

4. Acknowledge students' efforts and praise their successes.

The Importance of Strokes

Children and teens need some strokes, or units of attention, for simply being who they are, unrelated to their academic progress. In TA (Transactional Analysis) these are called *unconditional strokes*. Young people will often perform better for grown-ups who like them just for being who they are rather than always pegging strokes to performance. Teens may feel, "I want you to see me for who I am and not just for how well I do. My purpose in your life shouldn't just be to make you look good."

Besides unconditional strokes, children and teens also need strokes for their accomplishments. These are called *conditional strokes*. It is desirable to provide a combination of unconditional and conditional strokes. The phrase, "Your hard work paid off," is a more powerful motivator than "You are really smart" because it puts control in the student's hands. Praise should be genuine. In TA, an insincere or condescending compliment is called a *marshmallow*. Avoid throwing marshmallows. Insincere praise belittles students. For further reading, see Carol Dweck's (2007) "The Secret to Raising Smart Kids."

With this review, we have reached the end of *SMART! A Reading Tutor's Guide*. Now all that remains is for you to make the lessons your own through consideration and practice. This will happen by a process similar to gardening. You take the seeds from this book, plant the most promising ones, water, see what comes up, cull, tend, cultivate, and love. I hope the results will reward you many times over for your initial expenditure of care and effort.

Finally, as the spiritual teacher Martín Prechtel (1999) says, remember that "All can bless and all need blessing." We don't have to be saints to bestow the blessings our students and those around us need. In the meantime, prepare yourself to receive the many blessings your students have for you.

Appendices:

Supporting Materials for Student and Tutor

A | Materials for the Initial Evaluation

Student Information

Date_____

Name_____ Nickname (if preferred)_____

Age_____ Date of Birth_____

Parent's name_____

Parent's name_____

Home Phone_____

Mother's work phone/cell phone_____

Father's work phone/cell phone_____

Student's address

Street_____

City_____ Zip_____

Email address_____

Parent's address and home phone if different from above; please include for shared custody

Street_____

City_____ Zip_____

Home phone_____

In case of emergency, if I cannot reach you, whom should I call (include phone number)?_____

_____

Referred by_____

Student's school_____

Grade_____

Teacher (or counselor) if you want me to contact the school.
Please include phone numbers_____

_____

Indicate the subjects in which you're interested:

___Reading 　　___English 　　___Writing 　　___Study Skills

___Vocabulary ___Social Studies 　　___Test Taking

___ACT/SAT Preparation

Has student ever been tested for learning problems?_____

If so, when?_____

What were the conclusions/recommendations?_____

_____

_____

_____

What remediation has the student received and when? (tutoring, resource room, vision therapy, occupational therapy)_____

_____

_____

_____

_____

How would you describe the student's problems?_____

_____

_____

_____

_____

What are the student's recreational interests? _____

_____

_____

_____

_____

If the student reads recreationally, what kinds of books does he or she enjoy?_____

_____

_____

_____

For grades 9 and up:

Does the student wish to attend college?_____
_____
_____

Which colleges have been considered? _____
_____
_____
_____

What are the student's career interests?_____
_____
_____

Tutoring Policies

Note: Parents, please read and go over these policies with your student. For you to keep.

1. Payment: My fee is $ _____ an hour. You may pay at each lesson, or ask me to bill you monthly. If you pay weekly, send either a check or cash with the student to each lesson. If you'd like to pay monthly instead, let me know and I will send you a statement around the 1st for the preceding month. Please pay by the 10th.

2. Cancellations: 24 hours notice is required to cancel appointments. You will be charged the hourly fee for late cancellations and missed sessions. The only exception I can make is for sudden illness. If your child misses because he or she forgot the appointment, I suggest you have the student pay part of the charge. Please make sure the student knows this beforehand. If I'm late (rare, but it does happen), please wait 10 minutes. If you are late I'll wait 20 minutes before leaving to do something else.

3. Parent/tutor time: Lessons are an hour. Parents may come in to meet with me the last 10 minutes of each lesson. Phone consultations are also recommended. You might wish to call every other week or so the first couple of months to see how things are going, and as needed after that.

4. Books: Since I regularly lend books to students, I'd appreciate it if you'd have your child keep materials together and bring everything in to each lesson, whether it's finished or not. I buy all my own materials, and lost books can really add up, so please help your child keep track. Sometimes I may ask you to buy a book, but I try to keep purchases to a minimum.

5. School visits: I would be glad to visit your child's school. I charge my hourly fee for the time actually at the school, and the same fee for writing reports.

6. Waiting: Students, when you come for your appointment, please ring the doorbell and then come on in. Don't wait for me to come to the door, since I may be working with someone else. Parents, when you come in to talk to me, please just come on in and knock on my office door.

7. Parking: On the north side of the drive only, please. Bikes may be parked in the front yard.

Skills Checklist

This checklist can be used to make notes about a student's educational needs and to discuss your plan of action with parents.

Informal evaluation
    Oral reading
    Silent reading
        fiction
        nonfiction
    Comprehension and memory check
    Writing sample
    Introduction to test-taking ("How to Take a Test")
Reasoning and reading ("brain exercises")
Phonics (sounding out words)
Oral reading for fluency and phrasing
Reading comprehension, memory and concentration exercises:
    Count facts on fingers
    Form a mental image
    Read and tell about one paragraph, then an entire section
Main idea
    How to identify the main idea (There's a formula for this.)
    Practice in textbook
    Outlining: sort note cards into topics, outline subjects, do factual articles
Reading speed
    Long smooth underline, phrasing, pacing
    Graphing and timing
    Skimming
Introduction to understanding a novel, what to look for
Listening skills
Note-taking
    Reading notes
    Lecture notes
    Underlining
SQ3R technique for reading a textbook chapter
Memorization
Writing skills
    Penmanship
    Spelling
    Composition
Vocabulary
Test preparation: PSAT, ACT, SAT

Fiction Reading Test Story: "Two Were Left"*

ON THE THIRD NIGHT of hunger, Noni thought of the dog. Nothing of flesh and blood lived upon the floating ice island with its towering berg except Noni and the dog.

In the breakup of the ice, Noni had lost his sled, his food, his furs, even his knife. He had saved only Nimuk, his great devoted Husky. And now the two of them, alone on the ice, eyed each other warily—each keeping his distance.

Noni's love for Nimuk was very real. It was as real as the hunger, as real as the cold night. It was as real as the pain of his injured leg in its home-made brace.

But the men of his village killed their dogs when food was scarce, didn't they? They killed them without thinking twice about it.

And Nimuk, he told himself, when hungry enough would seek food. "One of us will soon be eating the other," Noni thought. "So . . . ."

He could not kill the dog with his bare hands. Nimuk was powerful and much less tired than he. A weapon, then, was needed.

Removing his mittens, he unstrapped the brace from his leg. He had hurt his leg a few weeks before. To help it heal, he had made the brace from bits of harness and two thin strips of iron.

Kneeling now, he wedged one of the iron strips into a crack in the ice. He began to rub the other one against it with slow, firm strokes.

Nimuk watched him intently, and it seemed to Noni that the dog's eyes glowed more brightly as night faded.

He worked on, trying not to remember why. The strip of iron had an edge now. It had begun to take shape. Daylight found his task completed.

Noni pulled the finished knife from the ice and felt its edge. The sun's glare reflected from it. The brightness stabbed at his eyes and almost blinded him.

Noni steeled himself.

"Here, Nimuk!" he called.

Nimuk came closer. Noni saw fear in the animal's gaze. He read hunger and pain in the dog's labored breathing and dragging crouch. His heart wept. He hated himself and fought against it.

Closer Nimuk came, wary of Noni's intent. Now Noni felt a lump in his throat. He saw the dog's eyes, and they were wells of suffering. Now! Now was the time to strike!

A great sob shook Noni's kneeling body. He cursed the knife. He swayed blindly, flung the weapon far away from him. With empty hands outstretched, he stumbled toward the dog. He fell.

The dog growled as he warily circled the boy's body. And now Noni was sick with fear.

In throwing away his knife, he had left himself defenseless. He was too weak to crawl after it now. He was at Nimuk's mercy, and Nimuk was hungry.

The dog had circled him and was creeping up from behind. Noni heard a fearful rattling in the savage throat.

He shut his eyes, praying that the attack might be swift. He felt the dog's feet against his leg, the hot rush of Nimuk's breath against his neck. A scream gathered in the boy's throat.

Then he felt the dog's hot tongue rubbing his face.

Noni's eyes opened, staring. Crying softly, he thrust out an arm and drew the dog's head down against his own. . . .

The plane came out of the south an hour later. Its pilot, a young man of the coast patrol, looked down. He saw the large, floating floe, with the berg rising from its center. And he saw something flashing.

The sun was gleaming off something shiny, which moved. His curiosity aroused, the pilot banked his plane and flew lower, circling the floe. Now he saw in the shadow of the peak of ice, a dark, still shape that appeared to be human. Or were there two shapes?

He set his seaplane down in a water lane and investigated. There were two shapes, boy and dog. The boy was unconscious but alive. The dog whined feebly but was too weak to move.

The gleaming object that had caught the pilot's was a crudely made knife. It was stuck point down into the ice a little distance away, and quivering in the wind.

---

*Cave, Hugh B. 1983. "Two Were Left" in *Aiming High: Stirring Tales and Poems*, Annette Sloan and Albert Capaccio, eds. Used by permission of the Hugh B. Cave Irrevocable Trust.

B | How to Take Tests

Sample Test

The source of this test is unknown. I got it 30 years ago at the Reading Group, a speed-reading instruction business in Denver, now closed.

1. Match the following with the correct description from the list.

   _____Planting a sloping field with rows of corn, then rows of wheat, then rows of corn, etc.

   _____Plowing a crop under instead of harvesting it.

   _____Removing brush and weeds along the fence between the fields.

   _____Planting around the hillside in level rows instead of planting up and down the hill.

   _____Planting a field one year with wheat, the second with oats, the third with alfalfa, and the fourth with corn.

   Descriptions

   a.   Clean Farming
   b.   Contour Farming
   c.   Crop Rotating
   d.   Green Manuring
   e.   Strip Cropping

2. South Dakota was admitted to the Union as the:

   a.   Fourth state
   b.   Fourteenth state
   c.   Fortieth state
   d.   Forty-ninth state

3. "A shepherd's boy (he seeks no better name) /Led forth his flocks along the silver Thame, /Where dancing sun-beams on the water played,"

   The above are the first three lines of Alexander Pope's poem, "Summer: The Second Pastoral." Which of the following is the fourth line?

   a.   Where wigs were worked and fancy watches made

   b.   As never yet to love, or to be loved

   c.   He jumped a brook, and the trumpets played

   d.   And verdant alders formed a quivering shade

4. Three is to triple as—

   a.   12 is to a dozen

   b.   multiply is to many

   c.   pair is to trousers

   d.   two is to double

5. The order of mammals known as *Chiroptera* possesses members, commonly termed *bats*, which (1) have wings and fly, (2) possess a pseudocoelom, (3) will not die when infected with rabies, and (4) feed largely on gemmules. Which of the above four statements is (are) correct?

   a.   only (3)

   b.   only (4)

   c.   both (1) and (3)

   d.   both (2) and (4)

   e.   all are correct except (1)

6. The main advantage of using Huntington's axioms of Boolean Algebra is:

   a.   If a theorem is provable from the axioms, its dual is immediately provable.

   b.   Not all theorems of Brigg's Boolean Algebra can be proved from them.

   c.   They are the simplest Boolean Algebra axioms to prove.

   d.   They are consistent with the properties of the models of Boolean Algebras.

7. Name one important way these two things are the same and one important way they are different.

   smile   laugh

   same _____

   different _____

8. Shoulder is to wrist as hip is to _____.

9. Which one does not belong? cellar, cave, tunnel, bridge, mine

   What do the others have in common? _____

Observe and Teach

For all questions: Will the student try a question again if she doesn't get it right the first time? (Encourage the student to stick with a problem and not just drop it if she doesn't get it right away.) Does she use a process of elimination in answering multiple choice questions? (If she doesn't, teach her to weigh answers by going over each item aloud: Is this the right answer? Why or why not?)

Question 1: Soil conservation

The answers are 1-e, 2-d, 3-a, 4-b, 5-c.

Did your student start by answering the easy questions first? "There is much unfamiliar material here. Start with what you know. Getting the easy answers out of the way will narrow down the choices for the material you don't know."

Even if the student did not know the answer to a question at the outset, was she able to derive the answer by using clues? For instance, which agricultural practice would you associate with the word "clean" in clean farming? Also, your student is probably not familiar with the term "green manuring," but she can look for a practice that enriches the soil by adding something to it.

Did your student know where the question began and ended? Occasionally students only work on part of the question because they don't understand how the questions and answers are arranged on the paper. If your student made this error, it could indicate problems with visual organization. To remediate, teach an organized method of note-taking, include outlining, and point out to the student the organization of textbooks by heading and subheading. (Also see the case of Nicky in "Summarizing," Chapter 6.)

Question 2: South Dakota

Did your student use information with which she was already familiar to solve this puzzle? To deduce the answer, the student has to possess and use the following information: There were 13 original colonies; they were located on the East Coast; and South Dakota is in the North Central part of the country. Using this information, the student could rule out the 4th state and the 49th because the 4th was already a colony and with 50 states, it makes sense that the 49th would have been further west. The 14th probably would have bordered on the original 13, the wrong location for South Dakota. By a process of elimination, that leaves the 40th, the correct answer.

Show your student how to solve the South Dakota question by drawing a sketch of the U.S. and having her indicate locations of the original colonies and of South Dakota. If she had the information in her mental filing cabinet but did not use it, problem-solving exercises can help. See "Reasoning" in "Suggestions for Remediation," Chapter 3.

If a student did not know the basic facts, check further on the extent of her background knowledge. You may not be able to help students build a great deal of background knowledge in tutoring alone, but it is possible to work with parents and encourage them to provide more educational experiences and to devote more time discussing these and other experiences with their teens. Though it might seem like too little too late, I have seen surprisingly good results come from these efforts. One possible cause for lack of background knowledge is poor auditory skill. See Chapter 18 for tips on how to help teens improve their listening.

Question 3: A shepherd's boy

This question is from a college literature exam, but younger students are frequently able to understand it and choose the correct answer. The question tests a student's ability to make use of several pieces of information at the same time. This is similar to the South Dakota question except that the student only has to consult the clues on the page rather than needing to have them in mind. The line to complete the poem must fit its meaning, have the correct rhythm, and end with a rhyme. The answer is "d." If she missed the clues, help her see them now. To show the student what is needed, read aloud, ask for, or provide an explanation of the meaning, and try each line for "fit." Even if your student doesn't know what an alder is, she may be able to guess correctly that a tree or a shrub would be most likely to make a shadow moving on the water.

Question 4: The word analogy

This question reflects ability to see relationships, part of abstract reasoning. The answer is "d." Explain to your student that this question is like a mathematical ratio except that it uses words. (Most students are familiar with ratios.) The process for finding the answer could be expressed this way. "You have to see what the relationship is between the first two words and find a pair that has the same relationship. *Three* is a number. *Triple* means to multiply by three.

So you have a number and an action you do with that number. Look for the same relationship between a pair of words in the answer. It's "d" because *two* is a number and *double* is something you do with that number, so this matches the pattern of the first pair."

For a student who missed this question, *Reasoning and Reading* provides excellent practice on word analogies (Carlisle 2000, 20-25). This is an easy question, however, so a student who had trouble with it would probably benefit from not only studying the analogies but an entire unit on reasoning skills.

Question 5: Bats

The answer is "e." A correct answer indicates the student will use logic to answer the question and not be thrown off by words she doesn't know. A student who answers incorrectly but who seems to have fairly good skills otherwise could benefit more from encouragement than from any particular exercise. "Don't assume you can't do something just because there are things about it you don't know. Ignore the words you don't know and think about what you do know. Take it one step at a time and see what you could figure out."

Question 6: Algebra.

The answer is "a." Again, explain to the student she does not need to know all the words to get the answer right. Translating into simplest terms, the correct answer could be stated, "If you know how to do one thing, you also know how to do this other thing." Most students understand that doubling your knowledge without putting in any extra work would be an advantage. The student also should reflect on who it is who writes test questions and what that person's bias is likely to be. Teachers write these test questions, and a typical teacher would think that doubling one's knowledge would be a bigger advantage than having things be simple to prove.

Question 7: Same and different

Answer: Same: A smile and a laugh are both expressions of happiness. Different: A smile is silent; laughter makes noise. A student who missed the question can practice on similarities and differences, as well as reasoning in general in *Reasoning and Reading*.

Question 8: Word analogy

The answer is *ankle*: "shoulder: wrist, hip: *ankle*." If the student answered incorrectly, point physically to each part of the body, stopping just before ankle, and see if she guesses correctly this time. Missing this question indicates the student is not asking herself what she can do to make the problem understandable for herself. In this case, for example, it's necessary to form a clear mental image. As you proceed with tutoring, turn questions back to the student and ask, "What would help you learn or understand this the best?"

Question 9: Which one doesn't belong?

"Bridge" doesn't belong. Everything else is underground. Practice on grouping and classification can help students who missed this question.

C | Magic: A Reading Passage for Speed and Comprehension

THIS SHORT ARTICLE ON MAGIC may be used as part of the informal evaluation to test speed and comprehension (Fry 1975, 18-19, 20, 179). The process is described in "Reading speed" under "Nonfiction: Textbook Reading" in Chapter 3.

Time your student to see how long it takes her to read the passage. (Use a timer, not a clock for this exercise.)

Determine your student's reading speed by dividing the number 1000 (the number of words in the passage) by the number of minutes and seconds it took her to read it. (Turn the seconds into a decimal by dividing the number of seconds by 60.)

Questions and answers follow the passage. Have the student check her work and come up with a percentage score.

Magic, or *conjuring*, is a form of entertainment that is based on pretending to do things which are impossible. The magician is a specially trained actor. He tries to make the audience believe that he has the power to do things which are against the laws of nature.

Magic shows are entertaining as long as the audience does not discover how the tricks are done. The magician always tries to keep his tricks a secret.

The magician usually depends on his skill with his hands, on his knowledge of psychology, and, sometimes, on mechanical devices. Since magic tricks are meant to fool people, the use of psychology is important. The magician must keep people from noticing all the movements of his hands and from thinking about the secret parts of his equipment. He must also lead the audience to draw false conclusions. The magician's success depends on the fact that many things seen by the eye do not register on the mind.

Two basic magic tricks are making objects seem to appear and making objects seem to disappear. A combination of these two tricks makes for some interesting effects. For example, the magician puts a small ball under one of several cups. The ball then seems to jump from one cup to another or to change color. What actually happens is that the magician, employing quick hand movements or a mechanical device, hides one ball. While doing this he talks to the audience and waves a brightly colored cloth with one hand. The audience is too busy watching the cloth and listening to the magician's words to notice that his other hand is hiding the ball.

Another favorite trick is to cut or burn something, and then make it appear whole again. What actually happens is that the magician makes the cut or burned object disappear by quickly hiding it while the audience watches something else. Then he "magically" makes it appear whole again by displaying another object that has not been cut or burned.

There are a number of so-called "mind-reading" tricks in which the magician purports to tell a person what he is thinking about. For some of these tricks the magician has a person write down his thoughts. Then the magician secretly obtains the paper. Another "mind-reading" technique is to have a trained helper blindfold the magician. Then the helper has the audience hand him various objects. The helper can tell the magician what the objects are, without mentioning their names, by using keywords or code words as he talks to the magician. This trick may take the magician and his helper many months to learn.

A magician's powers are really quite limited, but he makes people believe that he can do most anything by changing or combining several tricks.

Tricks in which the magician apparently cuts people in half or makes them disappear are called illusions. The word *illusion* derives from the fact that mirrors are often used to perform these tricks. A famous illusion trick is to saw a woman in half. The woman is put into a long box with her head sticking out of one end and her feet sticking out of the other end. The magician takes an ordinary wood saw and cuts the box into two halves. The audience is shocked, thinking that perhaps he has killed the woman. A few moments later, however, the magician puts his "magic" cape over the box and the woman comes out. The woman that the audience saw being cut in two was only an image in a mirror—an illusion.

Conjuring is as popular today as it was in ancient times. Records show that over 2,000 years ago magic performances were being given in ancient Egypt, India, Rome, China and Greece. These early magicians only performed for small groups of people on a street corner or for a king and his friends. The magicians in those days used small objects that they could carry with them or borrow, such as cups, pebbles, knives, and string.

Early conjurers frequently wore a large apron with many pockets in which they could carry their props. The bag-like apron served as identification and as a place to hide things while performing. Conjurers also carried a small folding table on which to perform their tricks.

About 1400, more elaborate tricks were invented which used larger equipment, such as boxes and barrels with false bottoms. Under these false bottoms the magician could hide a bird, rabbit, plant, or whatever he wanted to make appear suddenly. From one barrel he could make several different liquids pour forth while he told the audience that he was changing the entire contents of the barrel by magic. People of that time knew very little about mechanical devices, so it was easier for the magician to deceive them.

Some conjurers made enough money to buy a donkey, a horse, or even a horse and wagon so that they could carry bigger equipment. Conjurers also began to rent halls or empty stores so that they could give their shows indoors. Some conjurers used a large room in a local inn to give their performances. Others had a large van that could be opened in the rear to make a stage.

The most successful magicians would move only three or four times a year. They decorated their stages with lots of equipment, but used only a small part of it in each show. In this way they could entice the same people back over and over again. Some of their equipment was of no use at all. It was only used to decorate the stage and impress the audience.

Modern magic did not really start until the 1800s. Its father is considered to be Jean Houdin, a Frenchman, who developed rules for conjuring. Houdin was also a highly skilled mechanic and watchmaker. Today modern magicians can perform feats of magic that would have been impossible years ago because they now have better mechanical equipment and greater knowledge of audience psychology.

Comprehension: Answer the questions without looking back at the passage.

1. The magician pretends to do things which
   - ☐ a. people like.
   - ☐ b. are impossible.
   - ☐ c. are secret.
   - ☐ d. make people laugh.
2. An important part of a magic trick is that
   - ☐ a. it does not take too long.
   - ☐ b. it has a combination of interesting effects.
   - ☐ c. the audience doesn't discover how it is done.
   - ☐ d. a bright colored cloth is used.
3. If a magician cuts something, such as a cloth, he usually makes it appear whole again by
   - ☐ a. displaying a duplicate.
   - ☐ b. using special glue.
   - ☐ c. not really cutting it.
   - ☐ d. showing you only the part not cut.
4. In the 1400s some of the favorite new tricks used
   - ☐ a. cups and balls.
   - ☐ b. cloth and knives.
   - ☐ c. mind reading.
   - ☐ d. false bottoms.
5. A mark of a magician's success was that
   - ☐ a. he used big equipment.
   - ☐ b. he didn't move often.
   - ☐ c. he performed in an inn.
   - ☐ d. his tricks involved illusions.
6. The audience draws false conclusions because
   - ☐ a. the magician is smart.
   - ☐ b. they are led to believe them by the conjurer.
   - ☐ c. they like to be deceived.
   - ☐ d. there could be no other explanation.
7. After reading this article, you would conclude that mind reading
   - ☐ a. couldn't really work.
   - ☐ b. requires much concentration.
   - ☐ c. requires a special talent.
   - ☐ d. could work only for some people.

8. What is one valid conclusion you can draw from this article?
    ☐ a. Magicians are now extinct.
    ☐ b. People today don't like to be fooled.
    ☐ c. Magic is only for children.
    ☐ d. It is more difficult to be a magician today than it was 400
        years ago.
9. Another good title for this article would be
    ☐ a. "Magic Is a Lost Art."
    ☐ b. "How to Fool Your Friends."
    ☐ c. "The First Actors."
    ☐ d. "An Introduction to Conjuring."

Magic: Answers

b
c
a
d
b
b
a
d
d

D | Developing Active Reading with Effective Questions

After reading the first chapter or part, ask . . .

- What has the author told you about the main character? What does the character look like? Act like? Say? Think? Feel?
- What do you think the problem or conflict will be in the story?
- How do the illustrations contribute to the story?
- What questions do you now have about this story?
- What do you think is going to happen next in the story? Why?

During the reading, ask . . .

- How is the setting important to the story?
- Who are the minor characters in the story? How do they contribute to the plot?
- What can we learn about the characters from what they say and do?
- What is the relationship between the minor character(s) and the main character?
- What problem(s) does the character have to solve?
- What is the most important event in each chapter or section of the story?
- Does the author make you want to keep reading? If so, how?
- Did you make a picture in your mind while reading? Describe the picture and tell the words that helped to give you this picture.
- Can you relate any part of this story to an event in your life?
- How do you think the story will end?
- What questions do you have about an event or character in the story?
- What do you think is going to happen next in the story? Why?

After reading, ask . . .

- How accurate were your predictions? What clues did you miss when you made your predictions?
- How did the story end? How was the problem or conflict resolved?
- Did you like the ending of the story? Did you expect the story to end in that way? Would you have ended the story differently? How?
- What clues did the author use to create the ending of the story?
- How did the minor characters contribute to the story ending?
- What could be an alternative ending for this story?
- What was the most exciting/interesting part of the story?
- Was there a part of the story that you didn't like or found uninteresting? How would you change it?
- How did the main character change during the story?
- In what ways can you relate to the characters?
- What words would you use to describe the characters in the story? How and when did the characters show these traits?
- How did the problems/conflicts contribute to the pace, humor, or drama of the story?
- Why do you think the author chose this genre to tell the story?
- In what ways did the story fit the genre?
- How did the author's writing style contribute to the telling of the story?
- How did the author use imagery to tell the story?
- How did the author use dialog to tell the story?
- Would you use a different title if you were the author?
- What did the author make you think about as you read the story?
- What questions do you have for the author?
- How is this story like/unlike other stories you have read?
- What are some questions you would ask someone else who has read this story?
- Would you recommend this story to your friends and family members to read? Why or why not?

These effective questions were developed under a grant from the U.S. Department of Education. However, the contents do not necessarily represent the policy of the U.S. Department of Education, and you should not assume endorsement by the federal government. ©2006 PBS. All rights reserved. PBS TeacherLine Tips for Developing Active Reading. PBS LearningMedia.

E | Book Report Form

Title

Author, Publisher, Date

Type of book (adventure, mystery, sci fi, etc.)

Setting, including when and where

What the story is about generally

Example: "This is the story of a girl who becomes a sailor." Or, "A wise judge makes decisions that are both creative and fair." Or, "The book is about street life in a tough part of town in the sixties."

Plot (what happened), one paragraph

To keep from including too many incidents, think of *categories* of happenings rather than simply listing them. Here is an example of a plot summary from S. E. Hinton's novel *That Was Then, This Is Now*:

> Bryon and Mark live a tough life on the streets. They hustle pool and meet up with M&M, a young hippie. Mark gets beat up trying to prevent a fight. Verne, the bartender, is shot protecting the boys. They take revenge on Angela, Bryon's self-centered ex-girlfriend. Bryon falls in love with Kathy, M&M's sister. Bryon grows more responsible, while Mark starts dealing drugs. The two grow apart and at the end Bryon turns Mark in for dealing drugs.

Theme

For older students: write one paragraph or more on the theme or on some issue the author brings up. (See discussion of theme in Chapter 6.)

Characters, one to three paragraphs

Describe one or several of the people in the story. Use adjectives, tell about personality. For example, brave and cheerful, or self-centered and arrogant. Give examples from the book of people's actions that back up what you say.

Evaluation

What did you like or not like about the book? This could include your favorite scene or a part you thought was boring or unrealistic. Explain why you felt as you did. Be specific.

F | Maps and Timelines

EVEN THOUGH MAP READING is taught in school, many students don't learn to interpret the maps and graphs in their textbooks, and as a result they miss much essential information. Though map literacy is not a reading skill per se, it is a prerequisite for reading comprehension. The following is a lesson on teaching map reading.

Introducing Maps

Using a social studies textbook, pick a map and have the student explain the "main idea" of the map. It helps to ask the student to "pretend to be a teacher" for the purposes of the exercise. An ideal answer would be thorough and concise. For instance, "This is a map of early civilizations of the world. It is color-coded and shows the date and location of each civilization. This whole area is the Middle East, and this part is Egypt."

Unfortunately, few students will be able to come up with an answer that is clear and concise, either because they are not used to taking the role of teacher or because they are unfamiliar with maps. If you find that your student lacks basic map-reading skills, you will have to make a decision about how much remediation you want to provide at this time. If you decide to keep it short and simple, you might just review the cardinal directions and show how they correspond to the directions in "real life." Then, in the interests of keeping things moving, make a mental note to return to the basics of map-reading later and proceed to the map memorizing exercise.

If you do decide to spend some time now with map interpretation, point out clues and ask questions to encourage the student to observe the map in detail. Have the student draw a simple map by *following written directions*. (See the example of Mr. Smarty in Chapter 18, "Following oral directions," but give the directions in writing.) Students usually love doing this exercise, and it is a good way to teach following directions along with basic map skills. You can write your own directions for drawing a map and even have students write them for each other.

Finally, give a pep talk on the importance of paying attention to maps and graphs. I believe this anecdote hits the nail on the head. One year I tutored several seventh-graders at a private college prep school. My students asked if I could help them study for a science test that was coming up. It was their first test in junior high, and they weren't sure how to prepare. Besides the usual how-to-study tips, I saw to it that they memorized the diagrams in the text on organs of the body. The students were oblivious to the drawings at first and thought the whole exercise was fairly useless. That was until they got their grades on the test. Every one of my students got an A and everyone else in the class failed the test! Kids who hear this story are usually cooperative about working with maps and diagrams.

How to Memorize a Map or Diagram

Here is a method for teaching students how to memorize maps or diagrams. It has the added advantage of strengthening visual perception and memory. In brief, the student memorizes locations of countries or other geographical features by looking carefully at the map then looking away and seeing them "in her mind's eye." The student memorizes the locations of three countries at a time, *sketches them from memory*, and then checks her work against the book.

LEARNING TO USE VISUAL AIDS

Jeff, age 12, bright but disorganized, usually skipped the visual aids in the book (maps, graphs, etc.), and ignored assignments that required him to memorize, so when his teacher told him to learn the locations of all the countries of Europe, he felt that he had been given an impossible task. Even so, using the following method, Jeff not only learned the locations of all the countries, but was also able to draw a simple map of Western Europe from memory!

Here's how we did it. From an atlas, I found a clear, readable map of Europe that had the countries in different colors. Working aloud, I demonstrated how to learn the general shapes and locations of three of the easiest countries in Europe: Spain, Portugal, and France. Next—and this is an important step—I closed my eyes and gestured to show where each country stood in relation to the others, naming them as I went. It was as if I were touching an imaginary map in the air.

I then opened my eyes and, without looking back at the book, drew on paper, in extremely simplified form, outlines of the three countries, showing how they fit together. "Simplified form" means I reduced them to their simplest geometric shapes. Spain, Portugal, and France were all rectangles. I labeled this hand-drawn map and when it was done, checked it against the atlas. I then learned three adjoining countries in the same way and drew, not only the new ones, but all six I had learned so far.

Next it was Jeff's turn. He learned, if not quickly, at least thoroughly, and not surprisingly got an A on his test at school. He had successfully learned all the countries of Europe, but that was not all. In the process, he had learned how to memorize maps and diagrams, and most importantly had made brain connections that would help him in learning other visual material.

Timelines

On the subject of visual learning, many people have trouble remembering dates—but even dates can lend themselves to visual images in the form of timelines. For most people it is easier to remember a location on a timeline than an isolated number. If needed, stop here and make a timeline to show students how to visualize dates (Figure F.1).

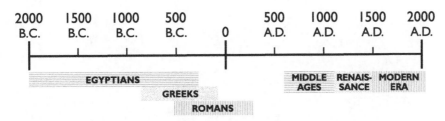

Figure F.1. History timeline.

You and your student can build the timeline using colored pencils. Fill in a couple of dates and have him come up with the rest. Explain that the dates are approximate and that the timeline gives a rough idea of when a civilization was at its height or when an era began and ended. You'll find that some teens aren't clear on the terms B.C. and A.D., so some clarification may be in order. As a further activity, you might have the student memorize the dates, eras, and main events represented on the timeline in Figure F.1, and then, as with the map activity, reproduce the whole thing from memory.

Many teens like learning about timelines even if they have previously ignored them, and you may find that a timeline provides a ready "jumping-off place" for some great discussions about history and culture. Even the least studious kids often have a natural curiosity about the past. They are interested in knowing about when and where different groups of people lived and what their lives were like. However, since poor readers haven't had much chance to satisfy their curiosity in school, they may welcome the chance to find out more through discussion in tutoring. Also, away from peers, they are removed from the worry of being pegged as "uncool" for asking questions.

You might even set aside a few minutes at the end of each session for the student to ask her own history questions, using the timeline as a prompt. As before, prime the pump with some stories. Students want to know what people ate, what they wore, and what their arts and crafts were like. They might want to know more about famous people and about some of the differences between the various religious and ethnic groups.

Another good thing about the timeline is that it can be used to break up the monotony of a study skills lesson without being too far removed from the official subject.

G | Human "Moms" Teach Chimps
It's All in the Family

FOLLOWING IS AN EXCERPT from Maxine Rock's *Smithsonian* article, "Human 'Moms' Teach Chimps It's All in the Family." A script in the right-hand column can be used to guide discussion. The script is just to give you ideas about questions and possible answers. It is not necessary to follow it word for word. Start by having the student read the title above.

Article Excerpt	Comments and Script
A nursery school at the Yerkes Primate Center gives lessons to the offspring of lab chimps on how to live like their wild-born relatives On a warm spring day in Atlanta, Kathy Gardner and Kelly McDonald are taking the little ones out to play. A couple of the youngest are riding on the women's backs, and five toddlers are romping along beside. In a few minutes Kim Bard appears and greets the adults and children with a wide, open-mouthed expression—a rather forced-looking grin by most standards, but the youngsters respond enthusiastically, and 10-month-old Rosemary beams a delighted grin back in response.	Do a regular tellback for the first paragraph (main idea and detail). Q: What is the purpose of this paragraph? A: It is to introduce the main characters and set the scene in a way that makes you curious. Continue with tellbacks on the next two paragraphs.
The youngsters are chimpanzees, and to them Bard's smiley expression means that fun is on the way. For the rest of the afternoon, for the sake of science and the endangered primate species, Bard will become a mother chimpanzee.	Q: What is the point of the entire article, in one sentence, based on what you know so far? A: Some women are raising baby chimpanzees in a research center.

Article Excerpt	Comments and Script
Bard and her research assistants, Gardner and McDonald, work at the Yerkes Regional Primate Research Center at Emory University in Atlanta, raising 22 baby chimps ranging in age from a few days to four years. All the babies are offspring of laboratory animals. Legal and social pressures have led Yerkes, like other science centers, to cut back on its use of chimps, except for reproductive, psychological and urgent medical research. And it has initiated programs such as Bard's to improve the animals' environment. In addition to teaching captive-born chimps how to act like their wild relatives, Bard's work is prying open some of the secrets of human infant development.	Main idea of the paragraph: The researcher is teaching offspring of lab chimps to act like their wild relatives. Q: How does the current paragraph relate back to the title? A: This paragraph explains the phrase in the title "Human 'Moms' Teach Chimps . . ."
There are between 200,000 and 300,000 chimpanzees remaining in the wild in Africa, but their future is in peril. The chimps are still hunted by some indigenous peoples for meat, and their body parts are prized as souvenirs. Mother chimps are killed so their infants can be snatched and sold as pets. Chimp habitat is also quickly being destroyed as their homeland is rapidly developed. There is a growing consensus that chimps in the wild may disappear entirely within 20 years.	Main idea of the paragraph: Chimps in the wild are threatened. Q: Why might the researchers be trying to teach lab chimps to act like their wild relatives? What could that have to do with chimps being threatened? You may not know enough to answer yet, but that's something to look for as you read.

Article Excerpt	Comments and Script
There are approximately 2000 chimps now in captivity in the United States, and many of the captive chimps are in the care of researchers like Bard, a developmental psychologist. Her project at Yerkes is changing the way captive chimps are treated; she insists that humans in the business of raising apes in research labs, zoos or animal parks adopt the behavior of the chimps, not force the chimps to fit in with human behavior.	Notice the transition in the first sentence of this paragraph. Q: How does it relate to what came before and lead into what comes after? A: It's still talking about numbers of chimps, but this time in captivity. It leads into more information about the research center mentioned earlier in the article. Q: Now what do you think about the article as a whole? A: Maybe the women are teaching the chimps wild behavior so they can return them to the wild since their numbers are threatened. Q: What new theme has come up in this paragraph? A: Chimps should be treated like chimps, not humans. Q: What themes you've seen so far might be repeated in the rest of the article? A: There are several ideas to choose from, so the direction the article will take is hard to say. It could be about returning chimps to the wild, protecting chimps in labs, treating chimps as chimps, or some combination of these. Q: Could it be about preserving wild chimps? A: No, because that's not mentioned in the title.

412   SMART! A Reading Tutor's Guide

Article Excerpt	Comments and Script
"In the past, when newborn apes were taken away from their captive mothers because they lacked the nurturing skills to care for them, the babies were treated by researchers as little people," Bard says. "We meant well, but the result were terrible!"	Main idea, this paragraph: Treating chimps as humans doesn't work. Main idea, article, so far: Since chimps in the wild are in trouble, it matters even more how we treat lab animals; it's important not to raise them like humans.
In the wild, female chimps learn from their mothers and other female relatives. When they are removed from their maternal group and isolated from one another, none of the nurturing skills are passed along. The offspring of the captive chimps have no role models, so when they grow up they are afraid of their own kind and don't know how to behave. If young chimps are placed with wild-born chimps in a zoo, they just scream and hang on to the humans who raised them. They never learned chimp techniques for mating or for getting along socially. If they do produce offspring, the animals rarely have the skills to care for their own babies.	Q: What's new here? A: Mother chimps teach the young how to behave, but without mothering, chimps lack social skills and can't relate to their own kind at all. Q: Where are we heading? A: The human researchers are going to take the place of chimpanzee mothers in teaching the young how to behave. Q: How do you know? A: It's implied in the title and it's stated in the first paragraph, "Bard will become a mother chimpanzee."
The result? "More orphans in more nurseries," says Bard, "and more chimpanzees with hang-ups that come from being raised by humans."	Putting the first paragraph together with the one we just read helps us understand a little about why it's important for the women to work with the baby chimps.

H | Multisensory Language Programs

EXAMPLES OF MULTISENSORY language programs are the Wilson, Hill, Orton-Gillingham, and Lindamood-Bell systems—all intensive, sequential methods for teaching phonemic awareness and other language skills using multisensory modalities. Translation: Intensive may mean going to a special class one or two hours a day. Sequential refers to a highly organized, incremental approach to teaching. Phonemic awareness begins with helping students hear speech sounds in words and continues to use sound and letter patterns to teach other aspects of reading and spelling. A multi-sensory approach encourages students to learn through seeing, hearing, and feeling.

The Wilson and Hill methods are based on ideas originated by Orton-Gillingham in the 1930s. Lindamood-Bell uses their own system. I've heard the Wilson and Hill systems recommended as balanced and effective. Critics say the Lindamood-Bell and traditional Orton-Gillingham systems excessively dissect the language and drill on phonics patterns in an unnecessarily detailed way; proponents say the detail is necessary and the programs work for kids who have failed at all other methods. You would no doubt wish to compare programs yourself before referring a student. Also, ask about prices, as some are quite expensive. Here's information to help you begin exploring multisensory language programs. An internet search will provide even more alternatives.

The Wilson Reading System is a research-based reading and writing program. Call for a list of tutors trained in their system. Their website (www.wilsonlanguage.com) has many links to good information pertaining to dyslexia, worth looking at even if you're not in the market for a specialist.

The Hill Methodology, as it's called, is taught at the Hill Center (www.hillcenter.org), a school in North Carolina that provides language education to students with dyslexia and other reading problems. They also provide training programs to educators from around the world. Their program is based on Orton-Gillingham methods.

Lindamood-Bell teaches auditory discrimination in depth. They do clinical evaluations and instruction at learning centers around the country using the LiPS, or Lindamood Phonemic Sequencing program (www.lindamoodbell.com).

The website of the Academy of Orton-Gillingham Practitioners and Educators (www.ortonacademy.org) lists accredited Orton-Gillingham training programs for educators. Call a training center to locate a tutor.

I | Phonics

ALMOST ALL STUDENTS KNOW the sounds of the consonants, so we can safely skip them for now and begin with the vowels.

Short and Long Vowels

Short vowels are usually taught first. To help your student learn the short vowel sounds, use the sentence, "Fat Ed is not up," or some equivalent. The sentence contains all five short vowels, *a, e, i, o* and *u*, in alphabetical order. Have the student learn the sentence and then the respective vowel sounds in that order. To help the student remember the sounds, have him make a large card or sign with the "Fat Ed" sentence on it, mark the vowels to indicate they are short, and practice the sounds at home. (The diacritical marks, below, indicate how to mark vowel sounds.) Kids report they like to put the "Fat Ed" sign up on a mirror, the fridge, or at their desk to review every time they go past. All practice should be done aloud, as silent review and practice does next to no good.

As soon as the student can say the short vowel sounds in isolation while *looking* at the "Fat Ed" words, cover the sentence and have him recite the sounds with only the written letters as prompts. At this point, ask the student to "think the (Fat Ed) words but only say the sounds." After he knows the sounds in order, have him do them in random order. Students usually need to review the short vowel sounds at each lesson for several weeks.

Next, teach long vowel sounds by asking your student to tell you the names of the vowels. Write them down, have him mark them with the "long" mark, and then do a dictation exercise mixing both long and short vowel sounds. You say a sound, either alone or in a word, he writes the letter that spells that sound and supplies the appropriate long or short mark. Examples of words with short vowels are *clam, bed, list, lock* and *bus*. Words with long vowels are *pole, used, blame, roam, beach, clay, file* and *mute*.

415

Writing the words from dictation and marking the vowels, as you just did, is a great exercise to develop phonemic awareness (an awareness of sounds) and should be repeated over a period of several weeks. Though teaching long and short vowel sounds seems like a simple activity, it can sometimes mark a turning point for a teen who has bypassed unfamiliar words for years.

Diacritical Marks

Here is a list of diacritical marks for the single vowels to use as a reference if you don't already know the marks and their sounds. (We'll go over the schwa sound later.)

Long Vowel Mark

The long vowel mark placed over a vowel indicates that it will be pronounced just as it sounds when we recite the alphabet:

ā as in *ate*
ē as in *evil*
ī as in *ice*
ō as in *open*
ū as in *use* or in *flute*

Short Vowel Mark

The short vowel mark placed over a vowel is as follows:

ă as in *apple*
ĕ as in *elephant*
ĭ as in *Indian*
ŏ as in *octopus*
ŭ as in *umbrella*

Schwa Mark

The schwa mark ə, sometimes shown as a dot under a vowel, represents the indistinct vowel sound that is the unaccented or unstressed syllable of a multisyllabic word:

ạ as in *a*go
ẹ as in happ*e*n
ị as in leg*i*ble
ọ as in comm*o*n
ụ as in s*u*ggest

In teaching phonics, individual sounds are usually taught first, as we are doing here, but some students do better if they learn about syllables first so they can gain an overview. Secondary students may also do well working on letter sounds and syllables in the same lesson. (Syllables are introduced in Chapter 13.)

Though we are focusing on teaching phonics as a way to improve reading, phonics is extremely useful in teaching spelling, too, and there's no reason reading, writing, and phonics can't be taught together. Here is a series of steps that works well with any phonics learning. First make flash cards of the sounds you want your student to know. When he is proficient with the individual letters and sounds on the flash cards, have him read words containing those elements from a list, then write them from dictation. If he needs more practice, ask him to read nonsense words similar to those on the phonics pretest. Keep practicing until your student knows the sounds and their spellings and can quickly and accurately read new words that contain them. Finally, ask him to read aloud from a challenging book while you keep track of his ability to apply the phonics skills he's learned so far.

Digraphs, Diphthongs, and Phonics Flash Cards

So far you have been working only on individual vowels. The next step is to have your student learn the sounds of the letter combinations, also known as *digraphs* and *diphthongs*. (An internet site that explains these terms clearly is www.madison.k12.al.us/central/first/reynolds/phonics-page.html.) Using the list below, make a set of flash cards to teach your student the sounds. This concept is from *The Writing Road to Reading* (Spalding 2003, 213-221). Write the letter combinations on the front of the card and a word using those letters on the back. In the sample words on the back, underline the letters whose sounds are to be learned.

Begin by pretesting to see which sounds your student already knows. To do this, show him the letter or combination of letters on the front of the card and ask him the sound. Then have him come up with an example—a word in which the letters have the same sound as those on the card. (For short *a*, ă, his answer might be "apple.") The student may make up his own words or use the sample words you have provided on the cards. Just make sure he uses real words, not slang or made-up words.

Some students with learning disabilities have trouble thinking of words that meet certain parameters—even words with which they are quite familiar. If this is the case, simply have the student memorize the words you provide. If your student misses sounds or takes more than a few seconds to answer, have him study the cards at home and then quiz him at each lesson to check his progress. Aim for three seconds or less per card. The purpose of the time limit is to assure the student has this knowledge at an automatic level. Explain the purpose of the time limit to the student: "You probably won't sound out the words if you have to think too long to remember the sounds." Practicing with students to meet a speed limit is especially helpful for those with dyslexia.

I like to have the student make his own copy of the cards—just the ones he needs to learn—so that he can take them home without my worrying about the originals getting lost. If he has quite a few to learn I don't send all the cards home with him at once. Instead, we decide together on a reasonable number for him to study each week and he takes those home. Cutting the task down to size can make all the difference in whether the job gets done or not.

Here is a list of graphemes (the written symbols for sounds) to use for making the flash cards. Short vowels should be included as a review. The graphemes in the first column go on the front of the card, the words in the second column on the back. (Explanations in parenthesis are my notes and not meant to be put on the cards.)

For flash cards:

ă	*apple, fat*
ĕ	*elephant, Ed*
ĭ	*Indian, is*
ŏ	*octopus, not*
ŭ	*umbrella, up*
ir	*bird*
ur	*fur*
er	*her*
ar	*star*
or	*or*
sh	*ship*
th	*thin*
th^2	*the* (The number 2 indicates this is a second sound for this digraph. Include the number 2 on the card to help the student keep the sounds straight. Teach the sounds without the numbers first.)

-x	*six*	*ks*	(The dash means the letter appears at the end of a word)
-y	*my*	long *i* sound	
-y²	*baby*	long *e* sound (The two *y* sounds say *my baby*.)	
w	*we*		
wh	*where*	(Many kids don't pronounce the *wh* sound. Pronounce words containing *wh* clearly and have students practice by holding a finger in front of the lips to feel the air rushing out.)	
ai	*rain*	(*ee, ea, oa, ai,* and *ay* are grouped together because they are the five most common combinations in which the first vowel is long and the second is silent. When the student has learned the sounds separately, put all five on one card and have him learn and reproduce both the graphemes and sample words from memory. To make them easy to remember, arrange *ee, ea, ai, ay* in the corners and *oa* in the middle of the card.)	
ay	*play*		
oa	*boat*		
ee	*feet*		
ea	*eat*		
ow	*cow*	(On the back of the card write *ow = ou*.)	
ow²	*bowl*	(Kids can learn the *ow* sounds by remembering the "*cow* drank out of the *bowl*.")	
ou	*house*		
oi	*oil*	*oi = oy*	
oy	*boy*		
au	*haunt*	*au = aw*	
aw	*saw*		
ew	*new*	*ew = oo* (sort of)	
ch	*church*		
ing	*sing*	(All the *-ng* sounds and words go on one card.)	
ang	*sang*		
ong	*song*		
ung	*sung*		
ink	*pink*	(All the *-nk* sounds and words go on one card.)	
ank	*thank*		
onk	*honk*		

unk	*bunk*
oo	*boot*
oo^2	*foot* (Teach the two *oo* sounds thus: "The *foot* goes in the *boot*.")
ck	*black*
qu	*queen* kw
igh	*night*
kn	*knee n*
wr	*write r*
ph	*phone f*
g	*goat*
g^2	*gym, giant* (Put both *g* sounds on the same card. The *g* must have *e, i,* or *y* after it to sound *j.*)
c	*cat*
c^2	*city, bicycle* (Put both *c* sounds on the same card. If *c* has an *e, i,* or *y* after it, it must sound *s*. The *g* "has a choice.")

Consonant Blends

When your student knows the phonetic elements introduced so far, start on consonant blends, letter combinations such as *bl* and *sp*. The list below introduces blends and reviews much of what your student has already learned. The list is divided into sections that may be used separately or combined.

The list may contain more than you need, or less, so adjust for the needs of the individual student. The nonsense syllables make it possible to quiz students on sounds rather than known words. Each step introduces or reviews several sounds, as noted.

1. Review short vowels ă and ŭ, consonant digraphs *sh* and *th*: *nish rith tham fum fath pib*
2. Same sounds as in #1, with ě, *ing, ung, ong,* and *ang* added: *tish fing tang deg tef gung gup shag*
3. Add ŏ, *ch, ank, onk, unk, ink*: *tink kef lunk sush cham chish pank chonk*
4. Add *ck, wh, qu*: *yaf whag whub yuth whux vank joth whick zish quif quath*
5. Consonant blends with short vowels: (To read these, the student should imagine a consonant where the blank is. For example, *sla-*

becomes *slap*.) *sla- sli- sle- slo- slu- blu- ste- fli- swu- dri- pla- gli- pru- sto- spre- sma- snu- cre- sku-*

6. Real words with initial consonant blends: *slip blank prank slum gland brag drunk splash pluck spring sprung swish strap clink stick glob*

7. Nonsense syllables with initial blends: *slan brip sprish spret grom drush plonk*

8. Real words with various endings: *next bump lash raft slump tramp*

9. Review of vowel diphthongs and digraphs:

    Ask the student the following questions until she can answer accurately and quickly. Since you're doing this from dictation, you obviously don't show this sheet to her before she writes.

    Q. Write two ways to spell the /ou/ sound and give a word for each one.
    A. *ou* as in *house*, *ow* as in *cow*.
    Q. Write two ways to spell the /au/ sound.
    A. *au* as in *haunt*, *aw* as in *saw*
    Q. Two ways to spell the /oi/ sound.
    A. *oi* as in *oil*, *oy* as in *boy*
    Q. Two ways to write the /ee/ sound using two letters.
    A. *ee* as in *feet*, ea as in *eat*
    Q. Two ways to write the /ay/ sound using two letters.
    A. *ai* as in *rain*, *ay* as in *play*
    Q. How do you write the /ew/ sound?
    A. *ew*
    Q. How do you write /oa/?
    A. *oa* (also *o* in the middle of a word with a silent *e* on the end)

10. Real words containing vowel diphthongs and digraphs can be used as a test of the student's skill in reading "double vowels": *bleed railway moist peanut haystack goose food main thaw screech mailman moose tooth sailboat sheer toadstool launch beak railroad soy proof oatmeal hoist fault grouse glimpse moonbeam Troy maintain*

11. (Mostly) words with the /k/ sound; these are good words to use for dictation since most kids can read them, but don't think about how they're spelled: *back bake brake sack sake stoke soak stark cube cub cuke lack cake coke mack make rake rock lake mask mark mock murk stack stake*

This is the end of the phonics list. As mentioned, some students will go straight from phonics flash cards to reading books, but others will need the intermediate step of using this phonics practice list. Make sure your student has consigned the material to long-term memory before discontinuing the list.

References

Achieve, Inc. 2005. *Rising to the challenge: Are high school graduates prepared for college and work?* Washington, D.C. A study conducted for Peter D. Hart Research Associates. http://achieve.org.

ACT, Inc. 2006. *Reading Between the Lines: What the ACT reveals about college readiness in reading.* Iowa City, IA: ACT National Office. Accessed 3/9/2014. http://www.act.org/research/policymakers/reports/reading.html

Adams, Richard. 2005. *Watership Down.* New York: Scribner.

"Special Education and Reading Intervention: The Need." *Administrator Magazine.* 2009. http://scholastic.com/administrator/theneed.htm

Anderson, Laurie Halse. 2006. *Speak.* New York: Penguin Group.

Babcock, Dorothy Ellen, RN, and Terry D. Keepers, Ph.D. 1976. *Raising Kids O.K.: Transactional Analysis in Human Growth and Development.* New York: Grove Press, an imprint of Grove Atlantic.

Becker, Wesley C. 1971. *Parents Are Teachers.* Champaign, IL: Research Press.

Berne, Erik, M.D. 1996. *Games People Play: The Basic Handbook of Transactional Analysis.* New York: Ballantine Books.

———. 1985. *What Do You Say After You Say Hello? The Psychology of Human Destiny.* New York: Bantam Books.

Blume, Judy. 2010. *Tiger Eyes.* New York: Delacorte Press.

Boorstin, Daniel J. 1983. *The Discoverers: A History of Man's Search to Know His World and Himself.* New York: Random House, Inc.

Bulfinch, Thomas. 1913. *Bulfinch's Mythology: The Age of Fable; The Age of Chivalry; Legends of Charlemagne.* New York: Grosset and Dunlap.

Burnford, Sheila. 1996. *The Incredible Journey.* New York: Delacorte Books for Young Readers, an imprint of Random House.

Campbell, Joseph. 1949. *The Hero with a Thousand Faces,* Bollingen Series XVII. Princeton, NJ: Princeton University Press.

Carlisle, Joanne. 1987. *Beginning Reasoning Skills: Beginning Reasoning and Reading.* Cambridge and Toronto: Educator's Publishing Service, Inc.

————. 2000. *Reasoning and Reading*, Level 1. Cambridge and Toronto: Educator's Publishing Service, Inc.

Carson, Rachel. 2002. *Silent Spring*. 40th anniversary ed. New York: Houghton Mifflin.

————. 1991. *The Sea Around Us*. Special Edition. New York: Oxford University Press.

Cather, Willa. 1999. "Paul's Case." *Coming, Aphrodite! And Other Short Stories*. New York: Penguin Books.

Cave, H. B. 1983. "Two Were Left." In *Aiming High, Stirring tales and poems*, edited by Annette Sloan and Albert Capaccio. Originally published in 1942. New York: Amsco School Publications, Inc.

Cayton, Andrew, Ph.D. 1999. *America: Pathways to the Present*. Needham, Massachusetts: Prentice Hall.

Chadron State College. Last accessed 2/23/2014. http://www.csc.edu/learning-center/study/studymethods.csc.

Christ, Henry I. 1992. *Building Power in Reading*. New York: Amsco School Publications, Inc.

Cisneros, Sandra. 1997. *The House on Mango Street*. San Diego, CA: Jane Schaffer Publications.

Cruse, Amy. 1930. *The Englishman and His Books in the Early Nineteenth Century*. London: George G. Harrap and Company, Ltd.

Cutler, Wade E. 2003. *Triple Your Reading Speed: The Proven Self-Study Plan*, 4th ed. New York: Pocket Books.

DK Illustrated Oxford Dictionary. 1998. New York, Oxford: Dorling Kindersley Limited and Oxford University Press.

Drummond, Dorothy, and Bruce Kraig. 1988. *Our World Yesterday and Today*. Glenview, IL: Scott Foresman and Company.

Dweck, Carol S. 2007. "The Secret to Raising Smart Kids." *Scientific American Mind* 18:6:36-43.

Elliot, Kathleen, Carmen Geraci, and David Ebner. 2013. *Barron's SSAT/ISEE: High School Entrance Examinations*, 3d ed. Hauppauge, NY: Barron's Educational Series, Inc.

Ericson, Bonnie O. 2001. "Reading in High School English Classes: An overview." *Teaching reading in high school English classes*. Bonnie O. Ericson, ed. Urbana, IL: National Council of Teachers of English.

Frender, Gloria. 2013. *Learning to Learn: Strengthening Study Skills and Brain Power*, 3d ed. Nashville, TN: Incentive Publications.

Fry, Edward. 1975. *Reading Drills for Speed and Comprehension, Advanced Level*. Providence, RI: Jamestown Publishers. ISBN 0-89061-039-8.

George, Jean Craighead. 2003. *Julie of the Wolves*. New York: HarperTrophy.

————. 2004. *My Side of the Mountain*. New York: Puffin Books.

Golding, William. 1959. *Lord of the Flies*. New York: Perigee Books.

Hallowell, Edward M., and John J. Ratey. 1995. *Driven to Distraction: Recognizing and Coping with Attention Deficit Disorder from Childhood Through Adulthood*. New York: Touchstone Books.

Haynes, M. 2005. *Reading at risk: How states can respond to the crisis in adolescent literacy*. Alexandria, VA: National Association of State Boards of Education.

Hinton, S. E. 2008. *That Was Then, This Is Now*. New York: Puffin Books.

Hoyt, Linda. 1999. *Revisit, Reflect, Retell: Strategies for Improving Reading Comprehension*. Portsmouth, NH: Heinemann.

Huxley, Thomas H. 1877. *Collected Essays*, vol. III. London: Macmillan.

Joffe, Irwin L. 1980. *Opportunity for Skillful Reading*, 3d ed. Belmont, CA: Wadsworth Publishing Company, Inc.

Jung, Carl. 1966. "The Problem of the Attitude Type," *Two Essays on Analytical Psychology*, 2d ed., vol. 7 of *The Collected Works of C. G. Jung*. Princeton, NJ: Princeton University Press.

————. 1976. *Psychological Types*, vol. 6 of *The Collected Works of C. G. Jung*. Princeton, NJ: Princeton University Press.

International Dyslexia Association. Accessed 3/7/2014. http://www.interdys.org/FAQ.htm.

Keirsey, David. 1998. *Please Understand Me II: Temperament, Character, Intelligence*. Del Mar, CA: Prometheus Nemesis Book Company.

Keirsey, David, and Marilyn Bates. 1984. *Please Understand Me: Character and Temperament Types*, 5th ed. Del Mar, CA: Prometheus Nemesis Book Company.

Kimball, John W. 1965. *Biology*. Palo Alto, CA: Addison-Wesley Publishing Company, Inc.

Kottmeyer, William. 1989. *Conquests in Reading*, 2d ed. Honesdale, PA: Phoenix Learning Resources.

Lawrence, Gordon. 2009. *People Types and Tiger Stripes: Using Psychological Type to Help Students Discover Their Unique Potential*, 4th ed. Gainesville, FL: Center for Applications of Psychological Type, Inc.

Lasky, Kathryn. 2005. *The Night Journey*. New York: Puffin Books.

Leokum, Arkady. 1989. *Big Book of Tell Me Why*. New York: Barnes and Noble.

Lerer, Seth, Ph.D. 1998. *The History of the English Language*, 2d ed. The Great Courses, 2250. Chantilly, VA: The Teaching Company. Accessed 3/7/2014. http://thegreatcourses.com/tgc/courses/course_detail.aspx?cid= 2250

Lowry, Lois. 1989. *Number the Stars*. New York: Laurel Leaf Books.

Mann, Charles C. 2006. 1491: *New Revelations of the Americas Before Columbus*. New York: Vintage.

McDonald, Betty. 1994. *Mrs. Piggle-Wiggle*. New York: HarperTrophy.

Meltzer, J. 2002. *Adolescent literacy resources: Linking research and practice*. South Hampton, NH: Center for Resource Management.

National Endowment for the Arts. 2007. "To Read or Not to Read: A Question of National Consequence." Report #47. Accessed 3/7/2014. http://arts. gov/ publications/read-or-not-read-question-national-conse-quence-0

National Geographic Society. *National Geographic*. Washington, DC: National Geographic Soc. Accessed 3/9/2014. http://ngm.nationalgeographic.com/

Official SAT Questions and Study Guides. Accessed 3/7/2014. http:// sat.college-board.org/

Okimoto, Jean Davies. 2000. *Jason's Women*. Lincoln, NE: iUniverse, Inc. Originally published in 1986 by Dell.

Orwell, George. 1996. *Animal Farm*. New York: The Penguin Group.

Parker, Bertha Morris. 1960. *Ghosts to House Plants*. vol. VII of *The Golden Encyclopedia*. New York: Golden Press Inc.

Pauk, Walter. 1999. *Six-Way Paragraphs: Introductory*, 3d ed. New York: Glencoe/McGraw-Hill.

Pauk, Walter, and Ross J.Q. Owens. 2013. *How To Study in College*, 11th ed. Boston, MA: Wadsworth/Cengage Learning.

PBS Online. 2006. "Developing Active Reading with Effective Questions." PBS TeacherLine Tips for Developing Active Reading. Accessed 3/7/2014. www. pbslearningmedia.org

Peterson's Four-Year Colleges. 2013. Paramus NJ: Peterson's.

Prechtel, Martin. 1999. Lecture, "Love Letters to the Flowering Earth" Conference, Ghost Ranch Conference Center, Abiquiú, New Mexico, October 3.

Quinn, Shirley, and Susan Irvings. 1991. *Active Reading in the Arts and Sciences*, 3d ed. New York: Longman Publishing Group.

Rand McNally *History Encyclopedia: Civilizations, Explorers, Conflicts, Inventions*. 1985. Deborah Manley and Andrew Sich, eds. New York: Rand McNally and Company.

Region 10 Education Service Center. 2002. "Dyslexia Definition." Accessed 3/7/2014. http://www.region10.org/dyslexia/information/dyslexia-definition

Rock, Maxine. 1995. "Human moms teach chimps it's all in the family." *Smithsonian* 25:12:70-75. Accessed 3/10/2015. http://www.smithsonian-mag.com/science-nature/human-moms-teach-chimps-its-all-in-the-family-1-31784237/?no-ist

Rocky Mountain Health Plans. 2005. *Good Health*. Winter.

Sadlier, William H. 2001. *Sadlier Oxford Vocabulary Workshop*. New York: William H. Sadlier, Inc.

Sharman-Burke, Juliet, and Liz Greene. 1986. *The Mythic Tarot*, illustrated by Tricia Newell. New York: Fireside Books, Simon and Schuster.

Shaywitz, Sally, M.D. 2003. *Overcoming Dyslexia: A new and complete science-based program for reading problems at any level*. New York: Alfred A. Knopf.

Shelley, Mary. 1994. *Frankenstein*, 3d ed. Mineola, NY: Dover Publications.

Sherman, Kathy. 2009. Personal communication. Ms. Sherman is co-founder of Bridge School and founder of Hillside Learning Center.

Silverman, Linda Kreger, Ph.D. 1991. "Understanding Introverted Kids," *Making the grade*. Denver: KCNC-TV, Channel 4. May.

Simos, P. G., Ph.D., J. M. Fletcher, Ph.D., E. Bergman, M.D., J. I. Breier, Ph.D., B. R. Foorman, Ph.D., E. M. Castillo, Ph.D., R. N. Davis, MA, M. Fitzgerald, BA, and A. C. Papanicolaou, Ph.D. 2002. Dyslexia-specific brain activation profile becomes normal following successful remedial training. *Neurology* 58:8:1203-1213. Accessed 3/2/2014. http://www.neurology.org/content/58/8/1203.

Spalding, Romalda Bishop, with Walter T. Spalding. 2003. *The Writing Road to Reading: The Spalding Method for Teaching Speech, Spelling, Writing, and Reading*, 5th ed. New York: Collins Reference.

Sperry, Armstrong. 1990. *Call It Courage*. New York: Aladdin Paperbacks.

Spielvogel, Jackson J. 1999. *World History, The Human Odyssey*. Mason, OH: South-Western Educational Publishing Company.

Tanaka, Hiroko, Jessica M. Black, Charles Hulme, Leanne M. Stanley, Shelli R. Kesler, Susan Whitfield-Gabrieli, Allan L. Reiss, J.D.E. Gabrieli, and Fumiko Hoeft. 2011. The Brain Basis of the Phonological Deficit in Dyslexia Is Independent of IQ. *Psychological Science* 22:11:1442-1451. Accessed 3/3/2014. http://pss.sagepub.com/content/22/11/1442

Temple, Elise, R. A. Poldrack, and A. Protopapas, S. Nagarajan, T. Salz, P. Tallal, M. M. Merzenich, and J.D.E. Gabrieli. 2000. Disruption of the neural response to rapid acoustic stimuli in dyslexia: evidence in functional MRI. *Proceedings of the National Academy of Sciences* 97:25. Accessed 3/2/2014. http://www.pnas.org/content/97/25/13907

Tolkien, J.R.R. 2007. *The Hobbit, or There and Back Again*. Boston: Houghton Mifflin Co.

———. 2005. *The Lord of the Rings*. Boston: Houghton Mifflin Co.

Voigt, Cynthia. 2005. *Izzy Willy Nilly*. New York: Simon Pulse.

Wallbank, T. Walter, Arnold Schrier, Donna Maier, and Patricia Gutierrez-Smith. 1990. *History and Life*, 4th ed. Glenview, IL: Scott Foresman and Company.

Wallis, Velma. 2004. *Two Old Women: An Alaska Legend of Betrayal, Courage and Survival*. New York: Harper Perennial.

Walsh, Jill Paton. 1993. *Matthew and the Sea Singer*. New York: Farrar Straus & Giroux.

Yale Center for Dyslexia and Creativity. "I Have Dyslexia. What does it mean?" Accessed 3/7/2014. http://www.dyslexia.yale.edu/Stu_whatis-dyslexia.htm

Annotated Bibliography

Books for Students

The selections in the student book list are based on these criteria:

- The student said this book changed his or her life.
- Or I thought it did.
- It was the first book a student ever enjoyed reading.
- It was a book that led to a breakthrough in the student's skills or understanding.

Some of these titles are suggested for exercises described in the text and so are included in the list of references as well.

Anderson, Laurie Halse. 2003. *Speak*. New York: Puffin Books.

Brautigan, Richard. 2006. *The Revenge of the Lawn*. Edinburgh: Canongate Books Ltd.

———. 2010. *Trout Fishing in America*. New York: Mariner Books.

Cave, H. B. 1983. "Two Were Left." *In Aiming High, Stirring tales and poems*, edited by Annette Sloan and Albert Capaccio. Originally published in 1942. New York: Amsco School Publications, Inc.

Dahl, Roald. 1980. *The Twits*. New York: Puffin Books.

———. 1964. *Charlie and the Chocolate Factory*. New York: Puffin Books.

Farley, Walter. 1941. *The Black Stallion*. New York: Random House.

George, Jean Craighead. 1991. *My Side of the Mountain*. New York: Puffin Books. First published in the United States in 1959 by E. P. Dutton, Penguin Books.

Hinton, S. E. 1967. *The Outsiders*. New York: Laurel-Leaf Books.

———. 1969. *Rumble Fish*. New York: Laurel-Leaf Books.

———. 1998. *That Was Then, This Is Now*. New York: Viking Press.

Lasky, Kathryn. 2005. *The Night Journey*. New York: Penguin Putnam, Inc.

Lewis, C. S. 2001. *The Chronicles of Narnia*. New York: HarperCollins

Publishers. There are numerous editions of The Chronicles of Narnia, some containing one volume and others several, as here. This edition, illustrated by Pauline Baynes and published by HarperCollins, is a deluxe paperback edition that includes "The Magician's Nephew," "The Lion, the Witch, and the Wardrobe," "The Horse and His Boy," "Prince Caspian," "The Voyage of the Dawn Treader," "The Silver Chair," and "The Last Battle."

Lowry, Lois. 1989. *Number the Stars*. New York: Yearling Books, Bantam Doubleday Dell Publishing Group, Inc.

McDonald, Betty. 1994. *Mrs. Piggle-Wiggle*. New York: HarperTrophy.

McKissack, Patricia C., and Frederick McKissack. 1992. *Sojourner Truth, Ain't I a Woman?* New York: Scholastic Books.

Okimoto, Jean Davies. 2000. *Jason's Women*. Lincoln, NE: iUniverse.com Inc. Authors Guild backinprint.com ed. First published 1986 by Dell.

Paulsen, Gary. 1990. *Woodsong*. New York: Scholastic Books.

Rand, Ayn. 1937. *Anthem*. New York: Signet.

Schar, Louis. 1998. *Holes*. New York: Yearling Books, a Random House imprint.

Sperry, Armstrong. 1990. *Call It Courage*. New York: Aladdin Paperbacks.

Walker, Alice. 1982. *The Color Purple*. New York: Washington Square Press.

Books for Tutors

Brain development

Begley, Sharon. 2007. *Train Your Mind, Change Your Brain: How a New Science Reveals Our Extraordinary Potential to Transform Ourselves*. New York: Ballantine Books.

Gage, F. 1999. "Exercise makes mice smarter, Salk scientists demonstrate." Online. www.salk.edu News Release.

Schiller, P. 1999. *Start smart! Building brain power in the early years*. Beltsville, MD: Gryphon House.

Schwartz, Jeffrey M., and Sharon Begley. 2003. *The Mind and the Brain: Neuroplasticity and the Power of Mental Force*. New York: HarperCollins. This book has some fascinating research on retraining dyslexics' brains to hear sounds more accurately.

Study skills

Buzan, Tony. 1984. *Make the Most of Your Mind*. New York: Touchstone Books, Simon and Schuster.

Elliot, Kathleen, Carmen Geraci, and David Ebner. 2013. *Barron's SSAT/ISEE: High School Entrance Examinations*, 3d ed. Hauppauge, NY: Barron's Educational Series, Inc.

Fry, Edward. 1975. *Reading Drills for Speed and Comprehension, Advanced Level*. Providence, RI: Jamestown Publishers. ISBN 0-89061-039-8. This book is out of print, but I have permission from the author, now deceased, to make copies available for educational purposes. The book can also be bought online. Oddly, there is a book by the same author bearing the same title, published in 2000, with completely different content. I do not recommend it.

Pauk, Walter. 1999. *Six-Way Paragraphs: Introductory*, 3d ed. New York: Glencoe/McGraw-Hill. This three-level series teaches the basic skills necessary for reading factual material through the use of the following six types of questions: subject matter, main idea, supporting details, conclusions, clarifying devices, and vocabulay in context.

Pauk, Walter, and Ross J.Q. Owens. 2013. *How To Study in College*, 11th ed. Boston, MA: Wadsworth/Cengage Learning.

Paul, Kevin. 2009. *Study Smarter, Not Harder: Use the genius inside you*, 3d ed. Bellingham, WA: Self-Counsel Press, Inc.

Robinson, Adam. 1993. *What Smart Students Know: Maximum Grades. Optimum Learning. Minimum Time*. New York: Three Rivers Press, Random House, Inc.

Vocabulary

Bear, Donald R., Marcia A. Invernizzi, Shane Templeton, and Francine Johnston. 2011. *Words Their Way: Word Study for Phonics, Vocabulary, and Spelling Instruction*, 5th ed. New York: Pearson, Inc.

Ganske, Kathy. 2000. *Word Journeys*. New York: Guilford Press.

See also Johnston in the "How To Tutor" section below.

Writing

Calkins, Lucy McCormick. 1994. *The Art of Teaching Writing*. Portsmouth, NH: Heinemann Publishing.

Daniels, Harvey "Smokey," Steven Zemelman, and Nancy Steineke. 2007. *Content-Area Writing: Every Teacher's Guide*. Portsmouth, NH: Heinemann Publishing.

Fletcher, Ralph. 2003. *A Writer's Notebook: Unlocking the Writer Within You*. New York: HarperCollins.

Fletcher, Ralph, and JoAnn Portalupi. 2007. *Craft Lessons, Teaching Writing K-8*, 2d ed. Portland, ME: Stenhouse Publishers.

How to Tutor

Blumenfeld, Samuel L. 1973. *How To Tutor: How To Teach Phonics, Arithmetic and Handwriting*, 10th ed. Boise, ID: Paradigm Company. Useful detail, but misses the big picture; assumes that if kids know phonics, they'll be able to read.

Jensen, Eric. 1995. *Super Teaching*. San Diego, CA: The Brain Store, Inc. For classroom teaching, but gives a good overview of teaching ideas.

Johnston, Peter H. 2004. *Choice Words: How Our Language Affects Children's Learning*. Portland, ME: Stenhouse Publishers.

Rabow, Jerome, Tiffani Chin, and Nima Fahimian. 1999. *Tutoring Matters: Everything You Always Wanted To Know About How To Tutor*. Philadelphia, PA: Temple University Press. Contains a lot about relationships but not much on academics.

Schumm, Jeanne Shay, Ph.D., and Gerald E. Schumm Jr. 1999. *The Reading Tutor's Handbook: A Commonsense Guide to Helping Students Read and Write*. Minneapolis, MN: Free Spirit Publishing, Inc. This is more for teaching elementary students but has some good ideas.

Shapiro, Eileen Kaplan. 2001. *Tutoring as a Successful Business, An Expert Tutor Shows You How*. Burbank, CA: Nateen Publishing Co. This author is an expert and never lets you forget it.

Books for Classroom Reading Teachers

Frey, Nancy, and Douglas B. Fisher. 2013. *Rigorous Reading: 5 Access Points for Comprehending Complex Texts*. Newbury Park, CA: Corwin Press, Inc.

Wood, Karen D., Diane Lapp, James Flood, and D. Bruce Taylor. 2008. *Guiding Readers through Text: Strategy Guides for New Times*. Newark, DE: International Reading Association.

Wilhelm, Jeffrey D. *"You Gotta BE the Book": Teaching Engaged and Reflective Reading with Adolescents*. 2d ed. New York: Teachers College Press.

Online Resources

For more on literature discussion questions, the internet is full of helpful websites. One is www.readinggroupguides.com. (Enter a book title and click "discussion questions.") Individual publishers have their own sites, many with reading guides and thought-provoking study questions. Search Google for the title of the book and "discussion questions."

For more difficult material, depend on CliffsNotes (www.cliffsnotes. com) or a similar guide. In the same category, a website called Pink Monkey (www.pink-monkey.com) has detailed summaries of many of the books you are likely to ask your students to read.

The discussion leader's guides for the Junior Great Books discussion groups are also helpful, not so much to learn about discussing a specific piece of writing, but to see what kinds of questions other teachers ask. The Junior Great Books program is part of the Great Books Foundation. You can find their website at www.greatbooks.org. Follow this route to download a free copy of the excellent discussion leader's handbook: Click on K-12, Parents and Homeschoolers, Lead Great Books Discussions at Your Child's School, Volunteer Handbook and Training Courses, Handbook for Volunteer Leaders, fill out the form, and download.

Many libraries host Junior Great Books discussion groups and have training for discussion leaders along with the books and discussion guides used by the leaders. Any of these Great Books connections would be excellent. While you're investigating Great Books, you may also wish to read about their philosophy of Socratic inquiry, a subject that fits in perfectly with the topic of discussing literature with young people.

A variety of book summaries written by teens can be found at http://teenink.com. The state associations of the IRA also publish concise, interesting book reviews suitable for students.

Index

CPSIA information can be obtained at www.ICGtesting.com
ted in the USA
703s0754140814
LV00002B/2/P